PSYCHOLOGY AND LAW IN EUROPE

When West Meets East

PSYCHOLOGY AND LAW IN EUROPE

When West Meets East

Edited by
Pär Anders Granhag | Ray Bull
Alla Shaboltas | Elena Dozortseva

CRC Press
Taylor & Francis Group
Boca Raton London New York

CRC Press is an imprint of the
Taylor & Francis Group, an **informa** business

CRC Press
Taylor & Francis Group
6000 Broken Sound Parkway NW, Suite 300
Boca Raton, FL 33487-2742

First issued in paperback 2019

© 2017 by Taylor & Francis Group, LLC
CRC Press is an imprint of Taylor & Francis Group, an Informa business

No claim to original U.S. Government works

ISBN-13: 978-1-4987-8098-8 (hbk)
ISBN-13: 978-0-367-88993-7 (pbk)

Library of Congress Cataloging-in-Publication Data

Names: Granhag, Pär-Anders, author.
Title: Psychology and Law in Europe : When West Meets East / Pär-Anders Granhag [and three others].
Description: Boca Raton, Fl. : CRC Press, [2017]
Identifiers: LCCN 2016027103| ISBN 9781498780988 (hardback) | ISBN 1498780989 (hardback) | ISBN 9781315317038 (web pdf) | ISBN 1315317036 (web pdf)
Subjects: LCSH: Law--Psychological aspects. | Law--Psychological aspects--Russia (Federation) | Law--Psychological aspects--Europe. | Forensic psychology.
Classification: LCC K346 .G73 2017 | DDC 340/.19--dc23
LC record available at https://lccn.loc.gov/2016027103

Visit the Taylor & Francis Web site at
http://www.taylorandfrancis.com

and the CRC Press Web site at
http://www.crcpress.com

Contents

Section III

PERSONALITY: PSYCHOPATHY AND RISK TAKING

Foreword

We are very grateful to the rector of St. Petersburg State University, Nikolay Kropachev, for agreeing to host and support the meeting from which the chapters in this volume emerge. We would also like to acknowledge the support from the many brilliant psychologists and lawyers of St. Petersburg State University. We would like to extend particular appreciation to the dean of the Faculty of Psychology, Professor Alla Shaboltas, and the dean of the Faculty of Law, Professor Natalia Sheveleva. Without your support, this volume would never had materialized. We are also in debt to Moscow State University of Psychology and Education. Scholars at this university provided valuable support in preparing and running the European Association of Psychology and Law congress in St. Petersburg. We are particularly grateful to Professor Elena Dozortseva of Moscow State University of Psychology and Education. We would also like to thank Dr. Lisa Öhman for all her efforts working with this book.

Editors

Pär Anders Granhag is a professor of psychology at the University of Gothenburg, Sweden. For 25-plus years he has conducted research on interviewing, deception detection and eyewitness testimony. He has published more than 250 scientific reports, and he has presented his work worldwide. He is the past president of the European Association of Psychology and Law (EAPL) and the founding director of the research unit for Criminal, Legal and Investigative Psychology (CLIP).

Ray Bull is a part-time professor of criminal investigation at the University of Derby. In 2014 he became (for 3 years) president of the European Association of Psychology and Law. In 2012 he was made the first Honorary Life Member of the International Investigative Interviewing Research Group. In 2010 he was elected an Honorary Fellow of the British Psychological Society 'for the contribution made to the discipline of psychology' (this honour is restricted to 40 living psychologists). In 2008 he received from the European Association of Psychology and Law the Award for Life-time Contribution to Psychology and Law. In 2005 he received a commendation from the London Metropolitan Police for 'innovation and professionalism whilst assisting a complex rape investigation'. He regularly acts as an expert witness and conducts workshops/training on investigative interviewing.

Alla Shaboltas, PhD, has been the dean of the Psychology Department at St. Petersburg State University since 2011. Starting her career as a faculty member at the university in 1988, she successfully defended her PhD dissertation in psychology in 1998. Since 1999, after a one-year postdoctoral fellowship at Yale University and Medical College of Wisconsin, Shaboltas's scientific interests moved to health psychology and, particularly, to the topic of development and longitudinal evaluation of HIV prevention interventions. Since 2006 she has served as the chief of the Division of Behavioral Psychology and Prevention of Behavioral Deviations at St. Petersburg State University and managed the educational programs on behavioural health psychology and criminal psychology. In 2014 Shaboltas received an award from the Russian Ministry of Education for 'Significant contribution into High Education and Training of High-qualified Specialists'.

Elena Dozortseva is the head of the Laboratory for Child and Adolescent Psychology at the Serbsky Medical Research Center for Psychiatry and Narcology (Moscow). She acts as a consultant forensic psychologist and an expert witness for the most complicated criminal cases concerning minors. For 30 years her work has involved juvenile forensic psychology, including issues of juvenile offenders' personality development, forensic assessment and rehabilitation of child victims of crimes, and she has published more than 200 scientific reports. In 2004 she was an organiser and the first dean of the Department of Forensic and Legal Psychology at Moscow State University of Psychology and Education. She now works in the department as a professor and the chair of Forensic & Legal Psychology and Law.

Contributors

C. Bailey
Faculty of Society and Design
Bond University
Gold Coast, Australia

Inna Bovina
Moscow State University of Psychology
    and Education
Russia, Moscow

N. Brooks
Faculty of Society and Design
Bond University
Gold Coast, Australia

Ray Bull
University of Derby
Derby, England

S. Croom
School of Business Administration
University of San Diego
San Diego, California

Olga Deyneka
St. Petersburg State University
St. Petersburg, Russia

Elena Dozortseva
Moscow State University of Psychology
    and Education
Russia, Moscow

Nikolay Dvoryanchikov
Moscow State University of Psychology
    and Education
Russia, Moscow

K. Fritzon
Faculty of Society and Design
Bond University
Gold Coast, Australia

Sergey V. Gorbatov
St. Petersburg State University
St. Petersburg, Russia

Pär Anders Granhag
University of Gothenburg
Gothenburg, Sweden

J. V. Granskaya
St. Petersburg State University
St. Petersburg, Russia

Anastasiya Gutnick
Moscow State University of Psychology
    and Education
Moscow, Russia

Tina Hahnemann
Department of Psychology
Technische Universität Chemnitz
Chemnitz, Germany

Laura Hammond
International Research Centre for
    Investigative Psychology
University of Huddersfield
Huddersfield, England

Maria Ioannou
International Research Centre for
    Investigative Psychology
University of Huddersfield
Huddersfield, England

Maria A. Kapustina
St. Petersburg State University
St. Petersburg, Russia

André Körner
Department of Psychology
Technische Universität Chemnitz
Chemnitz, Germany

Olga Logunova
Moscow State University of Psychology
    and Education
Moscow, Russia

Djenevra I. Lukovskaya
St. Petersburg State University
St. Petersburg, Russia

Galit Nahari
Department of Criminology
Bar-Ilan University
Ramat Gan, Israel

Paula Sismeiro Pereira
Department of Psychology
High School of Education
Polytechnic Institute of Bragança
Bragança, Portugal

C. Gabrielle Salfati
John Jay College of Criminal Justice
City University of New York
New York, New York

Rose Schindler
Department of Psychology
Technische Universität Chemnitz
Chemnitz, Germany

Alla Shaboltas
St. Petersburg State University
St. Petersburg, Russia

Julia Shaw
London South Bank University
London, England

Marina Sorochinski
John Jay College of Criminal Justice
City University of New York
New York, New York

Colin G. Tredoux
Department of Psychology
University of Cape Town
Cape Town, South Africa

Gayane A. Vartanyan
St. Petersburg State University
St. Petersburg, Russia

Annelies Vredeveldt
Department of Criminal Law and
    Criminology
VU University Amsterdam
Amsterdam, the Netherlands

Aldert Vrij
Psychology Department
University of Portsmouth
Portsmouth, England

Marina Igorevna Yudina
St. Petersburg State University
St. Petersburg, Russia

V. A. Zaicev
St. Petersburg State University
St. Petersburg, Russia

Introduction

Pazdravleniya! Congratulations – you have just picked up a unique book! 'Psychology and law' is a bourgeoning field of research, and new books are produced at a steady and high pace. But this volume stands out; this is something different. For the very first time, Russian scholars have joined forces with their western colleagues to produce an international volume covering some of the more central themes within 'psychology and law'. We are proud to present a truly pioneering volume, a volume that we hope will be the starting point for increased cross-border collaboration.

The chapters in *Psychology and Law in Europe: When West Meets East* emerges from the international congress that took place at St. Petersburg State University in 2014 – Russia's oldest and most prestigious university. The congress, which was the first international conference on 'psychology and law' ever to be held in Russia, was a great success. This significant event was organised under the auspices of the *European Association of Psychology and Law* (EAPL), which is one of the world's leading organisations within this field of research (established in 1990).

The scientific program of the St. Petersburg meeting was exceptionally strong, and scholars from more than 30 different countries came together to present and discuss their research. Not very surprisingly, a large proportion of the research presented at the meeting had been carried out by Russian experts.

The title of the congress was *Actual Problems of Psychology & Law: From Research to Effective Practice* – this theme held a promise, and there was an ambition to pay particular attention to research that can make a difference. The theme fits neatly with a new wave of psycho-legal research; research that is not only about 'what went wrong', and about errors and biases. The new wave of research has a constructive and positive dimension; it is about developing and nurturing constructive factors – it is about 'what works'. In brief, the new wave of psycho-legal research is about preventing crime and factors that promote justice. It will always be important to learn the right lessons from explaining miscarriages of justice, but psycho-legal research needs to make contributions beyond looking back. The congress in St. Petersburg contributed to this new wave of research.

Those familiar with 'psychology and law' research know that papers from Russian researchers are a rare treat. In brief, turning to traditional scientific journals in the field, one finds very few papers from Russian researchers. However, from this one should not conclude that the field is new and/or not very strong in Russia. The truth is that the field of 'psychology and law' is very strong in Russia – and we believe that this is reflected in the present volume. Furthermore, the field of 'psychology and law' in Russia has a rich and fascinating history – something that we will learn all about in the opening chapter of this volume. The main reason for why Russian research on 'psychology and law' is unknown in the West is that Russian scholars prefer to write and publish in their own language. The present volume will remedy the barriers of language. Half of the chapters are written by Russian researchers. In fact, no less than 13 Russian scholars have contributed to these fascinating chapters; the majority of these scholars are from the field of psychology, but there are also scholars from the field of law. These chapters offer important insights with respect to what is taking place behind the curtain, not only in terms of the topics studied (e.g. sexual offenders and financial crimes) but also with respect to the methodology used and, importantly, the actual outcome of the research. It is safe to say that such insights are long overdue.

At the beginning of the field, Russian researchers of 'psychology and law' worked in pace with their European colleagues. However, the social and political changes in Russia during the last century hampered the development of Russian experimental and applied psychology for many years. Despite these difficulties, it did not prevent original thinking and researchers' strive forward. The last decades of the century were marked by an increasing interest for psychological issues in the legal context in Russia. The same tendency could be seen in Europe. During the conference in St. Petersburg, all this came together and made possible an exchange of views and experiences, some of them presented in this book. Differences in legislations, social contexts and traditions sometimes make a direct transfer of knowledge, experience and research difficult; at the same time, such differences enrich and stimulate creative ideas. Topics such as interviewing techniques, especially in cases of child victims and witnesses, lie detection and memory problems are actively debated by Russian specialists in the field of investigative and forensic psychology. Hence, all the new results and opinions of European colleagues are highly relevant. The problem of offenders' personalities is vital for forensic and penitentiary psychologists, and a major difference in traditional understanding of the term 'psychopathy' in the Western and Russian psychiatry and clinical psychology is a source of special interest. The same can be said about many other issues in the field of 'psychology and law'. It was also important for Russian psychologists and lawyers to have the opportunity to introduce topics of particular significance to the foreign colleagues. Some examples of such topics are the reflection about legal and social consciousness in the country and risk behaviour in different spheres. The chapters in this volume book represent a small 'tip of the iceberg', as the range of studies in Russian legal and forensic psychology is very wide.

We received over 40 manuscripts from researchers that aspired to contribute to the book. Only the very best, all in all 15 papers, were accepted. Hence, we have a volume of high-quality chapters. In fact, all chapters are written by top scholars within the field; and besides Russia, there are contributions from the United Kingdom, the United States, Australia, Portugal, the Netherlands and South Africa. Hence, the volume is truly international.

The chapters in this pioneering volume address a number of fascinating topics, and they are organised in four different sections. The first section sets the stage and commences with a unique historical overview of the development in Russia of forensic and criminal psychology. This is followed by an interesting chapter on 'legal consciousness', and the section ends with a chapter that focusses on a historical and legal analysis of paternalism in Russia. The second section is on crimes related to sex and money, and is opened by a revealing review of young Russian adults' social representations/thinking about sexual murderers and victims. This is followed by a chapter from the United States on seeking to link crimes committed by the same offender via his/her behaviour. Next we find a fascinating chapter from Portugal on the narratives of abused women who have killed their partners. The ensuing chapter from the United Kingdom examines would-be jurors' understanding and perception of forensic science evidence validity and utility. The section is closed by a chapter from Russia on victims of financial debt. The third section of the volume highlights 'psychopathy and risk taking' and is opened by a chapter from Australia on assessing psychopathic personality traits in business settings. This is followed by a chapter from Germany on the relationships between moral emotions, such as shame and guilt, and recidivism. The section is closed by two chapters from Russian scholars: one examining the personality traits of juveniles convicted of sexual assault and one on the high number of serious road traffic accidents and 'street racing', comparing 'street racers' and 'ordinary drivers' in their attitudes regarding traffic safety and risk taking. The fourth and final section is on different aspects of 'interviewing' and commences with a chapter from the Netherlands and South Africa on the effects of asking witnesses to close their eyes during the interview. The next chapter improves our understanding of how false memories may arise/be created. The volume's final chapter is co-authored in the United Kingdom and Israel, and it addresses verbal veracity assessment procedures. Overall, this book presents a truly international ('East meets West') perspective.

We hope that this volume will attract the attention of both students and researchers within the field, eager to learn about the 'psychology and law' scene in Russia. We also foresee that the book will be of interest to practitioners who want to take part in the latest research findings.

Pär Anders Granhag
Ray Bull
Alla Shaboltas
Elena Dozortseva

Setting the Stage I

Forensic and Criminal Psychology in Russia
History of Development and Current State

1

ALLA SHABOLTAS

Contents

1.1 Psychology and Law in 18th Century: The Beginning

It was in the 18th century that the idea of interconnection between psychological and forensic aspects of law experienced rapid development in Russia, like in many other countries. The need to take into account the psychological make-up of the criminal when investigating crimes and the insight into criminal behaviour was expressed by Ivan Pososhkov (1652–1729), a prominent Russian economist, writer and public figure. In his work titled *A Book on Poverty and Wealth* (1724), he suggested various methods for interviewing and interrogating the accused and the witnesses, and explained how to explore the evidence given by false witnesses in order to obtain extensive information that will expose their lies, and also recommended to break criminals into groups to avoid the bad influence of the worst ones over the less depraved ones (Pososhkov, 2010).

Vasiliy Tatishchev (1686–1750), an eminent historian, geographer, economist and statesman, was an ardent supporter of compulsory, long-term instruction and education of the population in legal matters starting from the childhood years as a strategy of crime prevention. He convincingly argues this in his *Talk about Benefits of Sciences and Schools* written in 1733 (Tatishchev, 1887).

Prince Mikhail Shcherbatov (1733–1790), who was a historian and a philosopher, emphasised in his works, particularly his *History of Russia from the*

Earliest Times, the necessity for a lawmaker to know the 'human heart' and the need to create laws with due account for the psychology of the people (Shcherbatov, 1777). Shcherbatov was amongst the first to bring up the issue of possible early release of reformed criminals and the need to use prisoner's labour.

Fedor Ushakov (1748–1770), a Russian philosopher and legal expert, was a vocal opponent of any violence. In his treatise *On Law and the Purpose of Punishment* (1770), Ushakov emphasised the importance of creating psychological conditions when punishing and influencing a criminal. The essential point for him was leading the criminal to repentance (Radishchev, 2005). The most important achievements of scientific and social thought with relation to the issues of psychology and law which were formulated in Russia in the 18th century were classifications of criminals, attention to the procedures of interviewing and interrogating witnesses and suspects as well as the need to increase legal awareness amongst the population in order to prevent crime.

Amongst the prominent people and the most important works in the field of psychology and law which appeared at the same time in Europe we should name the prominent English humanist John Howard (1726–1790), whose efforts led to tremendous progress in the area of reforming the system and incarceration conditions of correctional institutions. In this regard it is interesting to mention one of his first works, *The State of Prisons in England and Wales* (1777), where he emphasised the importance of humanisation of prison conditions as an essential factor in rehabilitation (Sliozberg, 1891). It is noteworthy that Howard visited Russia several times. The first time he came to Russia was in 1781. His main purpose was to take a survey of Russian prisons and correctional institutions. Howard's particular interest in Russia's penitentiary system was due to the fact that Russia at the time was the only country in Europe where, even if just on paper, the death penalty was abolished. Howard came to Russia a second time in 1789, mainly to survey the state of the military hospitals in the southern part of the country, as the issues of organising medical care in the event of such socially dangerous diseases were also amongst his primary interests. Arriving at Kherson (at that time located on the territory of Ukraine), where an epidemic of typhus was raging, Howard actively participated in the fight against this infection. He also planned to visit Crimea, but it was not to be, since at the beginning of 1790 he fell ill, catching typhus most probably from one of his patients, and despite the help given to him by Prince Grigoriy Potemkin's personal physician, died on January 20, 1790, and was buried in Kherson.

The German writer and philosopher Carl Von Eckartshausen (1752–1803) was best known for his works in the field of mysticism and theosophy. He served as adviser on legal matters to the Elector of Bavaria and was regarded in Europe of that time as an expert in the field of jurisprudence, who placed special emphasis on the psychological aspects of criminal investigation. In this respect, his work *The Need for Psychological Insights in Assessing Crime* (1791) is especially noteworthy.

Around the same time, the German scientist Johann Schaumann (1768–1821) published his work *Thoughts on Criminal Psychology* (1792), which contains analysis of separate criminal law concepts. In general, one can conclude that at the end of the 18th century both in Russia and Europe a specialised branch of psychological and legal knowledge emerged, namely, criminal – and later in a broader sense – forensic psychology.

1.2 Psychology and Law in the 19th Century

The development of psychology and law in the 19th century in Russia is marked by several important achievements, including a greater emphasis on the idea that application of psychological knowledge in legal matters is important and the publication of a large number of works on criminal psychology, typology, motivation and the mental state of criminals. In the 19th century, forensic psychology and forensic psychiatry were united into one subject area, and the possibilities and the nature of rehabilitation of criminals were clearly identified.

A major role in the development of criminal psychology was played by the works of the Russian writer, philosopher and prominent public figure, who advocated the revolutionary transformation of the society and the legal sphere, Alexander Radishchev (1749–1802). In his work *On Legislation*, written in 1802, he made one of the first attempts in history to formulate a typology of crimes and criminals, to describe the main motives and causes of criminal behaviour, and also emphasised the importance of taking into account the individual characteristics of offenders when developing and implementing preventive measures (Radishchev, 1952).

Alexander Galich (1783–1848), a Russian idealist philosopher, who studied in Germany, is known for one of Russia's first works on traits and patterns of human character, *Picture of a Human* (1834). Galich insisted that judges should be good psychologists in order to understand the psychology of criminals and various personalities (Ananiev, 1947).

The beginning of the 19th century in Russia was marked by the introduction, in 1806, of the first criminal psychology courses for law students at Moscow State University, taught by Professor Christian Steltzer.

In the early 19th century, the idea of using psychological data in criminal investigations started to appear in the works of European authors as well, in particular, in *Psychology in its Major Applications to the Administration of Justice* (1808) by the German scholar Johann Hofbauer and in the works of Johann Friedreich, *Systemic Literature on Medical and Forensic Psychology* (1833) and *A System of Forensic Psychology* (1842). Amongst those interested in psychological issues connected with evaluation of human evidence was the prominent French mathematician Pierre-Simon Laplace. In his *Philosophical Essay on Probabilities* published in France in 1814, Laplace attempts a materialist interpretation of the reliability of judicial decisions.

The first definition of forensic psychology as a scientific discipline in Russia was given in the late 19th century by the Russian psychiatrist, Professor Alexander Frese (1826–1884) in his *Essay on Forensic Psychology* (1871), where he describes it as application of knowledge about abnormal mental life to the solution of legal problems (Frese, 1874). Frese contributed greatly to the implementation of psychological and psychiatric knowledge in practical work aimed at crime prevention. On his initiative and with his direct participation, the first orphanage for young offenders was established in Kazan in 1872.

Leonid Vladimirov, a prominent lawyer and expert in the field of criminalistics at the time, expressed the belief that criminalists in their work should first and foremost be guided by psychiatrists and psychologists, not by lawyers. Justification of such statements can be found in his works titled *Psychological Peculiarities of Criminals According to the Newest Studies* (1877) and *Psychological Studies in Criminal Court* (1901). Vladimirov stressed that investigation of crimes should be based on medical and psychological data. He supported the need for judicial proceedings to engage experts in the field of psychology, who would have the right to familiarise themselves with case files, examine the defendant and question participants of the trial. He pointed out that a crime could result from a mental condition; therefore, in order to avoid errors in the analysis of the crime, medical and psychological investigation should be applied. Vladimirov believed that just like a disease affected first of all those organisms death of which would be favourable for disease's development, the social causes of crime looked for favourable soil in the individual character.

Subsequently, Vladimirov's ideas laid the foundation for the development of forensic psychological investigation and its problems. He introduced the term 'psychology of the criminal procedure', by which he meant 'a psychological examination of both the crime and the proof' (Vladimirov, 1901).

The development of the interdisciplinary field of psychology and law at the end of the 19th century was greatly influenced by the works of Dmitriy Dril' (1846–1910). Dril' was an outstanding legal scholar, statesman and public figure, the recognised leader of the Russian branch of the positive school in criminal anthropology. Dril' received his first degree in the field of law and, dissatisfied with the dogmatic practices that prevailed at that time in Russian jurisprudence, went to a medical school to study psychiatry, natural and medical sciences and their application for a comprehensive examination of the offender and his personality. He went on a three-year business trip to Western Europe, studying inmates of prisons, juvenile homes, workhouses, pauper asylums and psychiatric clinics. His master's thesis titled 'Juvenile Offenders' caused a heated discussion in the scientific community due to its explicit promotion of the anthropological school in criminal law (Dril', 1884). He was particularly interested in the individual factors of crime, which, in contrast to West European anthropologists, were in his view completely subordinated to social factors. In his opinion, two main factors – the personal and the social – were at the bottom of any crime, with the latter determining the former. In 1908, Dril' together with Vladimir Bekhterev founded the Psychoneurological Institute, which included the development of the course on 'Forensic Psychology' into its programme. In 1909, the Criminological Institute was founded within this institute, with its main purpose being interdisciplinary research of human personality, the necessity of which Dril' had always supported. Dril' himself referred to his main work, *Crime and Criminals*, as studies on criminal psychology; this work can serve as an indispensable reference book for modern criminologists as well. Whilst criticising the idea of innate criminality, Dril' nevertheless highly valued the scientific basis of Western European anthropology. He regarded Cesare Lombroso's famous treatise *Criminal Man* (1898) as the turning point in the development of the science of criminal law and believed that mental abnormalities played an important role in determination of criminal behaviour. In all of his works Dril' remains staunchly opposed to the 'classical school' of criminal law, recognising that crime is an expression of congenital and acquired abnormalities in mental organisation and the nervous system of the criminal, who should therefore be treated rather than punished (Dril', 1899). His fundamental works can with good reason be regarded as the basis for the development of Russian legal psychology. 'Psychologisation' of law and humanisation of attitude towards criminals in the late 19th century was greatly influenced by Russian literature. The prominent, worldwide renowned Russian writers Fedor Dostoevsky, Lev Tolstoy and Anton Chekhov in their works turned to the analysis of the causes of crime, stressing the ambivalent character of criminal personality, which combines contradictory impulses and emotions. The writers paid much attention to their own studies of moral and religious aspects of crime, psychological conflicts, sufferings, feelings of guilt and remorse. Literary works of the time contained detailed descriptions of Russian prisons and the horrifying living conditions of the prisoners. The need to integrate achievements of various sciences, including psychology, into legal and criminological practice was also extensively discussed in the late 19th century by prominent Western European scientists and experts.

Hans Gross (1847–1915), a prominent Austrian scholar who is regarded as the creator of Western European forensic science and legal psychology, when working as an investigator and studying the techniques of criminal investigation, called attention to the negligence, characteristic of Austrian police at the time. Gross worked on classification of successful investigation techniques; took interest in chemistry, physics, botany, microscopy and psychology and declared that knowledge of criminal law and criminal procedure law alone was not enough for successful criminal investigation. Gross emphasised the need to examine criminals, their personality, criminal methods and techniques used to commit crimes. Being an ardent advocate of comprehensive training for future investigators and despite the strong opposition on the leadership of law schools, Gross managed in 1895 to obtain permission to read his lectures to law students. Starting from that time, criminalistics appeared in the curriculum of law schools. In classroom, Gross made wide use of role-playing games and carried out psychological experiments. He was interested in the problem of detecting lies in testimony, the perception of the incident by the witness and its peculiarities. In order to perfect his *Handbook for Coroners, Police Officials, and Military Policemen* (1895) and to collect information on criminal and investigative experience, Gross began publishing *Archives on Criminal Anthropology and Criminalistics*, a journal that is still published today. Gross contributed immensely to the development of legal psychology. His *Criminal Psychology* (1898), where he analyses the psychology of interrogating witnesses and defendants, and the psychology of judicial work, has become a notable achievement in the development of legal psychology. In this book Gross for the first time used the term 'forensic psychology', regarding it as an applied branch of general psychology. He defined forensic psychology as the entirety of psychological knowledge that can be useful for a criminalist.

The problem of using psychological knowledge in the legal field was extensively studied by Edouard Claparède (1873–1940), a prominent Swiss psychologist. He was distinguished by the breadth of his interests in the field of psychology, including such topics as sleep, activity of the intellect, problem solving and education. He was also interested in neurology and psychiatry. In addition to his theoretical, experimental and applied work in the field of psychology, Claparède devoted much time to professional and administrative duties. He founded the *Archives de Psychologie* and made a significant contribution to international cooperation of psychologists through the work of the International Congress of Psychology. Besides, in 1912 he founded the Jean-Jacques Rousseau Institute, which he conceived as a centre for innovative research and practical studies in the field of education. Claparède was the person who entered the term 'legal psychology' into scientific use (1906), the term later being adopted in Russia as a general definition for all applicable areas in psychology and law. In the same year he introduced the course of legal psychology at the University of Geneva. Claparède significantly expanded the range of problems addressed by forensic psychology.

Russian scholars working in the field in psychology and law in the late 19th century in Russia also paid great attention to the works of European authors on psychological aspects of testimony. In this connection it is important to mention Albert von Schrenck-Notzing (1862–1929), a German physician, psychiatrist and notable psychic researcher, who devoted much of his time to the study of paranormal events, connected with mediumship, hypnotism and telepathy, but as a practitioner testified at a murder trial about the effects of suggestibility on witness testimony. It is noteworthy that at the time, both in Europe and the United States, there appeared works discussing experimental studies of processes of information reproduction by different people, which exerted considerable influence on the application of psychology in judicial practice. First, it is necessary to mention the works of William Stern (1871–1938), a German psychologist and philosopher, and the creator of the IQ concept, who is considered to be one of the pioneers of differential psychology and personality psychology and who had a great influence on the nascent legal psychology. Stern wrote that accurate and exact testimonies and memories were rather an exception than the rule. We should also mention the American psychologist James McKeen Cattell (1860–1944); the French psychologist Alfred Binet (1857–1911), who created the world's first test for the assessment of intelligence and Hugo Munsterberg (1863–1916), a philosopher and psychologist of German origin who pioneered the use of applied psychology in education, medicine and business, whilst choosing legal practice as the primary field for application of psychological knowledge.

1.3 Psychology and Law in the 20th Century

The late 19th and the early 20th centuries in Russia are connected with intensive development of psychology and psychiatry as well as a number of legal disciplines. Many scholars who worked in these fields at the time had progressive views and attitudes (Ivan Sechenov, Vladimir Spasovich, Dmitriy Dril', Leonid Vladimirov, Ivan Foynitsky, Vladimir Bekhterev, Sergey Korsakov, Vladimir Serbskiy, Anatoliy Koni and others). The active development of problems of psychology, psychiatry and law resulted in the necessity to formally establish legal psychology as a separate science. In 1899, the famous Russian psychiatrist and public figure Pavel Kovalevsky (1850–1931) raised the issue of the need to divide psychopathology and legal psychology and the introduction of these sciences into programmes of legal education.

At the beginning of the 20th century, experimental studies of legal psychology gained importance in both theory and practical work. A significant number of works from this period deal with the topical problem of the psychology of testimony (Vasilyev, 1998). These include the works by Portugalov (*On Testimony*, 1903), Goldovsky (*Psychology of Testimony*, 1904), Elistratov (*On Influence of Non-Suggestive Questions on Accuracy of Testimonies*, 1904), Kulisher (*Psychology of Testimony and Court Investigation*, 1904), Zavadsky and Elistratov (*On the Accuracy of Testimonies*, 1906). In 1922, the famous

Russian lawyer, judge and public figure Anatoliy Koni (1844–1927) published a brochure titled 'Memory and Attention', which set forward problems connected with testimony. Koni played an important role in the integration of psychology and law, possessing extensive knowledge in both areas. In his works Koni spoke critically about direct conclusions made on the basis of experimental studies, in particular the conclusions made by Stern, laying emphasis on the fact that experimental conditions in research differ significantly from the actual conditions of crime (Koni, 2000).

In the same period, a significant number of works that examined the psychology of the criminal's personality appeared. First, we should mention the works of Lev Petrazhitsky (1867–1931), the Russian and Polish scientist, lawyer, sociologist, philosopher and member of the first State Duma, and in particular, his *Theory of Law and State in Connection with Theory of Morality* (1907). Petrazhitsky emphasised the need to develop the psychological theory of law. According to him, law observance is determined by psychological factors, such as experiences and emotions (Petrazhitsky, 2000).

Solutions to methodological problems of legal psychology continued to attract attention after the establishment of the Soviet system. The issue of applying psychological knowledge during interrogations, preliminary investigations and trials was given much attention. After the establishment of juvenile courts in 1910 in Russia, special attention was paid to the study of the personality and behaviour of juvenile offenders. The law of evidence in the new system of justice placed particular emphasis on forensic examination, including the psychological one. During that period, intensive research was carried out by the psychologist Alexander Luriya (1902–1977). He studied the possibility of using the methods of experimental psychology in criminal investigation (Luriya, 2010). In 1927, on his initiative and with his direct participation, the laboratory of experimental psychology was established under the auspices of the General Prosecutor's office (1927), where researchers studied, for example, the method of 'conjugated motor dynamics' to evoke 'symptoms of the concealed situation', which was later used for the development of the polygraph. In Russia, during the first 15 years of Soviet power, conditions favourable for the development of almost every branch of legal psychology were created due to the social mandate and the establishment of organisational and institutional conditions for applied research. In 1925, the National Institute for Studies of Criminals and Criminality was established in Moscow, which contributed to the growth of psychological and legal knowledge. Diverse research tools for examining the personality of criminals and for influencing them were developed. Amongst the most significant works of the period were *Essays on Criminal Psychology* (1925) by the philosopher and psychologist Konstantin Sotonin (1893–1944), *Criminal Psychology: Criminal Types* by the lawyer and psychologist Sergey Poznyshev (1870–1943), *In Prison: Essays on Prison Psychology* (1926) by the legal expert and criminalist Michael Gernet (1874–1953), *Studying the Personality of the Criminal* (1928) by the psychiatrist and psychologist Vladimir Bekhterev (1857–1927) and *Forensic Psychiatric Evaluation* (1929) by the forensic psychologist Brusilovsky. Amongst the significant events of that time one should name the establishment in St. Petersburg, on the initiative of Bekhterev and Dril, of a research institute with a course of forensic psychology (1907) and the establishment at its premises of the Criminological Institute in 1909. In 1925, the National Institute for Studies of Criminals and Criminality was founded in Moscow. In many cities, including Moscow, Leningrad, Kiev, Odessa and others, research centres (departments) of forensic psychology were established. At the time when the First Congress for the Study of the Human was held in 1930, legal psychology was already an established area of applied psychology, and achievements of scientists working on the problems of criminal, judicial and penitentiary character received recognition.

The development of psychology in general, and legal psychology in particular, in the 20th century in Soviet Russia experienced a tragic period of more than 25 years, when as a result of the government resolution 'On pedological perversions in the system of People's Commissariats of Education' of July 4, 1936, experimental studies were almost completely halted. Psychology as a science, including forensic and legal psychology, was subjected to severe criticism. The government banned experimental psychology and all laboratories were closed. Introspection became the only recognised research method.

Studies in the field of legal psychology were only resumed in the 1960s. Applied psychological studies were launched to cater for the purposes of law enforcement, administration of the law and crime prevention. During the last 50 years, Russian experts in the field of legal psychology have been examining a wide range of topics. These topics include using forensic psychological expert examination, the psychology of interrogation and investigation, psychological problems of crime issues of the psychology of a criminal's personality, the psychology of judicial procedure and good behaviour. Psychological knowledge is now widely used in the criminal investigation process. In the 1960s to 1980s, active implementation of psychological and psychiatric evaluation in criminological practice began; psychological studies started within the penitentiary system. Courses in psychology were widely introduced in the educational programmes at law faculties of universities and institutes. Starting from 1964, courses in forensic psychology were included in all educational programs for training lawyers.

During that time, the modern independent national school of legal psychology developed, which is represented by a number of distinguished scholars and practitioners. First, we should mention one of the founders of Russian legal psychology, the prominent legal expert Alexander Ratinov (1920–2007). Ratinov made an enormous contribution to the development of modern legal psychology. Publication of his main work, *Forensic Psychology for Investigators* (1967), was a major event in the field. This book was the first fundamental work after years of stagnation experienced by legal psychology in the USSR. It determined the main directions in the development of legal psychology. In the late 1960s and the early 1970s, Ratinov organised, within the National Institute for the Study of Causes and Development of Measures for Crime Prevention at the Prosecutor's Office of the USSR (now the Research Institute of Strengthening the Legality and the Rule of Law at the General Procuracy of the Russian Federation), the country's first research branch of legal psychology, which became the backbone of his school of thought. Here major projects were carried out in the field of legal awareness and public opinion, the psychology of criminal personality, psychological mechanisms of investigative actions, understanding the processes of witness testimony development, reasons for perjury and self-incrimination, principles behind the application of expert psychological knowledge in criminal procedure and so forth. Ratinov, when heading the division of Legal Psychology at the Research Institute of Strengthening the Legality and the Rule of Law, contributed immensely to the coordination of the research in the field of legal psychology. He participated in the development of the legislation with respect to mass media, the development of legal education and to the fight against extremism and organised crime.

A very important role in the development of psychology and law in Russia was played by Michael Kochenov (1935–1999), a prominent expert in the field of clinical and legal psychology. Kochenov started his career as a general and clinical psychologist, but then, in the course of his research work, created a highly integrated field of forensic psychological work. Thus, the forensic psychology, first, consolidates the achievements from separate areas of psychology (clinical, social, developmental, etc.) and, second, serves as a source of new theoretical knowledge in general psychology and its main sections. Kochenov became known as a brilliant clinical psychologist in at least two areas: in his pathopsychological studies of motivation in schizophrenia and in justifying the need for comprehensive forensic psychological and psychiatric examination, which is now the prevailing form of expert psychological knowledge used in forensic examination. Kochenov carried out in-depth research on the issues of multi-disciplinary psychological and psychiatric expert examination of juvenile offenders with different types of dysontogenesis and victims of sexual abuse suffering from borderline mental disorders. Works published by Kochenov, starting with the outstanding *Forensic Psychiatric Examination* (1977), determined the development of forensic examination with participation of a psychologist for many decades to come. In addition to his work on the problem of forensic psychological examination, Kochenov also greatly contributed to the development of such areas of legal psychology as criminal victimology, psychology of interrogation and application of psychological knowledge by investigators in their professional work.

A very important role in the development of psychology and law in Russia was played by the work of Vladislav Vasilyev (1930–2011), who, possessing both practical and research experience as a lawyer and psychologist, placed emphasis on psychological aspects of the lawyer's work. He created a course of psychology for law students and began teaching this course at the Law Faculty of St. Petersburg (then Leningrad) State University. The result of this work was a monograph titled *Legal Psychology* (1974), the first work of its kind, which covered a full range of psychological problems in law enforcement. In recent years, Vasilyev, without interrupting his active research work, was developing the methodology for the use of forensic psychological expert examination. Being a recognised forensic psychologist, he carried out examinations, often serving as an expert during re-examinations and in cases when there were inconsistencies in the results of previous examinations. In 1995, serving the needs of real-world practice, he organised and headed the study of religious totalitarian sects. Vasilyev's research interests also included psychological aspects of the shadow economy, organised crime and terrorism as a socio-psychological phenomenon.

The end of the 20th century can be described as a period of active development of research and practical methods in the field of psychology and law in Russia. That time was associated with the establishment of psychological laboratories and departments in the Police Office, the State Prosecutor's Office and Investigative Committee Office, the development of the psychological service in the penitentiary system and the increased use of forensic psychological examination in criminal and civil cases.

1.4 Psychology and Law in Modern Russia

At the present stage of development of psychology and law in Russia, the following areas have already formed and are in existence: legal psychology, criminal psychology, investigative psychology, forensic psychology, penitentiary psychology, preventive psychology, juvenile forensic psychology and psychology of professional work in legal practice. The practice of applying psychological knowledge in the field of law includes more than 15,000 psychological and psychiatric examinations per year. The penitentiary system employs more than 2,500 psychologists working with inmates and correctional officers. Psychological services continue to be established on the basis of police departments. A large number of leading universities in Russia today are engaged in professional training and research in the field of psychology and law. The first master's programme of studies with specialisation in 'legal psychology' in the USSR was established at St. Petersburg State University (SPbU) to satisfy the need of the Ministry of Internal Affairs and Police Departments for psychologists (Kurbatova & Lyskov, 1978). Courses in legal psychology were included in educational programs for all students in law school. Since 2012, two specialised educational programmes of forensic psychology and criminal psychology were introduced at SPbU as part of a 6-year 'clinical psychology' educational programme. Departments of forensic psychology were established at Moscow State University, Rostov-on-Don University and Ryazan Police Academy. The Faculty of Forensic and Legal Psychology was established at the Moscow State University of Psychology and Education, where three levels of educational degrees are provided: BS, MS and PhD. There are three professional journals in Russia (*Forensic Psychology, Applied Forensic Psychology, Psychology and Law*) publishing the latest research data and practical experience of Russian experts in psychology and law.

Current challenges and goals for psychologists in the field of psychology and law in Russia are related to several major issues, such as the reflection of the current state of society from the point of view of legal psychology and application of psychological knowledge to the problems emerging in the field of law; conceptualisation of forensic and legal psychology as a single branch of applied psychology, its theoretical grounds, its subject and aims, structure and functions; the adoption of an ethical code of practice; the development of best standards of practice and certification of professional activities (such as forensic psychological assessment) and the development of professional scientific and practical exchange at the national and international level. From this point of view, international cooperation in psychology and law, including research and educational programmes as well as conferences, is important for the achievement of major goals. That is why the 24th International Conference of the European Association of Psychology and Law held in St. Petersburg State University in Russia in 2014 has been seen as one of the strongest resources for scientific and educational development, creating new perspectives for psychology and law both in Russia and abroad.

References

Ananiev, B. G. (1947). *Essays on the history of Russian psychology in the 18th and the 19th centuries* (pp. 74–79). Moscow: Gospotilizdat (in Russian).

Dril', D. A. (1884). *Juvenile offenders: History of the latest studies* (Issue 1). Moscow: Publishing House of A.I. Mamontov & Co. (in Russian).

Dril', D. A. (1899). *Criminality and criminals: Essays on criminal psychology* (2nd ed.). St. Petersburg: Nobel-Press (in Russian).

Frese, A. U. (1874). *Essay on forensic psychology*. Kazan (in Russian).

Kochenov, M. M. (1977). *Forensic psychiatric examination*. Moscow: Research Institute on Law Empowerment (in Russian).

Koni, A. F. (2000). *Selected writings and speeches*. Tula: Avtograph (in Russian).

Kurbatova, T. N., & Lyskov, B. D. (1978). *Foundations of legal psychology.* St. Petersburg: St. Petersburg State University (in Russian).

Luriya, A. R. (2010). *Experimental psychology in judicial and investigative work.* Moscow: Yuwrite (in Russian).

Petrazhitsky, L. I. (2000). *Theory of law and state in connection with theory of morality.* St. Petersburg: Lan (in Russian).

Pososhkov, I. (2010). *A book on poverty and wealth: A father's will.* Moscow: Russian Political Encyclopaedia (in Russian).

Radishchev, A. N. (1952). *Selected philosophical and socio-political writings.* Moscow: State Publisher of Political Literature (in Russian).

Radishchev, A. N. (2005). *The life of Fyodor Vasilyevich Ushakov including some of his writings* (Version 1.0). Retrieved from http://www.rvb.ru/18vek/radishchev/01text/vol_1/03prose/019.htm?start=1&length=1 (in Russian).

Ratinov, A. R. (1967). *Forensic psychology for investigators.* Moscow: Research Institute High Police School of Russian Federation (in Russian).

Shcherbatov, M. M. (1777). *History of Russia from the earliest times* (Vol. 7, Part I). St. Petersburg: Imperator's Academy of Science (in Russian).

Sliozberg, G. (1891). *Howard: His life and his public and charitable work. A biography* (Lives of Great People Series). St. Petersburg (in Russian).

Tatishchev, V. N. (1887). *Talk about benefits of sciences and schools.* Moscow: University Printing House (in Russian).

Vasilyev, V. L. (1998). *Legal psychology.* St. Petersburg: Piter (in Russian).

Vladimirov, L. E. (1901). *Psychological investigation in criminal court.* Moscow: Publishing House of A.A. Levenson (in Russian).

Legal Consciousness
The Nervous Chord
of a Legal System

2

DJENEVRA I. LUKOVSKAYA
MARIA A. KAPUSTINA

Soviet legal theory all but ignored the concept of legal consciousness. Up until the 1970s, it signified only the degree to which people exercised law, or the attitude of social classes to the existing body of legal rules. Such an approach was relevant because the law was understood strictly as a body of legal rules; this understanding was dominant and officially maintained.

Later, in the 1970–1980s, researchers started to develop the concept of a legal system and broadened its scope from one single component (a body of legal rules) to several components. The terms 'legal system' and 'body of legal rules' are often used interchangeably in Russian and foreign law books, which is a tribute to the established tradition. However, it does not mean that these concepts are treated as theoretically identical. Adherents to the so-called broad understanding of law used the legal system concept in their polemic against legal positivists (etatists). Therefore, 'the legal system' is a Russian version of a broad (integral) understanding of law which comprises not only the body of legal rules, but also legal consciousness and legal relations.

Researchers turned to the notion of a legal system because they recognised the need for a comprehensive study of legal reality. Besides, the idea was considered a tacit compromise between the advocates of a narrow and broad comprehension of law – a fortunate way out of a methodological dead end. The concept of a legal system included legal rules established by the government, legal relations and legal consciousness. This concept complied with the broad understanding of law. The academic community also approved this interpretation of law; a compromise had thus been found. Consequently, Russian legal scholars laid the groundwork for an integral understanding of law from the perspectives of various philosophical and methodological approaches.

What comprises a legal system is an issue of debate. A legal system normally includes: (a) positive law, that is, a set of rules expressed in legislation and in other forms of positive law approved by the government; (b) the ideology of law and (c) the practice of law (Alekseev, 1999). Some authors associate the ideology of law only with the dominant ideology of law. Others believe it should include both the dominant and non-dominant ideologies of law. We wholly agree with the latter view. There is an opinion that in its static form the legal system contains the ideology of law, whilst its dynamic form includes legal thinking (Vasilev, 1986). This statement does not sound convincing as it belittles legal consciousness, which is a crucial element of any legal system.

We believe it is legal consciousness that reflects and accommodates people's values; and these values, including positive law, enable us to judge what legal culture society has. Legal culture is not an independent element of a legal system. It is determined by the workings and evolution of the entire legal system including the legal consciousness level, the behavioural level, the institutional level and the level of development of law as a body of legal rules ('law in books'). For this reason, a comparative study of various legal systems implies identification of their cultural and historical backgrounds, including factors and preconditions of legal development.

There is a discussion about the relation between the legal system and legal reality. Legal reality is viewed as 'the legal life', 'the legal field' or 'the legal sphere' of society – a standpoint which, beyond doubt, broadens a lawyer's horizons. Some authors isolate the legal system from legal reality, because the former includes only positive components of the latter; meanwhilst, legal reality comprises also legal pathology – for example, violations of law (Polyakov & Timoshina, 2005; Zatonsky & Malko, 2006). We do not agree with these authors for different reasons. We think, however, that legal pathology – not only the infringement of law, but also, for instance, deformed legal consciousness – belongs to the legal system, but not as its component. Rather, it serves as an indicator of the degree of violation which characterises a certain profile of the legal system at a given point of time. Eventually, deviant behaviour indicates the attitude of legal subjects (participants of legal life) to the regulatory values of a legal system. It shows the degree to which society accepts the goals of the legal system and the means of their achievement.

Finally, the totality of legal phenomena forming a legal system (not only the basic ones) allows us to judge about the legal culture and legal consciousness of a particular society. Legal consciousness determines lawful or unlawful behaviour. Indeed, deformed legal consciousness often excites unlawful behaviour. Can a legal system help eradicate negative phenomena from legal reality, if these phenomena are not included in the legal system itself? Any system structures its own elements, but it cannot organise those outside its scope.

What element integrates all others into a legal system? Most authors think it is positive law in its regulatory or sociological sense. This approach demonstrates, at best, a neutral attitude to the quality of law (positive law) and, thus, to the quality of the entire legal practice. The role of legal consciousness amounts only to the improvement of an existing normative order, regardless of how this order is perceived by subjects of law. However, all legal institutions develop and function solely due to the conscious activity of people. Activity and information, which Polyakov and Timoshina (2005) refer to as two separate pillars, form a major component of the legal system. In this case, we can hardly overestimate the role of legal consciousness in putting a legal system together. Unlike our colleagues, we also identify a regulatory complex within a legal system, although we do not consider it to be foundational. Still it is legal consciousness that integrates all the components into a legal system. It is an instrument with which cultural values are reproduced and distributed in the legal sphere.

We believe that too much importance is often attached to identifying an integrating component. Scholars tend to fail to see that the component, identified as an integrating one, acquires new characteristics in the structure of the system through interaction with other components. The same component possesses different properties in its autonomous, isolated existence. The legal system is a dynamic structural unity. Its basic properties, ways of interaction with external environment and self-organising capacity are determined by the *relations* between system components rather than by the components themselves. The contemporary systematic approach seeks to establish integrative relations between components rather than identify an integrating one (Lukovskaya & Kapustina, 2012). Cultural and historical features of the legal system as well as its authenticity in a given society develop precisely in the aforementioned relations.

Therefore, legal consciousness integrates all components of a legal system, interacting with all phenomena of legal reality. Legal consciousness activates legal relations subjects. This activity becomes possible only after the subjects realise their mutual rights and obligations. A subject in a legal system realises and evaluates these phenomena 'from the inside', as a participant in the society's legal life, by interacting with other people; but not 'from the outside' as an external observer. Ilin (2003) even claims that

> The dictates of law presuppose that citizens consciously seek to observe the law because *legal order rests on the interaction between citizens at the level of their legal consciousness*. If citizens do not have the aforementioned striving, legal order turns into incessant, systematic violence … Good government views its citizens as virtuous and desired partners in state-building. Such a government trusts their intentions and believes in public approval. It counts on citizen support and does not fear their free initiative: winning its citizens' trust, the government comes to trust itself; and the trust in itself allows it to be confident in its citizens.

Interacting with each other at the level of legal consciousness, subjects of law, as participants of social legal life, realise their mutual rights and obligations at the rational and non-rational (emotional) levels, as well as at the level of professional and non-professional knowledge. Legal consciousness reflects the attitude to the legal sphere held by individuals, groups and society.

Is the researcher of legal phenomena a participant of legal reality? Or is he or she an outside observer? Obviously, a legal scholar (as any social scientist or humanities scholar) cannot just 'observe' legal phenomena 'from the outside'. In 1922, Frank wrote,

> In social science the subject of knowledge coincides, to a known degree, with its object; and this is a methodological peculiarity of social science. A researcher of an anthill does not participate in its life; a bacteriologist and the microorganisms he studies are two different phenomena; however, a social scientist directly participates – consciously or unconsciously – in the life of the society he investigates.

Today, even physics shares the same peculiarity: a research object is not independent of a research subject any more due to the development of quantum theory.

Polyakov (2013) uses the notion of 'an outside observer' when he refers to law as a coherent whole: in particular, virtual law in unity with actual law (the law viewed by 'a participant' of legal relations). Aleksi views the issue from a different angle. He says that there is an important connection between law and morality. According to him, acknowledgement of this connection depends on the perspective from which the law is viewed: from the point of view of an observer or participant, that is, from an external or internal perspective on law (Hart suggested to differentiate between internal and external perspectives on law). The observer is a scientist for whom it is important to strictly differentiate between law and morality. The participant of legal life cannot be indifferent to the ethical bases of legal rules (Aleksi, 2011, 2012).

The preceding example differentiates between 'an observer' and 'a participant'. Most probably, the difference lies between scientific (professional) and non-scientific (non-professional) knowledge. The philosophy of science views it as a problem of scientific knowledge limits. In the 1970s, this problem became the starting point of the criticism of scientific knowledge, which is science as rationality in its classic understanding that implies a belief in the omnipotence of reason and its power of transformation, and so forth. Should we abandon our search for these limits? According to Feyerabend, the answer is positive. And if not, there are other questions. Can these boundaries change? Or are they beyond the scope of science, various theories being merely the result of convention? And so on.

Whilst classical science claimed that there was an unavoidable gap between scientific and non-scientific knowledge, modern (postmodern) science turns to the logic of the latter. It does not contrast unscientific and scientific knowledge, but, on the contrary, insists on their harmonisation and continuity. At the level of non-scientific knowledge, citizens develop under-lying, internal strata of legal consciousness, which implies the legal mentality and legal culture of a society. A legislator, a judge and a legal scholar have both scientific (professional) legal consciousness and everyday consciousness with its 'legal myths', guidelines and so on (i.e. accusatory bias in criminal procedure).

In the early 20th century, the concepts of legal consciousness emphasised its psychological component. According to Petrazhitskiy, law itself consists of imperative and attributive emotions. Jhering (1991) denied that legal con-sciousness could have any rational nature. He asserted that it was the feeling for law rather than human reason formed the psychological origins of law. Ilin (1994) defined legal consciousness as 'a natural feeling for law and right-ness', 'a special sort of instinctive feeling for law'. However, he added that legal consciousness also included thought, will, imagination and the whole sphere of subconscious experience.

Between the mid-1930s and the mid-1950s, Soviet legal theory excluded the psychological aspect of legal consciousness. Legal consciousness was lim-ited to a set of views, ideas and notions about existing law. Any evaluative attitude to law and any desired ideals of law were ruled out. The rational (ideological) element of legal consciousness was made absolute.

The preceding absolutisation has its origins in the 17th–18th century doctrine of natural law. The doctrine glorified the legislative reason which is never wrong (like Rousseau's common will of citizen legislators). Classical rationalism considered both the legislator and the judge to be representa-tives of a unique reason, which is unavailable to ordinary citizens. We agree with Chestnov that Dworkin's famous Judge Hercules is of the same kind (Chestnov, 2013).

In Russian jurisprudence (both theoretically and practically oriented), the legal system is still presented primarily as the product of an exclusively rational mechanism of legal (i.e. state-legal) regulation. Government, repre-sented by its legislative bodies, occupies the central role in legal regulation. Therefore, it also finds itself in the centre of the legal system, which is the product of legal regulation. From this point of view, the legal system develops in purposeful and rational regulation of social relations through legal rules. The rational (professional) component is still considered dominant in the structure of legal consciousness. The point is that individuals to whom legal actions are addressed do not have professional legal skills. Therefore, they are only supposed to embody in their behaviour the dictates of law generated by professional lawyers. The psychological (emotional) part of legal conscious-ness, be it a legislator's, a judge's or a private person's legal consciousness, is taken into account only in a limited number of cases. These cases are mainly associated with the sphere of criminal law: for example, a motive for committing a crime. As a rule, the motive for a civil or administrative offence has no legal significance unless it involves harm.

We cannot agree with this view, as contemporary research indicates the opposite. Legal consciousness and, perhaps, mainly its psychological component play a considerable role in legal regulation of social relations. Non-professional legal consciousness not only shows a citizen's attitude to effective law and its practice, but also affects the content and results of legal regulation in general. To be more exact, both rational and non-rational legal consciousness influence legal regulation. For this reason, a legal system develops not only by virtue of a rationally organised mechanism for state-legal regulation, but also under the influence of unordered processes and self-organising social relations.

Legal consciousness performs an important role in all spheres of legal regulation. However, legal regulation of healthcare is, perhaps, the most representative example because it concerns everyone. There is very little research on how people and medical workers perceive and legitimatise Russian healthcare law. One such study was conducted by a St. Petersburg State University research team. It was part of the Law Enforcement Monitoring Research Project aimed at assessing judicial opinion (judicial practice), and actions taken by public prosecutors and other state bodies. The Ministry of Justice of Russia and other government bodies provided assistance to the team in collecting law enforcement data. The resulting empirical data yielded important theoretical and practical observations regarding the role rational and irrational legal consciousness plays in legal regulation of healthcare. The data also shows what meaning is ascribed to regulatory rules by various participants of legal regulation.

The project was carried out in 2012. It included the following data: citizen requests submitted to St. Petersburg State University; online submissions on specialised medical forums providing space for private requests; the practice of general jurisdiction and commercial courts of the Russian Federation; inspections carried out by the Public Prosecutor's Office in St. Petersburg between 2010 and 2013 and interviews with district prosecutors and their deputies in St. Petersburg. The research was focused, amongst other topics, on common violations of the immunoprophylaxis law.

We think that these violations clearly prove the interdependence between rational and non-rational (or emotional) legal consciousness. They show that individual legal consciousness is an integral part of government officials' legal knowledge.

In compliance with Article 4 of Federal Law No. 157-FZ of 17 September 1998, 'On Immunoprophylaxis of Infectious Diseases' (hereinafter 'the immunoprophylaxis law'), the government policy on immunoprophylaxis is aimed at preventing, curbing and eliminating infectious diseases. The Government of the Russian Federation and regional authorities ensure the implementation of this policy. Lack of prophylactic vaccinations entails unfavourable legal consequences for citizens. The consequences are connected with certain restrictions of citizens' rights and legitimate interests in the following three cases. First, without prophylactic vaccinations a citizen will be forbidden to enter the countries where such vaccinations are required. Second, such a citizen will be temporarily denied access to educational and healthcare institutions in case of mass infectious diseases or under threat of an epidemic. Third, he or she will not be allowed to fill, or will be removed from, a position which is associated with a high risk of contracting an infectious disease. The researchers came to the following conclusions: Although the first two cases hardly ever occurred in the studied period, the third case – the denial of access to work or removal from work due to absence of necessary vaccinations – is a widespread problem, as the judicial practice and the work of public prosecutor's offices reveal.

The list of jobs involving a high risk of catching infectious diseases and requiring obligatory vaccinations is established by Government of the Russian Federation Regulation No. 825 of 15 July 1999. Persons holding such jobs will lose their employment unless they have prophylactic vaccinations. As part of the monitoring we researched law enforcement acts connected with the firing of employees of medical and educational institutions. We should note the type of vaccination appearing practically in all the cases examined is flu vaccination. As for other vaccinations included in the national prophylactic vaccination schedule, workers get vaccinated in a timely manner. The peculiarity of this vaccination is that it is done every year in accordance with the national prophylactic vaccination schedule.

Mass media form a diverse public opinion on the effectiveness of the flu vaccination. There is a wide discussion about potential adverse consequences of this vaccination – for example, various allergic reactions. Judging by the examined data, people refuse this very vaccination. They doubt its effectiveness and fear harmful consequences for their health. For the most part, courts approach the cases of firing quite formally. They consider the absence of prophylactic vaccinations sufficient grounds for dismissal. Furthermore, in some cases judges ruled that a prophylactic vaccination was an obligation – but not a right – for the employees of educational institutions. Besides, they denied a defendant's argument that there had been no flu epidemic in the area for a long time.

However, in other cases judges stated that employees of educational institutions should be discharged from their duties only in the event of mass infectious diseases or under threat of an epidemic; and therefore the absence of flu epidemic may be considered a circumstance in which the dismissal is unnecessary, because there is no real danger to the life and health of the employee and other people.

Presuming the professional expertise of a federal regulatory body in the sphere of healthcare is adequate, immunoprophylaxis experts rather than lawyers (prosecutors, judges or legislators) should make decisions regarding the necessity of annual flu vaccination. This problem cannot obviously be resolved by legal measures alone (law enforcement). As the monitoring showed, medical employees, kindergarten teachers and schoolteachers refuse to be vaccinated even running the risk of being fired. At the same time, their employers, in a number of cases, do not follow public prosecutors' instructions to fire the employee, apparently thinking that the absence of the vaccination does not pose any danger to surrounding people.

The examined practice of legal enforcement characterises different types of legal consciousness in the immunoprophylaxis sphere. Two types of legal consciousness (individual and collective) and its two levels (rational and emotional) conflate in reality, though they might be separate in theory. Naturally, the ways of interaction between, for example, the rational and emotional components of legal consciousness change over time. Nevertheless, all of them – both legal consciousness in general and law itself – stem from the living world of a human. Polyakov (2013) emphasises that law is not an external object for a human; it forms part of a person's living world.

Legal consciousness is the nervous chord of the legal system and of the entire legal life of society. At the same time, we should consider the serious role of environment (context) in the development of legal consciousness, which is viewed as citizen's attitude to the legal life around them. This is because people interpret legal phenomena in a great number of ways. Special importance should be paid to the socio-cultural and legal-cultural contexts of the living world of an individual, a group or society.

References

Alekseev, S. S. (1999). *Gosudarstvo i pravo. Opyt compleksnogo issledovaniya* [Government and law. Experience in comprehensive research] (p. 47). Moscow: Statut Publ.

Aleksi, R. (2011). 'Sushchestvovanie prav cheloveka' [Existence of human rights], *Jurisprudence*, no. 4, 23–31.

Aleksi, R. (2012). 'Dualnaya priroda prava' [The dual nature of law], trans. (from English) by S. I. Maksimov, *Issues of Philosophy of Law* (Vols. 8–9, pp. 19–28). Kiev-Chernivtsi: Chernivtsi National University.

Chestnov, I. L. (2013). 'Dialogicheskaya kontseptsiya prava' [Dialogic concept of law], *Non-classical philosophy of law: Questions and answers* (p. 179). Kharkov: Biblioteka Mezhdunarodnogo zhurnala «Problemy filosofii prava» Publ.

Frank, S. L. (1922). *Ocherk metodologii obshchestvennykh nauk* [Essay on methodology of social science] (p. 36). Moscow: Bereg Publ.

Ilin, I. A. (1994). *Sobranie sochineniy v 10 tomakh* [Collection of essays, in 10 vols.], compilation and comments by Yu. T. Lisitsyn (Vol. 4, p. 231). Moscow: Russkaya kniga Publ.

Ilin, I. A. (2003). *Teoriya gosudarstva i prava* [Theory of law and state] (p. 363). Moscow: Zertsalo Publ.

Jhering, R. (1991). *Borba za pravo* [The struggle for law] (p. 30). Moscow: Feniks Publ.

Lukovskaya D. I., & Kapustina, M. A. (2012). 'Sistemny podkhod v teorii prava' [Systematic approach in legal theory], *Science of Theory and History of State and Law in Search of New Methodological Solutions* (p. 10). St. Petersburg: Asterion Publ.

Polyakov, A. V. (2013). 'Kommunikativno-fenomenologicheskaya kontseptsiya prava' [Communicative-phenomenological concept of law], *Non-Classical Philosophy of Law. Questions and Answers* (pp. 96, 105). Kharkov: Biblioteka Mezhdunarodnogo zhurnala «Problemy filosofii prava» Publ.

Polyakov, A. V., & Timoshina, E. V. (2005). Obshchaya teoriya prava [The general theory of law]. St. Petersburg: Izdatel'skii Dom Sankt-Peterburgskogo gosudarstvennogo universiteta Publ.

Vasilev, A. M. (1986). Pravovaya sistema sotsialisma: Ponyatie, struktura, sotsialnye svyazi [The legal system of socialism: The concept, structure, and social connections] (Vol. 1, p. 39). Moscow: Yuridicheskaya literature Publ.

Zatonsky, V. A., & Malko, A. V. (2006). 'Kategoriya "pravovaya zhizn": Opyt teoreticheskogo osmysleniya' [The concept of legal life: Experience of theoretical consideration], *Jurisprudence*, no. 4, 5.

The Origin of the Paternalistic Tradition in Russian Social Consciousness

3

MARINA IGOREVNA YUDINA

Paternalism (Latin *paternus* meaning 'paternalistic, fatherly') as the principles and practice of state governance is a mechanism of patronage on the part of the state authority, state control over all spheres of public life (Waitr, 1979). As etatism (From French *état* meaning 'a state'), paternalism orients a society to subordinate the public authorities but not to create mechanisms of social compromise and public mind consideration in the process of public decision-making.

It should be pointed out that paternalist consciousness has its roots in the theocratic and patriarchal traditions of the Russian Middle Ages, but it is still seen in Russia, including the law and legal consciousness spheres. Medieval orthodox consciousness was deeply theocratic. This was the root of the main peculiarity of the orthodox understanding of the authority. Besides as religion pervaded social life of that time, the theocratic elements inevitably accompanied all the medieval political theories. The attitude towards the authority was a part of the religious duties of a Christian. This fact itself affected the formation of paternalistic social consciousness.

The Christian doctrine on the supreme authority included the vision of the completeness of the world authority which was essentially related to the Divine authority. Orthodoxy aimed to convert the Kingdom of Caesar to the Kingdom of God, to hallow sovereignty. The doctrine of the orthodox kingdom, which was included in the Holy Writ, was in the basis of the notion 'kingdom'. A father – a chief father – was considered as the prototype of the reign on earth. His authority over his relatives had the divine origin. When families became bigger, the tribes appeared. Thus, kingdoms appeared. That is why all kings were God's vicars on earth and were considered as fathers of their nationals. Orthodox Christianity based on the idea that there was no authority given not by God (Yakovlev, 1867). Those words clearly meant that the authority was the extension of God's order on earth, expression of God's concern for people and divine plan for them (Yakovlev, 1867). According to that idea, orthodoxy considered any assaults on the authority as the assaults on God; accordingly, such assaults were regarded as a crime or as the religious opposition against the authority ('heresy').

Though, according to the official Moscow chronicle writing, the princely authority did not recognise the theocratic theory of the divine origin of the authority in full. In Rus* legality of the authority was stated not in its divine origin but in the divine origin of its inheritance. As a rule, in Muscovia, the monarch, who takes the throne by birthright ('born' tsar), was considered as the Chosen Tsar. Thus, the doctrine on the divine institution promoted monocracy of the prince authority. At that time monarchy was the most typical form of governance. It merged the feudal republics. Herewith, the order of the throne inheritance was typically autocratic – from sire to son (Vladimirskiy-Budanov, 1915).

Muscovy saw itself as a successor of the Byzantine Empire traditions (dynastic succession amongst grand dukes of Kievan Rus and ideological succession amongst the Byzantine emperors). But herewith, Muscovy continued to cultivate oriental despotism borrowed from the Golden Horde (the idea of the strong unlimited autocratic authority) which contributed to the final destruction of the popular assembly statehood and, therefore, of the democracy elements in Muscovy.

Ivan III changed an old predicate 'dominus' (dominium) or sovereign to the title 'monarch'. 'Monarch of all Russia' was considered as a master of the Russian land which was a fiefdom of the monarch (the state belongs to a monarch). Thus, a monarch was considered as a supreme owner and controller of the Rus land's wealth (Vladimirskiy-Budanov, 1915). The other people were his slaves or 'kholopy' within the political terminology of Rus of the 15th to 17th centuries.

Kholopy had the property given by a monarch which could have been taken by him as he was the supreme owner. Despite social position, nationals of a monarch of Moscow were considered as the monarch's kholopy. Their personal and civil rights existed insofar as they were needed for realisation of the state interests. Nobody was considered as a free man. Every national was included in the peculiar pyramid of hierarchic personal dependence. There was a prince (tsar) on the top of the pyramid (Zolotukhina, 1985). Thus, the relations between the nationals and a monarch of the Moscow state (fiefdom) were within the scheme 'a monarch – kholopy (slaves)'.

The monarch's kholopy (slaves) were divided into two main social groups: noblemen and tenants. Tenants (peasants of all kinds, trades people, staplers) were the major part of the population. Tenants paid taxes, performed works to the good of a monarch and 'fed' the machinery of government. Noblemen consisted of the court nobility children and servants amongst others. They

---

* Rus' is a large ethno-cultural region in eastern Europe, the historical name of East Slavic lands. The powerful Old Russian State has arisen in these lands and become the basis for the formation of a unified Old Russian nationality, language and culture.

ruled the state institutions of the country. The highest rank of noblemen consisted of a small range of nobility. They took the highest places in court, military and public positions. 'Monarchic genealogy' (Bytchkova, 1975) is a list of the noble families. Those families' members had the right to precede or aspire to one or another position. The list was composed in the middle of the 16th century (1555–1556) when Ivan the Terrible ruled.

All authority of legal patrimonial governance was concentrated in hands of a tsar and was enough for nationals' obedience. A power holder was beyond the nationals' assessment. Tsar authority was indivisible. Any intervention in its prerogative rights was impossible by virtue of its nature. A tsar was responsible before God only. Thus, a punishment for any tsar guilt was imposed mainly on his nationals and not on him. Governance of Ivan the Terrible is the best historical example of the values repositioning (ideological justification of total autocracy, moral and legal irresponsibility of a ruler, nationals' unhesitating obedience and unconditional submission to tsar authority, their self-sacrificing devotion to their monarch). This is an example of the situation when the advantages of a form of state governance could be totally absorbed by the regressive political regime.

The idea of the divine origin of the monarch authority was used for justification of the unlimited character of that authority. Autocracy in Moscow Rus was legitimated on the basis of dynastical and theological principles mixing. 'Since you haven't been minded to live under the rule of God and your monarchs, who were given to you by God, listen and obey us' (Vaneeva, Lurje, Rykova, & Tvorogova, 1986). Herewith, neither aims nor Christian standards of morality limited the monarch authority even dogmatically (the practice of life-guards is a good example). The monarch's authority extended to the souls of the nationals who were slaves of the monarch of Moscow even after their death. Being in the Crimean capture, Vasiliy Gryaznoy wrote the following to Ivan the Terrible in Moscow: 'You, sire, as God' (Lotman, 1996).

Though, there still were the residual notions of the monarch's responsibility before God, its criteria were deviating from the Christian ethic and moral standards and becoming indefinite. That fact meant that the idea of the monarch's responsibility was withdrawn out of the political doctrine of Moscow Rus. Even the church had no moral influence on the monarchs, thus, the Christian standards did not actually have an impact on the Moscow monarch's deeds.

It should be noted that the idea of a tsar, elected in public, was expressed by the Assembly of the Land in 1613, and from that moment the idea of divinely instituted tsar authority would have been associated with a way of obtaining the authority only indirectly.

The other ideas and theories could not be expressed in the Medieval Rus. For example, the contract theory of the origin of state could not be expressed, as Russian people considered the service under the contract as a deceitful one because it could have been violated and the service to a tsar as God could not have been. The service to the monarch supposed the absence of any conditions between the sides. From one side there had to be unconditional and full devotion, from the other side there was mercy. In that case, there were religious feelings towards the monarch, and the service became devotion. Dignity of a nobleman was defined by the degree of mercy from a monarch towards him or her only. The rights and privileges were considered as a reward for the proper service to the state (Lotman, 1996).

A monarch could sacrifice property, freedom and lives of his nationals without any limits, as the interests of the state on whole were the aims of the Moscow monarch rule and not the interests of nationals. The aims of the monarch's exercising of his authority and his actions, taken for the purpose of achieving those aims, could not be apprehended by the nationals, thus, they were not the subject of the nationals' assessment. Exercising of any monarch's order was considered by a Moscow State national not only as his or her duty within the policy sense, but the divine call as well.

In the Moscow State the monarch's rule could not have been conceived as derived from the rule of the people. The interests and safety of the nationals were not taken into consideration even dogmatically when the monarch exercised his authority. Only some representatives of the intellectual elite could have expressed their ideas about the need to protect citizens from the iniquity in the process of governance (Patrikeev, 1863).

That is why the theocratic and patriarchal paternalism within governance characterised the Moscow State. The features of the patriarchal family (the monarch's paternalism – 'Father the Tsar', 'Mother the Monarchess') and the citizens' absolute dependence ('not sensible little children') were illustrative of paternalism. Theocratic and patriarchal understanding of the authority was reflected in the text of the well-known work of the 16th century *The Domestic Order* (Yakovlev, 1867): 'God is the head of the universe, a monarch is the head of the state, a father is the head of a family' and contributed to the conviction 'to please God' and 'reasonableness' of the paternalistic pretensions of a monarch. That authority was able to do everything: to give to eat, to give to drink, to clothe, to say how to live. On the contrary, what was official, formalised and went beyond the patriarchal structures was met with suspicion and seen as strange. That was the explanation for the fact that people held a head of the state in respect but did not trust the machinery of the authority.

Collective consciousness of the Russian Middle Ages endowed the authority with traits of holiness and truth. Value of the authority was considered as unconditional, as it was a form of the 'divine authority' and materialised the eternal truth. The rituals, common for it, were similar to the Divine order. In its face, a person was just a drop of water which inpoured into a sea.

Giving himself or herself, he or she asked for nothing in return, except for the right to give himself or herself, to be managed, 'obedient' and constantly patronised.

It's safe to say that people's desire to see on the throne the 'true', 'God-given' tsar, who could take care of people 'fatherly', has been observed during the whole period of the Moscow State existence. Herewith, none of the liberal initiatives of Boris Godunov and then of False Dmitry could not have changed the view of them as self-appointed tsars. In their paternal care people did not see the former monarchs. Thus, a desire to return to the paternalistic style of government brought the new dynasty of the Romanovs to the governance.

The developing Russian society was sociocentristic: a man in such a society was engrossed in that society. There were no irreconcilable contradictions between an individual and the society. In such a society a man should have been like everyone else. A person did not feel his or her personality, as any personality was engrossed in the community. The society suppressed any personality in itself. Freedom of a person was replaced with will. It was freedom only for themselves with indifference to other people's freedom. That view led to lawlessness, tyranny and anarchy; it blocked any individuality and activity of people, as the concept of 'freedom' was identified with the permissiveness and anarchy. As a result, as soon as the force of the state authority in Russia weakened, the Time of Troubles came.

Paternalism also implied the law at the legislative level. The attempts to take care of the individuals in the political and legal condition resulted in disregard for their freedom. The peculiarity of the Russian Orthodox sense of justice was and still is an inextricably link of the law with the moral and spiritual principles, moreover, with the Christian virtue. The moral law as a whole has always dominated over the legal one in the sense of justice of a Russian. In Rus it was customary to act not in accordance with the written laws but in accordance with the laws of conscience. It should be noted that the said fact is one of the reasons of the Russians' disparagement towards the legal norms and laws, especially towards those which disagree to some extent with the moral norms (Gantseva, 2001). People developed a distrust of law (legal nihilism) because they were often faced with the lack of legal regulation and replacing of it with the acts of the men in authority. It taught the Russians to evade and violate the law and the laws at the slightest opportunity. This fact is reflected in proverbs and sayings of the Russian people. For example: 'One law for the rich, and another is for the poor', 'A friend in court is better than a penny in purse', 'The horse loves oats; the earth loves manure, and the governor loves tribute', 'If your pocket is empty, the judge is deaf', 'The Law is like an axle – you can turn it whichever way you please, if you give it plenty of grease', 'Be righteous before God; be wealthy before a judge' (Dahl, 1999).

The Russian people were characterised by boundless love of authority which always put itself above the law creating legal nihilism (Gulina, 2000) on one hand; on the other hand, the Eastern obedience.

Despite the fact that in the middle of the 19th century the secular principle to service to the Motherland replaced the religious principle to serve the monarch, the state paternalism continued to be regarded as a good and the authorities' duty to people.

The centuries-old monarchy and autocracy led to the tradition of paternalism. It was expressed in the inculcation of the idea of the infallibility of a supreme ruler, his deification and, at the same time, of his unlimited tyranny, injustice, the nationals' subservience, the denial of freedom and democracy in the public mind.

The Russian centuries-old tradition of paternalism was embodied in the small bourgeoisie cult of a leader which was peculiar to the multi-million peasant country. The psychology of the leaderism and bureaucratic deification of the authority became the nutrient medium of the personality cult of Stalin (Alekseev, 1985).

During the years of Soviet authority the citizens' were affected by the ideology of the Communist Party where the decision of the supreme authority of the party was above the law and the measure of responsibility of a person depended on interests of the party leaders. The command-administrative system continued to cultivate the paternalistic consciousness in society. Relations with the state were within the scheme 'paternalism – gratitude'. A subconscious lack of self-confidence and hope for help from 'above', which were the foundation of paternalism, and excessive tolerance for actions of the state authority combined with disrespect for the law from both the top and bottom. Paternalism made a person not a citizen but a national, whilst continuing to cultivate dependency relations in society and training a person to passive expectation (Walicki, 1991).

If we compare the situations in the Soviet state and the post-Soviet state, it can be concluded that an essential element of the civil society, which is the respect for the law, still cannot become perpetuated in modern Russia.

As a consequence, elements of legal nihilism and anarchism persevere in the sense of justice. Moreover, these elements sometimes combine with a boundless faith in the omnipotence of a head of the state.

Public consciousness, which continues to perceive the authority of a head of the state as a patriarchal, 'fatherly' (especially in the context of economic and social crises), usually sees the way out in the governance of a 'strong hand'. And people do believe that only such governance is able create the firm order in the country. Herewith, the order is not necessarily based on the law. The basis of it is a subconscious lack of self-confidence (which remains nowadays as well), the human desire to live at the expense of state support (subsidies, grants) and, as a consequence, the silent delegation of a part of the human's rights to a head of the state.

It is obvious that the Russian society has to eliminate paternalism in the relations between the state and the society and establish relations within the scheme 'citizen – society – state'. Thus, the problem of the impact of the phenomenon on the paternalism on Russia and law is still relevant in modern times.

References

Alekseev, S. S. (1985). *The theory of the state and the law*. Moscow: Law Books.

Bytchkova, M. E. (1975). *The books of genealogy of the 16–17th centuries as a historical source*. Moscow: Nauka.

Dahl, V. I. (1999). *Proverbs of the Russian people* (pp. 98, 101–102, 153). Moscow: Olma-Press.

Gantseva, L. M. (2001). The peculiarities of the development of the legal awareness of the Russians in modern conditions. *Vestnik of Bashkir State University*, no. 1, 44–48.

Gulina, O. R. (2000). The roots of the legal nihilism. *Vestnik of Bashkir State University*, no. 2–3: 70–72.

Lotman, Y. M. (1996). *Outline of history of the Russian culture of the 18th – the beginning of 19th centuries* (p. 34). Moscow.

Patrikeev, B. (1863). The polemic works of a monk – Tsar. *Orthodox Interlocutor*. Part 3.

Vaneeva, E. I., Lurje, Y. S., Rykova, Y. D., & Tvorogova, O. V. (1986). The messages of Ivan the Terrible. *Monuments of ancient Rus literature. The later half of the 16th century* (pp. 22–73, 78–83, 108–217). Moscow.

Vladimirskiy-Budanov, M. F. (1915). *Review of the Russian law history*. Kiev.

Waitr, J. (1979). *Sociology of political relations*. Moscow: Progress.

Walicki, A. (1991). Morality and the law in the theories of the Russian liberals of the late 19th–early 20th centuries. *Philosophical Items*, no. 8, 25.

Yakovlev, V. (1867). *The domestic order* (p. 11). St. Petersburg: The publishing house of Kozhantchikov, D.E.

Zolotukhina, N. M. (1985). *Development of the Russian medieval political and legal thought*. Moscow: Law Literature.

Crimes: Sex and Money

II

Lay Thinking about 'Sexual Murderer' and 'Victim' in Groups of Young Russian Men and Women

4

NIKOLAY DVORYANCHIKOV
INNA BOVINA
OLGA LOGUNOVA
ANASTASIYA GUTNICK

Contents

4.1 Introduction

The questions about the offender's personality, as well as about the reasons of criminal activity are amongst the most interesting ones in legal psychology. The psychological typology of the criminal personality is a method to analyse the criminal behaviour. The typology should be based on the general and stable characteristics of offenders, and these characteristics need to be detectable in the offender's behaviour. The problem of serial murderers typology and of psychological profiling of them is in the focus of many studies in the fields of legal and psychological knowledge (Godwin, 2001; Logunova, 2014; Logunova, Demidova, & Dvoryanchikov, 2012). The results of these studies have implications for the practice of law enforcement.

The analysis of different typologies conducted by Logunova and colleagues (2012) led the authors to conclude that one of the most promising typology in terms of practical purpose is the one proposed by Sitkovskaya and Konysheva (2002). According to this typology, three types of serial sexual murderers are distinguished: *situational offenders, sexual murderers* and *force users* (Sitkovskaya & Konysheva, 2002). This typology is based on motivation of criminal behaviour of offenders. The insufficient social mediation of motives corresponds to the situational offenders. The disturbance of sexual motivation manifested in sadistic domination in sexual relationships is a criterion to distinguish the category of offenders named sexual murderers. In other words, the ways that they use to murder gave them satisfaction of their sexual needs. Finally, the motivation of criminal behaviour of force users becomes apparent by violent ways to satisfy the need for self-affirmation. To put it differently, this category of offenders commits murder in order to accomplish control and power. In the recent study conducted by Logunova (2014), this typology of sexual murderers got additional empirical support.

Another interesting line of research on sexual murderers concerns their personality and gender identity. The analysis proposed by Dvoryanchikov, Nosov and Salamova (2011) found an interesting description done by Brittain in his seminal paper 'The Sadistic Murderer' in 1970. The portrait of the serial sexual murderer contained the following characteristics: reserved, timid and anxiety-ridden, he feels inferior in his everyday relations with others and as result, he prefers to dominate and to humiliate women because they are not accessible for him in real life. These results were obtained in other studies as well (Dvoryanchikov et al., 2011). This person is sexually restrained and inexperienced, has sexual deviations (such as fetishism and transvestism) and has rich sadistic fantasies, its implementation is motivated by low self-esteem. The accuracy of this description was confirmed repeatedly in other studies (Dvoryanchikov et al., 2011). Langevin and colleagues (1985) demonstrated that the majority of sadistic offenders had disturbances of gender identity; it is manifested, at least, by gender indifference and femininity. From our point of view it could be very interesting to reveal how laypersons explain the sexual murderer's personality.

The analysis of the serial murderers attracts attention not only of the scientific community, but also attention of lay people who try to analyse the offender personality and behaviour by their proper methods. The mass media and cinema play the crucial role in supplying lay people with the images of offenders, as well as the ideas about their motivation and models of crime.

According to Godwin (2001) the serial murderers got the attention of the world of entertainment after the publication of profiling principles by the U.S. Federal Bureau of Investigation (FBI). From this point of view this topic became quite popular because of films like *Silence of the Lambs*, *Seven*, *Copycat* and *The X-Files*. This line of films is growing every year.

At the same time, the problem of serial murders became an important theme of public discussion as well. Being exposed to the different kinds of information circulating in the mass media, in cinema and in the popular literature lay people worked out their proper explanations to this kind of crimes, they built up their own classifications of aggressors and of victims, and they attributed particular characteristics to each of them. The purpose of this 'naïve scientific activity' is to understand the world and to make it controllable. Lay people also use different kinds of knowledge coming from scientific ideas and real live stories shared with friends and acquaintances and heard from strangers. As a result, people reduce the scare related to the murder itself and overcome the danger of the murderer.

The particularity of this topic is defined by the fact that in the discussion about the sexual murderer and victim, the gender identity of the interlocutors becomes salient. Men and women need to work out different strategies to overcome this danger. Our main objective in this reported study was to reveal and to compare lay thinking about sexual murderer and victim in groups of young Russian men and women. The productive theoretical framework to reach our objective was the social representations theory proposed by Moscovici (2000).

4.2 Social Representations Theory

According to one amongst many definitions, social representation is 'a form of knowledge, socially elaborated and shared, having a practical aim, and concurring to the construction of a common reality to a social whole' (Jodelet, 1989, p. 36). As Moscovici underlines it: 'the purpose of all representations is to make something unfamiliar, or unfamiliarity itself, familiar. What I mean is that consensual universes are places where everybody wants to feel at home, secure from any risk' (2000, p. 37).

The creation of the social representations helps people to adapt the strangeness related to objects, phenomena, events, other people and so on by putting it into the existing *frame of references*. This transformation definitely has a defensive function. The other functions of social representations are the following: the function of communication facilitation, the function of regulation of social behaviour and practice, the function of social identity construction and support and the function of justification of social relations (Abric, 2001; Breakwell, 2001; Doise, 1986).

Amongst several methodological approaches towards the social representations analysis, we prefer the structural approach proposed and developed by Abric and his followers (Abric, 2001, 2003). This approach gives an opportunity to compare the social representations of the same object worked out in different groups by revealing their structure as well as to analyse the relations between social representations of different objects elaborated by the same group by revealing the structure of the social representation. This structure is consisted of the central system (or central core) and the peripheral system. The central core, as Abric said, consists of 'one or several elements that give the representation its meaning' (2001, p. 43). The central system gives meaning to the whole representation, it maintains stability of the representation and it plays the main role in the organisation of the representation; the peripheral system plays a crucial role in the protection of the central system stability (and, therefore, in the protection of the representation itself against any transformations) and plays an important role in a concretisation and adaptation of the central system elements (Abric, 2001). The central system is 'linked to collective memory and to the history of the group' (Abric, 1993, p. 76) that shares the representations; whereas, the peripheral system is linked to individual memory and experience. The central system is consensual and it provides the homogeneity of the group. The peripheral system plays the main role in the adaptation of the central system to the changing context; this part of the representation is not consensual, it provides the heterogeneity of the group (Abric, 1993). As one can see there is a hierarchy in the structure of the social representation: the central system is formed by the main elements, and the peripheral systems are organised around the less important elements.

This theory can contribute to the domain of lay thinking about crime and offenders and this knowledge seems to have practical implications for the preventive programs. However, research in this field is very scarce. The analysis of the literature reveals that there are only few studies concerning the social representations of crimes and offenders. For example, in one study conducted in Switzerland (Hammer, Widmer, & Robert, 2009) the social representations of crime reasons and attitudes towards the punishment were analysed and it was revealed that there was a relation between the subjective proximity to crime and the attitudes towards punishment.

Goulevitch (2000) investigated the content of social representations of crime, offenders, victims and specialists of legal system; she found out that the social representations about crimes were not simply a list of crimes; people create their own understanding of hierarchy of crimes.

In a recent study concerning with the social representations of crime, offender and victim realised in structural approach to social representations (Bovina & Bovin, 2013), it was found that the representation of offender was crystallised around three main elements: murderer, thief and bad person. An offender is guilty of the crimes. The representation of victim was structured around two elements: innocent and complainant.

Taking into consideration these results as well as the key ideas of the social representations theory, we put forward several propositions. (1) The social representations of the sexual murderer and victim would be different in groups of young men and women as a result of different strategy defensive functions of the social representations. Namely, in groups of young men the central system of the social representations of sexual murderer and victim would consist of more elements than the central system of the social representations of sexual murderer and victim in groups of young women. (2) The elements of the central system of the social representations of sexual murderer and of victim would be more shared and concrete in groups of young women in comparison with the ones in groups of young men.

4.3 Sample

A total of 224 Russian students (117 females and 107 males) aged from 17 to 31 years (M_{age} = 19.70; SD = 2.07) participated in the study. The study was totally anonymous, subjects participated voluntarily and they were recruited at several universities of Moscow. The sample was composed by students on social sciences.

4.4 Method

The questionnaire consisted of several parts. In the first part the free associations task was used in order to reveal the social representations, the stimuli were 'sexual murderer' and 'victim'. The subjects were asked to write at least five words of expressions which immediately come into their minds. The free association technique is usually used in the analysis of social representations, because it reveals the latent dimensions of the semantic universe of the studied object (Abric, 2003). In the numerous studies where the free association technique was implemented, the subjects were presented with a key word (or key words) and they were asked to give from three to five words that come to their minds immediately (for example, Bonnec, 2002; Dany, Urdapilleta, & Lo Monaco, 2014; Flament & Rouquette, 2003). From these data the structure of the social representations in groups of males and females was revealed.

In the second part of the questionnaire, the socio-demographic questions (about age and gender) were asked.

The overall structure of the social representations of sexual murderer and victim was revealed by applying the prototypical analysis proposed by Vergès (1992), the so-called rank-frequency method (Dany et al., 2014). The rank-frequency method takes into account two main parameters: (1) associations' frequencies (it is a quantitative parameter*) and (2) rank of their appearance (it is a qualitative parameter†). The usage of these criteria allows us to reveal the most salient words.

The combination of these criteria forms a four-cell table that corresponds to different zones of social representation. As it was said before, the structure of the representation included the central and the peripheral systems. In the peripheral system two parts could be distinguished: potential change zone and peripheral system. The potential change zone is a part of the peripheral system that could bring the changes to the central system and change the representation as result of it. Further theoretical analysis is needed in order to understand the inner structure of the peripheral system (Sa & Oliveira, 2002).

1. Central system zone – This zone contains associations with high frequency and low rank of appearance; in other words, these associations come to mind immediately to many people when they think about the object of the representation, and the consensual elements are situated in this zone.
2. Potential change zone – This zone unites two cells. The first cell contains associations with low frequency and low rank of appearance; it means that these words are shared by a minority of people, and these associations come to subjects' minds immediately when they think about the object of the representation. The second cell contains associations with high frequency and high rank of appearance; in other words, these associations are shared by many people, but these associations do not come to the subjects' minds immediately when they think about the object of the representation.
3. Peripheral system – This zone contains the associations with low frequency and high rank of appearance; in other words, these associations are shared by few people, and these words do not come to the subjects' minds immediately when they think about the object of the representation. These elements are linked to the subjects' individual experience and individual memory.

---

* This parameter is linked to the collective dimension of the social representation (Dany et al., 2014).
† This parameter is based on the idea of the Marbe's law (Dany et al., 2014; Flament & Rouquette, 2003), and according to it there is a 'direct relation between the frequency of an associative response and the speed of its utterance' (Dany et al., 2014, p. 5), so the words that appeared at first are more cognitively available and more important in comparison with the words that appeared later.

4.5 Results

A total of 542 words were evocated by males and 640 by females in case of the stimulus *sexual murderer*; in case of the stimulus *victim*, 511 words were evoked by males and 596 evoked by females.

The prototypical analysis revealed the structure of the social representations. The answers done by at least 5% of subjects were analysed here.* The volumes of the central system systems were 32.13% and 41.18% correspondingly in the group of males and in the group of females in case of the representations of sexual murderer; 50.22% and 40.5% in case of the representations of victim.

4.5.1 Sexual Murderer: Content and Structure of Social Representations

The central system zone of the representation in groups of males (Table 4.1) is composed by the elements related to *murder* (murderer and murder) and to *violence* (violence, cruel, aggression). The sexual murderer is seen as an *evil person* (some concretisations could be found in the potential change zone [pitiless] and in the peripheral system [cold-blooded]), and he is seen as *suffering from mental illness* (ill person). Other references to the state of mental health are situated in the potential change zone (nutcase, pervert, unbalanced, crazy). A *swear word* is also presented in this zone (freak). The *context of the crime* is situated here (night), and other references to the context are in the peripheral system (forest, darkness).

Other elements of the potential change zone are the following: the particular *physical characteristic* of the sexual murderer that could be used in order to recognise the criminal (eyes of a maniac), a *highly negative affective reaction* linked to the crime (horror).

The potential change zone and the peripheral system are also composed by the elements concerning other aspects of crime: *a tool of crime* (knife), *an affective reaction* (fear), the evaluation of the object of the representation (danger) and the consequence of the crime (death). The comparison of the central system zone with the part of the potential change zone that contains the minority position shows that the minority vision of the sexual murderer refers more towards the state of the mental health of sexual murderer in comparison with the majority vision. The indicator of the affective reaction towards the object of the representation is also situated in this part of the potential change zone and not in the central system zone.

---

* The associations cited by less than 5% of subjects (sample size) were not included into the current analysis.

Table 4.1   **Structure of Social Representation of Sexual**
Maniac in Groups of Males

	Association Appearance Ranking	
Frequency	Low (<2.74)	High (≥2.74)
High (≥8)	Murderer (17; 2.06)	Knife (15; 2.93)
	Evil person (15; 2.00)	Danger (12; 3.50)
	Ill person (14; 2.57)	Fear (10; 3.20)
	Violence (13; 2.69)	Rapist (9; 2.78)
	Cruel (11; 2.45)	
	Aggression (9; 2.69)	
	Night (8; 2.25)	
	Freak (8; 2.52)	
	Murder (8; 2.63)	
Low (<8)	Nutcase (7; 1.86)	Blood (6; 2.83)
	Pervert (7; 2.43)	Forest (6; 3.43)
	Unbalanced (7; 2.57)	Death (6; 3.67)
	Pitiless (7; 2.71)	Darkness (5; 3.60)
	Eyes of a *maniac* (6; 2.50)	Cold-blooded (5; 4.00)
	Horror (5; 2.20)	
	Crazy (5; 2.40)	

Note: For each association the frequency and the rank of its appearance are indicated in parentheses.

The central system zone of the social representation in groups of females
(Table 4.2) is composed by the elements related to *violence* (violence, cruelty).
The sexual murderer is seen as a *person, suffering from mental illness* (mentally ill, crazy). Other references to this theme are in the potential change
zone and in the peripheral system zones (inadequate, ill, unbalanced, pervert). The *negative affective reaction* is situated in the central system zone
(fear); the *other indications of the affective reactions* are in the potential
change zone and in the peripheral system (anger, horror). A *tool of the crime*
is also situated in the central system zone (knife).

In the potential change zone there are also the following elements: *cat-
egorisation of the representation object* (murderer, rapist) and a *swear word*
(freak). The other elements of peripheral system refer to the *identity of the
sexual murderer* (man), the *context of the crime* (night, forest, blood and
darkness) the evaluation of the object of the representation (dangerous). The
comparison between majority and minority positions shows that the sexual
murderer is categorised as suffering from mental illness in the case of the
majority.

The comparison of the content of the social representations of sexual
murderer in groups of males and females shows the similarity of the main
themes of the representations (many elements are the almost same), but their
position in the zones of the social representation in each group is different,

Table 4.2 Structure of Social Representation of a Sexual Maniac in Groups of Females

Frequency	Association Appearance Ranking	
	Low (<2.89)	High (≥2.89)
High (≥8)	Violence (29; 2.31)	Ill (19; 3.05)
	Cruelty (25; 2.12)	Murder (17; 3.06)
	Mentally ill (22; 2.86)	Darkness (17; 3.59)
	Fear (20; 2.50)	Dangerous (15; 3.87)
	Knife (8; 2.20)	Man (9; 3.56)
	Crazy (8; 2.38)	Unbalanced (8; 3.50)
Low (<8)	Murderer (7; 1.43)	Pervert (7; 3.14)
	Sexual maniac (7; 1.86)	Horror (7; 3.14)
	Anger (7; 2.57)	Forest (7; 3.86)
	Freak (7; 2.71)	Night (7; 4.29)
	Inadequate (7; 2.86)	Blood (6; 3.00)
	Rapist (6; 2.67)	

Note: For each association the frequency and the rank of its appearance are indicated in parentheses.

and it allows us to conclude that the representations are different. The elements of the central system zone are more shared in the case of females in comparison with males (t (12) = –2.25, p < 0.042); there are fewer themes in the central system zone in the case of females in comparison with males. This fact proves that females have a more agreed and precise image of sexual murderer in comparison with males.

4.5.2 Victim: Content and Structure of Social Representations

The central system zone of the representation in groups of males (Table 4.3) is composed by different characteristics of victim and relations of empathy towards her. The victim is female, characterised as defenceless, and other characteristics attributed to victim are situated in the other zones of the representation: in the potential change zone (guilty, weak) and in the peripheral system (helpless). Her emotional state is described by the reference to the following elements in the central system zone: fear, unhappiness, scared and psychological trauma. The concretisation of these characteristics is situated in the potential change zone (suffering), and the other ones (horror, shock) are in the peripheral system. The *affective reactions towards victim* (pity, compassion, poor) are situated in the central system zone. One more characteristic in this category is placed in the peripheral system (empathy). Amongst the other elements of the potential change zone and in the peripheral system are the following: *reference to the physical state* (pain), *reference to the consequences of the crime* (death) and *crime type* (murder). Particular attention should be paid to the elements of the potential change zone (the

Table 4.3   **Structure of Social Representation of Victim in Groups of Males**

Frequency	Association Appearance Ranking	
	Low (<2.83)	High (≥2.83)
High (≥7)	Pity (22; 1.77)	Weak (21; 3.05)
	Female (18; 2.06)	Pain (15; 2.93)
	Fear (17; 2.76)	Death (11; 3.64)
	Defenceless (9; 1.56)	Victim (7; 3.00)
	Scared (9; 2.67)	Suffering (7; 3.43)
	Poor (8; 1.13)	Violence (7; 3.71)
	Compassion (8; 2.63)	
	Unhappiness (7; 1.57)	
	Blood (7; 2.29)	
	Psychological trauma (7; 2.71)	
Low (<7)	Guilty (5; 2.20)	Helpless (6; 3.17)
	To run (5; 2.60)	Murder (6; 3.50)
		Empathy (6; 3.67)
		Horror (5; 3.80)
		Vengeance (5; 4.00)
		Shock (5; 4.80)

Note: For each association the frequency and the rank of its appearance are indicated in parentheses.

minority position is situated in here). There are two elements – guilty and to run – in this part of the potential change zone. This is the position of blame; victim is seen as guilty of being violated and being attacked by sexual murderer. This position is contrasted with the position of the majority situated in the central system zone.

The central system zone of the social representation of victim in group of females (Table 4.4) is composed by different *characteristics of victim* (almost concerning her emotional state) and *relation towards her*. The victim is characterised as defenceless; other characteristics are in the other zones of the representation: in the potential change zone (innocent, helpless), in the potential change zone and in the peripheral system (weak, unlucky). Her *emotional state* is described by the reference to the following elements in the central system zone: fear, unhappy, frightened. The concretisation of these characteristics is situated in the potential change zone and in the peripheral system (scream, horror, panic, psychological trauma). The relation towards victim in the central system zone is presented by the elements (pity) and in the potential change zone (poor). Amongst other elements of the zone of the peripheral system there is a reference to the victim's identity (female, youth), as well as a reference to the consequences of the crime (death). The element of the peripheral system (carelessness) could be seen as a reference to the guilt of the victim, but it is situated in the zone that corresponds to the individual representations.

Table 4.4   **Structure of Social Representation of Victim in Groups of Females**

	Association Appearance Ranking	
Frequency	Low (<2.80)	High (≥2.80)
High (≥10)	Fear (39; 2.62)	Pain (22; 3.59)
	Pity (20; 2.20)	Weak (19; 3.00)
	Defenceless (19; 2.53)	Female (15; 3.00)
	Unhappy (13; 1.69)	Scream (11; 3.55)
	Frightened (12; 2.33)	Horror (10; 3.10)
		Death (10; 3.40)
Low (<10)	Innocent (9; 2.22)	Panic (8; 3.13)
	Poor (8; 1.13)	Psychological trauma (8; 3.13)
	Helpless (6; 2.17)	Blood (7; 3.57)
		Unlucky (6; 2.83)
		Youth (6; 3.00)
		Carelessness (6; 4.00)

Note: For each association the frequency and the rank of its appearance are indicated in parentheses.

The position of the minority presented by the elements (innocent, poor, helpless) is a kind of advocacy of victim against any possible blame.

The comparison of the prototypical analysis results in groups of males and females once again shows that the content of the representations of victim is quite similar; many elements are the same, but their position structure in each group is different, so it means that the representations of sexual murderer and victim are different in groups of males and females. The elements of the central system zone are more shared in the case of females in comparison with males (t (13) = –2.26, p < 0.042); there are fewer themes in this zone of the representation in groups of females in comparison with the group of males.

4.6 Conclusions

Following the ideas of the social representations theory (Moscovici, 2000) and using the methodological strategy of the structural approach (Abric, 2000, 2003) of this theory, we conducted a study in order to reveal the specificity of representations of sexual murderer and victim in groups of males and females.

The social representations of sexual murderer and of victim are different in group of females than in group of males; the social representations of sexual murderer and victim are more shared and concrete in groups of females than in groups of males. It could be seen as a different defensive function of social representations in two groups. So our predictions got empirical support.

Our study has some limitations. First, the sample was composed mostly by students in social sciences. The future study should take into consideration different groups of people; in particular it would be fruitful to analyse the professional social representations of the criminalists investigating serial sexual crimes.

Another limitation is linked to the usage of the rank-frequency method. Special attention should be paid to the methodological aspects of the importance-frequency method (Dany et al., 2014). This methodological point should get further attention; from our point of view these two methods are linked to different cognitive processes (automatic and controllable).

Nevertheless, the objective of our study was reached. The first steps towards the comprehension of what representations about sexual murderer and victim are used in everyday life were made, and the specificity of these representations in groups of males and females was revealed.

Acknowledgement

We would like to thank A. Rikel for his assistance in the data collection.

References

Abric, J.-C. (1993). Central system, peripheral system: Their functions and roles in the dynamic of social representations. *Papers on Social Representations, 2,* 75–78.

Abric, J.-C. (2001). A structural approach to social representations. In K. Deaux & G. Philogène (Eds.), *Representations of the social: Bridging theoretical traditions* (pp. 42–47). Oxford: Blackwell.

Abric, J.-C. (2003). L'analyse structurale des représentations sociales. In S. Moscovici & F. Buschini (Eds.), *Les méthodes des sciences humaines,* (pp. 375–392). Paris: Presses Univ. de France.

Bonnec, Y. (2002). Identité régionale, nationale et européenne. Organisation et statut de la mémoire sociale au sein des représentations sociales. In S. Laurens & N. Roussiau (Eds.), *La mémoire sociale: Identités et Représentations Sociales* (pp. 175–185). Rennes: Presses Univ. de Rennes.

Bovina, I. B., & Bovin, B. G. (2013). 'Do not kill! Do not steal!': Specificity of social representations about crime, offender and victim among students. In A. L. Zhuravlev & A. V. Yurevich (Eds.), *Psychological studies on morality* (pp. 219–239). Moscow: Institute of Psychology RAS.

Breakwell, G. (2001). Social representational constraints upon identity processes. In K. Deaux & G. Philogène (Eds.), *Representations of the social: Bridging theoretical traditions* (pp. 271–284). Oxford: Blackwell.

Dany, L., Urdapilleta, I., & Lo Monaco, G. (2014). Free associations and social representations: Some reflections on rank-frequency and importance-frequency methods. *Quality and Quantity, 48,* 1–19.

Doise, W. (1986). Les représentations sociales: Définition d'un concept. In W. Doise & A. Palmonari (Eds.), *L'étude des représentations sociales* (pp. 86–98). Neuchatel: Delachaux et Niestlé.

Dvoryanchikov, N. V., Nosov, S. S., & Salamova, D. K. (2011). *Sexual self-consciousness and its diagnostics.* Moscow: Flinta.

Flament, C., & Rouquette, M.-L. (2003). *Anatomie des idées ordinaires.* Paris: Armand Colin.

Godwin, M. (2001). Reliability, validity, and utility of extant serial murderer classification. In M. Godwin (Ed.), *Criminal psychology and forensic technology: A collaborative approach to effective profiling* (pp. 81–97). New York: CRC Press.

Goulevitch, O. A. (2000). *Social representations of offenders, crimes, victims, and specialists of legal institutions* (PhD dissertation). Moscow State University.

Hammer, R., Widmer, E. D., & Robert, C.-N. (2009). Subjective proximity to crime or social representations? Explaining sentencing attitudes in Switzerland. *Social Justice Research, 22,* 351–368.

Jodelet, D. (1989). Représentations sociales: Un domaine en expansion. In D. Jodelet (Ed.), *Les représentations sociales* (pp. 31–61). Paris: PUF.

Langevin, R., Bain, J., Ben-Aron, M. H., Coulthard, R., Day, D., Handy, L., … Wortzman, G. (1985). Sexual aggression: Constructing a predictive equation. A controlled pilot study. In R. Langevin (Ed.), *Erotic preference, gender identity, and aggression in men: New research studies* (pp. 39–76). Hillsdale, NJ: Lawrence Erlbaum Associates.

Logunova, O. A. (2014). *Psychological characteristics of personality and behavior of different types of serial sexual murderers* (PhD dissertation). Moscow State University of Psychology and Education.

Logunova, O. A., Demidova, L. Y., & Dvoryanchikov, N. V. (2012). Typological particularities of personality and behavior of serial sexual killers. *Psychological Science and Education, 2.* Retrieved from http://psyedu.ru/journal/2012/2/2903.phtml.

Moscovici, S. (2000). The phenomenon of social representations. In S. Moscovici & G. Duveen (Eds.), *Social representations: Explorations in social psychology* (pp. 18–77). New York: New York University Press.

Sa, C. P., & Oliveira, D. C. (2002). Sur la mémoire sociale de la découverte du Brésil. In S. Laurens & N. Roussiau (Eds.), *La mémoire sociale: Identités et Représentations Sociales,* (pp. 107–117). Rennes: Presses Univ. de Rennes.

Sitkovskaya, O. D., & Konysheva, L. P. (2002). Participation of a psychologist in the serial murder investigation. Moscow: Research Institute on Problems of Strengthening Law and Order at the General Prosecutor Office of the Russian Federation.

Vergès, P. (1992). L'Evocation de l'argent: Une méthode pour la définition du noyau central d'une représentation. *Bulletin de psychologie XLV,* 203–209.

Assumptions Underlying Behavioural Linkage Revisited

5

Ascertaining Individual Differentiation and Consistency in Serial Rape

MARINA SOROCHINSKI

C. GABRIELLE SALFATI

Contents

5.1 Introduction*

One of the key issues in the investigation of serial rape is the timely recognition of the multiple crimes as being part of a series, a process called linking. Whilst DNA and other physical evidence is the most reliable in linking serial crimes, such evidence is often absent from the crime scene (Grubin, Kelly, & Brunsdon, 2001). Behavioural evidence (i.e. everything known about what the offender did from the selection of the victim and the location of the crime to weapon choice and the way the offender fled the scene), however, is always present and therefore may provide the investigator with the necessary behavioural indicators in order to link offences (Salfati & Kucharski, 2005). The extent to which behavioural linking is feasible relies on two key hypotheses (Canter, 2000) both of which must be supported in order to conclude that behavioural crime linking is a valid and reliable investigative technique: (a) the *individual differentiation hypothesis* that states that the offences of one offender will be distinctively different from offences of other offenders, and (b) the *consistency hypothesis* that states that a degree of identifiable behavioural similarity across offence series will be evident.

Hence, the ultimate goal of the research on linking serial crimes is two-fold in that we must not only establish that offenders behave consistently across the series but also that their consistent behaviour is distinct from other offenders who commit the same type of crime (Bateman & Salfati, 2007). That is, if the consistent behaviours are also common to all offenders who commit these crimes, then they can only be considered characteristic of this crime type in general and are not useful in linking offences of an individual series. Thus, before testing whether an offender is consistent (i.e. if their different crime scenes can be linked to one another), it is crucial to decide what will be the *unit of analysis*. More specifically, one must identify the behavioural unit that will be expected to remain consistent across the series, for example, *individual* behaviour (e.g. binding), a particular *group* of behaviours (e.g. wounding behaviours) or the psychological *type* of behaviour or *theme* (e.g. controlling, violent) (Salfati, 2008).

Few empirical studies have fully investigated the issue of the salient components of offending behaviour that can be used reliably for linking individual crimes as part of a single series (Bennell, Mugford, Ellingwood, & Woodhams, 2014; Woodhams, Hollin, & Bull, 2007). Salfati (2008) highlighted that at present, more questions remain than we have answers to regarding the issue of the key behavioural components to be tested for consistency. Whilst differentiating between offences using specific individual behaviours

---

* This chapter represents a summary of several studies. For further details of methodology and results of the studies, please see Sorochinski, M., & Salfati, C. G. (2010), *A multidimensional approach to ascertaining individual differentiation and consistency in serial sexual assault: Is it time to redefine and refine?*, manuscript submitted for publication.

opens the door to too many idiosyncrasies thus making any attempt of generalisation impossible,* using broad over-encompassing typologies is also problematic in that many offences may not fit well into only one type (Terry, 2006). Canter, Bennell, Alison, and Reddy (2003) discussed the importance of considering the degree or level of violation as well as the type of violation as key dimensions in differentiating rapes. However, the *dimensional* differentiation of rape offenders' behaviours has not yet been fully tested empirically. Understanding the dimensionality of behavioural manifestation is an important step towards a fuller conception of behavioural consistency as a whole and may be especially useful in the understanding of consistency in criminal behaviour. For example, it has been argued in the literature that serial offenders generally exhibit some form of controlling (or organised) behaviours in order to complete their act (e.g. Canter, Alison, Alison, & Wentink, 2004), and thus looking at control behaviours as either present or absent only may not be as useful in finding consistency that is also practical for differentiating one series from another. On the other hand, looking at control as a dimension that can vary in both type and level can provide enough detail for differentiation whilst also helping identify potentially fluctuating patterns of behaviour where the offender may lose control (Hickey, 2006) or vice versa, become more controlling as his series progresses.

In addition to identifying the most appropriate unit of analysis, another key methodological issue that has yet to be resolved is how to operationally define consistency to be able to fully capture the *dynamic* nature of behavioural patterns across crimes. Studies that examined behavioural consistency in sexual offences (Canter et al., 1991; Grubin et al., 2001; Santtila, Junkkila, & Sandnabba, 2005) have all provided evidence that offenders are consistent to a degree in their offending behaviours, however, these levels of consistency are far from what is necessary for behavioural linking to be considered empirically validated and useful in practice. Recent studies (e.g. Hewitt & Beauregard, 2014; Leclerc, Lussier, & Deslauriers-Varin, in press; Sorochinski & Salfati, 2010) highlight the importance of looking beyond stability of behaviour and understanding the behavioural change patterns as a form of consistency. The general psychological literature (e.g. Fleeson & Noftle, 2008) also suggests that looking for consistent patterns (i.e. progression of behaviour along a certain dimension) rather than absolute consistency may be a fruitful approach. Thus, reframing our understanding of what constitutes consistency in crime series

---

* As explained by Grubin et al. (2001), although highly unique (consistent) behaviours, such as always travelling to the crimes dressed as a woman or riding a bicycle, may be useful during an investigation, it is impossible to use these behaviours to create generalised models and recommendations for a standard pro forma of crime scene information collection and recording of pertinent variables for the identification of consistency and linking, because the list of possible idiosyncratic behaviours that any offender could exhibit is nearly endless.

as a dynamic pattern rather than static behavioural matching may be the key for making empirical progress in the use of behavioural evidence for linking crimes. Using the right unit of analysis, it may be methodologically possible to develop an empirical model that would identify consistent patterns of behaviour within each series whilst also distinguishing one series from another. Thus, as summarised in Figure 5.1, in order to effectively link crimes using behavioural evidence, two basic assumptions must be validated: individual differentiation and consistency. In addition to the direct relationship of these two assumptions to behavioural linking, they are also inter-related (as shown by the two-sided arrows) because individual differentiation must be shown both at the level of crime scene (i.e. differentiate one crime committed by offender A from another crime committed by offender B) and at the level of series (i.e. differentiate multiple crimes committed by offender A from multiple crimes committed by offender B), and the search for consistency is contingent upon the identification of those differentiating factors. The two foundational questions are at the basis of the behavioural linkage structure shown in Figure 5.1: (a) the question of unit of analysis and (b) the question of whether a broader definition of 'traceability' of a behavioural pattern is more fruitful than the limited definition of behavioural 'stability'. This chapter presents an overview of a methodological reconceptualisation of the basic constructs that underpin behavioural linking in serial crime. Study 1 reframed the previously identified types of rape as behavioural dimensions and used quantitative (degree of behaviour present)

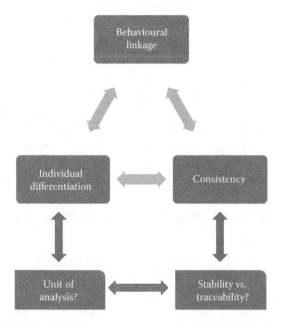

Figure 5.1 The conceptual structure that underlies behavioural linkage.

and qualitative (style of behaviour present) variants within those dimensions to differentiate between crime scenes. Study 2 aimed to test a redefined understanding of consistency in offending behaviour where, instead of only looking for behavioural stability (i.e. where offenders are expected to exhibit the same behaviours from one crime to the next), a progression of behaviour along identifiable trajectories (e.g. changing in degree through escalation, de-escalation or switching between subtypes of behaviour) along the aforementioned behavioural dimensions is seen as a form of dynamic consistency that can potentially be utilised for linking crimes.

5.2 Study 1: Dimensional Individual Differentiation

The identification of the most appropriate behavioural unit of analysis lies at the basis of being able to use behavioural evidence for linking serial crimes. Importantly, this unit of analysis must efficiently differentiate between offences before its consistency is tested for the purposes of linking. In serial rape, three subgroups of offenders' behaviours, namely, violence, control and sexual activity, have been consistently discussed in the literature as key in this type of offence (see Table 5.1). Although these behavioural categories

Table 5.1   Categories of Rape Identified in Previous Literature

Studies	Aggression/ Violence	Power/Control	Sexual Gratification
	Motivation-Based		
Cohen et al. (1969)	Displaced aggression		Sex-aggression diffusion
Groth et al. (1977)	Anger-retaliation	Power-assertive	Anger-excitation
Hazelwood and Burgess (2009)		Power-reassurance	
Groth and Birnbaum (1979)	Anger rape	Power rape	
Knight and Prentky (1990)	Pervasive anger		Non-sadistic sexual
	Vindictive		Sadistic sexual
Reid et al. (2014)	Aggression		Sexual
Vettor et al. (2014)	Anger	Compensatory	Sadistic
	Behaviour-Based		
Alison and Stein (2001)	Hostility	Dominance	
Canter and Heritage (1990)	Violence	Criminality	Sexuality
Canter and Youngs (2003)	Hostility	Control	Involvement
Hakkanen et al. (2004)	Hostility	Criminality	Involvement
Kocsis et al. (2002)	Brutality	Ritual	Intercourse
Salfati and Taylor (2006)	Violence	Control	Exploit

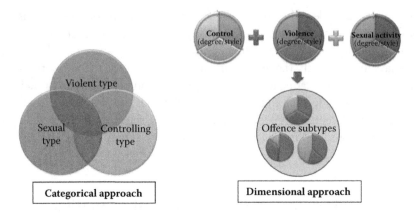

Figure 5.2 Categorical versus dimensional approach to differentiating sexual offences.

have been proffered as differentiating between types of rapists, studies consistently find that most rape offenders are likely to engage in behaviours from each of these categories at least to some extent, thus making a categorical approach impractical for differentiation and subsequent linking. In order to avoid the recurring issue of 'mixed types' in the empirical attempts of classifying sexual offences, it is necessary to examine the use of control, violence and sexual activity behaviours by the offenders dimensionally. Therefore, we proposed that reframing these categories as dimensions of rape offenders' behaviours and distinguishing between offences quantitatively (based on the specific degree of behaviour present) and qualitatively (based on the specific subtype of behaviour present) may be more efficient, and subsequently lay the foundation for determining the extent to which offenders remain consistent or progress in an identifiable trajectory along these dimensions (see Figure 5.2).

Specifically, in this study: (a) a number of qualitative subtypes are hypothesised to emerge within each of the behavioural dimensions (control: *instrumental, violent/blitz, extreme*; violence: *instrumental, expressive, situational*; and sexual activity: *pseudo-pleasing, demeaning, instrumental*), and (b) distinct quantitative differentiation into *low, medium* and *high* degree of enactment were hypothesised to emerge within each dimension.

5.3 Data

The data for this research were taken from closed, fully adjudicated state and local cases of serial rape that were contributed from law enforcement agencies from around the country for the purpose of research. All identifiers, including names of victims, suspects, offenders, officers, department and correctional agencies, were removed. Only aggregate data were reported on. The data set consisted of 30 rape series, all committed by male offenders acting alone who together were responsible for a total of 192 distinct assault incidents.*

5.4 Defining the Behavioural Dimensions

The three crime behaviour dimensions of violence, control and sexual activity are comprised of a variety of components described next.

5.4.1 Control

The dimension of control is comprised of behaviours that had been described in the literature (see Table 5.1) as being characteristic of various rapist types. These can be organised into four elements: (a) verbal – where an offender controls the victim through verbal threats; (b) weapon – where the offender uses a weapon (e.g. a gun or knife) to threaten and thus control the victim; (c) physical – where the offender uses special tools, such as bondage or gagging, to control the victim and (d) violent – where the offender resorts to physical violence (e.g. manual beating or using blunt force to incapacitate the victim) as a way of gaining the victim's compliance.

The hypothesised scale of control has an additive (quantitative) feature ranging from very low control (i.e. where all elements have been coded as absent) to high levels of control (where all elements have been coded as present) over the victim. Thus, differentiation in the degree of control used by the offender is possible using the number of control elements that the offender engaged in (e.g. someone who used one element is exhibiting low control, whereas someone who used two or three elements is showing moderate control, whilst the use of all four elements of control constitutes a high degree).

The hypothesised qualitative (subtype) differences between crimes were expected to emerge through the presence of different combinations of actions. Specifically, the use of a weapon to threaten and force a victim into initial compliance together with bonding to complete the rape is consistent with the hypothesised instrumental style of control. Alternatively, using violence as the primary means of control is consistent with a violent/blitz type of control. An extreme type of control is expected to emerge through the combination of at least three control modes (e.g. verbal, physical and violent).

---

* Of the 192 incidents, 51 (26.5%) constituted attempted sexual assaults and the remaining 73.5% constituted completed sexual assaults.

5.4.2 Violence

Previous studies of sexual offending (see Table 5.1) describe the use of violence by various rapists at the different stages of the crime (i.e. during the approach, during the actual assault and at the end [prior to leaving or disposing of the victim]). Thus, an offender may be violent throughout the offence or he may only resort to violence (a) in the beginning to incapacitate the victim, (b) to engage in violence during the actual assault act (e.g. the so-called, sadistic rapist) or (c) to only appear violent at the end. Moreover, an offender may use exclusively (a) manual violence, or may (b) use a weapon, such as a knife or a blunt instrument, which may result in more severe injury and is also considered a more severe crime by the law enforcement (i.e. assault vs. assault with a weapon). The actual extent of injury to the victim has not been examined as part of the violence domain here due to the subjective nature of determining the severity of injuries that the victim suffered (in addition to the fact that there are individual differences in how the body reacts to wounding if the number or even mere presence of visible bruises are taken as an indication of injury severity).

The hypothesised quantitative scale of violence can be seen as a 3×2 (stage × type) matrix, indicating the degree of violence present throughout the offence, ranging from very low violence, where the offender refrains from using overt violence at any stage of the offence, to moderate levels, where the offender engages in violence at one or two stages of the offence, or uses both manual and weapon at any one stage of the offence, to high levels of violence, if the offender uses multiple wounding ways at each stage.

Different subtypes of violence were also expected to emerge. Specifically, when the offender only engages in minimal violence at the beginning of the offence to subdue the victim, this is consistent with an instrumental subtype of violence (i.e. violence used as a means to control and allow for the completion of the offence). Alternatively, when an offender who engages in multiple acts of violence throughout the offence (i.e. during approach, assault and at the end of the offence) this is consistent with an expressive use of violence (Salfati, 2000). Furthermore, situational violence was hypothesised to be evident from isolated violent outbursts appearing after the start of the offence (i.e. use of weapon violence at the assault or end of offence stages).

5.4.3 Sexual Activity

The complexity of sexual activities that the offender engages in with the victim during a rape offence has often been ascribed in the clinical and investigative literature to the degree and richness of fantasy involved (Hazelwood & Burgess, 2009; Hickey, 2006). Moreover, different types of offenders within the existing typologies (see Table 5.1) are said to differ in this complexity of fantasy and henceforth of sexual behaviour. Authors have also hypothesised that the sexual fantasy of an offender may evolve throughout a series (Douglas & Munn, 1992). A detailed analysis of the various behaviours that have been described in the literature as important resulted in the following elements to be analysed: (a) the use of sexual verbiage (i.e. whether the offender complements the victim sexually or uses profanity to insult her); (b) presence of 'foreplay' sexual activity – such acts have often been described to distinguish a subtype of rapists who fantasise that the rape is in reality a consensual act (e.g. power-reassurance rapist in Groth and Birnbaum, 1979); (c) penetrative sexual acts; (d) forcing victim participation (ranging from verbal scripts to active involvement, such as forcing her to perform oral sex) and (e) the use of foreign objects or anything other than the penis to penetrate the victim.

The complexity of the sexual activity exhibited by an offender herein can range in degree from minimal where the offender was unsuccessful in his attempt to rape the victim, to moderate, where the offender engaged in two or three sexual behaviours (e.g. kissing and penetration) to highly evolved where the offender engages in multiple sexual acts during the offence.

Importantly, distinct subtypes of sexual activity were expected to emerge. Specifically, offences characterised by the presence of 'foreplay' (e.g. kissing, fondling) in addition to penetration would constitute a 'pseudo-pleasing' subtype of sexual activity. Alternatively, an offence characterised by forced victim participation, anal penetration or foreign object insertion is hypothesised to represent a demeaning subtype of sexual activity. Further, an offence characterised by vaginal penetration in the absence of other sexual behaviours may constitute an 'instrumental' sexual activity style (i.e. where the only purpose of the attack is basic physiological gratification).

5.5 Summary of Individual Differentiation Results

A Partial Order Scalogram Analysis with Coordinates (POSAC; Shye, 1985) was used to identify the behavioural differentiation in degree and style within the three behavioural dimensions of rape offences, namely, violence, control and sexual activity.

POSAC is a non-parametric multi-dimensional statistical technique that allows for a comparison between the profiles of individuals, or cases on multiple variables simultaneously (Shye, Elizur, & Hoffman, 1994). In addition to comparing cases on a qualitative dimension by creating profiles of scores across variables, POSAC assumes that there is a meaningful order to the variables, creating a quantitative scale in relation to the cumulative score of variables for each profile. The possibility of analysing both qualitative (subtype) and quantitative (degree) differences between cases across a behavioural dimension makes it particularly appropriate for the current study. POSAC has been used previously within the social scientific and investigative psychology research (see Bohm & Alison, 2001; Dancer, 1990; Guttman & Greenbaum, 1998; Last & Fritzon, 2005; Porter & Alison, 2001; and Taylor, 2002, for some examples) and has been propagated as a particularly useful technique for studying complex behavioural issues because of its ability to take into account multiple variables simultaneously and because of its sensitivity to both quantitative and qualitative differentiation.

In POSAC, numeric profiles are created using the scores each crime scene received based on the presence (2) or absence (1) of the variables that comprise the behavioural dimension in question (e.g. the control dimension is comprised of four variables: verbal, weapon, physical and violent, thus, a case where only verbal and physical control were present would receive a numerical profile of 2121, whereas a case where weapon and physical control were present would receive a profile of 1221, and so on). These profiles are subsequently represented as points in a geometrical space based upon both the order of the profiles (i.e. quantitative differences) as well as the types (i.e. qualitative differences). The overall interpretation of the analysis involves the identification of regions on the plot where all (or most) cases have the same score.

The results of the analysis substantiated the hypothesised differentiating methods, confirming that each sexual offence crime scene could be classified as having a particular degree and being characterised by a particular subtype of control, violence and sexual activity. One especially important conclusion that followed from this study was that the dimensions of control and violence may be best understood and differentiated quantitatively. This is in line with previous literature pointing to the fact that violence in sexual offences may be best understood as operating on a quantitative continuum (e.g. Salfati & Taylor, 2006) and that the degree of control plays a pivotal role in these types of offences (Terry, 2006). Conversely, sexual activity was found to be most meaningfully differentiated into qualitative subtypes of *instrumental*, *pseudo-pleasing*, *demeaning* and *extreme/fantasy*. These subtypes are in line with previously discussed motivation-based and behaviour-based typologies (summarised in Table 5.1), but because the proposed framework teases apart the different aspects of offence behaviour, the differentiation into these subtypes is focused only on the sexual activity facet, and thus it may provide the necessary degree of specificity allowing each crime scene to be appropriately classified.

Overall, the differentiation findings within each of the behavioural dimensions here are consistent with many aspects of previous literature and theory, whilst also providing an improvement on previous classification attempts in the degree of specificity of the differentiation as well as in that both the qualitative and the quantitative aspects of differentiation are taken into account. Previous behaviour-based (e.g. Kearns, Salfati, & Jarvis, 2011; Salfati & Bateman, 2005; Sorochinski, Salfati, & Labuschagne, 2014) as well as motivation-based (e.g. Groth and Birnbaum, 1979; Keppel & Walter, 1999) studies of crime scene classification consistently encountered the issue of overlap between types or themes, with a fairly large proportion of crime scenes being non-classifiable (or hybrid), and even those crime scenes that could be classified into a dominant theme still had a substantial number of behaviours from the other theme present (e.g. Kearns et al., 2011; Salfati & Bateman, 2005). With the dimensional approach used here, 100% of crime scenes can be allocated into a specific level and style for each of the examined behaviours.

Importantly, in an ad-hoc analysis, the possibility of putting the dimensions of control, violence and sexual activity back together into a single combined classification system (with broad types that include a degree of control and violent and a subtype of sexual activity) was tested. The analysis revealed that offenders used a wide variety of combinations of these behavioural dimensions and the few common subtypes that were identified accounted for only a minor proportion of crime scenes and did not provide a meaningful differentiation. Therefore, it was concluded that using the dimensional approach to classification, with specific subtypes and degree of presence within (rather than across) behavioural domains allows for more flexibility in individually differentiating crime scenes, whilst also avoiding the formation of mixed types, and thus laying a solid foundation for subsequent consistency analysis in serial crime.

5.6 Study 2: Dynamic Behavioural Consistency

The *Consistency Hypothesis*, as it applies to criminal behaviour, was outlined by Canter (1994) and states that 'the way an offender carries out one crime on one occasion will have some characteristic similarities to the way he or she carries out crimes on other occasions' (p. 347). As explained by Woodhams and Toye (2007), 'if offenders were not consistent in their criminal behaviour, it would be impossible to assign crimes to a common offender on the basis of their behavioural similarity' (p. 62). Thus, if empirical research is to aid law enforcement in identifying the salient crime scene features for linkage purposes, then understanding criminal behavioural consistency is crucial.

Whilst the reliance of investigators on behavioural cues for the purposes of linking crimes to a series has probably been present for a long time, its empirical validity has only recently started to be scrutinised. Investigative literature (e.g. Douglas & Munn, 1992; Holmes & Holmes, 1998; Keppel, 1995, 2000) maintains that serial offenders exhibit highly consistent behaviours that manifest themselves in behavioural signatures that are both unique and stable and thus can be used to link series whilst also differentiating one series from another. Empirical evidence to back up such claims, however, has yet to be accumulated.

At present, there have been a total of 36 empirical studies that directly address the issue of linking serial crimes, including burglary, robbery, rape, arson and homicide using behavioural evidence (see Table 5.2). Most of these studies have specifically focused on resolving the methodological dilemma of how to best use crime scene behaviours to link serial offences. However, of these 36 studies, only 11 involved series of sexual offences (Bennell, Jones, & Melnyk, 2009; Grubin et al., 2001; Harbers, Deslauriers-Varin, Beauregard, & van der Kemp, 2012; Hewitt & Beauregard, 2014; Kearns et al., 2011; Leclerc et al., in press; Santtila, Junkkila, & Sandnabba, 2005; Winter et al., 2013; Woodhams et al., 2007, 2008; Woodhams & Labuschagne, 2011).

Kearns et al. (2011) highlighted an important methodological concern relating to the number of crimes per series that is most often included in studies on linking (i.e. whether any reliable conclusions can be made regarding the general consistency of offenders' behaviour based on the degree of similarity between two crimes from a series). Indeed, as can be seen in Table 5.2, over half of studies to date examined the possibilities of behavioural linking using only two crimes from a series – either two consecutive crimes (e.g. Davies, Tonkin, Bull, & Bond, 2012; Tonkin, Grant, & Bond, 2008; Woodhams & Toye, 2007) or a random pair of two crimes (e.g. Bennell & Canter, 2002; Bennell & Jones, 2005) from series – and determining the predictive validity of various methods in linking the two crimes together. Such an approach may be problematic in that it does not allow for the examination of progression of consistency and change over time. The evidence is emerging, however, that offenders may become less consistent as their series progress (Kearns et al., 2011; Salfati, Horning, Sorochinski, & Labuschagne, 2014), highlighting the importance of fully investigating behavioural patterns across a larger number of crimes within series.

As shown in Table 5.2, previous literature has examined consistency in serial crime using either individual behaviours (e.g. approach method, victim type, binding), groups of behaviours (either pre-selected by researchers or identified through cluster analysis – e.g. control behaviours, planning behaviours) or theory-driven behavioural themes (e.g. expressive/instrumental model, interpersonal model). None of these approaches, however, yielded a fully satisfactory result in terms of great linking potential of consistent behavioural sets that are also well differentiated across series, and thus can be used reliably in the investigative process. A reframed understanding of what constitutes consistency in a crime series as a *dynamic pattern* rather than static behavioural matching has been proposed as key for making empirical progress in the use of behavioural evidence for linking crimes.

Table 5.2 Linking and Consistency Literature Organised by Unit and Type of Analysis

	Individual Behaviours	Groups of Behaviours	Behavioural Themes	Behavioural Patterns
Linking randomly selected crime pairs	Bennell, Jones, and Melnyk, 2009; Tonkin, Santtila, and Bull, 2012; Tonkin, Woodhams, Bull, Bond, and Palmer, 2011; Woodhams, Hollin, and Bull, 2008	Bennell and Canter, 2002; Bennell and Jones, 2005; Markson, Woodhams, and Bond, 2010; Melnyk, Bennell, Gauthier, and Gauthier, 2011; Tonkin, Woodhams, Bull, Bond, and Santtila, 2012; Woodhams, Grant, and Price, 2007; Woodhams and Labuschagne, 2011	Ellingwood, Mugford, Bennell, Melnyk, and Fritzon, 2013	Hewitt and Beauregard, 2014; Leclerc, Lussier, and Deslauriers-Varin, in press; Lussier, Leclerc, Healey, and Proulx, 2008
Linking consecutive crime pairs	Deslauriers-Varin and Beauregard, 2013; Harbers, Deslauriers-Varin, Beauregard, Van der Kemp, 2012	Burrell, Bull, and Bond, 2012; Davies, Tonkin, Bull, and Bond, 2012; Tonkin, Grant, and Bond, 2008; Woodhams and Toye, 2007		Sorochinski and Salfati, 2010
Consistency or discriminatory power across 3 or more crimes	Bateman and Salfati, 2007; Salo, Siren, Corander, Zappala, Bosco, Mokros, and Santtila, 2013	Bouhana, Johnson, and Porter, 2014; Green, Booth, and Biderman, 1976; Grubin, Kelly, and Brunsdon, 2001; Winter, Lemeire, Meganck, Geboers, Rossi, and Mokros, 2012	Canter, Heritage, Wilson, Davies, Kirby, Holden et al., 1991; Fox and Farrington, 2014; Kearns, Salfati and Jarvis, 2011; Salfati and Bateman, 2005; Salfati, Horning, Sorochinski, and Labuschagne, 2014; Santtila, Fritzon, and Tamelander, 2004; Santtila, Junkkila, and Sandnabba, 2005; Santtila, Pakkanen, Zappala, Bosco, Valkama, and Mokros, 2008	

The basis for an empirically sound analysis of consistency is the identi-fication of the most appropriate behavioural unit of analysis (i.e. what will be expected to remain consistent or change in an identifiable trajectory). In Study 1, it was determined that a useful way of differentiating between rape offences is within three broad dimensions of sexual offenders' behaviours, namely, violence, control and sexual activity. Specifically, it was concluded that the control and violence are most meaningfully differentiated *quantita-tively* (into none, low, moderate and high degree) and sexual activity is most appropriately differentiated *qualitatively* (into pseudo-pleasing, instrumen-tal, demeaning and extreme/fantasy subtypes).

Whilst Study 1 examined differentiation between individual crime scenes, the next step in understanding serial rape offences and establish-ing the grounds for behavioural linkage is to investigate the behavioural traceability (consistency and behavioural change trajectories) across offence series. In order to fully investigate how the offender's behaviour progresses along the three behavioural dimensions, it is necessary to not only exam-ine whether they remain consistent or change in a particular direction (e.g. escalate, de-escalate or switch between specific subtypes) from one crime to the next in the series (as has been done in e.g. Hewitt & Beauregard, 2014), but also whether an overall behavioural trajectory could be identified, and how these trajectories from the three distinct behavioural domains correlate with each other (i.e. whether the way offender's behaviour changes in one behavioural dimension is related to behavioural changes in the other two dimensions).

Thus, Study 2 aimed to determine whether offenders remained consistent or followed an identifiable quantitative (in control and violence) and qualita-tive (in sexual activity) behavioural trajectory exhibited across their series. It was hypothesised that (a) consistency as well as identifiable behavioural trajectories will be seen in the way offenders transition *from one crime to the next*, and (b) that *overall* behavioural trajectories of consistency and change over multiple crimes in the series could be identified in each behavioural dimension. Additionally, the study aimed to identify the cross-dimensional relationships between behavioural trajectories across crimes in the series, that is, determine how consistency or change within one behavioural dimen-sion correlates with changes or consistency in the other two.

5.7 Data

In order to be able to examine the pattern of behavioural consistency or change across the series, a subsample of the data was used. Because series varied significantly in length, it was necessary to select a fixed number of crimes in the series to compare. Whilst the mean number of crimes per series was 6.4 (*SD* = 3.14), the distribution was highly skewed, and therefore, the mode was used to determine the most appropriate cutoff. The largest proportion of series had four crimes (*n* = 11; 36.67%). Thus, to maximise the number of series that could be included in the study, the first four crimes in each series were analysed for consistency and behavioural trajectories. Two series that consisted of three crimes were, therefore, excluded from the analysis. This resulted in a total sample of the 28 series and a total of 112 crime scenes.

5.8 Summary of Behavioural Consistency Results

Study 2 examined the patterns of offenders' behaviours along the dimensions of control, violence and sexual activity in the way they transition from one crime to the next in the series as well as the overall progression across first four crimes in the series. It appears that using these two ways of examining offenders' behaviour provides complementing insights into how their behaviour evolves. For example, it was determined that offenders who engage in moderate or high degree of control, most commonly, remain consistent in the first two consecutive crimes. But only a quarter of offenders in the sample remained consistent in their degree of control when looked at across the first four crimes, suggesting that whilst they may exhibit consistency at a certain point in the series, they are also highly likely to deviate from the initial level as the series progress. This finding further highlights the methodological importance of going beyond the examination of consistency within pairs of crimes and extending the analysis to include multiple crimes from the series.

When the trajectories in the degree of violence are analysed, it was found that offenders are most commonly consistent in the first two crimes of their offence series, regardless of the initial level (i.e. those who started off with low violence remained in the low violence degree for the second crime, those who started with moderate violence remained moderate, etc.). However, nearly a third of the sample was found to escalate in their violence at some point during the first four crimes in the series, which is in line with previous research on violence (e.g. Hazelwood, Reboussin, & Warren, 1989; Hewitt & Beauregard, 2014) and may highlight the proneness of this behavioural dimension to situational factors. Importantly, whilst offenders who committed short or long series generally did not differ in the first four crimes, when the later part of the long series was analysed, it was found that offenders' levels of violence were more likely to be higher (in fact, very few offenders engaged in no or low violence in these later crimes of long series) and consistently so, suggesting that the situational use of high degrees of violence that may have occurred earlier in the series, becomes more habitual and, thus, consistent as the series progress. Alternatively, in line with the motivation-based literature (e.g. Cohen, Seghorn, & Calmas, 1969), the sex-aggression fusion becomes more prominent as the series progress and offenders may exhibit a higher degree of violence as part of the sexual assault to satisfy their sexual needs.

In examining the behavioural patterns within the sexual activity dimension, it was found that the presence of interrupted attempts severely handicaps the methodological possibilities of analysing the specific transitions from one crime to the next in this behavioural dimension (this limitation and possibilities for future investigation will be further discussed later). When interrupted attempts (i.e. where offenders failed to engage in any sexual activity behaviours) are not taken into account, over a third of offenders remain consistent across their first four crimes in the series. Offenders who were not consistent, for the most part switched between two subtypes of sexual activity. These findings are in line with the conclusions of Hewitt and Beauregard (2014) and Leclerc et al. (in press) that many serial offenders appear versatile in the kinds of sexual activity they engage in with the victims across the series. Furthermore, three of the four switching patterns observed included instrumental sexual activity (that consisted of vaginal penetration and was deemed to be indicative of basic need for sexual gratification) as one of the two types and one of the more 'fantasy-driven' types (i.e. pseudo-pleasing, demeaning or extreme) as the other type. This may be indicative of experimentation within this behavioural subgroup, as theorised by Canter and Youngs (2003) and as has previously been found in Sorochinski and Salfati (2010), or it may indicate an evolution of the offender's fantasy over the series (Douglas & Munn, 1992). Alternatively, it may be the case, as hypothesised by Hewitt and Beauregard (2014), that in some offences, offenders were unable to engage in the full gamut of sexual activity they had initially planned due to situational interference. Further investigation of factors that may influence the way offenders change their behavioural trajectory within this dimension may be necessary to fully substantiate these hypotheses. However, in line with previous studies (e.g. Bateman & Salfati, 2007), it is clear that, in contrast to what the early investigative literature (e.g. Dietz, Hazelwood, & Warren, 1990; Ressler, Burgess, & Douglas, 1986) had suggested, offenders are not highly consistent in the sexual fantasy-related, or 'signature' behaviours.

In order to gain a fuller understanding of the way offenders' behavioural patterns are manifested, we also examined the combined progression of offenders' behaviour *across* the three dimensions of control, violence and sexual activity. The results revealed that offenders were much more likely to exhibit consistency at the single behavioural dimension level than at the overall crime scene behaviour level. That is, over half of the offenders were consistent in at least one of the behavioural dimensions over the first four crimes in their series, but none were consistent across all three dimensions. Furthermore, when the trajectories of change were examined in those series where offenders did not exhibit consistency in any of the dimensions, it was found that these trajectories are also best understood when considered individually rather than in combination. These findings are in line with the Leclerc et al.'s (in press) conclusions that there is often a lack of synchronicity in the various subgroups of offending behaviours, and again highlight the importance of choosing the most appropriate behavioural unit for analysing offenders' behavioural continuity. Finally, using the reframed definition of consistency that included behavioural trajectories, only one series in this sample was found to exhibit complete inconsistency, which constitutes a substantial improvement on previously identified levels of behavioural consistency across series (e.g. Bateman & Salfati, 2007; Grubin et al., 2001; Kearn et al., 2011; Salfati & Bateman, 2005). Together, these findings suggest that the quantitative (control and violence) and qualitative (sexual activity) differentiation within behavioural dimensions, identified in Study 1, is a useful *unit of analysis* for crime scene classification and can also become a promising way for the identification of *behavioural traceability* (consistency and behavioural trajectories) across series.

Furthermore, an ad-hoc analysis conducted to examine the way failed attempts of sexual assault may contribute to how offenders change their control and violent behaviour in the following crimes revealed that there are individual differences in the offenders' behavioural patterns following a failed attempt in terms of the degree of control and violence observed. Specifically, four patterns were identified: (a) *rigid* – where complete consistency in both violence and control were observed, thus, these offenders remained rigid in their behaviour and did not attempt to change the degree of used control or violence to make sure that the subsequent attack is successful; (b) *strategic* – where offenders remained consistent in one of the dimensions, whilst changing in the other. These offenders made adjustments to the degree of either violence or control whilst keeping the other one constant in the crime following the attempt. Interestingly, of these offenders, all but one remained consistent in their violence degree and changed the degree of control, again highlighting the key role that control plays in these crimes. The third pattern of behaviour observed following the failed attempt was (c) *frustration* – a change in both the degree of control and the degree of violence in the same direction. These offenders, most commonly (in three out of four cases) escalated in both control and violence in response to the previous failed attempt, which may be evidence of increasing frustration (Hickey, 2006) as a result of failing to satisfy their sexual needs and finally the fourth pattern was (d) *switching gears* – a change in both control and violence in opposite directions. These are offenders who make adjustments to their behaviour in switching between the levels of control and violence, suggesting that they may view these two aspects of the offence as interchangeable. The fact that two thirds of the offenders did make adjustments to the degree of either violence, control or both in the crime following the interrupted attempt sub-stantiates the hypothesis that learning based on previous experience may affect the offenders' behavioural patterns across series.

These differences in how offenders react and adjust to the situational fac-tors affecting their criminal path are in line with what has been proposed as the interaction process between the influence of the situation and the differ-ences in personality (Bartol & Bartol, 2008; Fleeson & Noftle, 2008), and sug-gest that whilst situational factors are important to take into consideration when determining *why* the offender's behaviour may have changed, the key individual differences relevant to both the theory and the practice of behav-ioural linkage may lie in *how* the offenders are dealing with the situation. In other words, the emphasis should not be on whether the situational factors affected the individual, but in the way the effect is manifested in offenders' decision-making process of how to re-strategise their behaviour. This analy-sis also further supports the importance of analysing crime series in detail and including the attempted assaults in the behavioural analysis (as sug-gested by Salfati, 2008). Furthermore, fully expanding on such analysis by including other crimes that an offender may have committed (e.g. robberies or thefts that were committed between the sexual assaults) and determining how the offender's experiences during those crimes may have affected their behaviour in the other crimes can bring valuable insights into the under-standing of behavioural continuity across the full criminal path.

5.9 Implications and Conclusions

Behavioural linking is one of the central parts in the investigative process when faced with a possible series of offences (Grubin et al., 2001; Salfati & Kucharski, 2005). Although findings from recent studies (see Table 5.2) are promising for the future of behavioural linking, several important limita-tions were identified in how the key issues of individual differentiation and consistency in serial crime have been addressed to date that impede the fruitful development of this line of research. Researchers in the investiga-tive psychology and linking fields (e.g. Alison & Stein, 2001; Canter et al., 2004; Salfati, 2008; Woodhams, Grant, & Price, 2007) have stressed the importance of establishing valid and reliable methodological baselines for answering the questions underlying behavioural linkage (i.e. how to best dif-ferentiate between crime series, and how to define and identify behavioural consistency across crime series) to help move the field forward both in terms of understanding where it lands itself within the greater theory of human behaviour and in terms of evidence-based practical applications.

The studies summarised in this chapter add empirical evidence to the multidimensional conception of consistency in several ways. First, the fact that, in absence of complete stability, meaningful behavioural trajectories were evident in the way offenders' behaviour changed across series within each of the analysed behavioural dimensions suggests that consistency – defined more broadly as traceability – can be identified and can enrich our understanding of behavioural continuity. Second, it was found that most offenders, whilst exhibiting stability in one behavioural dimension across series, also exhibit a change pattern in the other. This confirms the notion that there are intra-individual differences in the way this behavioural continuity is manifested depending on the specific aspect of behaviour that is analysed. That is, Fleeson and Noftle (2008) suggested that one of the 'competing determinants' (p. 1364) of consistency is behavioural content, meaning that consistency can be manifested differently by the same person (either as stability or as change along a specified dimension) depending on the particular behaviour investigated. This idea (and the evidence identified here to support it) is pivotal for advancing the research on behavioural linking because it suggests a need to shift the focus from determining *which* of the relevant behaviours are consistent across series and which are not to determining *how* consistency is manifested in *each* of the various relevant behaviours. Furthermore, it highlights the importance of dissecting the totality of behaviours manifested during an offence into distinct behavioural dimensions (e.g. control, violence, sexual activity in sexual offences) and examining how offenders may exhibit consistency within each of those dimensions rather than broadly identifying the proportion of offenders who behave in a stable pattern across their series overall (e.g. in a broad behavioural theme that includes the full range of relevant behaviours).

The ultimate goal of this line of research is to be able to apply it during the investigative process. Thus, it is important to consider the extent to which the approach discussed here can inform the *practice* of behavioural linking. Previous literature (e.g. Canter et al., 2003; Robertiello & Terry, 2007; Terry, 2006) has highlighted the difficulties in classifying sexual offences into rigid types. Indeed, it appears that it may be advisable to refrain from making broad conclusions as to the motivation or the general behavioural theme when investigating these crimes. Instead, we believe it is important to emphasise a refined level of considerations in the analysis of sexual offending behaviour, both in terms of differentiating their offences within small and concrete behavioural dimensions, and in terms of the way the offenders' behaviour may change within each of the dimensions over their series.

Furthermore, previous studies on linking crimes have generally based their recommendations to law enforcement for determining whether two crimes are linked (Bennell et al., 2014) on the extent of similarity between the crimes in question. Based on the examination of behavioural change trajectories within specific dimensions of behaviour across crime series, these recommendations can be extended.

As summarised in the decision tree diagram in Figure 5.3, the first step in the linking process should be to look at whether the crime scenes have consistency (aka stability) in at least one of the behavioural domains. If there is no consistency in any of the behavioural domains, then, in the next step, specific behavioural trajectories need to be analysed in order to determine the likelihood of the series being linked.

Finally, if it is found that there is neither consistency nor an identifiable trajectory of change, unfortunately, at this stage, the behavioural evidence cannot be conclusively used to determine whether the crimes in question are part of the same series. In other words, it seems that, at this time, behavioural evidence can only be used to identify linked series but not to exclude linkage. Such a conclusion is problematic because it signifies that even distinctly behaviourally different offences could have been committed by the same offender, thus undermining the extent to which behavioural linking could be practically useful. Whilst studies that compare linked crime pairs to unlinked crime pairs (i.e. pairs of crimes that are known to not have been committed by the same offender; e.g. Bennell & Canter, 2002; Bennell & Jones, 2005; Markson, Woodhams, & Bond, 2010; Tonkin, Santilla & Bull, 2012) generally find that linked pairs are more similar than unlinked on a given set of elements, the present findings suggest

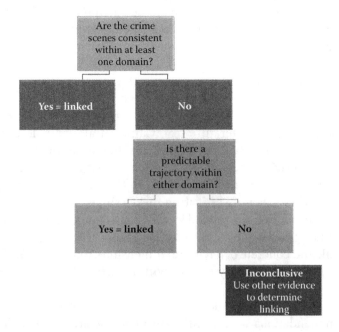

Figure 5.3 Investigative decision-making tree when using behavioural evidence to link crimes.

that at least a minority of crime series may be characterised by a complete lack of consistency or even discernible trajectory of change across their crimes. A further detailed examination of exactly how series characterised by inconsistency differ from unlinked crimes may be necessary to determine with any degree of certainty that apparently dissimilar crimes were not committed by the same offender.

In recent years, behavioural linking evidence, in addition to being used during the investigative process, has also been brought to court (e.g. *State v. Fortin I*, 2000; *State of California v. Prince*, 2007). In cases where sufficient direct (e.g. DNA) evidence is present to convict the offender of only one (or several) of the crimes he is suspected of committing, an expert may testify that the crimes, where there is not enough physical evidence, can be conclusively (behaviourally) linked to those where there is, and, thus, that whoever committed one of these crimes has also committed the others. Researchers (e.g. Ormerod, 1999; Risinger & Loop, 2002; Salfati, in press; Salfati & Curmi, 2014) have raised concerns regarding such premature use of behavioural linking, emphasising that the reliability and validity of the technique has yet to be fully established before any such consequential use of it can be implemented. The current findings, whilst adding support to the fundamental assumptions validating the use of behavioural evidence, also highlight that there is still much to be done in terms of fully developing, testing and fine-tuning the technique before it can be considered reliable in an investigation or in the court.

Another aspect of importance that needs to be addressed in relation to the focus of this chapter is that the proposed detailed examination of whether and how behavioural change may be viewed as a form of dynamic consistency may be practically useful when an investigator is faced with a limited number of crimes and needs to determine whether they should be investigated as part of a single series. However, in the case of crime analysis that aims to identify possible links between crimes in a large database of unsolved cases, such examination of trajectories may not be practically feasible because it would require the analyst to examine every possible combination of crimes in search of potential trajectories. Thus, in this type of crime linkage analysis, the only possibility is to concentrate on the subsample of offenders who remain truly stable in at least one aspect of their criminal behaviour. Nonetheless, the existence of these trajectories signifies that similarity-based crime linking is limited in its ability to detect and identify series because those series that are characterised by behavioural change will necessarily be overlooked.

In conclusion, whilst investigative use of behavioural evidence to help link and solve serial offences has been in use for a long time, the empirical and theoretical grounds for whether and how to use this evidence effectively has begun to emerge only in recent years. The theoretical framework, as described by Canter (2000), proposed that in order for behavioural crime linking to be validated, two base assumptions must be met: individual

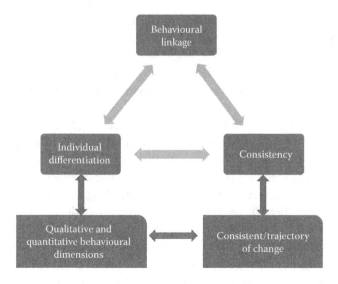

Figure 5.4 Conceptual structure that underlies behavioural linkage – revisited.

differentiation and consistency. The two key questions that underlie these assumptions, as outlined in the introduction to this chapter, are (a) what is the most appropriate behavioural unit – *unit of analysis* – that can best differentiate crime scenes, and (b) what is the most efficient way of defining the consistency of this unit – *stability or traceability* – that will maximise the potential for identifying series. Revisiting Figure 5.1 that summarised this basic underlying structure of behavioural linkage, the theoretical and empirical examination of the preceding questions allows for substituting the question marks in the base fields with the following answers (see Figure 5.4): (a) the unit of analysis that may be most appropriate for differentiating between crime scenes (at least in the case of sexual offences as analysed here) is the quantitative and qualitative distinctions within behavioural dimensions, and (b) in order to fully capture the consistency of behaviour across series, it must be analysed in terms of behavioural trajectories of change in addition to behavioural stability.

Acknowledgements

This project was supported by Award No. 2013-IJ-CX-0009, awarded by the National Institute of Justice, Office of Justice Programs, U.S. Department of Justice. The opinions, findings and conclusions or recommendations expressed in this paper are those of the authors and do not necessarily reflect those of the Department of Justice.

The authors would like to express their gratitude to the FBI's Behavioral Science Unit for coordinating access to the data used in this project. Authors' opinions, statements and conclusions should not be considered an endorsement by the FBI for any policy, program or service.

References

Alison, L. J., & Stein, K. L. (2001). Vicious circles: Accounts of stranger sexual assault reflect abusive variants of conventional interactions. *Journal of Forensic Psychiatry, 12*, 515–538.

Bartol, C. R., & Bartol, A. M. (2008). *Criminal behavior: A psychosocial approach* (8th ed.). Upper Saddle River, NJ: Pearson Prentice Hall.

Bateman, A., & Salfati, G. (2007). An examination of behavioral consistency using individual behaviors or groups of behaviors in serial homicide. *Behavioral Sciences and the Law, 25*, 527–544.

Bennell, C., & Canter, D. (2002). Linking commercial burglaries by modus operandi: Tests using regression and ROC analysis. *Science and Justice, 42*, 153–164.

Bennell, C., & Jones, N. J. (2005). Between a ROC and a hard place: A method for linking serial burglaries using an offender's modus operandi. *Journal of Investigative Psychology and Offender Profiling, 2*, 23–41. doi: 10.1002/jip.21.

Bennell, C., Jones, N. J., & Melnyk, T. (2009). Addressing problems with traditional crime linking methods using receiver operating characteristic analysis. *Legal and Criminological Psychology, 14*, 293–310. doi: 10.1348/135532508X349336.

Bennell, C., Mugford, R., Ellingwood, H., & Woodhams, J. (2014). Linking crimes using behavioural clues: Current levels of linking accuracy and strategies for moving forward. *Journal of Investigative Psychology and Offender Profiling, 11*, 29–56. doi: 10.1002/jip.1395.

Bohm, J., & Alison, L. (2002). An exploratory study in methods of distinguishing destructive cults. *Psychology, Crime, & Law, 7*, 133–165.

Bouhana, N., Johnson, S.D., & Porter, M. (2014). Consistency and specificity in burglars who commit prolific residential burglary: Testing the core assumptions underpinning behavioural crime linkage. *Legal & Criminological Psychology*. Advance online publication. doi: 10.1111/lcrp.12050.

Burrell, A., Bull, R., & Bond, J. (2012). Linking personal robbery offences using offender behaviour. *Journal of Investigative Psychology and Offender Profiling, 9*, 201–222. doi: 10.1002/jip.1365.

Canter, D. (2000). Offender profiling and criminal differentiation. *Legal and Criminological Psychology, 5*, 23–46.

Canter, D., & Heritage, R. (1990). A multivariate model of sexual offence behaviour: Developments in offender profiling. *Journal of Forensic Psychiatry, 1*, 185–212. doi: 10.1080/09585189008408469.

Canter, D., & Youngs, D. (2003). Beyond offender profiling: The need for an investigative psychology. In D. Carson, & R. Bull (Eds.), *Handbook of psychology in legal contexts* (2nd ed., pp. 171–205). Chichester, UK: John Wiley & Sons, Ltd.

Canter, D. V. (1994). *Criminal shadows*. London: Harper Collins.

Canter, D. V., Alison, L. J., Alison, E., & Wentink, N. (2004). The organized/disorganized typology of serial murder: Myth or model? *Psychology, Public Policy, and Law, 10*, 293–320.

Canter, D. V., Bennell, C., Alison, L. J., & Reddy, S. (2003). Differentiating sex offences: A behaviorally based thematic classification of stranger rapes. *Behavioral Sciences and the Law, 21*, 157–174.

Canter, D. V., Heritage, R., Wilson, M., Davies, A., Kirby, S., Holden, R. ... Donald, I. (1991). *A facet approach to offender profiling.* London: University of Surrey, Offender Profiling Research Unit.

Cohen, M. L., Seghorn, T., & Calmas, W. (1969). Sociometric study of sex offenders. *Journal of Abnormal Psychology, 74*, 249–255.

Dancer, L. S. (1990). Suicide prediction and the partial order scalogram analysis of psychological adjustment. *Applied Psychology: An International Review, 39*, 479–497.

Davies, K., Tonkin, M., Bull, R., & Bond, J. W. (2012). The course of case linkage never did run smooth: A new investigation to tackle the behavioural changes in serial car theft. *Journal of Investigative Psychology and Offender Profiling, 9*, 274–295.

Deslauriers-Varin, N., & Beauregard, E. (2013). Investigating offending consistency of geographic and environmental factors among serial sex offenders: A comparison of multiple analytical strategies. *Criminal Justice and Behavior, 40*, 156–179.

Dietz, P. E., Hazelwood, R. R., & Warren, J. (1990) The sexually sadistic criminal and his offenses. *Bulletin of the American Academy of Psychiatry & the Law, 18*, 163–178.

Douglas, J. E., & Munn, C. M. (1992). Modus operandi and the signature aspects of violent crime. In J. E. Douglas, A. W. Burgess, A. G. Burgess, & R. K. Ressler (Eds.), *Crime classification manual* (pp. 259–268). New York: Lexington Books.

Ellingwood, H., Mugford, R., Melnyk, T., & Bennell, C. (2013). Examining the role of similarity coefficients and the value of behavioural themes in attempts to link serial arson offences. *Journal of Investigative Psychology and Offender Profiling, 10*, 1–27.

Fleeson, W., & Noftle, E. E. (2008). Where does personality have its influence? A supermatrix of consistency concepts. *Journal of Personality, 76*, 1355–1386. doi: 10.1111/j.1467-6494.2008.00525.x.

Fox, B. H., & Farrington, D. P. (2014). Behavioral consistency among serial burglars: Evaluating offense specialization using three analytical approaches. *Crime & Delinquency.* Advance online publication. doi: 10.1177/0011128714540275.

Green, E. J., Booth, C. E., & Biderman, M. D. (1976). Cluster analysis of burglary MO's. *Journal of Police Science and Administration, 4*, 382–387.

Groth, A. N., & Birnbaum, H. J. (1979). *Men who rape: The psychology of the offender.* New York: Plenum.

Groth, A. N., Burgess, A., & Holmstrom, L. (1977). Rape: Power, anger and sexuality. *American Journal of Psychiatry, 134*, 1239–1243.

Grubin, D., Kelly, P., & Brunsdon, C. (2001). *Linking serious sexual assaults through behavior.* London: Home Office, Research, Development and Statistics Directorate.

Guttman, R., & Greenbaum, C. W. (1998). Facet theory: Its development and current status. *European Psychologist, 3*, 13–36.

Hakkanen, H., Lindlof, P., & Santtila, P. (2004). Crime scene actions and offender characteristics in a sample of Finnish stranger rapes. *Journal of Investigative Psychology & Offender Profiling, 1,* 17–32.

Harbers, E., Deslauriers-Varin, N., Beauregard, E., & van der Kemp, J. J. (2012). Testing the behavioural and environmental consistency of serial sex offenders: A signature approach. *Journal of Investigative Psychology and Offender Profiling, 9,* 259–273. doi: 10.1002/jip.1368.

Hazelwood, R. R., & Burgess, A. W. (Eds.) (2009). *Practical aspects of rape investigation: A multidisciplinary approach* (4th ed.). Boca Raton: CRC Press.

Hazelwood, R. R., Reboussin, R., & Warren, J. I. (1989). Serial rape: Correlates of increased aggression and the relationship of offender pleasure to victim resistance. *Journal of Interpersonal Violence, 4,* 65–78.

Hewitt, A. & Beauregard, E. (2014). Offending patterns of serial sexual offenders: Escalation, de-escalation, and consistency of sexually intrusive and violent behaviours. *Journal of Investigative Psychology & Offender Profiling, 11,* 57–80. doi: 10.1002/jip.1407.

Hickey, E. (2006). *Serial murderers and their victims.* Pacific Grove, CA: Sage.

Holmes, R. M., & Holmes, S. T. (1998). *Serial murder* (2nd ed.). Thousand Oaks, CA: Sage.

Kearns, E., Salfati, C. G., & Jarvis, J. (2011, November). *Serial rape: The relationship between geographic patterns, crime locations and offender demographics.* Poster at Annual American Society of Criminology Conference, Washington, DC.

Keppel, R. D. (1995). Signature murder: A report of several related cases. *Journal of Forensic Sciences, 40,* 670–674.

Keppel, R. D. (2000). Investigation of the serial offender: Linking cases through modus operandi and signature. In L. B. Schlesinger (Ed.), *Serial offenders: Current thoughts, recent findings* (pp. 121–133). Boca Raton, FL: CRC Press.

Keppel, R. D., & Walter, R. (1999). Profiling killers: A revised classification model for understanding sexual murder. *International Journal of Offender Therapy and Comparative Criminology, 43,* 417–437.

Knight, R. A., & Prentky, R. A. (1990) Classifying sexual offenders: The development and corroboration of taxonomic models. In W. L. Marshall, D. R. Laws, & H. E. Barbaree (Eds.), *The handbook of sexual assault: Issues, theories, and treatment of the offender* (pp. 27–52). New York: Plenum.

Kocsis, R. N., Cooksey, R. W., & Irwin, H. J. (2002). Psychological profiling of sexual murderers: An empirical model. *International Journal of Offender Therapy and Comparative Criminology, 46,* 532–553.

Last, S. K., & Fritzon, K. (2005). Investigating the nature of expressiveness in stranger, acquaintance and intrafamilial homicides. *Journal of Investigative Psychology & Offender Profiling, 2,* 179–193. doi: 10.1002/jip.36.

Leclerc, B., Lussier, P., & Deslauriers-Varin, N. (in press). Offending patterns over time: An examination of specialization, escalation and de-escalation in the commission of sexual offences. In A. Blokland & P. Lussier (Eds.), *Sex offenders: A criminal career approach.* Oxford, UK: Wiley.

Lussier, P., Leclerc, B., Healey, J., & Proulx, J. (2008). Generality of deviance and predation: Crime-switching and specialization patterns in persistent sexual offenders. In M. DeLisi & P. J. Conis (Eds.), *Violent offenders: Theory research, public policy, and practice* (pp. 97–118). Sudbury, MA: Jones & Bartlett Learning.

Markson, L., Woodhams, J., & Bond, J. W. (2010). Linking serial residential burglary: Comparing the utility of modus operandi behaviours, geographic proximity and temporal proximity. *Journal of Investigative Psychology and Offender Profiling, 7,* 91–107. doi: 10.1002/jip.120.

Melnyk, T., Bennell, C., Gauthier, D. J., & Gauthier, D. (2011). Another look at across-crime similarity coefficients for use in behavioural linkage analysis: An attempt to replicate Woodhams, Grant, and Price (2007). *Psychology, Crime & Law, 17,* 359–380.

Ormerod, D. (1999). Criminal profiling: Trial by judge and jury, not criminal psychologist. In D. V. Canter & L. J. Alison (Eds.), *Profiling in policy and practice* (Offender Profiling Series Vol. 2, pp. 207–261). Aldershot, UK: Ashgate.

Porter, L. E., & Alison, L. J. (2001). A partially ordered scale of influence in violent group behavior: An example from gang rape. *Small Group Research, 32,* 475–497.

Reid, J. A., Beauregard, E., Fedina, K. M., & Frith, E. N. (2014). Employing mixed methods to explore motivational patterns of repeat sex offenders. *Journal of Criminal Justice, 42*(2), 203–212.

Ressler, R. K., Burgess, A. W., & Douglas, J. E. (1986). Sexual killers and their victims: Identifying patterns through crime scene analysis. *Journal of Interpersonal Violence, 1,* 288–308.

Risinger, D. M., & Loop, J. L. (2002). Three card monte, Monty Hall, modus operandi and offender profiling: Some lessons of modern cognitive science for the law of evidence. *Cardozo Law Review, 24,* 193–285.

Robertiello, G., & Terry, K. J. (2007). Can we profile sex offenders? A review of sex offender typologies. *Aggression and Violent Behavior, 12,* 507–518.

Salfati, C. G. (2000). The nature of expressiveness and instrumentality in homicide. *Homicide Studies, 4,* 265–293.

Salfati, C. G. (2008). Linking serial crimes. In J. Fossi & L. Falshaw (Eds.), *Issues in forensic psychology* (Vol. 8, pp. 68–81). Leicester, UK: British Psychological Society, Division of Forensic Psychology Publications.

Salfati, C. G. (in press). *Profiling homicide: A sourcebook for students and researchers* (Offender Profiling Series). Aldershot, UK: Ashgate.

Salfati, G. C., & Bateman, A. C. (2005). Serial homicide: An investigation of behavioral consistency. *Journal of Investigative Psychology and Offender Profiling, 2,* 121–144.

Salfati, C. G., & Curmi, T. M. (2014, April). *Linking beyond the investigative process: Expert testimony and the role of linking in court.* Paper presented at the International Association for Investigative Psychology Conference, London.

Salfati, C. G., Horning, A. M., Sorochinski, M., & Labuschagne, G. N. (2014). South African serial homicide: Consistency in victim types and crime scene actions across series. *Journal of Investigative Psychology and Offender Profiling.* doi: 10.1002/jip.1428.

Salfati, C. G., & Kucharski, T. (2005). The psychology of criminal conduct. In J. Trevino & S. Guarino (Eds.), *The common subject of crime: A multidisciplinary approach.* New York: Anderson Publishing.

Salfati, C. G., & Taylor, P. (2006). Differentiating sexual violence: A comparison of sexual homicide and rape. *Psychology, Crime and Law, 12,* 107–126.

Salo, B., Sirén, J., Corander, J., Zappalà, A., Bosco, D., Mokros, A., & Santtila, P. (2012). Using Bayes' theorem in behavioural crime linking in serial homicide. *Legal and Criminological Psychology.* Advance online publication. doi: 10.1111/j.2044-8333.2011.02043.x.

Santtila, P., Fritzon, K., & Tamelander, A. L. (2005). Linking arson incidents on the basis of crime scene behavior. *Journal of Police and Criminal Psychology, 19,* 1–16. doi: 10.1007/BF02802570.

Santtila, P., Junkkila, J., & Sandnabba, N. K. (2005). Behavioural linking of stranger rapes. *Journal of Investigative Psychology and Offender Profiling, 2,* 87–103. doi: 10.1002/jip.26.

Santtila, P., Pakkanen, T., Zappala, A., Bosco, D., Valkama, M., & Mokros, A. (2008). Behavioral crime linking in serial homicide. *Psychology, Crime and Law, 14,* 245–265. doi: 10.1080/10683160701739679/.

Shye, S. (1985). *Multiple scaling: The theory and application of partial order scalogram analysis.* Amsterdam, ND: Elsevier Science.

Shye, S., Elizur, D., & Hoffman, M. (1994). *Introduction to facet theory: Content design and intrinsic data analysis in behavioral research.* Newbury Park, CA: Sage.

Sorochinski, M., & Salfati, C. G. (2010). The consistency of inconsistency in serial homicide: Patterns of behavioral change across series. *Journal of Investigative Psychology and Offender Profiling, 7*(2), 109–136. doi: 10.1002/jip.118.

Sorochinski, M., Salfati C. G., & Labuschagne, G. N. (2014). Classification of planning and violent behaviours in serial homicide: A cross-national comparison between South Africa and the US. *Journal of Investigative Psychology and Offender Profiling.* doi:10.1002/jip.1427.

State v. Fortin I, 162 N.J. 517 (2000).

State v. Prince, S036105 C.A. Super. Ct. No. CR130018 (2007).

Taylor, P. J. (2002). A partial order scalogram analysis of communication behavior in crisis negotioation with the prediction of outcome. *The International Journal of Conflict Management, 13,* 4–37.

Terry, K. J. (2006). *Sexual offenses and offenders.* Belmont, CA: Thomson Wadsworth.

Tonkin, M., Grant, T., & Bond, J. (2008). To link or not to link: A test of the case linkage principles using serial car theft data. *Journal of Investigative Psychology & Offender Profiling, 5,* 59–77. doi:10.1002/jip.74.

Tonkin, M., Santtila, P., & Bull, R. (2012). The linking of burglary crimes using offender behaviour: Testing research cross-nationally and exploring methodology. *Legal and Criminological Psychology, 17,* 276–293. doi: 10.1111/j.2044-8333.2010.02007.x.

Tonkin, M., Woodhams, J., Bull, R., Bond, J. W., & Palmer, E. J. (2011). Linking different types of crime using geographical and temporal proximity. *Criminal Justice and Behavior, 38,* 1069–1088. doi: 10.1177/0093854811418599.

Tonkin, M., Woodhams, J., Bull, R., Bond, J. W., & Santtila, P. (2012). A comparison of logistic regression and classification tree analysis for behavioural case linkage. *Journal of Investigative Psychology and Offender Profiling, 9,* 235–258. doi: 10.1002/jip.1367.

Vettor, S., Beech, A. R., & Woodhams, J. (2014). Rapists and sexual murderers: Combined pathways to offending. In J. Proulx, E. Beauregard, P. Lussier, & B. Leclerc (Eds.), *Pathways to sexual aggression* (pp. 285–315). New York: Routledge.

Winter, J., Lemeire, J., Meganck, S., Geboers, J., Rossi, G., & Mokros, A. (2013). Comparing the predictive accuracy of case linkage methods in serious sexual assaults. *Journal of Investigative Psychology & Offender Profiling, 10*, 28–56. doi: 10.1002/jip.1372.

Woodhams, J., Grant, T., & Price, A. (2007). From marine ecology to crime analysis: Improving the detection of serial sexual offences using a taxonomic similarity measure. *Journal of Investigative Psychology and Offender Profiling, 4*, 17–27.

Woodhams, J., Hollin, C. R., & Bull, R. (2007). The psychology of linking crimes: A review of the evidence. *Legal and Criminological Psychology, 12*(2), 233–249.

Woodhams, J., Hollin, C. R., & Bull, R. (2008). Incorporating context in linking crimes: An exploratory study of situational similarity and if-then contingencies. *Journal of Investigative Psychology and Offender Profiling, 5*, 1–23. doi: 10.1002 /jip.75.

Woodhams, J., & Labuschagne, G. (2011). A test of case linage principles with solved and unsolved serial rapes. *Journal of Police and Criminal Psychology*, 1–14. doi: 10.1007/s11896-011-9091-1.

Woodhams, J., & Toye, K. (2007). An empirical test of the assumptions of case linkage and offender profiling with serial commercial robberies. *Psychology, Public Policy, and Law, 13*, 59–85.

Victims or 'Fighters'? Narratives of Abused Women Who Killed Their Male Intimate Partners

6

PAULA SISMEIRO PEREIRA

Contents

6.1 Introduction

Intimate partner violence (IPV) has been addressed by professionals who work with women in healthcare and community facilities. They shed light on women's suffering and vulnerability as victims of their husbands or partners, and asking for protection.

The feminist perspective, which was the mainstream approach in the fight for women's equal rights in the 1960s, emerged as the major theoretical framework to conceptualise violence against women in intimate relationships (Dobash & Dobash, 1990; Walker, 1979; Yllö, 1983). This marked research and practice about intimate partner violence, sowing the seeds for confining it under the label of gender violence. Men are understood as being able to exert control over women, a belief that is deep-rooted in a patriarchal society that proclaims women's diminished judgement, judiciousness and self-sufficiency.

According to Holly Johnson (1998), attitudes and beliefs underlying gender asymmetry are deeply disseminated in society. Men use coercion and violence to subdue women, thwarting their access to academic, economic and social resources, and undermining their sense of worthiness, whilst keeping them under control (Dobash & Dobash, 1998; Saunders, 1990; Yllö, 1983).

The socio-cultural approach to gender asymmetry is enhanced by evolutionary psychology, which proposes that men need to ensure exclusive propriety over woman's reproductive competence. Any female behaviour that represents a real or perceived menace to male sexual proprietariness will be punished. Coercion and violence serves to maintain men's advantage in reproductive competition (Wilson & Daly, 1992, 1998).

These approaches establish violence as a univocal phenomenon: women as victims and men as aggressors. For the feminist perspective the key issue about intimate partner violence is 'Why do husbands beat up their wives?' (Bograd, 1990, p. 13). Any attempt to focus on men beaten by their female partners, according to Steinmetz's concept of mutual combat (1977/1978), would be immediately rejected with hostility by society. It is even argued that research on female violence against men was actively censored on the grounds that it would undermine the social and political commitment to defend women (Dobash & Dobash, 1990; Dobash, Dobash, Wilson, & Daly, 1992; Holtzworth-Munroe, 2005; Schwartz & DeKeseredy, 1993; White, Smith, Koss, & Figueredo, 2000). In addition, Saunders (2002) states that decreasing resources to support and provide shelter for female victims of violence will ultimately have negative consequences for men, because women left unprotected will undergo further abuse.

6.2 Women in Abusive Relationships

In these relationships, women are perceived as subdued by men who coerce them, undermine their free will and deprive them of their autonomy. Johnson (1995) uses the concept of patriarchal terrorism signifying that men control women persistently and pervasively. Men embody the role of 'norm enforcers upholding "high values"' (Dobash & Dobash, 2011, p. 114) through violence to keep women 'on track'. Hence, women live terrified. Johnson (2008) shows that physical violence is not a necessary requirement for women to become intimidated as psychological abuse and coercion is enough to trigger it. Walker (1979) describes how 'during an acute battering incident … [the woman] feels psychologically trapped and unable to escape' (p. 62).

Ineffective responses to control male violence lead to passivity. Extreme fear and helplessness, together with other symptoms (hypervigilance, numbed affect, perception of life threat, sleeping and eating disorders and flashbacks) are part of the battered woman syndrome, proposed by Walker (1983), which also includes post-traumatic stress disorder. This reveals that battering produces consequences similar to those experienced by people who have had other traumatic experiences. For battered women, the impact of trauma should be aggravated by the repetitive nature of the experience and the proximity between them and the aggressor (Holtzworth-Munroe, Smutzler, & Sandin, 1997).

Fear of the batterer and passivity commonly explain why women remain in abusive relationships. It is also accepted that being battered compromises women's reasoning skills and ability to make good decisions, such as leaving or protecting themselves and their children. Holtzworth-Munroe et al. (1997) and Rhodes and McKenzie (1998) review several studies where battered women seem less able to solve problems, as much related to the violence they suffer as to other topics of daily life. These women also seem unable to choose the most effective solution in comparison to non-abused women and generally show poor coping strategies.

6.2.1 Women as Perpetrators of Lethal and Non-Lethal Violence

Despite the appeal to hide data about female violence perpetration against male partners, several studies show that women may be violent as part of reciprocal violent relationships, either in response to man's violence or initiating violence, or as the only aggressor (Archer, 2000, 2002; Caldwell, Swan, Allen, Sullivan, & Snow, 2009; Ehrensaft, Moffitt, & Caspi, 2004; Kwong, Bartholomew, & Dutton, 1999; Langhinrichsen-Rohling & Vivian, 1994; O'Leary et al., 1989; Ridley & Felman, 2003; Schafer, Caetano, & Clark, 1998; Straus & Kantor, 1994; Vivian & Langhinrichsen-Rohling, 1996).

6.2.1.1 Non-Lethal Violence

Women as violent perpetrators are a great challenge to the explanation provided by the feminist perspective (Enander, 2011; Pereira, 2012), which maintains that this phenomenon occurs as self-defence. This is the reason for female violence being overlooked as this has consequences in two inter-related fields: social intervention and social research. For example, on the one hand, there is a tendency to disregard evidence that women retaliating to partner violence are more likely to increase man's violence in return (Bowker in Saunders, 1990; Leisring, 2009; Lorber & O'Leary, 2004; Straus, 1997,

2007). On the other hand, research reveals some incongruence between the widely accepted argument of self-defence and female explanations for their own violent behaviour.

Research shows that anger, frustration and distress and control and coercion over male partners emerge as major self-reported motives for women in the community (Caldwell et al., 2009; Weston, Marshall, & Coker, 2007), in treatment (Cascardi & Vivian, 1995) and a second major motive for women who are receiving treatment whilst having adjudication deferred (Babcock, Miller, & Siard, 2003). The loss of control of anger is the primary self-attribution for imprisoned females (Henning, Jones, & Holdford, 2005). There is a great similarity between men and women regarding self-explained violence perpetration. In couple therapy, both partners emphasise anger and coercion as major functions of violence (Cascardi & Vivian, 1995) and for male and female self-attributions regarding the last violent episode before detention (Henning et al., 2005). Gender converging self-explanations for violence defy the feminist perception of male violence as the result of typical 'psychological and behavioral patterns of most men' (Bograd, 1990, p. 17), a perception that supports the 'vilification of the batterer' (Cavanaugh & Gelles, 2005; Corvo & Johnson, 2003). Evidence that women may use physical violence to exert power, get control, coerce, pay back, draw closer or as loss of self-control or impulsive expression of anger or frustration, and brings a psychological framework to the IPV research agenda.

An in-depth analysis of the self-defence motive reveals inconsistency. Self-defence motives prevail in data gathered during mandatory treatment and arresting processes (Babcock et al., 2003; Hamberger, 1997) and are also suggested in hetero-attribution studies (Henning et al., 2005). Whilst these motives are equally present for females and males, there is a potential methodological bias. Self-defence may also be reported for women who have never been victimised (Hamberger, 1997) and for highly aggressive women (Babcock et al., 2003).

A closer analysis of self-defence reflects an entanglement with retaliation against previous abuse (Hamberger, 1997; Johnson, 2008). Agreeing that women actively engage in efforts to prevent future victimisation (Gondolf & Fisher, 1988; Walker, 1984), Johnson (2008) proposes violent resistance understood as physically 'fighting back' against a violent partner. This concept simultaneously means: (a) self-defence for women living in a relationship, outlined as intimate terrorism; (b) 'getting even' for women living in a relationship described as situational couple violence. Weston et al. (2007) explains the aggregation of self-defence items as a retaliation factor considering that women's violence is a way to prevent men's behaviour. Merging self-defence and retaliation concepts seems to uphold women's perception of violent behaviour as self-defence.

Female violence that is understood as mostly self-defensive and reactive to male violence seems to be too simplistic and maybe more ideologically than scientifically anchored (Dutton & Nicholls, 2005). Corvo and Johnson put it this way: 'how ideology may be suppressing theory development ... and how rhetoric tends to overwhelm science with respect to perpetrators of domestic violence' (2003, p. 260).

6.2.1.2 Lethal Violence

Intimate partner homicide (IPH) has had great impact on the community. However, only recently has it received attention by researchers (Pereira, 2015) and it is still at an embryonic stage of development (Dobash et al., 2007). Jurik and Winn (1990) examined data files of 108 men and 50 women convicted for homicide or non-negligent manslaughter for a 5-year period. They found that, compared to men 'women's offenses will more frequently occur at home, their victims will most often be opposite sex partners, and their relationships with these partners will involve past physical conflicts' (p. 232).

Wilson and Daly (1992) analysed data files of all homicides in Chicago and in other cities across the United States and in several countries for a period of time. For some other countries, only spousal homicides were analysed. They realised that men usually perpetrate more homicides than women. Yet, in several cities of the United States, women perpetrated more spousal homicides than men for the period considered. That happens particularly for couples, with a registered or *de facto* union and for Afro-American women. When analysing partner homicide between 1976 and 1987, Browne and Williams (1993) found a trend for diminishing homicide rates for married males and females, and for single males but, simultaneously, an increase for women as killers.

Explanation of female-perpetrated IPH usually follows three major interwoven guidelines and is permeated in feminist approaches. First, it is established that women who kill partners live in chronic conflictual relationships in which they are the victims. Jurik and Winn (1990) found that in 95% of the cases of female-perpetrated intimate homicides there is an early conflict history, which is just verbal in 10% of the cases but physical in 86% of the cases. Smith et al. (1998) reported that in almost 96% of the cases, domestic violence preceded homicide, with the man being the offender in all cases but one,* and with the homicide day being just an ordinary day without any extraordinary events.

Second, assuming the continuity between the intimate partner's violence and homicide, this promotes self-defence as the leading, even the exclusive explanation for women's perpetration of homicide. Women tormented by a

---

* Authors report male- and female-perpetrated homicide jointly.

life of victimisation, in a self-defensive (to protect themselves or their children) or retaliatory action, kill their intimate partners (Belknap, Larson, Abrams, Garcia, & Anderson-Block, 2012; Browne & Williams, 1993; Jurik & Winn, 1990; Schwartz, 2010; Smith et al., 1998; Wilson & Daly, 1992). The strength of the self-defence argument is reinforced by the plea that women were not the ones who initiated the physical aggression just before homicide (Johnson & Hotton, 2003; Jurik & Winn, 1990; Schwartz, 2010) and that they were defied by the men to kill them just preceding the homicide (Belknap et al., 2012). This supports the 'victim precipitation' concept (Wolfgang in Belknap et al., 2012).

Third, the self-defence thesis is kept even in the absence of a conflictive or aggressive event immediately prior to murder. This is sustained in Browne's concept of 'imminent danger' (in Schwartz, 2010). This explains that their previous relationship experience made women live fearful for themselves or their children, allowing them to develop aggressive or lethal actions 'in reaction to the level of threat and violence coming in' (Browne in Schwartz, 2010, p. 289). Schwartz asserts that 'female violence occurs mainly under extreme stress' (2010, p. 290). Smith et al. (1998) discussing women with emotional vulnerability due to battering experience, point to the differences between men or women perpetrating IPH. They embed their explanation of female-perpetrated IPH in the women's feeling of fear and their need to react to or reduce future danger. This perception serves the gender asymmetry established by the feminist approach and introduces a major bias in analysis by accepting dimensions for explaining aggressive female behaviour that were rejected for aggressive male behaviour.

Although this argument is very widespread, some researchers argue that it may not suffice to convey all the complexities of the phenomena. Schwartz (2010) infers that maybe some women could be motivated by revenge, or to obtain financial profits or guided by other illicit practices. Belknap et al. (2012) extended their range of types of women who perpetrate IPH beyond the self-defence explanation. They propose that some women may be driven by proxy/retaliation, that is, previously abused women had the opportunity to learn how to abuse and retaliate against a new partner. A third type is constituted by women whose violence against their partner can be explained by partner rejection or the threat to leave them and that is consistent with Wilson and Daly's (1998) sexual proprietariness theory.

The straightforwardness of the self-defence thesis conceals several questions. Research shows us that women who were not battered perpetrate some non-lethal violence. Might these women kill? How could these murders be understood? How do women who will kill their partners experience their couple relationship? Do they live in fear? Are they coerced or subdued by their partners in an asymmetric power relationship? These questions are addressed next.

6.3 Method

Research about women's intimate partner homicide is still emerging and may be ideologically permeated. Since the purpose is to analyse women's representations of their own experience, a qualitative methodology was used.[*]

Our main questions are

1. How do women talk about their relationships? (This included the decision to get married, relationship maintenance and dynamics and lethal and non-lethal violence.)
2. How do women explain the violence perpetrated by them against their husband?

Individual interviews were conducted, which are in line with the conversational perspective of Shotter (1993) and the contextualised perspective of Mishler (1991). It is accepted that talking is not merely a representational act of a pre-conceived reality with individuals trying to assess each other's referents, but is a rhetorical and responsive process (Shotter, 1993) instead, whose meaning is co-constructed by interlocutors (Ghiglione, 1990; Mishler, 1991; Shotter, 1993). For Mishler, a question should be perceived 'as part of a circular process whereby its meaning and that of its answer are created in the discourse between interviewer and respondent as they try to make continuing sense of what they are saying to each other' (pp. 53–54).

Accepting that people give meaning to their experiences through conversational events, and narrative production, contributes to refraining from understanding an interview as a methodology shaped by the rigid administration of a pre-determined and sequential list of questions through which the interviewer will reach the interviewee's ultimate thoughts or feelings. A script for an in-depth interview was originally designed with open-ended questions. Second-level questions were written more as the researcher's reminders for issues to talk about, rather than strictly guiding the interview. That script covers three domains. This study focuses on the relationship between the participants and the partner they murdered, by analysing the history of intimate relationships, physical and psychological violence and violent episodes. A clinical approach underlies the process, promoting a relationship of empathy, respect and acceptance of the participants[†]

---

[*] This is part of a larger research which deals with men and women convicted of partner homicide, and men convicted of battering (at the time of the survey, no woman convicted of battering her partner had been arrested in Portugal). The study only focuses on heterosexual relationships. The research has a quantitative component that assesses several dimensions: personality (through 16PF-5), attachment (RQ and ECR) and psychopathy (PCL-R, Interview Version).

[†] That does not mean acceptance of the crime.

and with various strategies being used to empower them* (Mishler, 1991). The interview context is, for some participants, the first opportunity to make sense of an emotional and cognitive experience of the relationship and violent episodes with a non-judgemental interlocutor. The researcher is not part of the legal system. Confidentiality of the interview content was guaranteed.

6.3.1 Participants

Six convicted women,† who served in prison, participated in the study. Four of them killed their partner and two hired the murderer. Four of them went through physical and psychological violence during the relationship, and the other two refer to having had undergone psychological violence. The women who were not physically victimised and two others reported that, sometimes, they had been physically violent towards their husband.

For these six women, the age at the research time was between 38 and 60, with a mean of 47 years; the age at the time of the crime varied between 27 and 52 with a mean of 38; when the crime was committed, the academic level varied between the 4th and the 11th grade with a mean of 6; the length of relationship varied between 7 and 26 years with a mean of 15; the sentence varies between 9 and 22 years with a mean of 15 and the time in prison, at the time of the research, ranged between 3 and 14 years with a mean of 9. All these women worked: four at the prison and two outside the prison. The women working outside the prison did so because they were serving a longer sentence, and their good behaviour in prison earned them the right to work outside occasionally. Almost all women studied or attended training pro-grammes. Some of them participated in cultural or religious activities inside prison. Two of the women got married again whilst in prison.

6.3.2 Data Source

Running for 4 h 40 m to 8 h 34 m or 5 h 47 m on average, interviews were the most relevant source of data. Each interview took place for 3 or 4 days according to the inmate's and the prison's availability. All interviews were

* These included explaining how the audio recorder works; that they can ask to stop recording; that they are free not to answer and showing them how their reasons were interpreted by the researcher. For example, the researcher might say 'So what you mean is ...', or 'It seems to me that you mean ...', or 'It seems to me that you are feeling ..., what do you think about this'? Thus the participants were given opportunities to clarify or give specific examples.
† These six women are half the total number of women arrested for IPH in a female central prison in the north of Portugal. Initially, twelve women agreed to participate but four gave up. Two women (out of eight) were excluded, because one did not live with a partner and the other had cognitive impairment.

conducted by the author of this chapter, and recorded with the consent of the prison director and the woman. The data from trial files and inmate files were also analysed.

6.3.3 Procedure

After the General Prison Service Directorate had given permission to develop the research in that female central prison and with the consent of the prison director, participants were screened through the Prison Information System (SIP) for identification of women who perpetrated a crime against persons. A second and more in-depth screening was carried out to identify whether husbands or partners were the victims of this crime against persons. Third, in a brief individual interview, the purpose of the study and the research procedures were explained and the women were asked to sign the informed consent. The participant files were analysed. The interview period took several weeks, and ended with administering quantitative measures.

6.3.4 Data Analysis

Data from trial files were the basis for identifying circumstances proven in court around homicide events and the weapons used. Data will be unveiled in a way to render case reconstruction impossible.* Every interview is transcribed verbatim. Content analysis (Bardin, 1977/2011) is the methodology used to explore the questions raised. All the transcripts were read several times. That first stage is very important because specific categories were looked for, and as part of the interview development procedure the same topics can be discussed in each interview at different moments. Since the purpose is to highlight how those women lived their experience, transcription excerpts of their narratives are provided. Attention will also be paid to consistencies in ways of experiencing life events across the women's narratives. Lethal and non-lethal violence episodes were analysed through a sequential analysis according to the A-B-C model† (O'Leary & Wilson, 1987).

---

* Since there are few cases in Portugal, small details would easily allow participants to be identified.
† The A-B-C model underlies a functional assessment process. It considers that Behaviour (B) is triggered or cued by immediately precedent events or Antecedents (A) and maintained or changed by Consequences (C). Understanding behaviour requires its contextualisation according to antecedents and consequences that influence it. External and internal events, namely, emotional, cognitive, behavioural and interpersonal experiences, were sought. The way perceived experience intervenes in the violent episode will be explored.

6.4 Findings

The trial files show that two out of four women used handguns, a third woman killed her husband with an axe and the other with a kitchen knife. The two men murdered by hired killers died as a result of physical aggression with cutting and slicing objects. The circumstances that preceded each homicide vary.[*]

One of the women made a comment to her husband on the street in the morning of the homicide. He punched her. They finished shopping and returned home. By mid-afternoon she asked him why he did not leave her. He insulted her. They did not talk again. After dinner, he went out for coffee. When he returned, he went to bed. After a whilst, she looked for a weapon and killed him in bed.

Another woman was talking with her husband and he saw an empty bottle. Then he called one of their daughters and said that the mother was drunk. She saw a weapon and went after him, menacing him with death. Suddenly, she used it on him. The third woman was home doing household chores. They had argued in the morning and he was physically aggressive against her. They were in the same room; he was behind her eating an apple. Suddenly, her oldest daughter shouts: 'He will kill you'. She turned around and used a weapon that she grabbed and killed him.

The fourth woman had plotted for days against her husband and killed him.[†] The most immediate remark is that in the first and fourth situation, the event that precipitated this occurred some hours or days before. Additionally, in the second case it is hard or impossible to ascertain that the women felt their life was physically threatened. So, at first glance, only the third case could fit the self-defence plea. Other menaces, particularly for the integrity of the self, may be present in the way those women were experiencing the relationship and some events will be discussed on the basis of interview analysis.

To try to understand how women experience relationship, the focus will be on establishing the relationship and maintaining it and its dynamics. Several topics emerge from women's narratives about the establishment of the relationship, namely, affects about man or about marriage; decision to marry; balance of power; self-commitment to relationship; perception of themselves; perception of man and man's commitment to relationship and perpetuation of relationship. The meaning given by women to homicide perpetration is expressed through two topics: homicide justification and responsibility for

---

[*] Facts from trial files and interviews with the four women that killed their husbands will be used. Distal circumstances for women who hired the murderer included their desire for estrangement from their partner.

[†] A more detailed description of events would allow identification.

Table 6.1   Emerging Topics and Illustrations

Topics	Description	Illustration
Affects about man or about marriage	Significant units of discourse expressing women's feelings towards men before marriage or about getting married.	I never loved him. (1A27, 1A32) I didn't want to marry him. (1A27, 1A31, 1A33, 1A34)
Decision to get married	Women's explanation for getting married.	I was pregnant. (1A27, 1A28, 1A34) Things were well on their way. (1A31)
Balance of power	Women's evaluation of power balance in the relationship. How they feel they can assert themselves or they are subdued.	I didn't feel dominated by him. (1A27) He doesn't agree, but I won't leave my family. (1A28)
Self-commitment to the relationship	How those women value their 'couple'.	Family [family of origin] always comes first. (1A28) I wanted a family. (1A27)
Perception of themselves	Women's self-image.	I'm a strong-willed woman. (1A28, 1A34) I'm a very embarrassed person and I like respect. (1A31)
Perception of man and man's commitment to the relationship	Women's image of men and of how they are committed to the relationship.	He was a good worker but he was not a good provider. (1A28) His only concern was himself. (1A27) He was afraid of losing me. (1A32)
Perpetuation of the relationship	Women's explanations for remaining in relationship.	I had never left him out of respect to my parents. (1A34) You always hope for better days. (1A28)
Justification to homicide	Refers to women's explanation for homicide perpetration.	It was only to scare my husband. (1A28) One of us has to die. (1A32) I got tired, overwhelmed! (1A31)
Responsibility for events	Women's appreciation of accountability to the course of events.	I think we all have a fate, and mine was already fated. (1A33) I also feel guilty for allowing things to reach that point. (1A32) The two of us are responsible for letting things getting that far. (1A27)

events. Table 6.1 shows each topic with transcription excerpts of women's experiences.

These women talk about relationships as if they were based on a series of mismatches. Several unexpected features seem to negatively mark the beginning of the relationship, namely, when they looked for someone to date. One woman said that although there was no love, after several years, she started liking him. Another woman said: 'We married to be free' (1A28).* At the same time, their future husbands do not seem to be aware of the lack of love, keeping them under pressure to remain in the relationship. Finally, their families did not seem to be aware of the situation. Families also seemed unable to protect their daughter effectively. At least two families were not able to give enough support for their daughters' desire to leave the young man that had once slapped them. Neither woman wished to get married. Even the one who intended to marry for freedom says: 'On our wedding day, I realised I would regret it' (1A28). Some of them thought about avoiding the wedding or trying to prevent it: 'Two days before the marriage I asked a friend to talk to my parents to stop it. She told me that I was crazy. I didn't get any support' (1A27).

How could these women decided to marry a man they did not love and with whom they did not want to marry? Table 6.1 shows that three women refer to being pregnant so they felt compelled to marry. One of those pregnant women further said that 'I was about to miss my own wedding, but the shame to my parents ...' (1A28). To prevent family, particularly parents, of being ashamed of their decisions or behaviours starts to emerge as a central dimension around which these women give meaning to their experience and construct their reality. Another women adds: 'He threatened me that he would tell my parents we had already had sex' (1A33); or 'It is just that things were well on their way [wedding arrangements] and, not to make things any uglier or shameful, I didn't say no and went ahead [got married]' (1A31). Obedience to parents extends after their death: 'He always liked me and I never liked him ... when my mother was dying, she asked him to take care of me' (1A32). Underlying that central dimension two others may be arising. On the one hand to get married could be also as much protective for the social image of those women as a practical decision. Maybe they anticipated that the family would not support a break-up decision and they were somehow in a dissonance cognitive reduction process (Festinger, 1957). On the other hand, those women seem to be entrapped in their own behaviours.

A central plea to the mainstream approach to IPV, even when women act as aggressors, is that the relationship between partners is permeated by gender asymmetry with the males exerting their manhood, imposing their views, ways of thinking and being in charge of decision-making, and where the female is subdued to the man, afraid and lacking power and resourcefulness to participate in decision-making. Yet, in some primordial domains of couples' life (choosing where to live or work) these women seem to be able to stand their ground: 'I always told him that I would not leave my parents'

---

* Participants' quotes are followed by a three level code between parentheses: the first digit, encodes the gender (1 is for female); the capital letter, encodes the nature of crime – battering or homicide – (A is for homicide) and the second set of numbers, encodes sequentially each participant.

house after marriage. He doesn't agree but I will not leave my family' (1A28); 'We got married, my husband wanted me to leave my job to go to work in the same place where he worked, and I made a stand and I didn't do it. [She explained her reasons] and he said, "You are right!"' (1A33). Nevertheless, in domains about which they may feel too ambivalent, they seem unable to assert their will: 'He didn't let me go to the 12th grade exam [1 month after marriage]' (1A27). Those women seem to be good workers and sometimes skilled entrepreneurs confronting men with ready-made decisions.

> I decided that I'll start to work at home [...] I went home and said to my late husband: 'Look here. I want you to vacate all these rooms in the back'. He had them full of his tools, motorcycles, full of cages, bird stuff. 'What do you want me to vacate them for?' 'Because my cousin is bringing over ... some sewing machines, because I'm going to start working at home'. He said: 'You're going to work at home? For whose sake?' 'Mine. Tomorrow I'm not going back to work. Tomorrow I'm going to the excise office to take care of paper work. I already have some ads on papers. I'm going ahead getting orders and work at home'. He said: 'You're crazy'. I said: 'I may be crazy but I fend for myself. And you're not crazy and you don't'. He said: 'Right. Have it your own way'. He never subdued me. (1A34)

This extensive quotation shows a woman that doesn't ask permission to make decisions. She is resourceful to devise a business plan and to deal with several issues, even if it may seem somewhat reckless or impetuous. These women feel superior to their husbands in their ability to 'run life'. The woman that did not take the 12th grade exam points out the negative impact of her ability to solve problems and to manage things for her husband.

> My husband started feeling angry; because he started seeing me as someone with the power to make things happen. He just fell into a habit. If he needs something, there it was the wife to provide it. He started feeling diminished. People didn't give him any credit, and if they did, it was on my account or because of our families (...). I didn't feel subjugated by him, he wasn't my master. (1A27)

This sense of mastery is consistent with their self-image as 'strong-willed', 'forceful', 'working woman', 'very determined', 'unassuaged'. That self-image and sense of mastery is very congruent with the results of the 16PF-5 personality test that presents these women as highly *self-reliant, self-disciplined* and *perfectionist*. They seem clearly *independent, suspicious* and somewhat *non-disclosing* (Pereira, 2012; Pereira & Gonçalves, 2011). These features suggest difficulties at the interpersonal level, particularly in trusting, which can be very damaging in relationships.

Simultaneously, women's self-image contrasts with their perception of their husbands as self-centred, away from the family project, careless and weak. The negative image they provide of their husbands is upheld by their lack of commitment to their family or wife: 'I've been always angry with my husband, because he never wanted to think about the future and the well-being [of the family]' (1A27); 'He was a good worker but he wasn't a good provider' (1A28), (1A33); 'He didn't care about me, he didn't spend any time with me' (1A31); 'He suffered accidents every week …. He was afraid of losing me' (1A32). These are husbands they could not count on, exhausting, demanding, derogatory and even contemptuous. The perceived lack of commitment co-exists with women complaining about men's demanding for them to be more estranged from their family of origin to which goes the women's commitment and loyalty: 'Family [origin family] always comes first. (…) I felt distressed and sad because he didn't listen to me and he wanted to separate me from the persons I loved more [her parents. Her husband wanted her to go to France with him]' (1A28).

Loyalty and honouring the family of origin, protecting it from shame, appears as the major motive to maintaining the relationship: 'I had never left him out of respect to my parents'; 'I didn't want my parents to suffer the shame of having a daughter who was a single mother'; 'I should honour my parents' (1A34). Discussions about how to murder their husband and be in jail for it could be less shameful or damaging for the family than divorce just reiterates the same idea. Obedience of social norms and family rules is also part of these women's features captured by 16PF-5 (Pereira, 2012; Pereira & Gonçalves, 2011). They are highly *rule-conscious, dutiful* and very *traditional* and *attached to familiar*. Yet, the idea of having a family could also be an important part of their self-image: 'If I leave him, he wouldn't have anybody to give him support. I didn't want to let him go', and as a woman 'I wanted a family… I didn't wanted destruction. But … I just let it run' (1A27). The idea of not being able to run the family conflicts with their image of competence as a problem solver, of integrity as someone who doesn't run from responsibilities and of self-sufficiency as someone who can sort out of complicated things by herself. That incongruence should be highly menacing for the integrity of the self of those women: 'Being able to help everyone and unable to help myself is like … I was unable to be autonomous. Suddenly, I felt surrounded, in a labyrinth, with no way out' (1A33).

Some women explained they remained in the relationship with ideas like 'fate', 'their lot' or 'hope for better days'. Besides being a threat to the self that would generate intense internal rebellious, the dismissal of taking charge of their lives may be also a protective strategy of the family of origin. After all, the family for which such great efforts are being made is not there to support them. Families send ambiguous and uncertain messages of sympathy for their daughters' troubled lives, but these messages are also so fragile that they are insufficient for these women to even dare to divorce. One of the women, who suffered physical violence, had run away to another town with her daughter. When her husband knew about where she was, he headed towards there and forced her to return home. She insisted on returning to her parents' home. After a few days, her father asked her to reconsider returning to her husband ' "It's your husband" he said'. She sadly commented: 'That broke me!' (1A34).

Homicide is explained differently by women who hire the murderer and by those who kill. The former allege that they just wanted to scare their husbands and to live apart from them, and that their husbands did not agree to this separation. One of the women who killed her husband put it this way: 'We had reached a point of no return, one of us had to die' (1A32). The perception that killing is inevitable, a way to end the relationship, pervades some narratives. In two other cases, the sequential analysis allows us to go further. The woman who heard the husband tell their daughter that she was drunk refers to feeling hurt. That repeated insult was felt as a huge offence,* a threat to their integrity. She took the gun, followed him and threatened, 'If you say that again, I'll use it on you'. She was feeling ashamed and humiliated and acted to assert her point, trying to coerce her husband to respect her, through intimidation. 'I just wanted to frighten him (…) I didn't know shooting was so easy', but suddenly her position turns into rage and revenge.

> He lay on the floor. He said: 'Oh, Mary'.† I was so … I was as confused as he was … I didn't mean to … all my life went through my mind […] and I thought 'If you're going to bring other women in, if I die […] my daughters are going to have a father, women, you ruin my life and you ruin my daughters' lives […] you're going to stand up and you're going to kill me.' after the first shot had gone off I shot everything else [all the other bullets]. In for a penny in for a pound.

The woman who killed her partner in bed hours after confronting him also felt intense rage. The insult that he called her was felt as an outrage for a woman who sees herself as someone who 'likes respect'. She had felt ashamed and humiliated in the morning and she gave up fighting for keeping family as a standard.

> I got tired, overwhelmed! […] He would like to master all, to be a 'gentleman' on my shoulders, right? Because I was the owner of everything, he had nothing. […] Well, I could live it to the end … but life was worse every day, the burden was each time heavier.

Again, shame, which Dutton (2002) refers as a threat to integrity of the self, is present. The woman tries in a first moment to make a point but her husband's response was outrageous. Rage emerged.

---

* She had had problems with alcohol consumption.
† Fictitious name.

6.5 Discussion

This study is an opportunity to bring to empirical scrutiny the widely accepted theoretical framework about female-perpetrated violence in intimate partner relationships. It represents a concern to 'give voice' to women who murder their husbands and to discuss their intimate partner relationship and homicide circumstances.

Careful reading of the women's narratives about the beginning and dynamics of the relationship allowed for the definition of previously referred to topics. They constitute a filter that gives meaning to female experiences. Findings are hardly reconcilable with the mainstream assertion of women's helplessness, powerlessness and use of violence as self-defence.

Usually, battered or psychologically abused women (Johnson, 2008) tend to be perceived as helpless. Although Walker (1984) had changed her conception of women passivity assigning them some agency, at least to try to escape from further victimisation, those women are understood as devoid of discernment and free will. They are simultaneously recognised for having an impaired ability to solve problems related to the relationship or in daily activities (Holtzworth-Munroe et al., 1997; Rhodes & McKenzie, 1998).

Contrasting with common explanations, the participants in this study seem to be able to run their lives and make decisions often more efficiently than their husbands. They seem to have more adroit management skills as much in the domestic context as, for some of them, in business. They are fully aware of their competence experiencing even a sense of superiority compared to their husbands. Questioned how they globally appreciated themselves and their husbands, as strong or weak persons, all of them self-evaluated as strong persons and judged their husbands as weak persons. That strength of the self is expressed in the way they talk about themselves as strong-willed and determined persons, sometimes even obstinate. These self-reported descriptions are supported by levels of self-reliance and perfectionism significantly higher than the norm for women, according to 16PF-5 results (Pereira, 2012; Pereira & Gonçalves, 2011). We might ask: If they weren't as vulnerable and diminished persons as expected, why would they remain in the relationship?

Again the most widely accepted theoretical frameworks unveil women in violent relationships as powerless, impotent, subdued to men's coercion, ineffective in their attempts to react (Bograd, 1990; Johnson, 2008; Saunders, 1990) and frame violence perpetrated by women as the culmination of a life of chronic victimisation. The last assertion is not corroborated by our participants' experiences in their relationship. The two who hired the killer were not battered by the husband and both reported to have assaulted them at least once. Of the other four (all suffered physical violence), two of them reported to have physically assaulted their husbands, even initiating violent acts against them; two received violence more frequently in return, one of them from a man who was physically disabled about whom the woman perceives herself as easily able to physically subdue him.

Women's narratives reveal the deep complexity of the dynamics of power in the relationship. On the one hand, women reported that they made decisions and imposed their own choices about where to live and about work. This happened since dating and continued during marriage. They seem to be imposed with more strength either when decisions involve activities external to them (e.g. work, home management) or are somehow related to their families of origin (for instance, live in parental home or nearby, take care of a sick or an elder family member). This inclination of power to the women's side is highly consistent with their self-image and 16PF-5 data. They seem very industrious and even resourceful. On the other hand, when decisions are about topics that are more intrinsically related to women, and probably more related to expected gender roles (continuing to study, how to spend time together as a couple or family and, in some cases, management of the family money), they seem more ineffective to make their viewpoint prevail or even to negotiate it. It is as if they simultaneously do not feel sure about what is the 'good choice' or at least as if they feel more dutiful about their legitimacy to choose or to fight for that choice. This self-doubt would be highly dissonant with their self-image.

The complexity of the women's experience of power gave rise to two questions. How does it happen that women so imperative in respect to some topics are simultaneously submissive about others? What will be the impact for those women living parts of their lives so incongruently with their self-image?

Explanation of the inconsistency pointed out in the first question leads us to the most striking idea that emerged from narrative analysis: those women have a strongly tied bond with their families of origin. Many decisions in their lives, including decisions as partner in an intimate relationship, are made on behalf of the family of origin's image. This includes the family's best interest, or honour, namely, in terms of getting married with someone they did not love and with whom they did not want to be with anymore, and the decision to remain in a relationship in a way that damages their self-image. Aspects such as not to damage the family of origin's 'peace' or disturb their well-being, and not to frustrate self-assumed family expectations for themselves will prevail over their own needs and the new couple's or family's best interest.

Those women seem to have an enmeshed relationship with their family of origin (Minuchin, 1974) proudly and stoically playing the role of 'family herald'. They were highly trained to be attentive to family needs and to be competent as problem solvers. This had consequences deeply rooted in their early life experiences and embedded into their psychological features (Pereira, 2012; Pereira & Gonçalves, 2013a,b) visible at two levels:

(a) increasing their sense of mastery and self-reliance; and (b) neglecting their emotional needs and ignoring the legitimacy of standing for themselves. This can simultaneously explain their selfless 'crusade' for the families of origin sake and their dismissing of fighting for their own sake. That dismissal is, partly still protective of the family's image for themselves, since it avoids testing family furtherance and availability to shelter and return loyalty to their daughter. On the other hand, it is protective of themselves as self-reliant persons. Nevertheless, remaining in the relationship partly 'feeds' their self-image as a responsible person, who do not give up without reaching what should be fulfilled according to high moral standards, as expected from persons as rule-conscious and conservative, as emerged from 16PF-5 data (Pereira, 2012; Pereira & Gonçalves, 2011). Paradoxically, their cohesion to their families does not allow them to attach to a partner (Alarcão, 2002; Relvas, 1996). The study of those women's attachment to parents and partners shows some proclivity to avoidant attachment (Pereira, 2012; Pereira & Gonçalves, 2013a).

The discussion around the first question gives us part of the argument for dealing with the second question. In the early years of life, the women did not have the opportunity to learn that their emotional needs should be recognised and satisfied by themselves. So, they kept going and expected 'better days' or some other magic solution and feeling doubly entrapped. On the one hand, between being loyal to the rules and expectations of the family of origin, whilst mobilising themselves to struggle for a life congruent with their own expectations. On the other hand, between their self-image of self-reliance and resistance, and the resignation with which they feel their married life is to be endured. The perception of being in control (knowing what would be done and doing what should be done), taking all the pieces together, the sense that they will be able to run their lives, no matter what, allows them to persevere in the relationship. Meanwhile, they are neither recognised by their family of origin, nor fulfil their expectations for their own family. The incongruence between them as valiant fighters and as resigned wives would be very disturbing, exhausting and even unbearable. Along these external or internal battles, women seem to be more and more at risk of becoming victims, or perpetrators or both at the same time.

The last of our topics of discussion refers to another widespread argument: women use violence against men in self-defence. For analysing narratives about homicide, two categories were drawn: justification to homicide and responsibility for events.

As reported, homicides perpetrated by our participants could hardly fit in that frame. They do not constitute retaliatory acts either, as proposed by Belknap et al. (2012); Browne and Williams (1993); Jurik and Winn (1990); Schwartz (2010); Smith et al. (1998) and Wilson and Daly (1992), at least as retaliatory acts for physical aggression. Neither does the homicide occur following physical aggression initiated by men, as opposed to the propos-als from Johnson and Hotton (2003); Jurik and Winn (1990) and Schwartz (2010), nor were perpetrators defied by the victim, contrasting to Belknap et al. (2012). The only case in which homicide could be a response against a potential aggression was not legally understood as such. Neither the argu-ment of 'imminent danger' (Browne in Schwartz, 2010) could be accepted to explain these homicides. Only one woman refers to sometimes feeling fear for her life due to her partner menaces, but her fear appears to be of a social embarrassment if divorce arises.

Even if some of them report that they just want to scare their husband, the partner's homicide seems to emerge in the mind of some of these women as a way to solve the impasse they are in, considering that divorce is not an option. The sequential analysis of feelings, behaviours and thoughts brings about motives for lethal violence that seem closer to the expression of anger, coercion and control referred to previously (Caldwell et al., 2009; Cascardi & Vivian, 1995; Weston et al., 2007). In these cases, homicide occurs when an event perceived as outrageous arouses intense negative emotions, namely, shame (Dutton, 2002), that threaten the integrity of the self. Homicide emerges as an attempt to receive respect and restore order in the chaos (Katz, 1988). At that moment it re-establishes balance and reduces internal tension. These are issues also found for some men who killed their female partners (Pereira, 2012, 2015).

6.6 Final Remarks

This study has important limitations: (a) the number of participants is too small (even if the overall population presents a very limited number of women arrested for IPH); (b) the reduced number of participants compromises any nuances of the experience, such as distinguishing between women who kill and women who hire the killer; (c) women convicted of co-authoring the partner homicide refused to participate at an early stage of research; (d) one cannot determine how battered women who do not murder their intimates partners make sense of their relationship and of the violence in it and (e) the focus is not on women with clinical levels of psychopathy or whose partner have clinical psychopathic levels.

Nevertheless, this study, going beyond a gendered explanation for women's perpetration of violence, deeply enlightened the women's experi-ence putting it in a new focus. It allows access to several layers of meanings about the dynamics of a relationship and the perpetration of lethal violence. Rejecting woman's deification and man's vilification, it opens new fields for intervention, namely, empowering each one to choose life contexts and rela-tionships that strength them, and increasing their sense of worthiness. Some of our participants unambiguously admit their responsibility or at least their share of responsibility for the relationship dynamics and the course of events.

> I also feel guilty for allowing things to reach that point. If I had stopped, maybe things wouldn't have gone so far. I let him do what he wanted … Maybe, if I had invested more in myself from the beginning. (1A32)
>
> The two of us are responsible for letting things getting that far. Him for having continued to behave the way he always did. And I didn't really look into the problem between us, to effectively solve it. (1A27)

Only a perspective that looks for each partner's responsibility for the relationship would help prevent as much the victimisation as the perpetration of violence.

Acknowledgement

The author is deeply grateful to Hugh Gash, PhD, for reviewing the use of English in this chapter.

References

Alarcão, M. (2002). *(des)Equilíbrios Familiares* (2nd ed.). Coimbra: Quarteto Editora.

Archer, J. (2000). Sex differences in aggression between heterosexual partners: A meta-analytic review. *Psychological Bulletin, 126*(5), 651–680.

Archer, J. (2002). Sex differences in physically aggressive acts between heterosexual partners: A meta-analytic review. *Aggression and Violent Behavior, 7*, 313–351.

Babcock, J. C., Miller, S. A., & Siard, C. (2003). Toward a typology of abusive women: Differences between partner-only and generally violent women in the use of violence. *Psychology of Women Quarterly, 27*, 153–161.

Bardin, L. (2011). *Análise de Conteúdo* (5th ed.). (L. A. Reto & A. Pinheiro, Trans.). Lisboa, Portugal: Edições 70. (Original work published 1977)

Belknap, J., Larson, D.-L., Abrams, M. L., Garcia, C., & Anderson-Block, K. (2012). Types of intimate partner homicides committed by women: Self-defense, proxy/ retaliation, and sexual proprietariness. *Homicide Studies, XX*(X), 1–21.

Bograd, M. (1990). Feminist perspectives on wife abuse: An introduction. In K. Yllö & M. Bograd, *Feminist perspectives on wife abuse* (pp. 11–26). Newbury Park, CA: Sage Publications.

Browne, A., & Williams, K. R. (1993). Gender, intimacy, and lethal violence: Trends from 1976 through 1987. *Gender & Society, 7*(1), 78–98.

Caldwell, J. E., Swan, S. C., Allen, C. T., Sullivan, T. P., & Snow, D. L. (2009). Why I hit him: Women's reasons for intimate partner violence. *Journal of Aggression, Maltreatment, and Trauma, 18*, 672–697.

Cascardi, M., & Vivian, D. (1995). Context for specific episodes of marital violence: Gender and severity of violence differences. *Journal of Family Violence, 10*(3), 265–293.

Cavanaugh, M. M., & Gelles, R. J. (2005). The utility of male domestic violence offender typologies: New directions for research, policy, and practice. *Journal of Interpersonal Violence, 20*(2), 155–166.

Corvo, K., & Johnson, P. J. (2003). Vilification of the 'batterer': How blame shapes domestic violence policy and interventions. *Aggression and Violent Behavior, 8*, 259–281.

Dobash, R. E., & Dobash, R. P. (1990). Research as social action: The struggle for battered woman. In K. Yllö & M. Bograd, *Feminist perspectives on wife abuse* (pp. 51–74). Newbury Park, CA: Sage.

Dobash, R. E., & Dobash, R. P. (2011). What were they thinking? Men who murder an intimate partner. *Violence Against Women, 17*(1), 111–134.

Dobash, R. E., Dobash, R. P., Cavanagh, K., & Medina-Ariza, J. (2007). Lethal and nonlethal violence against an intimate female partner: Comparing male murderers to nonlethal abusers. *Violence Against Women, 13*(4), 329–353.

Dobash, R. P., Dobash, R. E., Wilson, M., & Daly, M. (1992). The myth of sexual symmetry in marital violence. *Social Problems, 39*(1), 71–91.

Dutton, D. G. (2002). The neurobiology of the abandonment homicide. *Aggression and Violent Behavior, 7*, 407–421.

Dutton, D. G., & Nicholls, T. L. (2005). The gender paradigm in domestic violence research and theory: Part 1 – The conflict theory and data. *Aggression and Violent Behavior, 10*, 680–714.

Ehrensaft, M. K., Moffitt, T. E., & Caspi, A. (2004). Clinically abusive relationships in an unselected birth cohort: Men's and women's participation and developmental antecedents. *Journal of Abnormal Psychology, 113*(2), 258–270.

Enander, V. (2011). Violent women? The challenge of women's violence in intimate heterosexual relationships to feminist analyses of partner violence. *Nordic Journal of Feminist and Gender Research, 19*(2), 105–123.

Festinger, L. (1957). *A theory of cognitive dissonance.* Stanford, CA: Stanford University Press.

Ghiglione, R. (1990). Le qui et le comment. In R. Ghiglione, C. Bonnet, & J.-F. Richard, *Traité de Psychologie Cognitive: Cognition, représentation, communication* (Vol. 3, pp. 175–226). Paris: Dunod.

Gondolf, E. W., & Fisher, E. R. (1988). *Battered women as survivors: An alternative to treating learned helplessness.* Lexington, MA: D.C. Heath.

Hamberger, L. K. (1997). Female offenders in domestic violence: A look at actions in their context. *Journal of Aggression, Maltreatment, and Trauma, 1*(1), 117–129.

Henning, K., Jones, A. R., & Holdford, R. (2005). 'I didn't do it, but if I did I had a good reason': Minimization, denial, and attributions of blame among male and female domestic violence offenders. *Journal of Family Violence, 20*(3), 131–139.

Holtzworth-Munroe, A. (2005). Female perpetration of physical aggression against an intimate partner: A controversial new topic of study. *Violence and Victims, 20*, 253–261.

Holtzworth-Munroe, A., Smutzler, N., & Bates, L. (1997). A brief review of the research on the husband violence. Part III: Sociodemographic factors, relationship factors, and differing consequences of husband and wife violence. *Aggression and Violent Behavior, 2*(3), 285–307.

Johnson, H. (1998). Rethinking survey research on violence against women. In R. E. Dobash & R. P. Dobash, *Rethinking violence against women* (pp. 23–51). Thousand Oaks, CA: Sage.

Johnson, M. P. (1995). Patriarchal terrorism and common couple violence: Two forms of violence against women. *Journal of Marriage and Family, 57*(2), 283–294.

Johnson, M. P. (2008). *A typology of domestic violence: Intimate terrorism, violent resistance, and situational couple violence.* Lebanon, NH: University Press of New England.

Johnson, H., & Hotton, T. (2003). Losing control: Homicide risk in estranged and intact intimate relationships. *Homicide Studies, 7*(58), 58–84.

Jurik, N. C., & Winn, R. (1990). Gender and homicide: A comparison of men and women who kill. *Violence and Victims, 5*(4), 227–242.

Katz, J. (1988). *Seductions of crime.* New York: Basic Books.

Kwong, M. J., Bartholomew, K., & Dutton, D. G. (1999). Gender differences in patterns of relationship violence in Alberta. *Canadian Journal of Behavioural Science, 31*(3), 150–160.

Langhinrichsen-Rohling, J., & Vivian, D. (1994). The correlates of spouses' incongruent reports. *Journal of Family Violence, 9*(3), 265–283.

Leisring, P. A. (2009). What will happen if I punch him? Expected consequences of female violence against male dating partners. *Journal of Aggression, Maltreatment, and Trauma, 18*, 739–751.

Lorber, M. F., & O'Leary, K. D. (2004). Predictors of the persistence of male aggression in early marriage. *Journal of Family Violence, 19*(6), 329–338.

Minuchin, S. (1974). *Families and family therapy.* Cambridge, MA: Harvard University Press.

Mishler, E. G. (1991). *Research interviewing: Context and Narrative.* Cambridge, MA: Harvard University Press.

O'Leary, K. D., & Wilson, T. G. (1987). *Behaviour therapy: Application and outcome* (2nd ed.). Englewood Cliffs, NJ: Prentice-Hall.

O'Leary, K. D., Barling, J., Arias, I., Rosenbaum, A., Malone, J., & Tyree, A. (1989). Prevalence and stability of physical aggression between spouses: A longitudinal analysis. *Journal of Consulting and Clinical Psychology, 57*(2), 263–268.

Pereira, P. S. (2012). *Dinâmicas de Violência no Casal.* (Unpublished doctoral thesis), Universidade do Minho, Escola de Psicologia, Braga.

Pereira, P. S. (2015). Trajectories of intimate partner violence: From psychological and physical abuse to homicide. In E. Crespo (Ed.), *Cultures, social bonds and the dinamics of violence* (pp. 13–25). Available at http://www.inter-disciplinary.net/publishing/id-press/.

Pereira, P. S., & Gonçalves, R. A. (2011). Personalidad y apego en hombres y mujeres condenados por violencia u homicidio de pareja. *VI Congreso de Psicología Jurídica y Forense.* Palma de Maiorca: Sociedad Española de Psicología Jurídica y Forense.

Pereira, P. S., & Gonçalves, R. A. (2013a). Apego a los padres en ofensores de pareja. *VII Congreso (Inter)nacional de Psicología Jurídica y Forense.* Madrid: Sociedad Española de Psicología Jurídica y Forense.

Pereira, P. S., & Gonçalves, R. A. (2013b). Early childhood experiences of intimate partner violence. *33rd International Congress on Law and Mental Health*. Amesterdam: International Academy of Law and Mental Health.

Relvas, A. P. (1996). *O ciclo vital da família: Perspectiva sistémica*. Porto: Edições Afrontamento.

Rhodes, N. R., & McKenzie, E. B. (1998). Why do battered woman stay? Three decades of research. *Aggression and Violent Behavior, 3*(4), 391–406.

Ridley, C. A., & Feldman, C. M. (2003). Female domestic violence toward male partners: Exploring conflict responses and outcomes. *Journal of Family Violence, 18*(3), 157–170.

Saunders, D. G. (1990). Wife abuse, husband abuse, or mutual combat? A feminist approach on the empirical findings. In K. Yllö & M. Bograd, *Feminist perspectives on wife abuse* (pp. 90–113). Newbury Park, CA: Sage.

Saunders, D. G. (2002). Are physical assaults by wives and girlfriends a major social problem? *Violence Against Women, 8*(12), 1424–1448.

Schafer, J., Caetano, R., & Clark, C. L. (1998). Rates of intimate partner violence in the United States. *American Journal of Public Health, 88*(11), 1072–1074.

Schwartz, J. (2010). Murder in a comparative context. In C. J. Ferguson, *Violent crime: Clinical and social implications* (pp. 276–299). Thousand Oaks, CA: Sage.

Schwartz, M. D., & DeKeseredy, W. S. (1993). The return of the 'battered husband syndrome' through the typification of women as violent. *Crime, Law and Social Change, 20*, 249–265.

Shotter, J. (1993). *Conversational realities: Constructing life through language*. London: Sage.

Smith, P. H., Moracco, K. E., & Butts, J. (1998). Partner homicide in context: A population-based perspective. *Homicide Studies, 2*(4), 400–421.

Steinmetz, K. D. (1977–1978). The battered husband syndrome. *Victimology: An International Journal, 2*(3–4), 499–509.

Straus, M. A. (1997). Physical assaults by women partners: A major social problem. In M. R. Walsh (Ed.), *Women, men, and gender: Ongoing debates* (pp. 210–221). New Haven: Yale University Press.

Straus, M. A. (2007). Processes explaining the concealment and distortion of evidence on gender symmetry in partner violence. *European Journal of Criminology and Policy Research, 13*, 227–232.

Straus, M. A., & Kantor, G. K. (1994). *Change in spousal assault rates from 1975 to 1992: A comparison of three national surveys in the United States*. Durham, NH: University of New Hampshire.

Vivian, D., & Langhinrichsen-Rohling, J. (1996). Are bi-directionally violent couples mutually victimized? A gender-sensitive comparison. In L. K. Hamberger & C. M. Renzetti, *Domestic partner abuse* (pp. 23–52). New York: Springer.

Walker, L. E. (1979). *The battered woman*. New York: Harper & Row.

Walker, L. E. (1983). The battered woman syndrome study. In D. Finkelor, R. J. Gelles, G. T. Hotaling & M. A. Straus (Eds.), *The dark side of families - current family violence research* (pp. 31–48), Thousand Oaks, CA: Harper & Row Publishers.

Walker, L. E. (1984). *The battered woman syndrome*. New York: Springer.

Weston, R., Marshall, L. L., & Coker, A. L. (2007). Women's motives for violent and nonviolent behaviors in conflicts. *Journal of Interpersonal Violence, 22*(8), 1043–1065.

White, J. W., Smith, P. H., Koss, M. P., & Figueredo, A. J. (2000). Intimate partner aggression: What have we learned? Comment on Archer (2000). *Psychological Bulletin, 126*(5), 690–696.

Wilson, M. I., & Daly, M. (1992). Who kills whom in spouse killings? On the exceptional sex ratio of spousal homicides in the United States. *Criminology, 30,* 189–215.

Wilson, M., & Daly, M. (1998). Lethal and nonlethal violence against wives and the evolutionary psychology of male sexual proprietariness. In R. E. Dobash & R. P. Dobash, *Rethinking violence against women* (pp. 199–230). Thousand Oaks, CA: Sage.

Yllö, K. (1983). Using a feminist approach in quantitative research: A case study. In D. Finkelhor, R. J. Gelles, G. T. Hotaling, & M. A. Straus, *The dark side of families: Current family violence research* (pp. 277–288). Thousand Oaks, CA: Sage.

Mock Jurors' Understanding of Forensic Science and Its Perceived Importance in Judicial Processes

7

LAURA HAMMOND
MARIA IOANNOU

Contents

7.1 Introduction

A continually growing range of forensic science activities play an ever-increasing role throughout the criminal justice system, having notable implications for, and impacts on, case outcomes and the likelihood of conviction/acquittal. However, the ways in which they are understood by those involved in criminal justice processes (most notably jurors), and whether such understanding is accurate, has not been extensively explored or tested (Baskin & Sommers, 2010).

It is plausible that with ever-increasing exposure to popular programmes like *CSI: Crime Scene Investigation*, public understanding of forensic science methods may be heavily influenced by how and to what extent they are covered in such shows (Schweitzer & Saks, 2007). This, in turn, could have implications for the judicial decisions made by jurors (Podlas, 2006).

The present study examines and evaluates evidence presented within the literature for the existence of different forms of *CSI* influence on juror attitudes and expectancies regarding forensic science. On the basis of previously reported findings, a questionnaire is presented and tested, results from which provide the basis for an analysis of the relationships between crime series viewing and perceptions of the validity and utility of forensic science, and of its importance in judicial processes and criminal justice proceedings.

7.2 Background

7.2.1 Increasing Media Exposure to Forensic Science and Its Potential Impact

As a number of researchers have discussed (c.f. Elffers, de Keijser, van Koppen, & van Haeringen, 2007; Daftary-Kapur, Dumas, & Penrod, 2010), over the course of our lifespan few of us have any encounters with the criminal justice system. Most of us have no direct contact with it. Consequently, the average juror's experience of, and exposure to, real forensic practices and procedures is likely to be extremely limited (Tyler, 2006). Robbers (2008) argues that, as a result of this, their main source of information about the criminal justice system, and about forensic evidence in action, will be media accounts – in particular, what they watch on television. Indeed, empirical evidence suggests that most people learn about crime and criminal justice from television shows (Podlas, 2006). Baskin and Sommers (2010), for example, show that crime-show viewing habits affect potential jurors' pre-trial attitudes and predispositions to different forms of scientific evidence and testimony.

Shows depicting elements of the criminal justice process, such as *Law and Order* or *Without a Trace*, have exponentially increased in popularity

over the last decade or so (Baskin & Sommers, 2010). One in particular –
CSI: Crime Scene Investigation – has been elevated to what might now be
called cult status. The show, which first aired in 2000, is reported by Nielsen
Ratings Research to be the number one watched television programme in the
world for viewers over the age of 50 years, and the number five programme
for viewers aged 18–49 years. In addition, the programme's spin-offs (*CSI:
Miami* and *CSI: NY*) also feature in the top 20 most-watched programmes for
both age groups. *CSI* has been awarded the 'most watched drama series in the
world' title in 2007, 2008 and 2010, with an average of 73.8 million viewers
each new episode (Nielsen Media Research, 2010).

The ways in which forensic science techniques are portrayed in shows
like *CSI* have been argued to be distorted and unrealistic of their true
nature (Tyler, 2006). Houck (2006), a forensic consultant for the producers
of CSI, estimates that 40% of the science portrayed in the series does not
exist. Even the fact-based scientific techniques appearing on the show are
conducted in ways which are exaggerated and unrealistic, as Schweitzer and
Saks (2007) discuss. In particular, investigative timeframes are collapsed
(Mann, 2006), forensic evidence always reaches a conclusive and unbiased
conclusion (Schweitzer & Saks, 2007; Stephens, 2006) and court proceedings are not shown, resulting in trials being depicted as merely a formal-
ity (Stephens, 2006; Tyler, 2006). There is consequently a great deal of social
distance between popular media depictions of criminal investigations and
reality (Robbers, 2008).

One problem arising from this is that the general public, who have no
personal experience or knowledge upon which they can assess the credibility of forensic evidence or crime scene analysis methods, are likely to
develop unrealistic perceptions of forensic science, and of its investigative
utility or actual validity in the context of criminal trials. In actuality, much
of the technology that jurors expect to be utilised in criminal justice proceedings, and of the types of evidence that they expect will be present in
a criminal case, will not exist. Even if they do exist, their availability will
not necessarily correlate with their utility or admissibility (Dysart, 2012).
The types of crimes covered in such televisions programmes, such as sexual homicide and rape, are actually relatively rare (Peelo, Francis, Soothill,
Pearson, & Ackerly, 2004), and the procedures that are of value in these
types of cases are not routinely used in the investigation or prosecution of
more minor crimes, those that make up the bulk of criminal trials. Further,
the types of evidence that prove crucial in resolving cases in programmes
such as *CSI* are not actually that commonly prevalent in everyday cases
(Podlas, 2006).

On this basis, it is argued that general understanding and conceptualisations of the forensic sciences might be biased as a consequence of what has
been termed the 'CSI effect' (Tyler, 2006).

7.2.2 The CSI Effect

The now-ubiquitous term 'The CSI effect' has been used to describe the phenomenon whereby the way(s) in which forensic science is presented in popular media (i.e. television programmes like *CSI*) theoretically promotes unrealistic expectations amongst jurors of how reliably and definitively forensic evidence can be used to determine innocence or guilt (Dysart, 2012). It refers to the notion that jurors hold inaccurate beliefs about the validity of forensic science practices – including that they are infallible; that they are never wrong (Robbers, 2008) – which derive from the viewing of such shows and their distorted portrayal of the discipline. Very broadly speaking, it could be surmised as 'the impact that viewing fictional criminal investigation shows like *Crime Scene Investigation* ("*CSI*") is likely to have upon jurors' real life decision-making processes' (Lawson, 2009).

The central argument underlying any discussion of the CSI effect is that the pre-existing beliefs of the public may be shaped (and potentially distorted) by the inaccurate portrayal of forensic science and the criminal justice system in the popular media. This, it is suggested, could affect their ability to accurately evaluate forensic evidence, should they be called upon to be jurors. It is proposed that jurors are likely to be inherently 'biased' in their judicial attitudes towards the validity and utility of forensic science methods, and the evidence that they produce, by *a priori* media exposure. This possibility, it is argued, has notable implications in terms of judicial decision-making, and for the impartiality and fairness that are at the very heart of the notion of 'justice'.

Two key forms of the CSI effect have been proposed within the literature. The first focuses on the way that programmes like *CSI* elevate the status of forensic science, portraying it as equivocal, infallible and absolute. As Podlas (2006) discusses, such shows portray forensic science methodologies as mechanical, concrete indicia of certainty – which we know from empirical research (see Canter, Hammond & Youngs, 2013, for a summary) certainly isn't the case. These shows, Podlas (2006) argues, show forensics effortlessly identifying the culprit, but never show it 'just as easily' inculpating the wrong person. If such an effect is in operation, then it is more favourable to the prosecution than the defence in criminal trials, leading jurors to blindly believe forensic evidence and assign it undue levels of weighting in their considerations of case merit. A second variant of the CSI effect (and that which has so far received the most attention within the criminal justice literature) refers to inflated jury expectations regarding likely available forensic evidence (evidentiary proof). As Podlas (2006) discusses, in the typical *CSI* episode, each crime is solved with forensic tests, and these tests always discern the identity of the culprit. This, she argues, is likely to foster unreasonable juror expectations; that they will be conditioned to believe that every crime can be solved through forensic evidence, and that forensic evidence of guilt exists in every crime (Podlas, 2006). This, in turn, may impact upon jurors' assessments of evidence in criminal trials, playing a crucial role in determining whether they are likely to convict (Tyler, 2006). Such an effect, in operation, would place an increased burden on prosecutors to produce viable and believable forensic evidence. Tyler (2006) suggests that it is theoretically just as plausible (and, indeed probable) that a CSI effect might raise, as opposed to lower, the bar in terms of jurors' likelihood to convict.

7.2.3 The Influence of Media Exposure on the Perceived Accuracy/Reliability of Forensic Science

As Daftary-Kapur et al. (2010) discuss, research into the impacts of exposure to media coverage of forensic sciences is arguably still in its infancy. To date, only a handful of studies have explored the relationships between media exposure and the perceived accuracy/reliability of forensic evidence.

In 2006, Patry, Stinson and Smith demonstrated that viewing crime dramas had a significant, positive correlation with high expectations of forensic science. In a subsequent study they found that *CSI* viewing was associated with higher accuracy, reliability and fairness ratings for forensic evidence, including DNA and fingerprint evidence.

In another study investigating the effect of television viewing habits on the interpretation of forensic evidence, Schweitzer and Saks (2007) sampled 48 jury-eligible college students who were asked to read a transcript of a simulated trial involving one source of identification evidence. The forensic evidence presented in the scenario was in the form of expert testimony by a hair and fibre analyst, who testified that it was his professional opinion that a hair recovered from the perpetrator's ski mask originated from the defendant. Participants were asked to evaluate the usefulness of the trial evidence through a series of questions, and they were divided into two categories based on their viewing habits for both 'forensic related' and 'general crime-themed' programmes (p. 362). Results suggested that viewers of both forensic-related and general crime-related programmes rated themselves as having a higher level of understanding of the forensic technique presented than did non-viewers. Subsequently, forensic-related viewers also indicated significantly more confidence in their verdicts than did non-viewers. However, the difference between the groups in terms of their verdicts was not significant.

Lieberman, Carrell, Miethe and Krauss (2008) reported results from two studies investigating how mock jurors' attitudes relate to their perceptions of a criminal case. In the first study they surveyed participants (383 students and 233 jurors) about their perceptions of the accuracy and persuasiveness of different types of forensic evidence (e.g. DNA, fingerprints, hair, fibre, etc.). Participants also read either a rape or murder scenario in which evidence type was manipulated, and was either incriminating or exculpatory in nature, responding as to whether they would convict the culprit on the basis of the evidence presented. It was reported that DNA evidence was perceived to be the most accurate and persuasive form of evidence available, and incriminating DNA evidence led to 100% conviction rates. In the second study student participants ($N = 114$) were presented with a sexual assault trial which included multiple types of forensic evidence (semen, blood, hair, fingerprints). In each condition participants were told that only one of the sources of physical evidence was incriminating, whilst the remaining types of evidence yielded inconclusive results. By including both incriminating and inconclusive pieces of physical evidence within the same trial scenario, this study was able to determine which forensic evidence types led to conviction of the defendant, despite other physical evidence to the contrary. Results confirmed that there were significantly more convictions and higher probability of guilt estimates when the incriminating evidence type was a DNA or blood-type match, even when accompanied by damaging cross-examination within the scenario.

In one of the most recent empirical examinations of media exposure on the attitudes and beliefs of the general public, Baskin and Sommers (2010) explored perceived reliability of forensic evidence amongst mock jurors (jury-eligible voters). They found that the number of hours that respondents spent watching crime shows had a significant impact on assessments of different forms of testimony and evidence. Those who were more frequent crime-series viewers tended to view evidence derived using forensic science methods as more accurate and reliable than other forms of evidence (Baskin & Sommers, 2010). This study was limited, however, by the fact that the researchers were methodologically constrained in terms of how many questions they were allowed to ask participants. For example, they were unable to include any context for respondents to consider when making their assessments. As such, their study was, as they note, 'limited to obtaining black-and-white snapshots of public attitudes' (Baskin & Sommers, 2010).

7.2.4 The Influence of Media Exposure on Trial Expectancies and the Perceived Importance of Forensic Science in Judicial Processes

The bulk of the research that has been done into the CSI effect in action in trial settings has centred on surveys of practitioners, focusing on their opinions and experiences. As such, most of the accounts that have been provided of the influence of media exposure on trial expectancies and judicial processes have been primarily anecdotal in nature.

Robbers (2008) surveyed 290 American lawyers (both prosecution and defence) and judges about their experiences and opinions, and found that

79% cited specific instances in which they felt they had experienced juries who were influenced by forensic fiction on television. In addition, 85% of participants reported that the way they conducted their job had changed in recent years, in order to counter jurors' unrealistic perceptions of forensic science. Some of these changes included spending more time addressing these issues in *voir dire* hearings (36%) and use of negative expert testimony to explain missing evidence (23%), as well as specifically explaining to jurors the difference between television and real-life forensics (31%). Marquis (2007) reported similar opinions in his survey of prosecutors, highlighting a range of behavioural changes that have been deemed necessary by prosecutors as a result of defence attorneys exploiting the CSI effect to their advantage.

There are a number of problems with relying on feedback from members of the judiciary in isolating and characterising any CSI effects on jurors. As Baskin and Sommers (2010) argue, although prosecuting attorneys may be observing changes in juror attitudes, such studies provide no evidence that these changes emanate from crime-show viewing (or, indeed, any basis for inferring the root causes of such changes). Moreover, studies that are reliant on the (by nature – subjective) accounts of those with vested interests in the outcome of such research will of course suffer from potential threats to validity (Baskin & Sommers, 2010).

An alternative approach to exploring how pre-trial perceptions and attitudes, including those derived from media exposure, might impact upon jurors in a trial setting involves using mock-trial scenarios with samples of mock jurors. The first study to employ this kind of research paradigm was conducted by Podlas in 2006, and focused on determining whether there was an anti-prosecution bias held by jurors who reported viewing *CSI*. The participants in this study were classified as either frequent viewers of *CSI* (FV) or non-frequent viewers (NFV), based on self-reported viewing habits. They were given a trial summary of a rape case in which the only issue was consent (forensic evidence was not present and was not legally useful in determining the verdict). Reasons given for verdicts of not guilty were analysed in order to determine if *CSI* viewers were more likely to attribute a decision to acquit to the absence of forensic evidence. No significant differences were found between FV and NFV of *CSI* in terms of the reasons given for not guilty verdicts, which led Podlas to conclude that the findings did not support the claim that the CSI effect operates in such a way that jurors who view *CSI* are more likely to acquit on the basis that no forensic evidence is presented. The value of these findings in extrapolating evidence for or against the operation of CSI effects is somewhat limited, however, due to the fact that the researcher chose to use a case summary which did not rely on any forensic evidence, and therefore did not resemble a typical *CSI*-type scenario. If the mock jurors in the study were being influenced by any CSI effect, it would have been more likely to manifest in a scenario where they were being asked to evaluate forensic evidence (or lack thereof), under conditions which are more likely to activate any pre-existing schemas which have resulted from viewing typical CSI episodes (Cavender & Deutsch, 2007; Winter & York, 2007). Therefore, as evidence against the operation of CSI effects, the results of this study have to be approached with a degree of caution.

A different approach was taken by Shelton, Kim, and Barak (2006), who surveyed mock jurors about their expectations of forensic evidence, and then presented them with a trial transcript and examined their inter- pretations of the evidence presented. Participants were drawn from a list of people who had been summoned for jury duty ($N = 1027$), prior to their attendance at a trial. In the first part of the study participants were asked to report their crime-related viewing habits. They were then asked about what forensic evidence they would expect to be presented within a vari- ety of different types of criminal trial. Finally, they were presented with a series of scenarios, representing a range of criminal offences, and asked them to respond on a 5-point scale indicating their opinion of the likeli- hood of the defendant's guilt. Results indicated that the most frequently viewed law-related television programme was CSI, with less than half (44%) of participants indicating that they never watch it. Correlational analyses indicated that the more frequently participants reported watch- ing a particular programme, the more accurate they believed the por- trayal of forensic information in the programme to be. However, Shelton et al. (2006) only made comparison between viewers and non-viewers of television crime shows; no reference was made to the amount that such programmes were viewed. Such a crude distinction may have masked or downplayed the level of impact that media has on juror preferences and likely verdict decisions.

Rather than simply distinguishing between 'viewers' and 'non-viewers', Reardon, O'Neil, and Lawson (2007) explored differences in the judicial decisions made by frequent versus non-frequent viewers of television crime shows, examining in detail the impact(s) of level of media exposure on esti- mates of the probative value of forensic evidence. They found that when frequent viewers were presented with weak forensic evidence and strong non-forensic evidence, they were less likely to convict than non-frequent viewers. They subsequently explored the value of using a CSI 'warning' (emphasising that real forensic science is not on a par with fictional foren- sic science). This was found to have a direct impact on jurors' assessment of the probative value of fingerprint evidence; when the warning was not pre- sented, participants with high exposure to crime dramas tended to over- estimate the probative value of forensic evidence (Reardon et al., 2007). Overall, findings suggested that general belief in the diagnosticity of foren- sic evidence is significantly associated with an increased probability of con- viction (Daftary-Kapur et al., 2010).

Finally, Lieberman et al. (2008) explored whether participants' attitudes to forensic sciences were indicative of their likely verdict preferences. Students ($N = 130$) completed a pre-trial assessment before reading a murder trial scenario. Participants indicated their level of agreement with the items on a 10-point Likert scale, and these scores were analysed using logistic regression as predictors of verdict. Stronger beliefs in the validity and reliability of DNA evidence were found to significantly predict verdict preference and probability of guilt estimates (the higher participants agreement ratings, the higher their guilt estimates and the greater their preference for 'guilty' verdicts).

The aforementioned studies had varying approaches to addressing the question of whether media exposure impacts upon the perceived importance of forensic evidence to judicial processes, each with different aims and objectives, and, consequently, each producing very different and divergent findings. It is difficult to draw any firm conclusions from the results that are presently available.

Nonetheless, one common finding in these studies is that there does not appear to be any significant difference between jurors classified as 'CSI viewers' and those classified as 'non-viewers' in relation to the verdicts that they return at the end mock jury tasks. This lack of difference has been consistently observed, despite variations in the classification schemes employed and different types of juror decision-making activity. This might suggest that whilst the attitudes and general perceptions of jurors towards forensic science could be influenced by inaccurate media representations of forensic science techniques, this influence does not have a *direct* effect leading them to reach different verdict decisions from those jurors who are not exposed to the same media influence. This is not to say that exposure to *CSI*-type programmes does not have an *indirect* effect on jurors' decisions; indeed, more recent studies (e.g. Kim, Barak, & Shelton, 2009) suggest that treating the CSI effect as an indirect influence on juror verdict preference shows some promise.

However, it could also be the case that the types of task used in such studies are too crude to enable the true effects of media exposure on the perceived importance of forensic evidence in judicial decision-making to be delineated.

7.2.5 The Present Study

Much of the research into the likely effects of *CSI* exposure on jurors' perceptions of, and attitudes towards, forensic science in criminal trial settings has generally focused on only one outcome variable: the decision to convict or acquit (Baskin & Sommers, 2010). However, this – as Schweitzer and Saks (2007) discuss – is not a very sensitive measure of juror decision-making or of the factors (and potential biases) that underpin it. It is one clear and absolute judgement about the relative merits of the whole case. This is somewhat problematic because, firstly, it will be largely dependent on the information given and the general case merits; it will not necessarily reveal the subtle nuances of CSI effects or the relative weightings given to forensic science evidence in arriving at judicial verdicts. Secondly, recent research suggests that jurors' experiences and attitudes influence all aspects of decision-making in trial settings, including how closely jurors follow instructions given to them or what information they incorporate into their assessments, not just the final verdict that they choose (Baskin & Sommers, 2010). It is therefore suggested that what is now needed is research that is not limited to a test of whether jurors vote to convict or acquit, but rather on their general expectancies for forensic science in trial settings and how useful or valuable they perceive it to be as a whole. By moving away from the use of case scenarios, and thus stripping away contextual effects and confounding informational factors, it becomes feasible to explore how and in what ways forensic evidence is perceived to be reliable and of value in determining case outcome. This, in turn, facilitates the development of an enriched understanding of the merit and weighting assigned to it in juror decision-making throughout the whole trial process.

Previous research has tended to focus on just one of the range of variants of CSI effects that have been proposed within the literature (Schweitzer & Saks, 2007). However, as Tyler (2006) notes, it is feasible that a number of different CSI effects operate simultaneously in determining juror perceptions of the validity and utility of forensic evidence. It is proposed that in order to fully unpack the range of potential influences that media exposure has on jurors in criminal trial settings, research needs to consider both those effects that operate to the benefit and to the detriment of the prosecution. What is therefore needed is examination of pre-trial attitudes and biases, subsequent evaluation of the perceived importance and weighting assigned to forensic science evidence and – alongside both of these – determination of how they are impacted by exposure to different sources of forensic science information. It is suggested that this should be undertaken in relation to perceptions of forensic science generally, rather than with a focus on any specific forms of evidence or forensic science techniques (e.g. DNA recovery and analysis) or in the context of one case with its particular fact pattern (c.f. Schweitzer & Saks, 2007). This would remove any potential biases resulting from speciality-specific effects or stereotypes of different areas of forensic science/particular types of forensic evidence (Schweitzer & Saks, 2007).

The present study sought to establish what (if any) biases mock jurors have in relation to both the perceived reliability of forensic science and the perceived value of forensic evidence for judicial processes, and to determine where any such biases might derive from.

7.3 Method

A questionnaire/self-report format was used because – as Dysart (2012) discusses – juror questionnaires offer unique insight regarding (a) individual, personal biases and (b) beliefs (for example, in the accuracy of media portrayals of forensic science). Such insights cannot necessarily be gained from verdict decisions made in relation to a mock jury task. Further, this allowed participants' exposure to different forms of media depictions of crime, criminals and criminal trials to be established through self-report measures.

A questionnaire was developed which, firstly, surveyed where participants obtained their knowledge of forensic science. Secondly, it examined their perceptions of the accuracy and reliability of forensic science, and of the value and utility of forensic evidence for investigative/prosecutorial purposes.

In the first section of the questionnaire participants provided demographic information and answered questions about their interest in, and exposure to, media portrayals of forensic science. They were asked how much of their knowledge of forensic science, they felt, had come (a) from watching television programmes like *CSI*, (b) from reading crime fiction or crime non-fiction books, (c) from news programmes and news media or from factual documentaries or (d) other sources of information (including personal experience with the criminal justice system). They were also asked how many hours they spent on average, per week, engaging with these different forms of media.

To examine the public's views on the reliability and utility of different forms of forensic evidence, using a methodology similar to that employed by Baskin and Sommers (2010), participants were then presented with 25 statements and were asked to indicate their level of agreement with each, using a five-point scale ranging from 1 (*strongly agree*) to 5 (*strongly disagree*).[*] These were specifically designed to reflect the beliefs that jurors have been anecdotally reported to hold (within the CSI effect literature).

The questionnaire was piloted on a public sample of 60 jury-eligible individuals[†] – 30 males and 30 females.

---

[*] Some items were negatively worded and therefore these items were scored in reverse.
[†] The basic criteria employed required participants to be at least 18, but not more than 65, years of age and registered as a voter. They had to have lived in the United Kingdom for a minimum of 5 years, and could not have been convicted of a criminal offence for which they served a prison sentence or community order.

7.4 Results

7.4.1 Reliability of Questionnaire

Cronbach's alpha was used as a measure of reliability for this 25-item scale and was found to 0.921. This result is very high and indicates strong internal consistency amongst the questionnaire items (Field, 2009); respondents who tended to select high scores for one item also tended to select high scores for other related items; similarly, respondents who selected a low scores for one item tended to select low scores for the other related items.

7.4.2 Sources of Knowledge of Forensic Sciences

Seven per cent of the sample thought that their knowledge of forensic science was solely from watching television programmes such as *CSI*, and 35% thought that such shows constituted their primary source of forensic science information. None of the participants reported that books were their sole source of forensic science knowledge, although 17% said that crime fiction and non-fiction were their primary source of information on the forensic sciences. Two per cent of the sample cited news media and documentaries as their only information source and 18% as their primary information source. Finally, 16% said that their knowledge of forensic sciences came entirely from other sources or personal experience, and 33% reported that their knowledge had come from a wide range of sources.

7.4.3 *CSI*/Crime Series Viewing Habits

Fifteen per cent of the sample reported that crime dramas such as *CSI* were their preferred choice of viewing and that they watched them most days. More than a third reported watching such shows frequently (three or more times a week), and more than three quarters reported watching them regularly (at least once or twice a week). Sixteen per cent of the sample reported watching such shows for more than 7 hours a week, equating to an hour or more every day. Around 80% of the sample watched at least 3 hours of *CSI* or similar shows a week, at least three episodes. Only one participant reported never watching such shows.

7.4.4 Perceptions of the Accuracy and Reliability of Forensic Science

Levels of agreement with the different statements pertaining to the accuracy and reliability of forensic science methods and techniques are presented in Table 7.1. Thirty-five per cent of the sample indicated that they believed

Table 7.1 Levels of Agreement with Statements Pertaining to the Accuracy and Reliability of Forensic Evidence

Statement	Strongly Agree	Agree	Neither Agree nor Disagree	Disagree	Strongly Disagree
CSI dramas are a realistic portrayal of investigative behaviours and methods at a crime scene.	3.3%	31.7%	33.3%	25%	6.7%
The forensic science portrayed in CSI dramas represents actual crime-scene methods.	0%	26.7%	36.7%	36.7%	0%
Forensic evidence is the most accurate way to identify the perpetrator of a crime.	8.3%	23.3%	28.3%	28.3%	11.7%
Forensic evidence will always reveal the identity of the perpetrator of a crime.	3.3%	25%	35%	28.3%	8.3%
It is nearly impossible to commit a crime without leaving forensic evidence.	6.7%	21.7%	26.7%	38.3%	6.7%
Scientific evidence is absolute/unquestionable.	5%	25%	21.7%	35%	13.3%
Forensic evidence can be derived from methods that are not very scientific.	0%	20%	56.7%	21.7%	1.7%
An offender will always leave forensic evidence that can lead to their identity being revealed.	0%	11.7%	31.7%	53.3%	3.3%
Forensic evidence can solve every crime.	3.3%	18.3%	25%	31.7%	21.7%
An advantage of forensic science is that its methods are always conclusive.	1.7%	28.3%	25%	33.3%	11.7%
The strength of forensic science is that it only uses strongly scientific methods.	10%	25%	33.3%	30%	1.7%
Forensic evidence is reliable as it relies upon tightly controlled laboratory methods.	6.7%	20%	35%	31.7%	6.7%

programmes like *CSI* provide a realistic portrayal of forensic science methods, and more than a third indicated that they thought forensic science constituted the best or most reliable way of identifying the perpetrator of a crime. Around a quarter of the sample believed forensic science to be unquestionable and absolute, thought that all such methods relied upon strongly scientific techniques and that forensic evidence was universally robust and reliable.

Bivariate analyses were used to examine the relationships between agreement levels and frequency of viewing of *CSI*-type crime dramas. Significant correlations were found between viewing frequency and the level of agreement with the following statements:

- 'The forensic science portrayed in CSI dramas represents actual crime scene methods'. (0.337; $p < 0.01$)
- 'Forensic evidence is the most accurate way to identify the perpetrator of a crime'. (0.395; $p < 0.01$)
- 'It is nearly impossible to commit a crime without leaving forensic evidence'. (0.259; $p < 0.05$)
- 'An offender will always leave forensic evidence that can lead to their identity being revealed'. (0.254; $p < 0.05$)
- 'Forensic science can solve every crime'. (0.299; $p < 0.05$)
- 'An advantage of forensic science is that its methods are always conclusive'. (0.288; $p < 0.05$)
- 'The strength of forensic science is that it only uses strongly scientific methods'. (0.436; $p < 0.01$)
- 'Forensic evidence is reliable as it relies upon tightly controlled laboratory methods'. (0.232; $p < 0.05$)

There was a significant negative correlation between level of media exposure and level of agreement with the following statement: Forensic evidence can be derived from methods that are not very scientific (–0.240; $p < 0.05$).

7.4.5 Trial Expectancies and the Perceived Importance of Forensic Science in Judicial Processes

Levels of agreement with statements presented to participants which related to the utility and value of forensic science evidence in the courts (i.e. in relation to judicial processes) are presented in Table 7.2.

More than a quarter of the sample thought that forensic evidence should constitute a notable part of the prosecution's case in the majority of criminal trials, with a third stating that they agreed that it should be the foremost evidence from which convictions should be derived. More than 80% agreed with the statement that a jury should find a defendant guilty when there is substantial forensic evidence against them. Fifty per cent thought that forensic

Table 7.2   Levels of Agreement with Statements Pertaining to the Importance and Value of Forensic Science to Judicial Processes

Statement	Strongly Agree	Agree	Neither Agree nor Disagree	Disagree	Strongly Disagree
If there is no forensic evidence relating to the offender then the jury should not convict.	0%	11.7%	26.7%	40%	21.7%
Forensic evidence should be part of the prosecution's case in the majority of criminal trials.	3.3%	23.3%	31.7%	36.7%	5%
Forensic evidence is the foremost information from which criminal convictions should be derived.	3.3%	28.3%	33.3%	28.3%	6.7%
Forensic science evidence decreases the likelihood of wrongful convictions.	11.7%	40%	30%	18.3%	0%
Forensic scientists who testify in court are reliable experts as they give an unbiased account of the evidence.	3.3%	30%	40%	25%	1.7%
Eyewitness testimony is not scientific enough to convict an offender.	1.7%	13.3%	20%	48.3%	16.7%
When there are allegations of rape or sexual assault the conviction should be based on forensic science such as DNA evidence.	8.3%	10%	26.7%	40%	15%
Without forensic evidence the conviction of an offender can be easily overturned.	1.7%	31.7%	33.3%	25%	6.7%
Forensic science can also present strong evidence for the conviction of an innocent person.	0%	10%	45%	38.3%	6.7%
DNA is the strongest possible evidence for convicting an offender.	6.7%	28.3%	26.7%	33.3%	5%
If no forensic evidence is recovered from a crime scene then the police are at fault.	3.3%	25%	25%	30%	16.7%
It is easy for forensic evidence to be tampered with or results contaminated.	1.7%	10%	26.7%	43.3%	18.3%
A jury should find a defendant guilty when there is substantial forensic evidence against them.	18.3%	65%	13.3%	3.3%	0%

evidence decreases the likelihood of wrongful convictions, and only a small minority (10%) thought that forensic science could present strong evidence for the conviction of an innocent person.

Bivariate analyses were used to examine the relationships between agreement levels and frequency of viewing of *CSI*-type crime dramas. Significant correlations were found between level of media exposure and the level of agreement with the following statements:

- 'Forensic evidence is the foremost information from which criminal convictions should be derived'. (0.223; $p < 0.05$)
- 'Forensic scientists who testify in court are reliable experts as they give an unbiased account of the evidence'. (0.294; $p < 0.05$)
- 'Forensic science evidence decreases the likelihood of wrongful convictions'. (0.535; $p < 0.001$)
- 'Without forensic evidence the conviction of an offender can be easily overturned'. (0.384; $p < 0.01$)
- 'DNA is the strongest possible evidence for convicting an offender'. (0.431; $p < 0.01$)
- 'If no forensic evidence is recovered from a crime scene then the police are at fault'. (0.643; $p < 0.001$)
- 'A jury should find a defendant guilty when there is substantial forensic evidence against them'. (0.439; $p < 0.01$)

There was a significant negative correlation between level of media exposure and level of agreement with the following statement: Forensic science can also present strong evidence for the conviction of an innocent person (−0.224; $p < 0.05$).

Interesting, there was also a significant negative correlation between level of media exposure and level of agreement with the following statement: When there are allegations of rape or sexual assault the conviction should be based on forensic science such as DNA evidence (−0.274; $p < 0.05$).

7.5 Discussion

In the present study a clear relationship between interest in (and exposure to) media coverage of crime/crime investigation and general understanding and perceptions of forensic sciences was found. Exposure to sources of inaccurate information (such as shows like *CSI*) appears to generate biases that manifest both in judgements of perceived accuracy and reliability of forensic science, and of its importance in investigative/prosecutorial processes.

The present findings highlight, firstly, the value of developing methods of evaluating the biases jurors may hold and where these may derive from.

Secondly, they go some way towards identifying potential means of reducing the biasing effects of prior exposure to inaccurate or misleading information in potential jurors.

Results from the present study could be helpful in informing criminal justice professionals about potential areas where risks of bias are high, having applications in terms of preparing for such biases and taking appropriate action accordingly. Robbers (2008) notes that, at present, criminal justice personnel have little available to them by way of guidance in such respects.

Dysart (2010) discusses a range of different tactics that might be utilised before, throughout and/or at the conclusion of a criminal trial as countermeasures against potential juror biases, including CSI effects. One that the present findings suggest might be particularly helpful is the use of juror screening during *voir dire*. In countries with adversarial legal systems such as England and Wales, Australia, Canada and the United States, the use of pre-trial hearings (or *voir dire* hearings) for identifying potential juror bias is relatively commonplace, although how these hearings are conducted varies greatly between jurisdictions (Brooks, 2004; Kaplan & Miller, 1978). During these sessions, potential jurors can be questioned regarding any pre-existing beliefs or biases.

Trial counsellors have already started asking potential jurors during *voir dire* whether they watch forensic television shows, in an attempt to draw out any potential *CSI*-type biases (Robbers, 2008). Potential jurors in the Conrad Murray trial were given questionnaires that specifically asked if they watched *CSI* in preparation for presenting the particular evidence taken from Michael Jackson's bedroom that, unlike on *CSI*, did not clearly show what caused Jackson's death (Dysart, 2012). Questionnaires, such as that developed and presented here, could potentially prove very valuable to such endeavours. They offer a solid basis for the derivation of more detailed and robust methods of assessing potential juror bias.

If, during screening, potential jurors are found to have strong biases resulting from their exposure to inaccurate media representations of forensic science, then there are a number of ways that this potential jury bias could be addressed. Firstly, those displaying strong biases could be removed from the process. There are two main processes which provide the means for excluding jurors presumed to have biases relevant to a particular case; challenges for cause and the peremptory challenge (Norton, Sommers, & Brauner, 2007). The bases for such challenges, and the value of such exclusions, are discussed elsewhere (e.g. Van Dyke, 1977; Hastie, 1991; Crocker & Bull Kovera, 2010). Excluding those suggested by screening procedures to be inappropriately biased from the trial process might be the most fruitful way of reducing jury bias (Brooks, 2004), for, as Crocker and Bull Kovera (2010) discuss, research has shown that pre-trial biases are very difficult, if not impossible, to remove or for jurors to ignore. Exclusion is argued by some to be the best means of securing an impartial jury (Gobert, 1997), to result in more effective deliberation processes (Hastie, 1991) and to reduce the likelihood of a hung jury (Rose, 1999). However, others argue that the use of challenges undermines the purpose of the jury system, being contrary to the concept of a representative jury (e.g. Rose, 1999). In addition, concerns have been raised that the use of pre-trial hearings may give jurors unfavourable views of the trial attorneys and the evidence, and that the motivation for lawyers to select jurors who are likely to favour their side of the trial renders hearings inherently impartial (Gobert, 1997; Greene, Heilbrun, Fortune, & Nietzel, 2007).

A second way of managing any potential biases identified during *voir dire*, which circumvents some of the issues generated by juror exclusion, would be through development of juror information sheets or training programmes in order to facilitate more effective and reliable decision-making in cases relying heavily on forensic science evidence. Again, the present findings offer notable assistance for such endeavours.

As Lawson (2009) discusses, the use of special jury instructions directing jurors to only use the standards articulated by the court to assess the potential value and reliability of forensic evidence, not standards learned from television or other sources outside the courtroom, might be of considerable value in the majority of criminal trials. They are likely to be especially helpful in cases involving novel methods or techniques or those that are known to be frequently misunderstood (in terms of how they work and how accurate they are likely to be).

Alternatively, training might be provided to jurors in order to improve their ability to evaluate physical evidence. DNA evidence in particular was the focus of a research project conducted by Goodman-Delahunty and Hewson (2009), in which the effectiveness of providing mock jurors a tutorial as part of the expert evidence was evaluated. At the outset of the study, participants' knowledge about DNA evidence was very low (on average 24% of questions were answered correctly), regardless of their demographics or television viewing habits (a similar finding was also reported by Brewer and Ley, 2010). Results from this pilot study suggest that the use of such a tutorial can improve participants' knowledge and accuracy by around 40%, which seems promising for overcoming difficulties with evidence interpretation in the courtroom.

On the basis of the findings presented here, alongside other previous commentary in the area (e.g. Robbers, 2008), it is suggested that a useful policy change for adversarial criminal justice systems would be the introduction of a compulsory, non-partisan briefing for jurors; one which provides an accurate depiction of criminal trials and criminal investigation/forensic science procedures. This, as Robbers (2008) discusses, could be delivered through the use of an educational video, shown to all potential jurors prior to their selection and consequent participation. Bradshaw, Ross, Bradshaw, Headrick and Thomas (2005) show that such orientation videos lead to fewer juror errors, although at present there is little detailed empirical research on the effects of juror education (Robbers, 2008).

7.5.1 Limitations and Directions for Future Research

There are a number of methodological issues with the present research and consequently a number of limitations to the potential applicability of the findings. One is that the accuracy of results obtained through the use of self-report questionnaires is of course dependent on participant honesty. It can be problematic asking mock jurors about their perceptions of trial evidence or verdict preferences because, as Gobert (1997) discusses, social desirability may play a role in determining responses to questions about judicial attitudes. There is no reason to believe that the responses provided by subjects in the present study were not genuine, as participation was entirely voluntary and withdrawal was possible at any time, no motivational incentives were provided and there were no right or wrong answers to any of the questions posited. However, further research should seek to develop further and test more widely the bias measurement scale presented here, in order that the ecological validity and reliability of the scale might be better assessed.

As Baskin and Sommers (2010) discuss, there are a wide range of salient factors that could viably influence attitudes that jurors hold and might potentially bring to the court room, all of which could potentially influence verdict preferences and case outcomes. As is the case with other research into potential CSI effects, the study here focused on certain key elements, particularly viewing frequency and self-reported information sources.

The research paradigm utilised here could certainly be expanded, so as to take into account other different juror attributes and contextual factors that may mediate the relationship(s) between media exposure and jurors' attitudes/beliefs and their perceptions of the importance of forensic evidence in the making of judicial decisions. This might be a particularly fruitful direction for future research works for, as Baskin and Sommers (2010) discuss, juror decisions are highly unlikely to be the result of some direct relationship between two particular and distinct variables or behaviours.

Here, only the core relationship between viewing habits/media exposure and the perceived reliability/value of forensic evidence was examined. It would be interesting to see how factors such as age, gender, occupation, educational level and background experience all impact upon this relationship, and whether there are any significant interactions between any of these factors.

More complex statistical models and multivariate analyses are perhaps what are now needed. It is unlikely, though, that a causal arrow between exposure to certain forms of media, such as *CSI*-type programmes, and juror attitudes and preferences will ever be able to be definitively drawn. As Schweitzer and Saks (2007) discuss, there is always the possibility that the causal arrow goes in the opposite direction, namely, that those with unusually high hopes for forensic science are drawn to forensic-science fiction.

It is unrealistic to hope that the psychological processes underlying the development of juror biases and their consequent impacts on judicial decisions will ever be fully delineated. However, there is still much that might be done to try to glean a more detailed understanding of these processes and how they operate. For example, research might use a similar type of scale to that employed here, but distinguish between different forms of forensic evidence or different types of forensic science methodologies. Further, forensic evidence is just one of many types of evidence that may be presented during a trial in order to determine a defendant's guilt or innocence. Other types of trial information include the alibi of the accused, eyewitness testimony, circumstantial evidence, CCTV footage and offending motives. Key questions for future research to address would be: How are these types of information valued compared to forensic evidence? What relative weightings are given to different forms of forensic evidence?

Finally, it may be that the type of crime that questions are asked about has an influence on the responses provided and on the forms of that bias that manifest. Research into variations in mock jurors' understanding of forensic science and its perceived importance in relation to different types of cases, possessing a range of different attributes, is certainly warranted.

References

Baskin, D. R., & Sommers, I. B. (2010). Crime-show-viewing habits and public attitudes toward forensic evidence: The 'CSI Effect' revisited. *Justice System Journal*, *31*(1), 97–113.

Bradshaw, G. S., Ross, D. F., Bradshaw, E. E., Headrick, B., & Thomas, W. N. (2005). Fostering juror comfort: Effects of an orientation videotape. *Law and Human Behavior*, *29*(4), 457–467.

Brewer, P., & Ley, B. (2010). Media use and public perception of DNA evidence. *Science Communication*, *32*, 93–117.

Brooks, T. (2004). The right to trial by jury. *Journal of Applied Philosophy*, *21*(2), 197–212.

Cavender, G., & Deutsch, S. (2007). CSI and moral authority: The police and science. *Crime, Media and Culture*, *3*, 67–81.

Canter, D., Hammond, L., & Youngs, D. (2013). Cognitive bias in lineup identifications: The impact of administrator knowledge. *Science and Justice*, *53*(2), 83–88.

Crocker, B., & Bull Kovera, M. (2010). The effects of rehabilitative voir dire on juror bias and decision-making. *Law and Human Behavior*, *34*, 212–226.

Daftary-Kapur, T., Dumas, R., & Penrod, S. D. (2010). Jury decision-making biases and methods to counter them. *Legal and Criminological Psychology*, *15*, 133–154.

Dysart, K. L. (2012). Managing the CSI Effect in jurors. *American Bar Association Article*. Retrieved from http://apps.americanbar.org/litigation/committees/trial evidence/articles/winterspring2012-0512-csi-effect-jurors.html.

Elffers, H., de Keijser, J., van Koppen, P., & van Haeringen, L. (2007). Newspaper juries: A field experiment concerning the effect of information on attitudes towards the criminal justice system. *Journal of Experimental Criminology, 3,* 163–182.

Field, A. (2009). *Discovering statistics using SPSS* (3rd ed.). London: Sage.

Gobert, J. (1997). *Justice, democracy and the jury.* Aldershot, UK: Dartmouth.

Goodman-Delahunty, J., & Hewson, L. (2009). *Improving jury understanding and use of DNA expert evidence.* Report to the Criminological Research Council. New South Wales, Australia.

Greene, E., Heilbrun, K., Fortune, W., & Nietzel, M. (2007). *Wrightsman's psychology and the legal system.* Belmont, CA: Thomson Higher Education.

Hastie, R. (1991). Is attorney-conducted voir dire an effective procedure for the selection of impartial juries? *American University Law Review,* 1–19.

Houck, M. (2006). CSI: Reality. *Scientific American, 295,* 84–89.

Kaplan, M., & Miller, L. (1978). Reducing the effects of juror bias. *Journal of Personality and Social Psychology, 36,* 1443–1455.

Kim, Y. S., Barak, G., & Shelton, D. E. (2009). Examining the 'CSI Effect' in the cases of circumstantial evidence and eyewitness testimony: Multivariate and path analyses. *Journal of Criminal Justice, 37,* 452.

Lawson, T. F. (2009). Before the verdict and beyond the verdict: The CSI infection within modern criminal jury trials. *Loyola University Chicago Law Journal, 41*(1), 119–173.

Lieberman, J., Carrell, C., Miethe, T., & Krauss, D. (2008). Gold versus platinum: Do jurors recognise the superiority and limitations of DNA evidence compared to other types of forensic evidence? *Psychology, Public Policy, and Law, 14,* 27–62.

Mann, M. D. (2006). The 'CSI Effect': Better jurors through television and science? *Buffalo Public Interest Law Journal, 24,* 157–183.

Marquis, J. K. (2007). *CSI Effect: Does it really exist?* National District Attorney Association. Retrieved from http://communities.justicetalking.org/blugs/day17 /archive/2007/10/16/csi-effect-does-it-really-exist.aspx.

Nielsen Media Research. (2010). Retrieved from www.nielsenmedia.co.uk.

Norton, M., Sommers, S., & Brauner, S. (2007). Bias in jury selection: Justifying prohibited peremptory challenges. *Journal of Behavioural Decision Making, 20,* 467–479.

Patry, M. W., Stinson, V., & Smith, S. M. (2006). *What do we know about the CSI Effect?* Paper presented at the Dalhousie University Forensic Psychology Practice Day, Halifax, Nova Scotia.

Peelo, M., Francis, B., Soothill, K., Pearson, J., & Ackerly, E. (2004). Newspaper reporting and the public construction of homicide. *British Journal of Criminology, 44*(2), 256–275.

Podlas, K. (2006). 'The CSI Effect': Exposing the media myth. *Media and Entertainment Law Journal, 16*(2), 429–465.

Reardon, M., O'Neil, K., & Lawson, K. (2007). *A new definition of the 'Crime Scene Investigation (CSI)' Effect.* Poster presented at the Association for Psychological Science Annual Convention, Washington, DC.

Robbers, M. L. P. (2008) Blinded by science: The social construction of reality in forensic television shows and its effect on criminal jury trials. *Criminal Justice Policy Review, 19*(1), 84–102.

Rose, M. (1999). The peremptory challenge accused of race or gender discrimination? Some data from one county. *Law and Human Behavior, 23*, 695–702.

Schweitzer, N., & Saks, M. (2007). The 'CSI Effect': Popular fiction about forensic science affects public expectations about real forensic science. *Jurimetrics, 47*, 357–364.

Shelton, D. E., Kim, Y. S., & Barak, G. (2006). A study of juror expectations and demands concerning scientific evidence: Does the 'CSI Effect' exist? *Vanderbilt Journal of Entertainment and Technology Law, 9*, 330–368.

Stephens, S. (2006). The CSI Effect on real crime labs. *New England Law Review, 41*, 591–607.

Tyler, T. (2006). Viewing C.S.I. and the threshold of guilt: Managing truth and justice in reality and fiction. *The Yale Law Journal, 115*, 1050–1085.

Van Dyke, J. M. (1977). *Jury selection procedures: Our uncertain commitment to representative panels.* Cambridge: Ballinger.

Winter, R., & York, R. (2007). The 'CSI effect': Now playing in a courtroom near you? *Monitor on Psychology, 38*(6), 54.

Dysfunctional Economic Behaviour
Victims of Financial Debt (The Case of Microfinance Organisation Clients)

8

OLGA DEYNEKA

Contents

8.1 Introduction and Background

Researchers note that complication of society structure (increasing diversity of goods and services, institutions and organisations, social roles and values, growing stratification) leads to the emergence of a variety of types of victims of unfavorable socialisation conditions. Thus, the attention of social victimology, a currently developing integrated study devoted to people in a state of crisis and to measures of helping them, is concentrated on real and potential victims, particularly of the adverse economic socialisation conditions and addictive behaviour. Indeed, a debtor's behaviour can be both constructive and destructive. An adequate attitude to debt usually stimulates financial activity of economic agent, whilst debt-related dysfunctions lead to a decrease in the standard of living and the quality of life, including such harsh consequences as addictions, loss of employment and disruption of normal family relations.

It is worth mentioning that debt-related dysfunctions of economic behaviour might be found at all levels of management up to macroeconomic level (for instance, consider the amount of national debt of the United States) and the level of the world economy. A relevant example of such a dysfunction is the European debt crisis provoked by growing indebtedness in both private and public sectors and resulted in various problems in area of investment. The European debt crisis might be explained by a combination of complex factors. They include globalisation of financial market, easy credit conditions in 2002–2008, high-risk lending, the world financial crisis in 2007–2012, international trade imbalances, real-estate bubbles that burst, low rate of economic growth since 2008, failed fiscal policies and governmental bailouts to the banking sector and private bondholders when the debts were assumed or losses were socialised (European debt crisis, 2012).

If we summarise the analysis of the debt crisis in the language of economic psychology, it was an input–output imbalance (for instance, the national debt of Greece was due to extravagant salaries and pension funds in the country) combined with excessive social stratification (executive-to-worker pay ratio was about 400), narrowed temporal perspective (some economic agents derived benefit from credit-default swaps and toxic assets that aggravated the world financial crisis and the European debt crisis), when greed (Kramnik, 2003), profit-seeking and financially irresponsible behaviour was legitimised and idealised in context of deficit in balance of payments (Krugman, 2009).

Analysing the European situation in terms of political psychology, we may speak about imbalance in a 'state/business' system with a shift towards deregulated economy (which led Iceland to bankruptcy in 2008), or fusion between state and business with drastic reallocations of financial resource, like governmental bailouts to the banking sector during a bond crisis (in Greece and in Spain). In addition, certain imbalance in structural policy of European Union (monetary union without fiscal one) could be noticed, as well as in regional policies (problem of national debts in context of bond volume increase in a few countries). The latter situation results in citizens' dissatisfaction with the economic policies of their own states, for instance, in Germany (Deyneka, 2011), in protests against other nations' actions (anti-German grudges in Greece) or inner separatist tendencies. Such political values as equity and stability are being corrupted. Deficiencies resulting from financial bubbles are being socialised. High unemployment rate, excessive social stratification, poverty, homelessness, increased college costs and medical expenses result in a situation when bank management is perceived as a unified enemy, and movements such as Occupy Wall Street are initiated. New problems associated with migration and refugees have emerged: the higher the level of economic decision-making, the greater the risk of potential victims' appearance.

Against the background of debt-related dysfunctions at the level of states, there occurs an increase in the same dysfunctions of economic behaviour amongst individuals. At the individual level, debt-related dysfunctions lead not only to loss and disappointment, but also to various forms of destructive behaviour, such as 'credit suicide' (Katasonov, 2012) and other dangerous deviations (fraud, stealing and murder). The number of the victims of these deviations has increased in Russia and neighbouring countries.

Terrence Shulman, the founder of the Shulman Center for Compulsive Theft, Spending and Hoarding, thinks that the United States, being burdened with a debt of $17 trillion, shows a poor example for other countries. According to the researcher, Americans are caught in a vicious circle of debt, because there is a strong connection between debt obligations at the national and individual levels. Americans have been working harder for less money over the years, so many spend to justify the hard work but then they get into debt and have to work harder and so on (Plummer, 2014). Now debt obligations (credits) have turned into standard practice not only at the macro-social level, but also at the level of personality and family, despite all the dangers of debt bondage.

Formerly, the issues related to the psychology of dysfunctional economic behaviour – such as constant financial debts – were hardly ever discussed in the review publications on economic psychology and psychology of money (Furnham & Argyle, 2000; Lewis, 2008). Meanwhilst, the authors of the last fundamental works in the field actively examine these topics. They emphasise that this social problem has international roots and bears global importance. For instance, the new book by Furnham (2014) contains a section called 'Money Madness'. Scientists and practitioners also employ such terms as money pathology, debt addiction, compulsive debting and compulsive shopping (compulsive buying disorder).

In recent years, researchers have observed a stable increase in the credit activity of Russians. This causes alarm amongst various scientists – specialists in economics and economic policy, lawyers and psychologists. These tendencies should be examined more carefully by psychologists who specialise in this area. It is not an exaggeration to say that at the moment there is a deficiency of empirical research in psychology of financial debt.

The results of four research projects, which were held in the different periods of transition, are summarised next. The research was focused on different social groups' attitudes to debt and to the monetary policy of the Russian state. All research projects were conducted by the same method based on the multi-level approach to psychological attitude. Psychological attitude is a key concept which can be used to explore people's perception of economic reality. I designed a multifactor questionnaire that was the main method of investigation.

8.2 Overall Results of the First Study

The first research study was conducted between 1999 and 2002. Students, workers and public employees were participants in the study (a total of 623 participants). They demonstrated a prominent shift in attitude to debt, from previously traditional debt aversion towards a more positive attitude to debts and loans (Deyneka, 2008; Deyneka, Ivanova, & Kuzmenkova, 2000). The research showed Russians' negative attitude to debt at a macro-social level (national debt) and a more positive attitude to debt at a micro-social level in all groups of respondents (students, workers and state employees). We found factors which influence the respondents' perception of debt relationships and debt behaviour. The factor of temporal perspective was important: it was easier for respondents to take a loan for shorter time in order to achieve their long-term goals (financial dependency is less burdening and more justified). The amount of debt was important too: the less was the debt, the less was the feeling of dependency and anxiety. Factor of scale and level of debt was manifested in the fact that debt related to the national budget was strongly disapproved. A qualitative characteristic of the debt was also expressed.

A significant difference was found between older and younger generations' attitudes to debt. For example, state-employed specialists from the elder generation showed a more cautious, doubtful and anxious attitude to debt, which had been traditional for Russia. The younger generation showed a more positive attitude to debt. In their opinion, debt is an appropriate form of economic behaviour. However, they made an additional classification: there might be 'good debt' and 'bad debt'. Bad debt is money one takes for entertainment and self-indulgence, whilst good debt is necessary to pay for one's education, medical treatment, business start-up or important purchase. In student sampling, a more positive attitude to debt behaviour was shown by business management students than by students in humanitarian professions. The former were also more competent, careful and rational in their debt behaviour.

In relation to personal qualities, success-oriented subjects were more willing to lend money to others than failure-avoiding individuals. Subjects with an internal locus of control were less willing to enter debt-related financial relationships than subjects with an external locus, and they projected their opinions on the macro-level.

8.3 Overall Results of the Second Study

The second research study was conducted in 2006; psychological components of attitude to current monetary policy and debt were explored. The sampling included 125 employees working in finance in Moscow and St. Petersburg.

The results showed a contradictory attitude from financial sphere professionals concerning Russia's monetary policy. They perceived it not as means for improving the quality of life but rather as a tool for deriving profits. The main statistic results showed the respondents' cautious attitude to loans, distrust of banking structures and mortgage because they were afraid to be given incomplete information about its terms and attempts to avoid the situation of debt. The most popular form of bank loan with the respondents was the business start-up loan. As was shown by correlation and factor analysis, respondents who had more knowledge about loans showed less trust to state organisations and were less willing to use them, whilst those with less knowledge in this area were more inclined to trust the state.

8.4 Overall Results of the Third Study

The third research carried out in the spring 2012 was a pilot study. Let us discuss its findings in more details. The aim of the research was to explore bank employees', in comparison with a control group's, attitudes to state monetary policy, bank loans and individual debt behaviour. The main method was an original scaled multifactor questionnaire 'Attitude to Monetary Policy'. Additional methods were used, which measured psychological factors related to the quality of life, such as the Scale of Subjective Well-Being (by E. Diener) and Tolerance Ambiguity Scale. Sampling included 79 people; 50 of them were bank employees.

The results of the research showed complex and contradictory attitudes to monetary policy and debt in both groups. Respondents showed a very high level of agreement with the idea that Russia should implement growth-stimulating economic policy. At the same time, they agree that the economy of the country should be more human regarding the social sector and that stability is the most important quality for the economy. The majority of respondents agree that the Central Bank should in any situation support the value of the ruble and should not resort to excessive money emission.

The research showed that national and personal debts are perceived by particular respondents in a similar way. According to the factor analysis, the subjects who are against debts demonstrate their negative attitude to credits at the level of both micro- and macro-economics.

Despite negative attitudes about debt in general, attitudes about debt at the macro-level can be called indifferent. Respondents are not anxious about Russian national debt, and they are not worried about macro-economic borrowing aimed at economic growth stimulation. Findings of the study conducted 10 years ago (Deyneka et al., 2000) were the opposite: it was national rather than individual debt that caused respondents' disapproval and anxiety.

Banks are seen by respondents as organisations which, first, encourage in-advance consumption and only secondarily assists with savings. At the individual level, the traditionally negative attitude to debt was reflected in the high level of respondents' agreement with the statement that a decent man should always have at least some money for emergency situations. At the same time, respondents showed a high level of tolerance (affective component) to people using in-advance consumption proposals, for instance, the respondents do not disapprove those who use payday loans and microloans.

Comparative analysis of bank employees' and control group's responses (the groups were balanced by age and gender) showed that the former have a significantly higher need for stability at the macro-economic level ($p < 0.01$) than the latter. Bank employees more often prefer to invest in real estate and to take loans for conspicuous consumption ($p < 0.05$).

Age differentiation was found in the respondents' attitudes about the monetary policy of the country. The older the respondents, the more they needed stability, the less they trusted the banking sector and the more they were concerned about the amount of their savings.

An analysis of personality factors about debt attitudes showed that respondents with a higher level of subjective well-being and ambiguity tolerance showed more a positive attitude to debts. It might be interesting for psychologists who work in the banking area that, according to our results, people's trust of the banking sector is connected, first, to their level of ambiguity tolerance. Respondents with higher ambiguity tolerance are less afraid of investing money in securities and keeping it in Russian commercial banks.

Subjective well-being and ambiguity tolerance significantly correlated with some components of debt attitudes at the individual and family level and, to a much lesser degree, with attitudes to monetary policy. Respondents who are more satisfied with their life show a more positive attitude to debt in general; they are less inclined to agree that savings are necessary for well-being, and they feel less discomfort when they need to borrow money. They rely upon a social network (They say, 'I will take a loan only if I cannot borrow money from my friends'). They also lend money more eagerly, and they are more inclined to see it as an investment. People who are more satisfied with their life have a higher level of trust of certain economic institutions. They are less afraid of investing their money in securities, and they are less worried about a possibility of such macro-economic measures as excessive money emission.

8.5 Overall Results of the Fourth Study

The fourth study was carried out between 2013 and 2014. It was devoted to the least rational pattern of credit behaviour – borrowing from microfinance institutions (MFIs). MFIs in Russia, unlike those in the Western world, have their own specifics. They are not focused on serving the needs of small-scale business, but on offering small easily drawn-up short-term consumer loans at high interest rates. Not surprisingly, the names of these organisations reflect the motivation of MFI consumers, for example, 'Till your salary comes', 'Your money', 'Immediate money', 'Your stash'. From the legal point of view MFI clients aren't victims, but from the psychological view their status is absolutely unsatisfactory.

The study focused on personal characteristics of the microcredit organisation's borrower and aimed to investigate the debt attitudes of customers and employees of MFIs in connection with their personality qualities. The status of an MFI is determined by Federal Law No. 151-FZ of July 2, 2010, 'On Microfinance Activity and Microfinance Organisations'. MFI employees can use the service of their company as clients. However, they are offered credits at a significantly lower interest. The total number of samples included 68 people (39 employees and 29 clients, the average age of 27 years, 27% men).

The research was based on comparative and person-centred approaches. Research methods embraced two units of techniques. For studying debt behaviour, we employed the Attitude to Debt questionnaire developed by our algorithm (Deyneka, 2013) and the Microcredit Borrowing Motivators author questionnaire. The unit of person-centred research techniques included Money Attitude Scale (Furnham, 1984), adapted by Deyneka (1999), Life Orientation Test and Tolerance Ambiguity Scale.

The results given by the Microcredit Borrowing Motivators questionnaire identified three basic reasons for obtaining a credit: (1) satisfaction of everyday needs, money is borrowed until payday; (2) payment of another credit or debt (relending); and (3) payment of medical treatment or purchase of medicaments.

The factor analysis of the questionnaire data confirmed the previous results indicating that subjects of debt behaviour divide loans into 'good' and 'bad' ones (Deyneka, 2008).

The factor bearing the highest loading may be termed 'the factor of debt incurred to satisfy vital needs and the needs for safety'. It includes the motivators associated with the basic needs of a research participant. Failure to meet them exposes a client to the risk of getting into a problematic situation.

The second factor may be termed 'the factor of non-functional demand'. It comprises the needs related to entertainment, maintenance of relations and a person's image.

The comparative analysis of the data from the Attitude to Debt Questionnaire filled in by a group of MFI clients and a group of MFI employees enables the following conclusion: MFI clients suffer from *the debtor syndrome*, because they use all possible types of credits: bank credits, consumer loans and 'promised payments' offered by mobile service providers which, like MFIs, charge a large commission fee. The results testify to the high importance of money for the clients, especially as an indicator of social standing, and identify their reluctance or inability to accumulate money for the future; this, in turn, shows an undoubtedly low level of financial self-control and a disturbance of temporal perspective. Although MFI employees make use of their company's credit services, they are irregular debtors. Meanwhilst, the clients resort to absolutely all possible ways of borrowing and are pathological debtors.

The analysis of the data obtained using the Money Attitude Scale (MAS) significantly adds to the psychological portrait of an MFI borrower. MFI clients, less often than the control sample, associate a person's income with his abilities and efforts ($p < 0.01$); are worse at controlling the price of a purchase ($p < 0.05$); fail to timely pay their bills ($p < 0.01$) and, in their financial behaviour, are less guided by their parents' experience and attitude towards money ($p < 0.01$). Besides, MFI clients have a higher fetish about money and exhibit a stronger addiction to it.

The correlation between the data from the Attitude to Debt questionnaire and the data from MAS not only confirmed the external validity of 'attitude to debt', but also added extra details to the description of the debtor. For example, the people who often use the 'promised payment' service of mobile network providers turned out to buy unnecessary products at a discount price ($R = 0.39$, $p < 0.01$) or in order to produce an impression on other people ($R = 0.32$, $p < 0.05$); prefer money to pleasure ($R = 0.40$, $p < 0.01$); feel ill at ease if they do not spend this money at the end of the week ($R = 0.27$, $p < 0.05$); buy friendship by means of their generosity and use money for manipulation and intimidation ($p < 0.05$); feel better or worse than others, depending on how much money they have, thus being envious of or feeling superior to others ($p < 0.05$) and firmly believe that money can settle all their problems ($R = 0.39$, $p < 0.01$).

The research participants, who associate the income level with a person's abilities and efforts and report good financial standing, are under no conditions ready to borrow until payday. Indeed, the people having a respectful and responsible attitude to their financial position are convinced they can control their finances in a proper way. At the same time, those who got stuck in debt spend significantly more money in a state of depression (at $p < 0.05$), or out of envy for people more successful financially (at $p < 0.05$), due to an inferiority complex.

Thus, the use of a wasteful, but immediate credit service unambiguously testifies to a consumer's financial accentuations and deformations of his financial behaviour.

The comparative analysis of the data related to MFI clients and employees identified statistically reliable differences in their level of financial self-control and in their need for using money to increase their social status and prestige or make purchases in a state of depression. By comparison with the employees, the clients are characterised by a lower financial self-control, a higher inferiority complex and a stronger desire to relieve it.

The analysis of correlation between the data from the Attitude to Debt questionnaire and the data from person-centred express techniques (Life Orientation Test and Tolerance Ambiguity Scale) indicated that inadequate financial behaviour, oriented at financial debts and credits at high interests, is more often observed amongst persons with low tolerance to ambiguity, especially to novelty and insolubility of problems, and with an insufficient level of dispositional optimism.

MFI clients' intolerance to novelty correlates also with discontent over the credit terms of financial institutions. The fear of novelty and therefore a negative attitude to risk underlie unfavourable views on financial organisations that symbolise the danger and ambiguity of financial relations.

Intolerance to insolubility of problems, as part of the general intolerance to ambiguity, appeared to have a tight connection (at $p < 0.01$) with some money attitudes (MAS). These attitudes are related to (a) the feeling of guilt about spending money despite sufficient financial means, and to (b) the belief that money is the only thing to rely on. Refusing to face a state of insolubility aroused by a problem, a person starts to consider money a symbol of safety and power (or strength) and a tool for resolving any problem. This, in turn, results in a self-restrictive behaviour and a fear of losing money.

It is important to emphasise that intolerance to insolubility proved to be a very sensitive indicator of using credit to display one's high social standing ($R = 0.43$, $p < 0.001$).

A high level of dispositional optimism and of openness to changes negatively correlates ($R = -0.35$, $p < 0.01$) with the degree of agreement with MAS statement, assessing a pathological suffering from shortage of money and dissatisfaction with one's financial standing. Hence, the people who are more open to (or more ready for) changes are more confident in their ability to satisfy their material expectations and to implement their plans.

There is a strong negative correlation between intolerance to novelty, as part of the general intolerance to ambiguity, and a person's age. This is quite natural for our research sample where participants' ages varied from 20 to 30 years. The older a person, the more experience he gained and therefore lower was his intolerance to novelty.

This research meets the public demand against the background of negative trends in the credit financing sphere. Trying to caution MFIs against bankruptcy, analysts suggest using a selective approach to clients as one of the ways to help companies avoid unreturned debts. By evaluation of a borrower's psychological portrait and a careful examination of a borrower's income and demands, MFIs can conclude that a client will have difficulty returning money, especially if he relends it to pay to other creditors. For mutual benefit, it is reasonable to deny such borrowers any credits, despite their good credit histories ('The Decrease of Trust', 2013; 'The Increase in the Number of Microfinance', 2014; Polukhin, 2013; Sorokina, 2013).

Thus, this research allowed description of certain psychological characteristics of borrowers who resort to the service of MFIs. The research indicated that inadequate financial behaviour, oriented at money debts and credits at high interests, is usually displayed by persons with financial addictions and accentuations, low tolerance to ambiguity (particularly, to novelty and insolubility of problems) and insufficient level of dispositional optimism.

8.6 Conclusion

In conclusion, there are a number of practical measures aimed at humanisation of credit policies and assistance to victims of debtor's behaviour. For instance, it is reasonable to further implement relief programmes connected with concessional lending, as well as to improve the loan insurance system. These steps will enhance the living standards of Russians.

Some researchers suggest banning the lending services offered by Russian microfinance institutions (in the same way as casinos were prohibited), because they do not serve any useful purpose, except enrichment of their owners (Polukhin, 2013). The first step towards this measure has already been made. The State Duma adopted the bill 'On Consumer Loans' at the second reading. It prescribes that the maximum interest rate for a credit shall not exceed the market average by more than 30%. Deputies also suggest adding a direct regulation specifying the maximum possible interest rate for consumer loans, in order to curb excessive appetites of banks and microfinance institutions. Finally, politicians are discussing the use of credit amnesty. First, credit amnesty presupposes that citizens should be exempt from all their obligations to debt collectors, whilst debt collectors should be paid an indemnity in the amount equal to the clients' financial obligations. Second, effective agreements between clients and banks should be re-examined in such a way that the interest rate does not exceed the legal level. The author is convinced that bankers are very likely to benefit from these measures, because clients will pay adequate sums and therefore the number of payment delays and bad credit histories will fall.

For Russian society, it is sound to introduce self-help groups for over-indebted borrowers (de Graaf, Wann, & Naylor, 2001). It might also be possible to implement such innovations as mutual aid funds, cooperation movement and barter exchange practice (Katasonov, 2012). Researchers recommend the following methods of psychological help to debt addicts: cognitive behavioural therapy, stress management techniques, training of assertiveness (Furnham, 2014) and group work similar to alcoholics anonymous (Moss & Dyer, 2010; Plummer, 2014). Finally, it is vitally important to increase financial awareness, primarily by means of education and training, including university curricular.

Acknowledgement

The study was sponsored by the Russian Foundation for Humanities, grant 14-06-00719.

References

'The decrease of trust in credits among Russians'. (2013, September 23). *MFO Russia*. Retrieved from http://mforussia.ru/snizhenie-kreditnogo-doveriya-rossiyan (in Russian).

de Graff, J., Wann, D., & Naylor, T. H. (2001). *Affluenza: The all-consuming epidemic*. San Francisco: Berrett-Koehler.

Deyneka, O. S. (1999). *Economic psychology: Social and political issues*. St. Petersburg: St. Petersburg State University (in Russian).

Deyneka, O. S. (2008). A man in economy. In A. A. Krylov (Ed.), *Psychology textbook*. Moscow: Prospekt (in Russian).

Deyneka, O. S. (2011). *The representation of modern economic policy in common consciousness citizens of Russia and Germany*. The 12th European Congress of Psychology. Istanbul, July 4–8.

Deyneka, O. S. (2013). Multivariate questionnaire in the diagnosis of socio-economic consciousness. *Psychology Economy Right*, 2, 23–26 (in Russian).

Deyneka, O. S., Ivanova, S. P., & Kuzmenkova, L. V. (2000). The attitude to monetary debts at the macro- and micro-social level. *Proceedings of the Second All-Russian Conference 'Contemporary Issues of Economic Psychology and Ethics of Business Communication'*. St. Petersburg: SPbGUEiF (in Russian).

European debt crisis. (2012, July 30). *Wikipedia*. Retrieved from http://en.wikipedia.org/wiki/European_debt_crisis.

Furnham, A. 2014. *The new psychology of money*. London: Routledge.

Furnham, A., & Argyle, M. (2000). *The psychology of money*. London: Routledge.

'The increase in the number of microfinance institutions may lead to a high debt load among the population'. (2014, February 6). *MFO Russia*. Retrieved from http://mforussia.ru/rost-mikrofinansovyx-organizacij-mozhet-privesti-k-zakreditovannosti-naseleniya (in Russian).

Katasonov, V. J. (2012). Bank-killers and credit suicides. Retrieved from http://www.sovross.ru/modules.php?name=News&file=article&sid=591681 (in Russian).

Kramnik, V. V. (2003). The devil of greed versus morals: Who wins? *The Bulletin of Political Psychology*, 1(4), 31–34 (in Russian).

Krugman, P. (2009, March 1). Revenge of the glut. *New York Times*. Retrieved from http://www.nytimes.com/2009/03/02/opinion/02krugman.html?_r=2&.

Lewis, A. (Ed.). (2008). *The Cambridge handbook of psychology and economic behaviour*. Cambridge, UK: Cambridge University Press.

Moss, A. S., & Dyer, K. R. (2010). *Psychology of addictive behavior*. London: Palgrave Macmillan.

Plummer, D. (2014, July 7). Debt addiction: Red is not the new black. *CNBC.com*. Retrieved from http://www.cnbc.com/id/101816105.

Polukhin, A. (2013, December 23). Credit slavery. *Novaya Gazeta* [*New Newspaper*]. Retrieved from http://www.novayagazeta.ru/economy/61573.html (in Russian).

Sorokina, V. (2013, April 24). Credit slavery. *The Essence of Time*, no. 25. Retrieved from http://gazeta.eot.su/article/kreditnoe-rabstvo (in Russian).

Personality: Psychopathy and Risk Taking III

Problem Personalities in the Workplace
Development of the Corporate Personality Inventory

9

K. FRITZON
C. BAILEY
S. CROOM
N. BROOKS

Contents

9.1 Introduction

The notion that individuals with psychopathic personality characteristics exist in the corporate world is both a logical extension of the estimated community prevalence rates of the disorder, as well as a scientific hypothesis based on the observation that a number of the characteristics of the disorder could convey an advantage within this context (Crant & Bateman, 2000; Kets de Vries & Miller, 1985). However, very little literature has actually tested the validity of the hypothesis, despite the proliferation of the idea in media portrayals and semi-academic publications (Babiak & Hare, 2006; Boddy, 2011b; Dutton, 2012). Given that psychopathy in its criminal manifestation has been shown to predict aggression and violent behaviour, the assumption has been that in a business setting those individuals with the disorder will be responsible for fraud (Blickle, Schlegel, Fassbender, & Klein, 2006), workplace bullying (Caponecchia, Sun, & Wyatt, 2012) and poor management (Babiak, Neumann, & Hare, 2010). Smith and Lilienfeld (2013) have, though, recently posited a 'double-edged sword' hypothesis, citing examples from studies that have shown positive characteristics including being a strategic thinker, being creative or innovative and successful leadership (Babiak et al., 2010; Lilienfeld, Waldman, Landfield, Watts, Rubenzer, & Faschingbauer, 2012). The present study seeks to further clarify the distinction between positive and negative manifestations of psychopathic personality characteristics in a corporate sample. The aims of the study include the development of an assessment tool to measure psychopathic personality traits in a business setting, as well as the elucidation of how these characteristics correlate with other validated measures relevant to psychopathy assessment.

Psychopathy is a pervasive psychological disorder that impacts interpersonal relationships and life domains such as employment, education and family (Kiehl & Hoffman, 2011). Despite cultural variations, documentation of individuals possessing psychopathic characteristics is far reaching and suggests universality of the construct (Kiehl, 2011). An interactive model suggests that the phenotypic interplay between biological disposition and environmental factors may best explain the disorder, and this may assist in explaining how different expressions of the disorder can result in differing subtypes, for example, criminal and non-criminal (Kiehl, 2011). The manifestation of psychopathy may be dependent on an individual's environmental circumstance (Kubak & Salekin, 2009), and involve mediating variables such as education and socio-economic advantages. This explanation for non-criminal psychopathy is known as the *compensatory process* perspective and assumes that the anti-social behaviour of criminal psychopaths is not part of the defining features of the disorder, but rather a consequence of it (Cooke, Michie, Hart, & Clark, 2004). This explanation resonates with the fearlessness hypothesis of psychopathy (Lykken, 1957, 1995) in which individuals with this temperament are resistant to socialisation and thus are likely to become anti-social. On the other hand, good parenting, high intelligence or greater economic opportunities can channel the fearless psychopathic individuals into socially sanctioned pursuits, including business, politics and athletics.

The triarchic model of psychopathy (Patrick, Fowles, & Krueger, 2009) also provides further clarification of the difference between psychopathy and anti-social personality disorder, emphasising the dimension of boldness as being a key defining characteristic of the former and absent in the latter (Ogloff, 2006; Venables et al., 2014). In addition to the construct of boldness, the triarchic model emphasises the traits of disinhibition and meanness. Disinhibition is characterised by impulse control problems, a lack of planfulness or foresight, immediate gratification and poor behavioural restraint (Patrick et al., 2009; Skeem et al., 2011). The trait of boldness concerns the capacity to remain calm and focused in pressured situations, the ability to recover from stressful events and a tolerance for unfamiliarity and danger (Patrick et al., 2009; Skeem et al., 2011). Meanness pertains to attributes including deficient empathy, a lack of close attachments with others, excitement seeking, rebelliousness, empowerment and exploitativeness (Patrick et al., 2009; Skeem et al., 2011).

The triarchic model is consistent with many of the leading theories and assessment measure of psychopathy, including Cleckley (1941), Karpman (1941), Hare (2003) and Lilienfeld (Lilienfeld & Widows, 2005). A strength of the model is that it provides a phenotypical account of psychopathy, allowing a diverse operationalisation of the construct across different samples, contexts and practical application. The advantage of an overarching conceptualisation, rather than a construct that is defined by a sole measure, is that it allows for a series of theoretical positions and assessment instruments to exist and demonstrate psychometric efficacy at various point in time (Skeem et al., 2011).

Although the majority of theory and research on psychopathy emphasises its criminal/anti-social manifestations, a number of possible explanatory models for non-criminal psychopathy have been posited (Hall & Benning, 2006). One of these is known as the *dual process* perspective, in which the interpersonal-affective components of psychopathy are etiologically distinct from the anti-social behaviour component, thus individuals could present with high levels of interpersonal-affective traits, and low or normal levels of anti-social behaviour. This perspective is compatible with the two-factor model of psychopathy (Harpur, Hare, & Hakstian, 1989), as well as the proposed etiological mechanisms of primary and secondary psychopathy (Kubak & Salekin, 2009).

The major global economic downfall of the late 2000s saw a detrimental shift in the financial and economic standings of various leading countries and multinational companies and corporations around the world (Boddy, 2011b). This saw a movement of researchers attempting to understand the leadership decisions, the moral climate of organisations and the high rates of staff turnover leading to depersonalisation of companies (Boddy, 2011b).

The focus of recent empirical attention has been largely geared towards development of assessment strategies for psychopathy in the corporate business context (Smith & Lilienfeld, 2013). The B-Scan 360 (Babiak & Hare, 2012) is based on Hare's (2003) four-factor model of psychopathy and comprises both self- and observer-report versions. No data have been reported for the self-report scale, but the observer-report version consists of 20 items and four factors: Manipulative/Unethical, Callous/Insensitive, Unreliable/Unfocused and Intimidating/Aggressive (Mathieu, Hare, Jones, Babiak, & Neumann, 2014). There are currently no convergent, divergent or criterion validity reported for this scale (Smith & Lilienfeld, 2013). In addition to this measure, Smith and Lilienfeld (2013) have reviewed a number of other possible assessment tools, including the Levenson Self-Report Psychopathy Scale (Levenson, Kiehl, & Fitzpatrick, 1995), and the Self-Report Psychopathy Scale-III (Paulhus, Neumann, & Hare, in press) that may be appropriate for use with a corporate sample. However the only measures that have actually been used with corporate samples have been the two Hare measures (PCL-R and B-Scan).

It is clear that the positive aspects of psychopathy may lend themselves to the appearance of strong leadership qualities, including charisma, confidence, passion and vision. However, individuals with psychopathic personalities also possess underlying dysfunctional characteristics that ultimately may precipitate their involvement in behaviour that is abusive, coercive, self-interested, unethical and manipulative (Babiak & Hare, 2006; Boddy, 2005, 2011b; Smith & Lilienfeld, 2013; Stevens, Deuling, & Armenakis, 2012). Unfortunately the identification of psychopathic leaders may not be a priority for organisations where the focus is on positive outputs including growth or financial increases (Babiak & Hare, 2006; Boddy, Ladyshewsky, & Galvin, 2010).

It is important to understand the balance between the potential detrimental influences as well as possible positive consequences of psychopathic individuals in organisations, as their influence can be pervasive (Henning et al., 2014; Smith & Lilienfeld, 2013). The presence of individuals with psychopathic personalities in the workplace also leaves non-psychopathic individuals potentially susceptible to manipulation without objectively recognising when it is occurring (Babiak et al., 2010; Henning, Wygant, & Barnes, 2014). Thus, it is important that we do not underestimate the impact of psychopathic individuals within a business context, and there is a need for effective identification and management. The current study aims to contribute to this emerging research area. A dearth of literature on non-criminal psychopaths currently exists, and, specifically, a distinct gap in the assessment of non-criminal psychopathy is evident. Thus, development of an assessment tool will assist in making further meaningful contributions to the literature, as it may assist in the detection of these individuals within corporate contexts.

9.2 Aim

The aim of the current study is to develop a self-report assessment inventory to effectively measure non-criminal psychopathy to aid in the detection of psychopathic personality traits in individuals within purchasing and supply professionals. This sample was targeted due to the nature of the occupational area, which involves significant responsibility and autonomy over corporate resources (typically purchasing expenditure accounts for more than 50% of the total costs of an organisation). It is anticipated that this will also assist in developing a greater understanding of this unique population, such that it may further inform our understanding of how to appropriately identify and manage individuals with psychopathic personality traits in business contexts. A key part of the scale development involves testing its construct, divergent and convergent validity, as well as reliability of the subscales identified through factor analysis. This will involve examining the bivariate correlations between the factors and subscales of the Psychopathic Personality Inventory–Revised (PPI-R) and Corporate Personality Inventory (CPI), as well as the Paulhus Deception Scale.

It is hypothesised that the CPI measure will obtain a factor structure similar to the triarchic model of psychopathy encompassing meanness, boldness and disinhibition.

It is hypothesised that the CPI will correlate highly with the PPI, such that individuals above the cut-off score for psychopathic personality on the PPI-R will also be detected on the CPI.

It is further hypothesised that impression management will form a core component of the factor structure of the CPI, given the need for individuals possessing psychopathic traits to adapt the more negative and emphasise the more positive qualities of their personalities. This is therefore hypothesised to be a unique point of differentiation for this population as compared to other groups of psychopathic individuals who have been shown not to engage in impression management (e.g. Verscheure et al., 2014).

9.3 Method

9.3.1 Participants

The initial survey sample comprised 325 participants recruited from a supply chain professional organisation via an e-mail list provided by the organisation. E-mails were sent to the full database of 1700 members, inviting them to complete the survey online via a link to the PsychData survey hosting website. Sixty-four participants were excluded on the basis of excessive missing data on the Psychopathic Personality Inventory. The final data set consisted of 261 participants. Participants consisted of 100 females (M_{age} = 46.97 years, SD = 10.03) and 161 males (M_{age} = 48.53 years, SD = 9.71). The overall mean age of the sample was 47.93 years (SD = 9.84) and overall age ranged from 27 to 75 years. The majority of the sample was married (n = 194; 74.3%), 26 (9.6%) were either divorced or separated and 32 (12.2%) were single. In terms of ethnicity, some interesting differences with respect to the Babiak, Neumann, and Hare (2010) study emerged. In the present study, 170 (65.1%) of the participants reported their ethnicity to be Caucasian, 47 (18%) were Asian and 18 (6.8%) were African-American. Seventeen (6.5%) reported their ethnicity as Hispanic or Mexican. The figures in the Babiak et al. study were 91.1% for Caucasian, 2.5% Asian, 1% African-American and 2.5% Hispanic.

The participants were highly educated with 37.5% possessing a bachelor's degree, 44.1% a master's and 3.8% a PhD qualification. Finally, participants were asked to report on their maximum budget for pricing negotiations, and these were as follows (all in U.S. dollars): <$1 million (8.4%); $1–$10 million (20.7%), $11–$50 million (14.2%), $51–$100 million (9.2%), $101–$999 million (16.5%) and $1 billion to unlimited (4.9%). The mode value was $50 million.

9.4 Measures

9.4.1 Participant Demographics

Questions included participants' gender, relationship status, highest educational qualification and ethnicity. Participants were asked to indicate (a) length in current role, (b) involvement in negotiating purchasing parameters, (c) maximum budget for purchasing negotiations and (d) management of staff as variables for examining criterion validity.

9.4.2 Paulhus Deception Scales: Balanced Inventory of Desirable Responding

The Paulhus Deception Scales (PDS; Paulhus, 1999) is a 40-item self report inventory designed to assess two forms of socially desirable responding, that being self deception and impression management. Use of this inventory enabled researchers to gauge the extent to which socially desirable responding had impacted the study. It was also utilised in the analyses to determine convergent validity with the social desirability items of the CPI. The inventory contains two scales: Impression Management and Self Deceptive Enhancement. Participants were instructed to indicate the degree to which each statement applies to them, including 'I sometimes tell lies if I have to' and 'I have never dropped litter on the street' on a 5-point Likert scale, ranging from 5 (*very true*) to 1 (*not true*). The inventory is scored at the extreme ranges of responding, such that only endorsed items 1 and 5 contributed to the overall score, with endorsed items 2, 3 and 4 not contributing to the overall score. The inventory demonstrates acceptable internal consistency, with Cronbach's alpha $\alpha = 0.85$ (Paulhus, 1999). For scoring purposes, raw scores are converted into *T*-scores. Raw scores range from 0 to 40, with higher scores indicating a higher likelihood of socially desirable responding. *T*-Scores ranging from 28 to 90, with scores above 70 and below 30 being concerning (Paulhus, 1999).

9.4.3 Psychopathy Personality Inventory–Revised

The Psychopathic Personality Inventory–Revised (PPI-R; Lilienfeld & Widows, 2005) is a 154-item self-report measure that assesses psychopathy and its component psychopathic traits. Use of the inventory enabled researchers to identify levels of psychopathic personality traits amongst the sample. The inventory can be utilised in both community and forensic settings for clinical and non-clinical purposes. Scores from the inventory comprise two scales: content and validity scales. The content scale consists of eight subscales: Machiavellian Egocentricity, Blame Externalisation, Carefree Nonplanfulness, Stress Immunity, Rebellious Non-Conformity, Social Influence, Cold-Heartedness and Fearlessness. The validity scales are Virtuous Responding, Deviant Responding and Inconsistent Responding. Participants were required to respond to items such as 'People are impressed with me after they first meet me' and 'When my life gets boring, I like to take chances' on a 4-point Likert scale of *false, mostly false, mostly true* and *true*. The inventory demonstrates adequate psychometric properties, demonstrating internal consistency ranging from $\alpha = 0.78$ to .092 (Lilienfeld & Widows, 2005). The measure also demonstrates convergent validity, as evidenced by significant correlations with other measures of psychopathy. Test-retest reliability is also high, ranging from $\alpha = 0.82$ to 0.93 over a 19-day retest period (Lilienfeld & Widows, 2005).

9.4.4 Corporate Personality Inventory

The Corporate Personality Inventory (Fritzon, Croom, Brooks, & Bailey, 2013) is a self-report measure designed to assess the presence of distinct personality traits in individuals employed in a corporate workplace environment. The measure was designed for the purposes of the present study due to the lack of an appropriate tool for assessing presence of psychopathic and other potentially problematic and dysfunctional personality traits within a business context. The development of the CPI was based on an exploratory approach to test construction. Items were generated by an expert panel ($n = 4$) comprised of academics with research and professional experience in business management and forensic psychology, specifically in psychopathic and other personality disordered offenders. An initial item pool of 120 items was drawn from the core personality descriptors of psychopathy as written into statements that would reflect the business environment, and a number of these items ($n = 47$) also reflected potentially positive constructions or manifestations of psychopathic personality traits in a business context (e.g. 'I am not afraid to make bold business decisions'; 'I am a talented communicator'), some of which also reflected the concepts of fearlessness and social influence as central features of the psychopathic personality. Finally, some items were drawn from previous research that found an association between high-functioning business executives and other personality disorder constructs, including histrionic and narcissistic personality types (Board & Fritzon, 2005). A list of original scale items can be found in the Appendix. Participants were instructed to respond to statements on a 4-point Likert scale: *true, mostly true, mostly false* and *false*.

9.5 Results

9.5.1 Descriptive Statistics

Correlations were performed on all continuous variables to examine the bivariate relationship between predictor variables. Table 9.1 presents the

Table 9.1 Summary of Means and Standard Deviations for Age, Psychopathic Personality Inventory-Revised (PPI-R), Paulhaus Deception Scale (PDS) and Corporate Personality Inventory (CPI) According to Gender

	M	*SD*
PPI-R	298.40	22.62
Male	297.72	21.88
Female	299.47	23.81
CPI	337.30	23.54
Male	336.10	24.76
Female	339.24	21.44
PDS	15.15	6.47
Male	15.07	6.53
Female	15.25	6.39
Age	47.93	9.85
Male	48.53	9.71
Female	46.97	10.03

Note: Means and standard deviations for age are presented in years. $N = 259$. PPI-R, ($N = 261$), PDS, ($N = 179$), CPI, ($N = 191$).

means and standard deviations for each measure and age according to gender. For the PPI-R, Lilienfeld and Widows (2005) suggest that offender samples obtain a mean of 283.86, $SD = 28.99$, which is well below the mean for both males and females within this sample. Additionally, for a community sample, expected mean scores for males with an average age similar to that of the current sample being $M = 284.29$, $SD = 33.07$ and for females being $M = 256.05$, $SD = 25.89$. This indicates that the current sample obtained a higher mean score than would be expected in an offending and community samples for both males and females. An alternative way of measuring the levels of psychopathic personality traits in the current sample was computed using 65T as a clinical cut-off score as per the PPI-R manual (Lilienfeld & Widows, 2005). This resulted in 55 (21%) individuals whose scores were within the clinically significant range. For the PDS, Paulhus (1998) suggests that normative data for the general population is $M = 8.9$, $SD = 3.7$. The current sample mean of 15.14, $SD = 6.5$ is thus very high.

9.5.2 Factor Structure of the Corporate Personality Inventory

Exploratory factor analysis was utilised as a means of selecting items for the constructs of interest and clarifying and modifying the constructs upon completion of data collection. The initial questionnaire consisted of 134 questions and the data from 191 participants initially violated the assumption of sampling adequacy, with a Kaiser-Meyer-Olkin (KMO) value of .45. Thus a series of Pearson correlations were run in order to eliminate items that did not correlate sufficiently. This resulted in a reduced item set of 61, giving an adequate KMO value of .68, and Bartlett's test of sphericity χ^2 (191) = 18239.14, $p < .001$, indicating that correlations between items were sufficiently large for principle components analysis. An initial analysis was run to obtain the eigenvalues for each component in the data. The scree plot was examined and showed an inflection at the fourth component. Due to the convergence of the scree plot and Kaiser's criterion on four components, this is the number of components that were retained in the final analyses. The final four-factor solution accounted for 23.14% of the variance. Table 9.2 presents the results of principle axis factoring on an orthogonal rotation (varimax) of the solution after rotation. Loading less than .4 were suppressed and excluded. Each question only loaded onto one factor. As presented in Table 9.2, Factor 1 (Boldness) had 23 variables that loaded onto that factor and accounted for approximately 8.7% of the variance. All items that loaded onto Factor 1 (Boldness) are conceptually similar and relate directly to being bold and making risky decisions. Factor 2 (Impression Management) consists of 18 items conceptually related to positive impression management and accounted for 7.1% of the variance. The 9 items that

Table 9.2   Principle Axis Factoring of Orthogonal Factor Rotation

	Factor			
	1	2	3	4
	Boldness	Impression Management	Interpersonal Dominance	Ruthless
I am willing to take risks and embark on difficult courses of action.	.678			
I would be good in a high stake or pressured situation as I make fast decisions.	.657			
I can handle being the centre of attention.	.631			
A fast paced workplace environment excites me.	.622			
I find it difficult to talk others into seeing my side or point of view.[a]	−.565			
I am able to remain calm in the face of danger.	.531			
I like being where the action is happening.	.521			
I am able to adapt to any situation or interaction.	.496			
Taking on multiple tasks at once is exciting.	.487			
I am able to adapt and change quickly to any task, job or requirement.	.487			
I am able to move on quickly from negative consequences.	.484			
When it is really matters, I can talk most people into anything.	.478			
I am quick-witted.	.471			
I am adept at noticing weakness in others.	.464			
Taking a risk for a big payoff would make me very nervous.[a]	−.463			
Being different and standing out from others has its benefits.	.462			

(Continued)

Table 9.2 (Continued)   Principle Axis Factoring of Orthogonal Factor Rotation

	Factor			
	1	2	3	4
	Boldness	Impression Management	Interpersonal Dominance	Ruthless
I am able to persuade people to see what matters.	.458			
I rarely get nervous in the workplace.	.430			
Once I have made a decision I do not doubt myself.	.427			
I am a talented communicator.	.423			
I possess the ability to read people at face value.	.420			
I am embarrassed easily.[a]	−.408			
I do not let negative events get on my nerves.	.401			
I have never eavesdropped on a conversation between other people.		.780		
I have never talked about someone behind their back.		.768		
I have never been tempted to tell someone off.		.699		
I never get upset when things do not go my own way.		.696		
I have never been disrespectful to another person that I dislike.		.681		
I never done something that I am ashamed off.		.674		
I have never been annoyed by another person.		.660		
I have never resented the success of another.		.643		
I have never tuned out to a conversation in which I have been involved.		.630		
I have never lost my temper at someone.		.609		
I am yet to meet someone in the workplace who I dislike.[a]		−.608		
I have never deliberately said anything offensive.		.596		

(*Continued*)

Table 9.2 (Continued)   Principle Axis Factoring of Orthogonal Factor Rotation

	Factor			
	1	2	3	4
	Boldness	Impression Management	Interpersonal Dominance	Ruthless
I've never been tempted to read someone else's printed papers that they have left in the print room/photocopy room by mistake.		.534		
I have never wished misfortune on another individual.		.522		
I never check my personal email when I'm at work.		.519		
I have never laughed at a joke I did not find funny.		.510		
I have never been late to an appointment in my life.		.509		
I've never used company resources, e.g. stationary, printers for my personal use.		.467		
People fail to accept when they have made a mistake.			.464	
I need new and exciting things in my life.			.456	
Although I value responsibility, it is often hard to say the same for others in the workplace.			.454	
I am careful to select my inner circle of supporters at work.			.454	
It is difficult for people to hear the truth.			.449	
It is not uncommon for others to try and show each other up at work.			.428	
Conflict amongst colleagues is inevitable.			.416	
Most people give up easily when facing a difficult task.			.412	
People can treat the workplace like a battlefield at times.			.403	

(Continued)

Table 9.2 (Continued) Principle Axis Factoring of Orthogonal Factor Rotation

	Factor			
	1	2	3	4
	Boldness	Impression Management	Interpersonal Dominance	Ruthless
It is acceptable to gain from other peoples weaknesses/ mistakes.				.602
I believe I am more important than other people in the workplace.				.544
Success at a cost to others can be justifiable.				.537
Lying and deceit are integral to successful business.				.480
Keeping appointments, even in busy times is important.				−.458
In some situations, honesty is not necessary.				.442
It makes me uncomfortable when colleagues are humiliated and intimidated by others.				.440
I wouldn't feel guilty making an employee cry if they made me look bad.				.429
When people make mistakes, they deserve a chance to rectify the situation.[a]				−.422
Thinking about consequences is always a factor in my decision making.				−.405
All staff members, regardless of authority/status meaningfully contribute to the company.				−.403
Eigenvalues	12.659	10.279	8.428	5.039
Percentage of total variance accounted for	8.7%	7.1%	5.8%	3.5%
Number of test measures	23	18	9	11
Cronbach's alpha (α)	.88	.92	.73	.76

Note: $N = 191$.

[a] Denotes reversed scored items.

load onto Factor 3 (Interpersonal Dominance) relate conceptually to disregard for social convention and impulsivity and accounts for 5.8% of the total variance. Factor 4 (Ruthless) consists of 11 items that are conceptually related to self-centredness and spitefulness and accounts for 3.5% of the variance.

Inter-item consistency was adequate to high for all scales, with Cronbach's alpha scores of $\alpha = .88$ for the Boldness scale, $\alpha = .92$ for Impression Management, $\alpha = .73$ for Interpersonal Dominance and $\alpha = .76$ Ruthless.

9.5.3 Discriminant and Concurrent Validity

The CPI was significantly correlated with the PDS ($r = .361$, $p < .001$), negatively correlated with age ($r = -.160$, $p < .05$) and relationship status ($r = -.194$, $p < .001$). The PPI-R was significantly correlated with the CPI ($r = .231$, $p < .001$), and negatively correlated with the PDS ($r = -.275$, $p < .001$) and age ($r = -.268$, $p < .001$).

Bivariate correlations between factors of the CPI and PPI can be found in Table 9.3. Factor 1 (Boldness) of the CPI was significantly negatively correlated with the Cold-Heartedness factor on the PPI-R ($r = -.189$, $p < .001$). As expected, Factor 2 (Impression Management) on the CPI was not significantly correlated with any of the Factors on the PPI-R, but was significantly correlated with the Impression Management subscale of the PDS ($r = .491$, $p < .001$). Factor 3 (Interpersonal Dominance) and Factor 4 (Ruthless) of the CPI were significantly positively correlated with all factors of the PPI-R, and negatively correlated with all factors of the PDS (Table 9.3).

9.5.4 Criterion Validity

The final analysis tested the external (criterion) validity of the CPI by examining the correlations between the subscales of the CPI and the purchasing parameters reported by individuals. For this analysis, the independent variable was created from the seven categories of purchasing limits (see descriptive section), and the CPI total score was the dependent variable. A one-way analysis of variance revealed that the differences in mean CPI scores for each of the seven groups was approaching significance, $F(6, 130) = 1.988$, $p = .072$. The box plot results are shown in Figure 9.1. These results indicate a curvilinear relationship between CPI score and pricing limits, such that as pricing limits increase towards approximately $50 million–$100 million, so does CPI total score increase. However, CPI score then decreases as pricing limit reaches the $1 billion.

Table 9.3 Summary of Intercorrelations Between Factor Structure of Corporate Personality Inventory (CPI) and Psychopathic Personality Inventory (PPI-R)

Variable	PPI-R; Self-Centred Impulsivity	PPI-R; Fearless Dominance	PPI-R; Cold-Heartedness	PDS Total	PDS; Impression Management	PDS; Self-Deceptive Enhancement
1. CPI (Boldness)	.097	.106	-.189**	.433**	.137	.568**
2. CPI (Impression Management)	.037	-.031	-.063	.322**	.491**	.039
3. CPI (Interpersonal Dominance)	.344**	.329**	.241**	-.213*	-.265**	-.085
4. CPI (Ruthless)	.419**	.304**	.294**	-.149*	-.260**	.014

*p .05, **$p < .01$. PPI-R ($N = 261$), PDS ($N = 179$), CPI ($N = 191$).

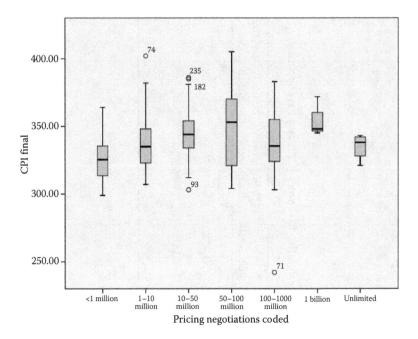

Figure 9.1 Box plot distribution of scores for Corporate Personality Inventory and purchasing limits.

9.6 Discussion

The aim of the current study was to develop a self-report assessment inventory to effectively measure non-criminal psychopathy to aid in the detection of psychopathic personality traits in individuals within business contexts. A key part of the scale development involved testing it's construct, divergent and convergent validity, as well as the reliability of the subscales identified through factor analysis. This involved examining the bivariate correlations between the factors and subscales of the Psychopathic Personality Inventory–Revised (PPI-R) and Corporate Personality Inventory (CPI), as well as the Paulhus Deception Scale (PDS).

It was anticipated that the CPI would obtain a factor structure similar to the triarchic model of psychopathy encompassing aspects of meanness, boldness and disinhibition. This was supported, as the CPI yielded a distinct four-factor model encompassing aspects of Boldness, Impression Management, Interpersonal Dominance and Ruthless. It is clear that although the factor analysis accounted for a modest amount of variance in the data, the CPI encompasses a similar factor structure to that which was previously identified within the literature, and may also capture further elements of non-criminal psychopathy, which may add to our theoretical understanding of this population. Furthermore, it was anticipated that the CPI would correlate highly with the PPI-R and this was ascertained by examining bivariate correlations between the total scores for each measure and also between factors of each measure. Significant correlations between Factor 3 (Interpersonal Dominance) and Factor 4 (Ruthless) on the CPI and all three factors of the PPI-R (Self-Centred Impulsivity, Fearless Dominance and Cold-Heartedness) were obtained.

A number of preliminary differences have been identified within the current analyses that could hold key information regarding the point of differentiation between the two subtypes (criminal and non-criminal) of psychopathy. It may also be possible that the CPI captures information about other dysfunctional personality characteristics in addition to psychopathic personality traits, for example, elements of the so-called *dark triad*, comprising Narcissism, Machiavellianism and Psychopathy. The key outcomes of this study provide a clear rationale for further investigation into this emerging area of research and encourage further refinement and validation of the CPI measure.

Within the regression analyses, the PDS was significantly positively predictive of psychopathic personality traits, as measured by the CPI. However, interestingly, a negative correlation exists between the PDS and the PPI-R. A study by Verschuere et al. (2014) found an inverse relationship between psychopathy and impression management based on the assumption that psychopaths have a disregard for social convention. This suggests that the current sample engaged in impression management and may provide evidence to support the idea that impression management may be a central part of the defining criteria for corporate psychopathy. Similar to this finding, a study by Vitale, Macoon, and Newman (2011) indicated that psychopathic participants showed activation of the emotional brain structures similar to that of non-psychopathic participants when instructed to engage in an emotional processing task. These findings are contrary to our traditional neurological understanding of psychopathy and may indicate that corporate psychopaths have the ability to imitate emotion at will, and this may be a distinguishing feature that differentiates corporate from criminal psychopaths (Kiehl & Hoffman, 2011; Kosson, Suchy, Mayer, & Libby, 2002; Vitale, Maccoon, & Newman, 2011). This suggestion may also explain the negative correlation between the Cold-Heartedness subscale of the PPI-R and Factor 2 (Impression Management) of the CPI.

Lilienfeld and Widows (2005) suggest that according to the normative community-based sample, males should score significantly higher on the PPI-R than females; however in the current sample, males and females obtained similar scores on the PPI-R. The authors also suggest younger individuals obtain higher scores on the PPI-R than their older counterparts, and this is consistent with the sample in the current study (Lilienfeld & Widows, 2005). These findings in relation to gender also raise an intriguing possibility in relation to the suggestion made previously, being that traditionally, females are generally conceived as possessing emotional qualities that enable them to form close social relationships more so than males (Carducci, 2009). It may be evident that females with psychopathic personality features have a distinct advantage over males in the corporate environment due to a suggested ability to channel their psychopathic personality characteristics more effectively in order to achieve success in the corporate environment. Further research would be needed in order to investigate this hypothesis.

9.7 Limitations and Future Directions

A major consideration for the current study was the high levels of attrition evident within the data set. This contributed to difficultly in data cleaning procedures and impacted upon the quality and quantity of data collected. When eyeballing the data set, it was clear that attrition affected the data set considerably, with measures early in the collection sequence obtaining a higher N than measures later in the data set. This was confirmed with missing patterns analysis conducted on the statistical software SPSS. To rectify this issue on future data collection of the CPI, it is recommended that this measure be entered first in the collection sequence, instead of last, to ensure that this measure is not as much affected by attrition as the other measures in the data set. The issue of attrition also had considerable effects on the requirements for adequate sampling size of the measure required for factor analysis. Although Cronbach's alpha for each factor reached acceptable levels, the KMO value for the total scale without deleting items was well below the recommended acceptable limit (Field, 2009), whereas including the full item set may have improved the total variance accounted for by the factor solution. Thus, for further validation of this measure, it is important for further studies to be conducted with a larger sample size, particularly so all assumptions of the factor analysis are met.

Given the infancy of this research area, it will be important to conduct future research in a variety of areas to increase our understanding of this unique population. Currently, there is a paucity of research within psychological literature surrounding the detection, assessment and management of individuals with psychopathic personality traits in a corporate context (Babiak et al., 2010). The construct of psychopathy generally attracts negative connotations related to the pathologic nature of the disorder (Boddy, 2011a; Smith & Lilienfeld, 2013). It is, however, important to consider that there may be some positive and adaptive qualities that psychopaths possess that can be highly advantageous in a corporate setting (Babiak et al., 2010). These adaptive qualities include a disinclination towards suicide as well as being creative, decisive, confident, strategic and skillful communicators who often possess strong personal presentation skills (Babiak et al., 2010; Cleckley, 1941; Smith & Lilienfeld, 2013). It is important for future research to focus on advancing our understanding of these individuals and gain insight into the strengths and weaknesses they possess in order to unlock their potential to contribute meaningfully to the business environment in the context of their disorder (Smith & Lilienfeld, 2013). Currently, we have a preliminary understanding of the impact corporate psychopaths have on the workplace environment. Thus, it is important for further research to examine and understand the specific impact of individuals with psychopathic personality traits on the business environment in order to highlight the potent influence of these individuals in business contexts, distinguishing between the distinct social, financial and economic impacts (Boddy, 2014). Longitudinal research would be advantageous in capturing an in-depth understanding of certain aspects of the workplace environment in the presence of these individuals.

In highly competitive corporate environments, psychopathic individuals may be viewed as a competitive advantage for organisations whose leaders propel the business in a creative and innovative direction, whilst not appreciating their destructive potential (Smith & Lilienfeld, 2013). It is likely that conducting further research on specific impacts of psychopaths on the business environment will grab the attention of businesses and will motivate them to actively cooperate and allow access to this unique population. It is highly important to communicate to businesses that psychopathy in the workplace is a highly important and beneficial research area (Boddy, 2006, 2014). It is also likely that some businesses may be hesitant to cooperate with researchers for fear of scrutiny. A major obstacle to future research is obtaining access to quality samples of psychopaths in corporate environments and reframing research as a possibility for growth rather than being primarily punitive in nature. Limited access to corporate samples is currently slowing the potential for quality research to be conducted with this population (Babiak et al., 2010). Thus, is it hoped that increased attention in this area will allow for more rigorous investigation of psychopaths in the corporate world. Furthermore, another avenue for future research could also focus on the development of measures that do not reply solely on self-report data for the detection of these individuals in corporate settings, rather than completed by other workplace colleagues to increase objectivity of the data and reduce socially desirable responding. It would be ideal if a correlation between self-report and other report data could be combined to produce an accurate depiction of psychopathy in the business environment.

Currently, it appears that although non-criminal psychopaths possess similar affective and behavioural characteristics to criminal psychopaths, there are a number of key areas of difference. As further research emerges in this field, it may be necessary to challenge and reorient our traditional understanding of psychopathy to keep up with modern advances in our understanding of the disorder (Smith & Lilienfeld, 2013). Further development of the Corporate Personality Inventory is crucial. The current study is preliminary and exploratory in nature, however, it has been conducted in response to a paucity of research in this emerging field. Further empirical and statistical validation of the Corporate Personality Inventory is highly important. Specifically, further data collection for this measure and conducting confirmatory factor analyses will be a key area for future research. The addition of a social desirability factor contributes a unique element to the measure, being that it captures a distinct component that indicates whether an individual's responses are biased in a socially desirable manner. Thus, further investigation into the utility of this factor within the Corporate Personality Inventory is warranted, particularly to further understand the direction of its contribution to corporate psychopathy. Additionally, examination of the presence of subscales within each factor of the Corporate Personality Inventory will be important as it may provide further explanatory power to the measure and provide further insight into what constructs the measure captures. It is anticipated that the Corporate Personality Inventory may fill a distinct void in the recruitment and vetting processes associated with the employment of such individuals. It may be advantageous for corporations to include assessment tools, such as the Corporate Personality Inventory, into standardised recruitment procedures to screen for individuals with disordered personalities, particularly psychopathic personality traits. With further research, it is anticipated that not only detection of these individuals will be possible, but also provision of intervention and management may be possible to manage these individuals in corporate settings.

Examination of the literature has identified inconsistency in the terminology used in this emerging research area. Thus, further revision of the definition for psychopathy in an organisational context is required, particularly given the distinction between the two subtypes: criminal and non-criminal. Current definitions and terminology demonstrate inconsistency within the literature and may increase confusion. Another aspect to consider is that it may be possible that non-criminal psychopaths, found in corporate organisational contexts, may conduct themselves in ways that are unethical, immoral and ultimately illegal, and may find themselves involved in the criminal justice system as a result of their conduct, often referred to as white-collar crime (Smith & Lilienfeld, 2013). The question would then be: Are these individuals classified as criminal or non-criminal psychopaths? Further revision and refinement of the definition and terminology surrounding corporate psychopathy must be considered to ensure consistency across the literature.

Possible implications for the results of the study lie within the potential to generalise results from the current sample to help inform detection, assessment and management of psychopathic individuals in corporate contexts. Particularly, an overarching aim of the current research is to assist corporations to effectively identify, manage and understand psychopathic individuals within a corporate context. Overall, the current study provides support for the presence of psychopathy in corporate contexts and provides preliminary support for the development of the Corporate Personality Inventory. On the basis of further research, replication extension, and further validation of these results and the Corporate Personality Inventory may provide both practical utility within recruitment and vetting procedures within a corporate business context. If replicated and extended based on the aforementioned recommendations, the contribution of the Corporate Personality Inventory to the research area of psychopathy could be substantial.

References

Babiak, P., & Hare, R. D. (2006). *Snakes in suits: When psychopaths go to work*. New York: Harper Collins.

Babiak, P., & Hare, R. D. (2012). *The B-Scan 360 Manual*. Manuscript in preparation.

Babiak, P., Neumann, C. S., & Hare, R. D. (2010). Corporate psychopathy: Talking the walk. *Behavioural Sciences and the Law, 28*. doi: 10.1002/bsl.925.

Blickle, G., Schlegel, A., Fassbender, P., & Klein, U. (2006). Some personality correlates of business white-collar crime. *Applied Psychology: An International Review, 55*(2), 220–233. doi: 10.1111/j.1464-0597.2006.00226.x.

Board, B. J., & Fritzon, K. (2005). Disordered personalities at work. *Psychology, Crime & Law, 11*(1), 17–32. doi: 10.1080/10683160310001634304.

Boddy, C. R. (2005). The implications of corporate psychopaths for business and society: An initial examination and a call to arms. *AJBBS, 1*(2), 30–40.

Boddy, C. R. (2006). The dark side of management decisions: Organisational psychopaths. *Management Decision, 44*(10). doi: 10.1108/00251740610715759

Boddy, C. R. (2011a). *Corporate psychopaths: Organisational destroyers*. London: Palgrave Macmillan.

Boddy, C. R. (2011b). The corporate psychopaths theory of the global financial crisis. *Journal of Business Ethics, 102*, 255–259. doi: 10.1007/s10551-011-0810-4.

Boddy, C. R. (2014). Corporate psychopaths, conflict, employee affective well-being and counterproductive work behaviour. *Journal of Business Ethics, 121*. doi: 10.1007/s10551-013-1688-0.

Boddy, C. R., Ladyshewsky, R., & Galvin, P. (2010). The influence of corporate psychopaths on corporate social responsibility and organizational commitment to employees. *Journal of Business Ethics, 97*, 1–19. doi: 10.1007/s10551-010-0492-3.

Caponecchia, C., Sun, A., & Wyatt, A. (2012). 'Psychopaths' at work? Implications of lay persons' use of labels and behavioural criteria for psychopathy. *Journal of Business Ethics, 107*(4), 399–408. doi: 10.1007/s10551-011-1049-9.

Carducci, B. J. (2009). *The psychology of personality* (2nd ed.). West Sussex, UK: Wiley Blackwell.

Cleckley, H. (1941). *The mask of insanity* (1st ed.). St. Louis, MO: Mosby.

Cooke, D., Michie, C., Hart, S., & Clark, D. (2004). Reconstructing psychopathy: Clarifying the significance of antisocial and socially deviant behaviour in the diagnosis of psychopathic personality disorder. *Journal of Personality Disorders*, *18*(4), 337–357.

Crant, J. M., & Bateman, T. S. (2000). Charismatic leadership viewed from above: The impact of proactive personality. *Journal of Organizational Behavior*, *21*(1), 63–75.

Dutton, K. (2012). *The wisdom of psychopaths: What saints, spies, and serial killers can teach us about success*. Heinemann.

Field, A. (2009). *Discovering statistics using SPSS* (3rd ed.). London: Sage.

Fritzon, K., Croom, S., Brooks, N., & Bailey, C. (2013). The Corporate Personality Inventory. Unpublished.

Hall, J. R., & Benning, S. D. (2006). The 'successful' psychopath: Adaptive and subclinical manifestations of psychopathy in the general population. In C. J. Patrick (Ed.), *Handbook of psychopathy* (pp. 459–478). New York: Guilford Press.

Hare, R. D. (2003). *The Hare Psychopathy Checklist – Revised* (2nd ed.). Toronto: Mutli-Health Systems.

Harpur, T. J., Hare, R. D., & Hakstian, A. R. (1989). Two-factor conceptualization of psychopathy: Construct validity and assessment implications. *Psychological Assessment: A Journal of Consulting and Clinical Psychology*, *1*, 6–17.

Henning, J. B., Wygant, D. B., & Barnes, P. W. (2014). Mapping the darkness and finding the light: DSM-5 and assessment of the 'corporate psychopath'. *Industrial and Organizational Psychology*, *7*(1). doi: 10.1111/iops.12123.

Karpman, B. (1941). On the need of separating psychopathy into two distinct clinical types: The symptomatic and the idiopathic. *Journal of Criminal Psychopathology*, *3*, 112–137. Retrieved from http://psycnet.apa.org/psycinfo/1942-00202-001.

Kets de Vries, P., & Miller, D. (1985). Narcissism and leadership: An object relations perspective. *Human Relations*, *38*(6), 583–601.

Kiehl, K. (2011). Peering inside the psychopath's mind. *The Forensic Examiner*, *20*(3), 24–29.

Kiehl, K. A., & Hoffman, M. B. (2011). The criminal psychopath: History, neuroscience, treatment, and economics. *Jurimetrics: The Journal of Law, Science, and Technology*, *51*(4), 355–397.

Kosson, D. S., Suchy, Y., Mayer, A. R., & Libby, J. (2002). Facial affect recognition in criminal psychopaths. *Emotion*, *2*(4). doi: 10.1037//1528-3542.2.4.398.

Kubak, F. A., & Salekin, R. T. (2009). Psychopathy and anxiety in children and adolescents: New insights on developmental pathways to offending. *Journal of Psychopathology and Behavioural Assessment*, *31*(4), 271–284. doi: 10.1007/s10862-009-9144-2.

Levenson, M. R., Kiehl, K. A., & Fitzpatrick, C. M. (1995). Assessing psychopathic attributes in a non institutionalized population. *Journal of Personality and Social Psychology*, *68*, 151–158. doi: 10.1037/0022-3514.68.1.151.

Lilienfeld, S. O., Waldman, I. D., Landfield, K., Watts, A. L., Rubenzer, S., & Faschingbauer, T. R. (2012). Fearless dominance and the U.S. presidency: Implications of psychopathic personality traits for successful and unsuccessful political leadership. *Journal of Personality and Social Psychology*, *103*, 489–505. doi: 10.1037/a0029392.

Lilienfeld, S. O., & Widows, M. R. (2005). *Psychopathic Personality Inventory-Revised.* Lutz, FL: Psychological Assessment Resources Inc.

Lykken, D. T. (1957). A study of anxiety in the sociopathic personality. *Journal of Abnormal and Clinical Psychology, 55,* 6–10. doi: 10.1037/h0047232.

Lykken, D. T. (1995). *The antisocial personalities.* New Jersey: Erlbaum.

Mathieu, C., Neumann, C. S., Hare, R. D., & Babiak, P. (2014). A dark side of leadership: Corporate psychopathy and its influence on employee well-being and job satisfaction. *Personality and Individual Differences, 59,* 83–88. doi: 10.1016/j.paid .2013.11.010.

Ogloff, J. R. P. (2006). Psychopathy/antisocial personality disorder conundrum. *Australian and New Zealand Journal of Psychiatry, 40*(6–7). doi: 10.1111/j.1440 -1614.2006.01834.x.

Patrick, C. J., Fowles, D. C., & Krueger, R. F. (2009). Triarchic conceptualization of psychopathy: Developmental origins of disinhibition, boldness, and meanness. *Journal of Development and Psychopathology, 21,* 913–938. doi: 10.1017 /S0954579409000492.

Paulhus, D. L. (1999). *Paulhus Deception Scales (PDS): Balanced inventory of desirable responding-7: User's manual.* Toronto, Canada: Multi-Health Systems.

Paulhus, D. L., Neumann, C. S., & Hare, R. D. (in press). *Manual for the self-report psychopathy scale.* Toronto: Multi-Health Systems.

Skeem, J. L., Polaschek, D. L. L., Patrick, C. J., & Lilienfeld, S. O. (2011). Psychopathic personality: Bridging the gap between scientific evidence and public policy. *Psychological Science in Public Interest, 12,* 95–162. doi: 10.1177 /1529100611426706.

Smith, S. F., & Lilienfeld, S. O. (2013). Psychopathy in the workplace: The knowns and unknowns. *Aggression and Violent Behaviour, 18.* doi: 10.1016/j.avb.2012 .11.007.

Stevens, G. W., Deuling, J. K., & Armenakis, A. A. (2012). Successful psychopaths: Are they unethical decision-makers and why? *Journal of Business Ethics, 105.* doi: 10.1007/s10551-011-0963-1.

Venables, N. C., Hall, J. R., & Patrick, C. J. (2014). Differentiating psychopathy from antisocial personality disorder: A triarchic model perspective. *Psychological Medicine, 44.* doi: 10.1017/S003329171300161X.

Verschuere, B., Uzieblo, K., De Schryver, M., Douma, H., Onraedt, T., & Crombez, G. (2014). The inverse relationship between psychopathy and faking good: Not response bias, but true variance in psychopathic personality. *The Journal of Forensic Psychiatry & Psychology, 25*(6), 705–713. doi: 10.1080/14789949 .2014.952767.

Vitale, J. E., Maccoon, D. G., & Newman, J. P. (2011). Emotion facilitation and passive avoidance learning in psychopathic female offenders. *Criminal Justice and Behaviour, 38*(7). doi: 0.1177/0093854811403590.

Appendix: Corporate Psychopathy Inventory Items

1. I never exceeded the speed limit when I am driving a motor vehicle.
2. I always ensure that I dispose of litter into a trash can.

3. I admit it every time I make a mistake.
4. I have never lost my temper at someone.
5. I have never been annoyed by another person.
6. I have never been tempted to tell someone off.
7. I am always happy and willing to help people out that ask favors of me.
8. Whenever I am criticised the other person always has a perfectly genuine reason for doing so.
9. I have never wished misfortune on another individual.
10. I have never been late to an appointment in my life.
11. I have never tuned out to a conversation in which I have been involved.
12. I have never talked about someone behind their back.
13. I have never laughed at a joke I did not find funny.
14. If I was undercharged for an item I had purchased I would make it known.
15. I have never deliberately said anything offensive.
16. I have never been disrespectful to another person that I dislike.
17. I have never done something that I am ashamed off.
18. I have never eavesdropped on a conversation between other people.
19. I have never resented the success of another.
20. I never get upset when things do not go my own way.
21. I never check my personal email when I'm at work.
22. I never log on to social networking sites when I'm at work.
23. I've never used company resources, e.g. stationary, printers for my personal use.
24. I've never been tempted to read someone else's printed papers that they have left in the print room/photocopy room by mistake.
25. I believe I am an amusing and entertaining conversationalist.
26. I am quick-witted.
27. My knowledge and skills far exceed the average person.
28. If I wanted to, I could be anything I wanted to be.
29. I like being where the action is happening.
30. I thrive off excitement and challenges.
31. I like to live life in the fast lane.
32. I get uninterested easily and constantly need a challenge.
33. I am able to adapt to any situation or interaction.
34. I am not perplexed or embarrassed when I am found to be wrong.
35. I am embarrassed easily.
36. Life is full of givers and takers.
37. I am adept at noticing weakness in others.
38. Tough decisions need to be made at times regardless of the cost to others.

39. Once I have made a decision I do not doubt myself.
40. I spend little time ruminating on trivial events.
41. I am able to move on quickly from negative consequences.
42. I am able to remain calm in the face of danger.
43. I would describe myself as an emotional person.
44. I try not to become emotionally attached to outcomes.
45. People often react to emotionally to small things in the workplace and should instead just move on.
46. Sometimes in life you need to put yourself first.
47. It is easy to get caught up in others problems.
48. People make their own decisions and must handle the mistakes.
49. Diversity is more important than stability.
50. Applying pressure to decision makers is a necessity at times.
51. I am able adapt and change quickly to any task, job or requirement.
52. People fail to accept when they have made a mistake.
53. I am often helping colleagues who struggle at keeping up with their work.
54. When a colleague makes a mistake I am quick to help point it out.
55. I am mentally stronger than others.
56. Most people give up easily when facing a difficult task.
57. I am good at noticing aspects to compliment another person on.
58. I need new and exciting things in my life.
59. I would be good in a high stake or pressured situation as I make fast decisions.
60. It is not practical to always make appointments on time.
61. It is enjoyable to test your own limits and learn about the limits of others.
62. I enjoy trying things for the first time.
63. I find it difficult to talk others into seeing my side or point of view.
64. I can usually tell if people are lying.
65. Taking a risk for a big payoff would make me very nervous.
66. I am able to persuade people to see what matters.
67. To achieve success, at times it may come at a cost to others.
68. It is difficult for people to hear the truth.
69. It has been necessary for me to make bold business decisions, that have caused others to suffer.
70. In my work environment, I do not care what others think of me, unless their opinion of me directly affects my business prospects.
71. Waiting patiently for others to complete work requirements that 'should have been finished' is arduous at times.
72. It is not uncommon for others to try to show each other up at work.
73. People can treat the workplace like a battlefield at times.
74. Although I value responsibility, it is hard to say the same for others often in the workplace.

75. I find I have often had to remind colleagues of imminent deadlines.
76. If I am confronted by a hostile colleague I am able to handle the situation with ease.
77. A positive presentation is a key ingredient in business.
78. It is important for me to be considered as a leader in the workplace.
79. When it is really matters, I can talk most people into anything.
80. Smiling is an easy way to attract the interest of others.
81. Sometimes I find I am nervous without knowing why.
82. I am often worried that I have hurt the feelings of others.
83. I know what to expect and how to handle people's reactions.
84. Making small talk with people I do not know is hard.
85. Asking a favor of someone makes me uneasy.
86. I can handle being the centre of attention.
87. Being different and standing out from others has its benefits.
88. I do not let negative events get on my nerves.
89. I am a talented communicator.
90. I rarely get nervous in the workplace.
91. I am willing to take risks and embark on difficult courses of action.
92. I often insist on having things my own way.
93. I possess a wide range of emotions.
94. I'm always looking for a new challenge.
95. I find no trouble in speaking out against unjust or unnecessary company policies.
96. A fast paced workplace environment excites me.
97. I'm the first to admit when I have made a mistake.
98. Challenging someone with authority does not bother me.
99. People perceive me as entertaining and theatrical.
100. I admire those who can work the system to get ahead.
101. I would resent anyone who challenged my work/position.
102. I am not afraid to publicly point out others' mistakes.
103. A persons first impression of me is always positive.
104. I don't worry about my future position in the company.
105. I would describe my mentality as being spontaneous.
106. Offering large bonuses to potential employees may attract individuals with misleading intentions.
107. Colleagues are often a useful resource in the workplace.
108. Sharing/allocation of company resources if often fair and just.
109. In some situations, honesty is not necessary.
110. Success at any cost to others is justifiable.
111. It is acceptable to gain from other peoples weaknesses/mistakes.
112. I feel guilty after reprimanding an employee or colleague.
113. I wouldn't feel guilty making an employee cry if they made me look bad.

114. Lying and deceit are integral to successful business.
115. I believe I am more important than other people in the workplace.
116. I have never deliberately said something to hurt a colleague's feelings.
117. I have never disliked anyone in the workplace environment.
118. When people make mistakes, they deserve a chance to rectify the situation.
119. Feelings of guilt and remorse are a sign of weakness in others.
120. Delaying gratification in the working environment is crucial.
121. Keeping appointments, even in busy times is important.
122. Thinking about consequences is always a factor in my decision-making.
123. It is acceptable to place extra pressure on colleagues to meet deadlines.
124. When others fail to meet deadlines, this may reflect badly on me.
125. I select people to be my allies at work.
126. Having allies helps me achieve my goals.
127. When conducting my work, I always stick to company rules and procedures.
128. Changing jobs is exciting.
129. Taking on multiple tasks at once is exciting.
130. Flexibility in the workplace is more valuable than strict constraints or rules.
131. Conflict amongst colleagues is inevitable.
132. It's good to challenge young people in the workplace to test their limits.
133. It's useful to have more junior staff in the workplace to do tasks that I find boring.
134. Some people in the workplace will be more valuable and important to me than others.
135. All personal information should be kept out of the workplace.
136. It makes me uncomfortable when colleagues are humiliated and intimidated by others.
137. All staff members, regardless of authority/status meaningfully contribute to the company.
138. In the past, I have found that most people are unreliable.
139. Most relationships in the workplace are superficial and impersonal.
140. I possess the ability to read people at face value.
141. I never hesitate before jumping into a conversation.
142. The content of a message is more important than the way it is delivered.
143. The present is more important than the past or future.
144. I like to create my own 'culture' at work.
145. When someone in my department has success, I believe my role in that should be acknowledged.

How Moral Emotions Affect the Probability of Relapse

10

ANDRÉ KÖRNER
ROSE SCHINDLER
TINA HAHNEMANN

Contents

10.1 Introduction

This chapter focuses on the so-called moral emotions, namely, shame and guilt. These emotions ensue from different attributional properties, which give rise to different predictions for recidivism of crime.

Emotions are an essential part of our lives. They often develop during interpersonal interactions, and they are very likely to direct and energise subsequent behaviour. With respect to criminal behaviour, emotions often play a crucial role, as they are able to directly promote or inhibit crime. Therefore, emotions are a key factor when it comes to correctional treatment and the prevention of criminal recidivism. As there are many potential causes for emotions, attributional theories have identified basic properties – the causal dimensions – to highlight the common structure of the emotional landscape. In this way, guilt is often based on the perception of controllability, and elicits a desire for reparation of the previous misdeed. In contrast, shame occurs when people interpret the causes of their actions as uncontrollable and elicits a desire to turn away or leave the field. Thus, guilt may reduce the likelihood of recidivism, whereas shame does not – in fact, shame may even promote deviant behaviour (Auchter & Hilgers, 1994; Ferguson & Wormith, 2013).

In what follows, we will present a brief overview of research on moral emotions and ways of correctional treatment. Then we will outline a study analysing the emotional reactions of adult prisoners in a German correctional facility in a scenario-based test. Our participants' emotions of guilt and shame were compared to those of a student sample. We also analysed the relation of shame and guilt to prisoners' scores on actuarial risk assessment instruments (e.g. Offender Group Reconviction Scale [OGRS 3]). The forensic sample showed lower emotional intensities than did their student counterparts. The results show that a tendency to experience shame (rather than guilt) might be associated with a higher risk of recidivism. Finally, we will discuss the implications for attributional and emotional training programs as well as relapse prevention promotion.

10.1.1 Moral Emotions and Their Attributional Underpinnings

Emotions are central elements of our lives because they accompany our thoughts and actions, especially when we interact with other people. Such interactions are regulated by various rules, norms, values and laws, in order to promote harmonious co-existence. Based on these norms, moral emotions serve the function of evaluating the quality of the perceived behaviour. This viewpoint, which focuses on attributional processes, has a long tradition in psychological research.

Within this theoretical framework, persons are seen as naïve scientists, who interpret their environment as a system of causes and effects, enabling them to predict and to control future events (Heider, 1958). In this way, attribution theorists aim to understand the naïve scientist. Since the number of subjectively perceived causes can be seen as endless, several attempts to structure the underlying causal dimensions have been made (see Försterling, 1980, for a comprehensive overview). The causal dimensions that have been identified are locus (internality versus externality), stability (stable versus variable) and controllability (controllable versus uncontrollable) (Weiner, 2014). Hence, when we ask for the emergence of a given emotion, the subjective causality as perceived by a person is of particular importance, because our attributional analyses and the configuration of the causal dimensions give rise to a variety of different emotions. For example, a student who classifies his bad mark on a test as caused by a lack of effort (rather controllable and variable) will feel regret and may try harder next time. In contrast, if a student interprets his failure as being caused by his poor ability (an uncontrollable and stable cause), he or she will feel ashamed and helpless, resulting in little or no confidence to achieve a better performance next time. These kinds of attributional calculations are part of our everyday life, and at the same time, they are hidden motivators of our emotional states and behaviours. This is not only the case for our own actions, but also in relation to our interaction partners. Consequently, Weiner (2006) has suggested the metaphor of a judge in the courtroom of life.

Therefore, Rudolph, Schulz and Tscharaktschiew (2013) have pointed out that moral emotions evaluate both our own actions (actor emotions) as well as the actions of other people (observer emotions), either as morally praiseworthy or blameworthy. A behaviour is morally praiseworthy if it is consistent with our social standards. If we perceive such a laudable behaviour, we will indicate so by exhibiting corresponding positive emotions. These positive emotions (such as pride or gratitude) are equivalent to a 'go' signal, which encourages others to repeat the evaluated behaviour. On the other hand, if a person's behaviour transgresses moral standards, negative emotions (such as guilt or anger) contain a 'stop' signal, which decreases the probability that the blameworthy behaviour is repeated. The go signal is transmitted via the fact that the generated emotion feels good to either the actor or the target. The mechanism underlying the stop signal works similarly, except that the transmitted emotion causes one or both interaction partners to feel bad (Rudolph & Tscharaktschiew, 2014).

Moral emotions like shame and guilt can be called 'self-evaluative' emotions. They also have been referred to as 'violation', or 'self-accusation' emotions (Roos, 2000). Shame and guilt belong to the negative actor emotions (see Rudolph et al., 2013) and are also labelled 'transgression emotions' or 'self-reproach-emotions' (Hosser, Windzio, & Greve, 2005; Roos, 2000). Shame and guilt are experienced when one's own behaviour is regarded as negative, when one pursues negative goals or when one fails to achieve positive goals (Rudolph et al., 2013). A transgression like achieving a negative goal disrupts social interactions and can range from minor (social etiquette) to severe (laws). The importance of a stop signal increases in the case of serious crimes. In addition to the internal stop signal, external criminal prosecution and judicial condemnation occur in almost all societies.

10.1.2 Moral Emotions and Recidivism

When it comes to relapse or recidivism, we ask whether he or she will do this again. Thus, we want to predict a specific behaviour that may emerge in different situations and under different circumstances. Because human behaviour is strongly driven by emotional forces, the so-called moral emotions, such as guilt and shame, play a crucial role in the regulation of interpersonal behaviour (Barrett, 1995). In recent years, there has been a growing interest in psychological research on relapse prevention. This also includes analyses examining the effects of cognitions and emotions on risk of relapse. Greenberg (2010) postulates that emotional processing (i.e. increasing awareness of emotion, expressing emotions, enhancing emotion regulation, reflecting emotion and transforming emotion) is centrally important to any good therapy.

Whether we feel ashamed or guilty following a negative event depends strongly on our causal attributions. A motivational sequence is assumed from causal attributions to emotional reactions to behavioural tendencies (for summaries, see Rudolph, Roesch, Greitemeyer, & Weiner, 2004; Rudolph & Tscharaktschiew, 2014). These attributional considerations postulate that an internal, stable and global causal attribution leads to shame. For example, when an individual attributes a failure to an uncontrollable lack of ability, the probability of shame is high. This pattern of thoughts and feelings results in a belief that one cannot change his own future behaviour. In addition, shame is a threat to self-esteem, and thus might lead to feelings of degradation or anger and can interfere with people's ability to empathise with others (Hosser et al., 2005; Tangney & Dearing, 2002). Anger, distrust and resentment caused by the feeling of worthlessness can go along with negative behaviour, which is morally blameworthy. Previous studies indicate that people who are more prone to shame will regulate feeling anger (and thus, their aggressive tendencies) less constructively (Tangney & Dearing, 2002; Tangney, Stuewig, & Hafez, 2011; Tangney, Stuewig, & Mashek, 2007).

In contrast, attributions of negative events to internal, unstable and specific causes lead to feelings of guilt (Tracy & Robins, 2004). Therefore, guilt is caused by attributions to a controllable lack of effort (Hareli & Weiner, 2002). Feelings of guilt elicit a need for reparation (Weiner, 2006), associated with prosocial behaviour, empathy and altruism (Hosser et al., 2005). Individuals who are prone to guilt are more likely to engage in behaviours valued positively and morally acceptable by others. In sum, shame is more likely when events or actions are attributed to uncontrollable causes, and more often leads to deconstructive behaviour. In contrast, guilt is more likely when negative events or actions are attributed to controllable causes and increases the likelihood of behaviours that aim to repair the damage done.

Therefore, when people have committed a crime, it appears useful to identify their emotional reactions and their attributional style in order to change their pattern of thoughts and feelings, thereby positively influencing their future behaviour. In addition to the punishment of illegal behaviour with potential imprisonment, it is very important to offer rehabilitative interventions to individuals who break the law. Therefore, the German justice system, as well as those in many other Western countries, measures the duration of imprisonment partly according to the extent and types of interventions that are seen as required (Hosser et al., 2005; Lösel & Bender, 1997). The central goal of intervention programs is to successfully change the offender's attitude towards social norms and to increase the likelihood of future prosocial behaviours. The foundation of the penal system is not only that any kind of treatment in prison will reduce the risk of relapse, but also that it offers an instrument for assessing future risks. A risk assessment and resulting prognosis are crucial for determining whether to ease detention conditions or offer an early release, both of which affect possible future victims. The importance of this system is grounded upon not only the protection of society but also on economic considerations. On the one hand, there are the calculable costs of police, courts, prisons and therapies, and the incalculable costs of the risk to potential future victims. On the other hand, there are the benefits (e.g. tax earnings or professionalism) of rehabilitating offenders so that they once again become productive members of society (Martinez, Stuewig, & Tangney, 2014). Thus, it seems reasonable and fruitful to keep these considerations in mind for correctional treatments, especially when the goal is to lower the risk of relapse.

10.1.3 Correctional Treatment of Prisoners

The usefulness and effectiveness of therapeutical intervention programs in general is often questioned. In almost all Western countries, the goal of resocialisation is a core principle of the correctional system (Laubenthal, 2008), based on the assumption that a suitable intervention reduces the likelihood of future offending behaviour, and/or prevents situations leading to further delinquencies. After a period of disillusionment and pessimism in the treatment of offenders ('Nothing works!'; Martinson, 1974; Sarre, 2001), research identified small effect sizes ($r = .10$) for overall preventive treatment on recidivism

(McGuire, 2002) and even larger effects ($r = .30$) for more elaborate methods of risk reduction (Lösel & Bender, 1997). Research tried to identify those programs with an effect on relapse prevention, which leads to the question of what works (Cornel & Nickolai, 2004).

In this vein, Andrews, Bonta and Hoge (1990) identified four general principles of effective rehabilitation programs: risk, need, responsivity and professional override. The authors summarise the principles as follows:

1. Higher levels of service are reserved for higher risk cases because they respond better to brief intensive service than to less intensive service. Cases of lower risk should do as well or better with minimal intensive service.
2. Targets of service should be matched to the criminogenic needs of offenders (e.g. procriminal cognitions or personal attitudes, values and thinking styles favourable to violations of law). Procriminal sentiments are basic to psychodynamic and social control perspectives (weak superego, disbelief in the validity of the law). Influencing these needs results in changes in the chance of recidivism.
3. Styles and modes of service should be matched to the learning styles and abilities of offenders.
4. Having considered risk, need and responsivity, decisions are made as appropriate under present conditions.

Following these principles, we need to distinguish between broader treatments and treatments with a focus on specific disorders.

10.1.3.1 Broader Treatments
Broader treatments take into account a wide range of different risk factors. For example, the Reasoning and Rehabilitation Program (R&R; Ross, Fabiano, & Ross, 1989) is a well-known instrument and is used in many countries. Several studies and meta-analytic findings confirm its effectiveness (Joy Tong & Farrington, 2006). Programs like R&R try to enhance cognitive skills that are associated with an adequate overall social behaviour. With methods like role-playing, group discussion, films and homework, the inmates mainly attend to these programs in group sessions. This training includes problem-solving, social competence trainings, regulation of emotions and reflecting moral values. The key factor for success is to put the prisoners in a positive position to master their lives, without committing a crime again. An influential program in this manner is also the Good Lives Model (GLM; Ward & Brown, 2004; Ward, Mann, & Gannon, 2007). Programs like R&R and GLM can be used in different kinds of correctional settings and for different populations of inmates.

10.1.3.2 Delict-Specific Programs

Most of the specific programs have a cognitive-behavioural background and focus on the underlying disorder that leads to criminal behaviour. One example is the Sex Offender Treatment Program (SOTP) of 1992 (see Mann & Thornton, 1998, for an overview). The key factor for these programs is to start with a treatment of the psychopathic causes of the deviant behaviour. Moreover, participants of these programs enhance their cognitive and social skills, problem-solving skills, creative thinking and critical thinking as well as social skills and regulation of emotions (Göbbels & Zimmermann, 2013). These kinds of programs are assumed to be superior to eclectic programs that do not follow a common structure or manual. This assertion is supported by meta-analytic findings (Brown, 2013; Friendship, Blud, Erikson, Travers, & Thornton, 2003; Landenberger & Lipsey, 2005; McGuire, 2002). In most of the specific programs, the regulation of emotions is a key factor for success. Emotions are crucial in terms of victim empathising or to start an attributional re-framing by focusing on the emotion-related causal interpretations of the clients. In Germany, special protocols such as the Behandlungsprogramm für Sexualstraftäter (BPS; Wischka, Foppe, Griepenburg, Nuhn-Naber, & Rehder, 2004) have been developed. These programs mainly deal with emotion regulation and include emotional components such as empathy training, and stress reduction.

As already seen, most of the existing correctional treatments include emotions and their regulation as a key factor for therapeutical change and to reduce recidivism. Unfortunately, many of these programs are not well informed about the attributional prerequisites of our emotional landscape. No matter to what extent treatment is seen as specific, the most common treatment measures still include one-on-one talks and unstructured discussion groups (Bosold, Hosser, & Lauterbach, 2007) that do not systematically address causal ascriptions and perceptions of responsibility. As Tangney (2002) puts it, it is surprising that a systematic research including a comprehensive consideration of moral emotions, namely, shame and guilt, has been lacking thus far in the area of criminal behaviour and recidivism.

10.1.4 Emotions within the Treatment of Prisoners

As mentioned earlier, shame and guilt are the result of different cognitive conditions. However, these conditions have not been distinguished from one another in a systematical way when it comes to offender treatment (Tangney, 1991). From an attributional point of view, reducing a person's feelings of shame and at the same time promoting feelings of guilt seems desirable, since perceptions of control will encourage reparative behaviours and reduce the likelihood of relapse. Thus, it seems necessary to distinguish between feelings of shame and guilt in the context of treatment programs for offenders. Therefore, the practitioner needs a practical instrument (free of demand characteristics), accurately assessing the proneness of shame versus guilt. With such an instrument, we would be better able to identify attributional styles, moral emotions and self-perceptions of the inmates within an intervention setting.

10.2 Testing the Relation of Emotional Reactions and Recidivism Rates in a Forensic Sample

10.2.1 A First Look into the Field; Aims of Our Investigation

First, we intend to examine prisoners' emotional responsiveness to shame and guilt relative to a non-prisoner control group. Moreover, we want to synthesise findings from the longstanding causal attribution research (Försterling, 1980; Försterling & Rudolph, 1988; Hareli & Weiner, 2002; Weiner, 2006) and newer work on recidivism (Hosser et al., 2005; Hosser, Windzio, & Greve, 2007; Tangney, Stuewig, & Mashek, 2007), with the goal of finding a specific score that distinguishes between people who prefer a more shame-orientated cognitive style rather than a more guilt-orientated style. We do not want to test this in the context of crime-related measures or scenarios, but rather by everyday life situations. Everyday life situations increase the probability that anybody (e.g. students and prisoners) is able to empathise with the scenarios, and thus give applicable answers which can be compared. Finally, we hypothesise that there is a significant relation between these specific attributional styles and a persons' individual risk of relapse.

10.2.2 Ethical and Legal Aspects

The study was evaluated and approved by the ethics committee of the University of Chemnitz (corresponding number: V-013-15-SM-UR) and the Research Unit of the Department of Justice of Saxony (corresponding number: 4557E-10/13). We thoroughly informed all participants about the procedures of the study and they consented to participation. Participation was voluntary and subjects were free to abort the study at any point in time. We encrypted all generated data and, therefore, no association exists between data points and participants' identity. Furthermore, we withheld the individual test scores from contractors and personnel at the Waldheim correctional facility. All collaborators on the study signed a confidentiality agreement.

10.2.3 Participants

The sample consisted of 21 male inmates at the federal correctional institution in Waldheim, Germany. Prisoners could take part in the study fully voluntary, which unfortunately resulted in a small sample size. The participants' ages ranged from 23 to 59 years in age, with a median of 31 years ($M = 34.57$, $SD = 10.36$). At the time of data collection, the participants had served a sentence between 1 and 19 years ($M = 3.96$, $SD = 4.60$). In terms of educational attainment, most of the sample had obtained a vocational school certificate (38.4%), followed by a certificate of extended Hauptschule (23.1%) or Realschule (23.1%) completion. We excluded people with apparent cognitive disabilities and illiterate individuals.

Furthermore, we tested a student subsample ($N = 37$) to compare the prisoners' sample to a sample with no prior criminal records. Students were also all male and their ages ranged from 19 to 29 years of age, with a median of 22 ($M = 22.51$, $SD = 3.30$). All students had no criminal records and received partial course credit for their participation.

10.2.4 Material

We designed a special scenario-based questionnaire consisting of eight vignettes of everyday life situations. Before we set in our study in the forensic and student sample, we pre-tested 28 scenarios with an anonymous sample of 81 people to extract the scenarios with the optimal level of item discriminative validity and item difficulty. This resulted in the final version of the test (the full version is available on request). The participants are instructed to assume the role of the described actor in the depicted situations. In addition, we asked participants to imagine being in the actor's position as realistically as possible. We described all situations as negative outcomes resulting from the actor's immoral or norm-breaking behaviour in terms of either low effort or a lack of ability. For example, people were instructed to imagine the following:

> You are trying to get into a parking space with your car when your mobile phone suddenly rings. You answer the phone although you do not have a hands-free system. With one hand on the wheel and distracted by the conversation, you try to get into the parking space. This is getting more and more difficult and finally you hit another parking car!

Participants indicated how much they would experience shame and guilt within these given scenarios on a 7-point Likert scale (from 1 = *not at all* to 7 = *very much*).

The students answered an online version of the questionnaire, whereas the prisoners completed a paper–pencil version. For both groups, the task lasted about 10 minutes. To control for ordering effects, we had four different versions of the questionnaire with a randomised order of the scenarios in both formats (online and paper–pencil).

10.2.5 Risk Assessment

To assess the participants' risk of relapse, we analysed the prisoners' files. In contrast to a complete assessment with face-to-face interviews or detailed clinical information, we chose this more economic examination methodology to avoid observer bias and to prevent the investigator from dangers of direct contact. The information that is required for an actuarial risk calculation is available through the prisoners' files (Endrass, Urbaniok, Held, Vetter, & Rossegger, 2009). We used four different actuarial instruments depending on the prisoners' actual offence. Overall risk assessment was done by OGRS 3, for the subgroup of violent offenders we used the Risk Matrix/V, and for the subgroup of sexual offenders we used the Risk Matrix/S and Static-99. These instruments all share good predictive validity as well as very good interrater reliabilities (Volbert & Dahle, 2010; Wakeling, Howard, & Barnett, 2011; Wakeling, Mann, & Milner, 2011). They all predict the future risk of one person based upon a large sample of prisoners' longitudinal recidivism data. Furthermore, the data needed for the actuarial risk calculation can be easily drawn from readily accessible sources (Thornton et al., 2006).

10.2.5.1 Revised Offender Group Reconviction Scale (OGRS 3)

Practitioners in England and Wales have used the Revised Offender Group Reconviction Scale (OGRS; National Offender Management Service, 2008) since the late 1990s. It has been modified many times and evaluates the general risk of relapse for a given person within the next 1 or 2 years (Howard, Francis, Soothill, & Humphreys, 2009). The instrument statistically utilises a person's age, sex and criminal history data, and calculates the individual's risk based on a special weighted formula. The specific values come from a regression model consisting of six easily collectable variables. This regression model was generated from a sample of over 79,000 former inmates in England and Wales. The instrument reliably predicts future convictions (Howard et al., 2009), and investigations using German samples revealed acceptable predictive coefficients, lying between $r = .32$ and $r = .37$ (Volbert & Dahle, 2010).

10.2.5.2 Risk of Violent Offending (RM2000/V) and Risk of Sexual Offending (RM2000/S)

Like OGRS 3, the Risk Matrix 2000 comes from the London Home Office, and has been designed and reconfigured by Thornton et al. (2006). Unlike the OGRS 3, the Risk Matrix is designed specifically to calculate the risk of relapse for sexual offenders (Wakeling, Howard, & Barnett, 2011). In comparison to other instruments, the Risk Matrix allows the user to easily distinguish between two types of relapse risks: sexual (RM2000/S) versus non-sexual violent (RM2000/V).

Although there is a two-step process for using the RM2000/V instrument to predict non-sexual violent reoffending within sexual offenders, it can be used as a rough estimate for predicting violent reoffending in a general population of former inmates (Volbert & Dahle, 2010). To do so, one can just calculate the first risk prediction step, which consists of the subject's actual age, violent offence history and history of burglaries. As a result, one obtains a four-stage risk category, which exhibits considerably good predictive validity for British samples (Thornton et al., 2006), as well as for German samples (Volbert & Dahle, 2010).

Similarly, the RM2000/S also only needs three variables in a first step (age at first offence, sexual convictions and overall criminal convictions). The resulting categorical score can then be raised by four aggravating factors (e.g. lack of a long-term age appropriate relationship). An ordinal score with four categories (low, medium, high or very high) is used to represent the final risk rating. Predictive validity of the sexual version is good ($r = .32$); however, there is little cross-validation with German-speaking samples (Volbert & Dahle, 2010). Fortunately, the instrument described next is used more frequently in Germany.

10.2.5.3 Static-99

Contextually, the Static-99 from Hanson and Thornton (1999; see also Harris, Phenix, Hanson, & Thornton, 2003) is related to a prior version of the mentioned RM2000/S. In addition, a German version is available (Rettenberger & Eher, 2006). Like the RM2000/S, the Static-99 calculates a risk of sexual reoffending by scoring nine dichotomous variables (e.g. history of living with a lover for at least 2 years, stranger as a victim) and one four-category variable (prior sex offences) assessing the criminal history of the subject. (Eher, Schilling, Haubner-MacLean, Jahn, & Rettenberger, 2011). The resulting score is divided into progressively risky categories (low, moderate-low, moderate-high and high). Interestingly, Dahle (2008) points out that the predictive validity of the risk score of the Static-99 and other sexual-related instruments is higher for recidivism in general than for a sexual offence recidivism specifically.

10.3 Shame and Guilt as Predictors for Recidivism

First, we compared emotional responsiveness to shame and guilt in the student and prisoner groups. We then computed a differential score for subjects' proneness to feel either more shame or more guilt within the scenarios. Finally, we address the relation between emotional style and prisoners' individual risk of relapse.

10.3.1 Comparing Inmates and Students

Figures 10.1 and 10.2 yield the outcome boxplots for both emotions separated by group (prisoners versus students). The sample distribution of both groups met the requirements for parametric testing. The Shapiro-Wilk test indicates normal distribution for shame ($W(58) = .97$, $p = .136$), as well as for guilt ($W(58) = .96$, $p = .080$). Students endorsed more shame proneness ($M = 4.94$, $SD = 0.79$) than their imprisoned counterparts ($M = 4.26$, $SD = 1.29$). This difference was significant ($t(28.68) = 2.19$, $p = .037$).

According to Cohen (1988), this is a medium effect size ($d = .63$). Similarly, the students experienced the emotion of guilt more intensely ($M = 5.13$, $SD = 0.78$) than the inmates ($M = 4.89$, $SD = 1.02$), but this was not a significant finding ($t(56) = 0.97$, $p = .336$). Nonetheless, the trend is in the expected direction, with an effect of $d = .26$, suggesting a small effect. Based upon calculations in G-Power (Faul, Erdfelder, Buchner, & Lang, 2009), one would need a sample size of 468 to find an effect of this size to be significant.

In order to determine guilt/shame proneness, we calculated a differential score by subtracting a person's mean guilt score from his mean shame score. That means that a positive value would indicate a higher tendency to experience shame, whereas a negative score would result in a higher guilt tendency. Both groups had mostly negative differential scores, with a mean score for inmates of $M = -0.63$ ($SD = 0.92$) and a mean score for students

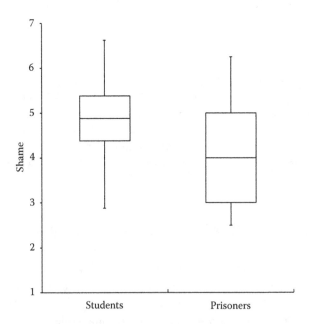

Figure 10.1 Box plots for experienced shame in students and prisoners. Areas around mean values indicate 95% confidence intervals.

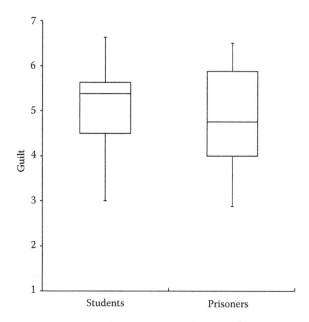

Figure 10.2 Box plots for experienced guilt in students and prisoners. Areas around mean values indicate 95% confidence intervals.

of $M = -0.19$ ($SD = 0.68$). It is visually apparent that prisoners' reported a greater tendency towards guilt (see Figure 10.3), but this was not significant ($U = 299.5, p = .075$).

10.3.2 Prediction of Relapse within Inmates

For all prisoners, we correlated the computed differential score for shame and guilt with the risk prediction values depending on the prisoners' specific offence. Table 10.1 shows the standardised regression coefficients for all prisoners as well as for the specific offence type. All relationships are positive, which indicates that greater shame proneness predicts a greater likelihood of relapse.

Only the relation between the OGRS 3 2-year risk and the prisoners' differential score was significant ($r = .44, p = .047$). In a regression model with the differential score for shame/guilt as the predictor and the OGRS 3 risk as the dependent variable, we found significant predictive validity for the emotional criterion we developed ($\beta = .44, t(20) = 2.13$). Due to the small sample size, the short-term prediction value for OGRS 3, which represents a 1-year recidivism rate, was marginally significant ($r = .42, p = .057$). As expected, due to the smaller sample sizes within the offence category subgroups, we found no significant correlations for the more specific instruments RM2000/S

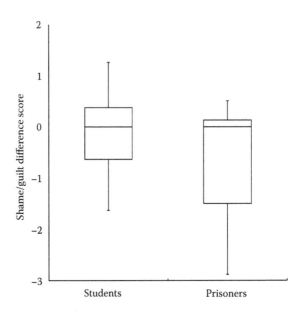

Figure 10.3 Box plots for differential scores of shame/guilt in students and prisoners. Areas around mean values indicate 95% confidence intervals.

Table 10.1 Correlation between Shame and Guilt Proneness and Relapse Risk by Specific Assessment Inventory

Instrument (Related Number of Participants)	Correlation (r) with Differential Score of Shame/Guilt	Needed N
Revised Offender Group Reconviction Scale (OGRS 3), 1 year ($n = 21$)	.42 ($p = .06$)	39
Revised Offender Group Reconviction Scale (OGRS 3), 2 years ($n = 21$)	.44 ($p < .05$)	–
Risk of violent offending (RM2000/V) ($n = 14$)	.47 ($p = .09$)	24
Risk of sexual offending (RM2000/S) ($n = 7$)	.62 ($p = .14$)	15
Static-99 ($n = 7$)	.67 ($p = .10$)	12

Note: For the needed N we set alpha = .05 and power $(1 - \beta)$ = .80, following Faul, Erdfelder, Buchner and Lang (2009).

($r = .62, p = .141$), RM2000/V ($r = .47, p = .093$) and Static-99 ($r = .67, p > .102$). Therefore, for the violent offender and sexual offender subgroups, non-significant findings were due to an even smaller number of participants ($n = 14$ violent offenders, $n = 7$ sexual offenders) relative to the sample assessed with the broader OGRS 3 instrument.

To overcome the constraints of our limited sample size, we again utilised G-Power to compute the sample size that would have been needed to detect a significant effect (Faul et al., 2009). As can be seen in Table 10.1 (column 'Needed N'), 39 (18 more than the current study) participants would be needed to detect a significant effect with OGRS 3 1-year relapse data. The same is true for the two subgroups of offenders, regardless of whether it is violent or sexual reoffending. The RM2000/V needs 10 more participants, the RM2000/S needs 8 more participants and the Static-99 needs 5 more participants.

10.4 Practical Implications and Outlook

In our own study, we examined the experience of the moral emotions of shame and guilt for prisoners as well as for a student sample. Overall, the results show lower emotional scores in the offenders' population in both of the predefined emotions. This could be either due to a lack in responsiveness to emotional content or a sign for restrain of shame and guilt expressions within the prisoners' sample. This finding supports a common assumption that responsiveness to emotional states or expression is lowered within imprisoned persons (Bereswill, 2004). An explanation for this might be that feelings of shame and guilt are hardly socially desired and might even be regarded as a weakness in the prisoner subculture. The students in our sample reported higher values of experienced shame and guilt than did the examined inmates. In the case of shame, the difference between students and inmates was significant even in our small sample. The significant lower values of shame in the prisoners are in line with the findings of Hosser et al. (2007) who found that feelings of shame and guilt decrease during the course of imprisonment.

Given the way that we constructed our scenario-based test, we were able to compute a reliable score for individuals' cognitive-emotional styles in terms of the moral emotions of shame and guilt. It was revealed that regardless of group (student versus prisoner) this differential score is universal, as prisoners and students did not differ in their absolute values. When investigating the results within the prisoners' sample, we found some interesting relations. As expected, a more shame-orientated emotional tendency predicts higher risks of recidivism. The risk of recidivism was assessed with established actuarial instruments (OGRS 3, RM2000 and Static-99), which predict population-based risk scores depending on the type of crime. All correlation coefficients support the hypothesis that a more shame-orientated cognitive style predicts a higher risk of recidivism. Although our results were only marginally significant because of low power, the relations are meaningful and could have easily been found significant in a slightly larger sample. More research is needed here, as our study was only a first attempt and we will need further investigation with support of policymakers as well. In the present study, our findings are based on correlations within a small sample. That means that causal inferences cannot be drawn from our investigation. However, our results support relations that have been found in other studies of moral development (Ferguson & Wormith, 2013). For example, Braithwaite and Mugford (1994) report comparable recidivism reduction effects when accounting for lower feelings of shame and stigmatisation amongst juvenile offenders. Another limitation is that we limited our study to probabilities for relapses that were calculated using actuarial instruments. We did not engage in further clinical investigation or utilise third-generation instruments. Furthermore, all instruments are validated on English and Welsh samples, rather than German samples. Nevertheless, these simple base-rate actuarial measures are simple to use and have good predictive validity (Endrass et al., 2009; Hanson & Bussière, 1998; Hanson & Morton-Bourgon, 2009; Harris, Rice et al., 2003; Volbert & Dahle, 2010). Finally, there are other measures for predicting risk, especially for violent reoffending. Future studies should use the Historical Clinical Risk Management-20 (HCR-20), Violence Risk Appraisal Guide (VRAG), Level of Service Inventory–Revised (LSI-R) or German adaptations of known instruments (Rettenberger, Mönichweger, Buchelle, & Schilling, 2010) as well to predict static risk rates. The usage of such instruments would require a deeper clinical interviewing by forensic experts and could lead to interesting insights, especially in terms of dynamic risk factors.

A recently published paper from Tangney, Stuewig and Martinez (2014) supports the theory and findings by investigating actual relapse rates. The authors show that perspective taking ultimately reduces crime. The authors emphasise the importance of the empathic triad (perspective taking, empathic concern and guilt proneness) and the fact that guilt has an inhibitory effect on criminal behaviour. Their findings from official crime reports and self-reports reveal a strong link between a person's attributional style and their likelihood of reoffending. Given this context, it should be noted that self-report measures of recidivism reveal much larger effect sizes ($r = .32$) than official reports of recidivism ($r = .09$; Van Vugt et al., 2011).

10.4.1 Practical Implications

A major advantage of the present study is the original, scenario-based questionnaire consisting of everyday life situations. Such a test could be utilised at the beginning of incarceration to assess present shame and guilt proneness, which could be used to guide development of specific cognitive-behavioural interventions. When looking at the pure values of the correlations, our results indicate that shame proneness has the strongest predictive value for scores in the sexual recidivism scales. Although this is just a trend and further investigation with larger samples is needed, one might speculate that an early investigation of the attributional styles and connected emotions might be especially effective for sex offenders.

Our research presents a newly created scenario test that could be useful for examining attributional styles and emotional states of shame and guilt. An assessment of these emotions could be fruitful for correctional treatment and relapse prevention. As highlighted earlier, it is possible to use our pre-tested instrument to compute an individual score that reflects the attributional style of a prisoner in terms of shame and guilt. Highly negative values on this measure might indicate a higher need for cognitive-emotional reappraisal interventions. In order to advance understanding in this important area, we need larger sample sizes and a long-term follow-up period to account for real relapse events.

10.4.2 Perspectives for Further Correctional Treatment and Relapse Prevention

Finally, it should be mentioned that shame and guilt are just two conditions amongst several others that control the reduction of deviant behaviour (Hosser et al., 2007). Studies so far have mainly highlighted the context of juvenile offenders. Further investigation is needed with broader samples and adult populations. Furthermore we should focus on other control groups (other than just students). We hope that cognitive therapist and correctional treatment personnel will more specifically focus on the underlying causal dimensions of prisoners' reasoning, attributional styles and emotional landscape. After the prerequisites of shame and guilt have been stressed in this chapter, inferences concerning important clinical variables like expectancy changes, emotional responses and interpersonal evaluation can be made. It is then up to the clinician's judgement and the client's goals which attributions can be altered. The ultimate goal should be to reflect the prisoners' emotions and to establish an attributional style that brings the patient in a role where he sees his actions as controllable.

Attribution theory is based on the premise that individuals are motivated to gain a realistic causal understanding of their environment as well as their own actions to predict and control the events in their lives (Försterling, 1985). In this light the prisoners' motivation to change will be a vital precondition. In order to prevent maladaptive cognitive styles and emotions of the prisoners' we should also assess the motivation to therapy itself. Attribution theory delivers practical inputs to address this. Most cognitive therapies in these attributional re-trainings assume that dysfunctional or maladaptive emotions and behaviours are caused by unrealistic thinking. The therapeutic strategies derived from these ideas then consist of the collection and processing of information in regard to the unrealistic cognitions in order to help the prisoners have more realistic thoughts. This, in turn, can lead to more functional behavioural and emotive consequences. Thus, a more elaborate implementation of attributional re-training could lead to significant reduction of relapse.

Acknowledgements

We thank Sylvia Johne and Bjoern Hommel for their help within the investigation and analysis of the prisoners' files. Furthermore, we want to thank Sven Hartenstein from the Ministry of Justice in Saxony, Germany, as well as Michael Brinkmann, Harry Kempf and Steffen Rost from the correctional facility in Waldheim, Saxony, Germany, for their cooperation and support. Udo Rudolph provided valuable contributions.

References

Andrews, D. A., Bonta, J., & Hoge, R. D. (1990). Classification for effective rehabilitation: Rediscovering psychology. *Criminal Justice and Behavior, 17*(1), 19–52. http://doi.org/10.1177/0093854890017001004.

Auchter, T., & Hilgers, M. (1994). Delinquenz und Schamgefühl. Zur Bedeutung von Stolz und Scham bei Straftätern. *Monatsschrift für Kriminologie und Strafrechtsreform, 77*(2), 102–112.

Barrett, K. C. (1995). A functionalist approach to shame and guilt. In J. P. Tangney & W. Fischer (Eds.), *Self-conscious emotions: The psychology of shame, guilt, embarrassment, and pride* (pp. 25–63). New York: Guilford Press.

Bereswill, M. (2004). Inside-out: Resocialisation from prison as a biographical process. A longitudinal approach to the psychodynamics of imprisonment. *Journal of Social Work Practice, 18*(3), 315–336. http://doi.org/10.1080/0265053042000314401.

Bosold, C., Hosser, D., & Lauterbach, O. (2007). Psychosoziale Behandlung im Jugendstrafvollzug – Erste Ergebnisse einer Längschnittstudie. *Praxis der Rechtspsychologie, 17*, 265–284.

Braithwaite, J., & Mugford, S. (1994). Conditions of successful reintegration ceremonies: Dealing with juvenile offenders. *British Journal of Criminology, 34*(2), 139–171.

Brown, S. (2013). *Treating sex offenders: An introduction to sex offender treatment programmes.* London: Routledge.

Cohen, J. (1988). *Statistical power analysis for the behavioral sciences* (2nd ed.). Hillsdale, NJ: Lawrence Erlbaum Associates.

Cornel, H., & Nickolai, W. (Eds.). (2004). *What works? Neue Ansätze aus der Straffälligenhilfe auf dem Prüfstand.* Freiburg: Lambertus.

Dahle, K.-P. (2008). Aktuarische Prognoseinstrumente. In R. Volbert & M. Steller (Eds.), *Handbuch der Rechtspsychologie* (pp. 453–463). Göttingen: Hogrefe.

Eher, R., Schilling, F., Haubner-MacLean, T., Jahn, T., & Rettenberger, M. (2011). Ermittlung des relativen und absoluten Rückfallrisikos mithilfe des Static-99 in einer deutschsprachigen Population entlassener Sexualstraftäter. *Forensische Psychiatrie, Psychologie, Kriminologie, 6*(1), 32–40. http://doi.org/10.1007/s11757 -011-0146-z.

Endrass, J., Urbaniok, F., Held, L., Vetter, S., & Rossegger, A. (2009). Accuracy of the static-99 in predicting recidivism in Switzerland. *International Journal of Offender Therapy and Comparative Criminology*, 53(4), 482–490. http://doi.org/10.1177/0306624X07312952.

Faul, F., Erdfelder, E., Buchner, A., & Lang, A.-G. (2009). Statistical power analyses using G*Power 3.1: Tests for correlation and regression analyses. *Behavior Research Methods*, 41(4), 1149–1160. http://doi.org/10.3758/BRM.41.4.1149.

Ferguson, L. M., & Wormith, J. S. (2013). A meta-analysis of moral reconation therapy. *International Journal of Offender Therapy and Comparative Criminology*, 57(9), 1076–106. http://doi.org/10.1177/0306624X12447771.

Försterling, F. (1980). Attributional aspects of cognitive behavior modification: A theoretical approach and suggestions for techniques. *Cognitive Therapy and Research*, 4(1), 27–37. http://doi.org/10.1007/BF01173353.

Försterling, F. (1985). Attributional retraining: A review. *Psychological Bulletin*, 98(3), 495–512. http://doi.org/10.1037/0033-2909.98.3.495.

Försterling, F., & Rudolph, U. (1988). Situations, attributions, and the evaluation of reactions. *Journal of Personality and Social Psychology*, 54(2), 225–232. http://doi.org/10.1037/0022-3514.54.2.225.

Friendship, C., Blud, L., Erikson, M., Travers, R., & Thornton, D. (2003). Cognitive-behavioural treatment for imprisoned offenders: An evaluation of HM Prison Service's cognitive skills programmes. *Legal and Criminological Psychology*, 8(1), 103–114. http://doi.org/10.1348/135532503762871273.

Göbbels, S., & Zimmermann, L. (2013). Rehabilitation von Straftätern. *Forensische Psychiatrie, Psychologie, Kriminologie*, 7(1), 12–21. http://doi.org/10.1007/s11757-012-0199-7.

Greenberg, L. (2010). *Emotion-focused therapy*. Washington, DC: APA Books.

Hanson, R. K., & Bussière, M. T. (1998). Predicting relapse: A meta-analysis of sexual offender recidivism studies. *Journal of Consulting and Clinical Psychology*, 66(2), 348–362. http://doi.org/10.1037/0022-006X.66.2.348.

Hanson, R. K., & Morton-Bourgon, K. E. (2009). The accuracy of recidivism risk assessments for sexual offenders: A meta-analysis of 118 prediction studies. *Psychological Assessment*, 21(1), 1–21. http://doi.org/10.1037/a0014421.

Hanson, R. K., & Thornton, D. (1999). *Static 99: Improving actuarial risk assessments for sex offenders*. User Report 1999-02. Ottawa: Department of the Solicitor General of Canada.

Hareli, S., & Weiner, B. (2002). Social emotions and personality inferences: A scaffold for a new direction in the study of achievement motivation. *Educational Psychologist*, 37(3), 183–193. http://doi.org/10.1207/S15326985EP3703_4.

Harris, A., Phenix, A., Hanson, R. K., & Thornton, D. (2003). *STATIC-99 Coding Rules Revised – 2003*. Ottawa: Department of the Solicitor General of Canada.

Harris, G. T., Rice, M. E., Quinsey, V. L., Lalumière, M. L., Boer, D., & Lang, C. (2003). A multisite comparison of actuarial risk instruments for sex offenders. *Psychological Assessment*, 15(3), 413–425. http://doi.org/10.1037/1040-3590.15.3.413.

Heider, F. (1958). *The psychology of interpersonal relations*. New York: John Wiley & Sons. http://doi.org/10.1037/10628-000.

Hosser, D., Windzio, M., & Greve, W. (2005). Scham, Schuldgefühle und Delinquenz. *Zeitschrift für Sozialpsychologie*, 36(4), 227–238. http://doi.org/10.1024/0044-3514.36.4.227.

Hosser, D., Windzio, M., & Greve, W. (2007). Guilt and shame as predictors of recidivism: A longitudinal study with young prisoners. *Criminal Justice and Behavior*, *35*(1), 138–152. http://doi.org/10.1177/0093854807309224.

Howard, P., Francis, B., Soothill, K., & Humphreys, L. (2009). *OGRS 3: The revised Offender Group Reconviction Scale*. London: Ministry of Justice.

Joy Tong, L. S., & Farrington, D. P. (2006). How effective is the 'Reasoning and Rehabilitation' programme in reducing reoffending? A meta-analysis of evaluations in four countries. *Psychology, Crime & Law*, *12*(1), 3–24. http://doi.org /10.1080/10683160512331316253.

Landenberger, N. A., & Lipsey, M. W. (2005). The positive effects of cognitive–behavioral programs for offenders: A meta-analysis of factors associated with effective treatment. *Journal of Experimental Criminology*, *1*(4), 451–476.

Laubenthal, K. (2008). *Strafvollzug*. Berlin: Springer.

Lösel, F., & Bender, D. (1997). Straftäterbehandlung: Konzepte, Ergebnisse, Probleme. In M. Steller & R. Volbert (Eds.), *Psychologie im Strafverfahren* (pp. 171–204). Bern: Hans Huber.

Mann, R. E., & Thornton, D. (1998). The evolution of a multisite sexual offender treatment program. In W. L. Marshall, M. Fernandez, & M. Hudson (Eds.), *Sourcebook of treatment programs for sexual offenders* (pp. 47–57). Boston: Springer US. http://doi.org/10.1007/978-1-4899-1916-8_4.

Martinez, A. G., Stuewig, J., & Tangney, J. P. (2014). Can perspective-taking reduce crime? Examining a pathway through empathic-concern and guilt-proneness. *Personality and Social Psychology Bulletin*, *40*(12), 1659–1667. http://doi.org /10.1177/0146167214554915.

Martinson, R. (1974). What works? Questions and answers about prison reform. *Public Interest*, *35*, 22–54.

McGuire, J. (2002). Integrating findings from research reviews. In J. McGuire (Ed.), *Offender rehabilitation and treatment: Effective programmes and policies to reduce re-offending* (pp. 3–38). Chichester: Wiley.

National Offender Management Service. (2008). *Offender Group Reconviction Scale – Version 3: Guidance*. London: Ministry of Justice.

Rettenberger, M., & Eher, R. (2006). Actuarial assessment of sex offender recidivism risk: A validation of the German version of the Static-99. *Sexual Offender Treatment*, *1*(3), 1–11.

Rettenberger, M., Mönichweger, M., Buchelle, E., & Schilling, F. (2010). Entwicklung eines Screeninginstruments zur Vorhersage der einschlägigen Rückfälligkeit von Gewaltstraftätern. *Monatsschrift für Kriminologie Und Strafrechtsreform*, *93*(5), 346–360.

Roos, J. (2000). Peinlichkeit, Scham & Schuld. In J. H. Otto, H. Euler, & H. Mandl (Eds.), *Emotionspsychologie – Ein Handbuch* (pp. 264–271). Weinheim: Beltz.

Ross, R. R., Fabiano, E. A., & Ross, B. (1989). *Reasoning and rehabilitation: A handbook for teaching cognitive skills*. Ottawa: The Cognitive Center.

Rudolph, U., Roesch, S., Greitemeyer, T., & Weiner, B. (2004). A meta-analytic review of help-giving and aggression from an attributional perspective: Contributions to a general theory of motivation. *Cognition & Emotion*, *18*(6), 815–848.

Rudolph, U., Schulz, K., & Tscharaktschiew, N. (2013). Moral emotions: An analysis guided by Heider's naïve action analysis. *International Journal of Advances in Psychology*, *2*(2), 69–92.

Rudolph, U., & Tscharaktschiew, N. (2014). An attributional analysis of moral emotions: Naïve scientists and everyday judges. *Emotion Review, 6*(4), 1–9. http://doi.org/10.1177/1754073914534507.

Sarre, R. (2001). Beyond 'What Works?' A 25-year jubilee retrospective of Robert Martinsons famous article. *Australian & New Zealand Journal of Criminology, 34*(1), 38–46. http://doi.org/10.1177/000486580103400103.

Tangney, J. P. (1991). Moral affect: The good, the bad, and the ugly. *Journal of Personality and Social Psychology, 61*(4), 598–607. http://doi.org/10.1037/0022-3514.61.4.598.

Tangney, J. P. (2002). Self-conscious emotions: The self as a moral guide. In A. Tesser, D. A. Stapel, & J. V. Wood (Eds.), *Self and motivation* (pp. 97–117). Washington, DC: American Psychological Association.

Tangney, J. P., & Dearing, R. L. (2002). *Shame and guilt.* New York: The Guilford Press.

Tangney, J. P., Stuewig, J., & Hafez, L. (2011). Shame, guilt, and remorse: Implications for offender populations. *Journal of Forensic Psychiatry & Psychology, 22*(5), 706–723. http://doi.org/10.1080/14789949.2011.617541.

Tangney, J. P., Stuewig, J., & Martinez, A. G. (2014). Two faces of shame: The roles of shame and guilt in predicting recidivism. *Psychological Science, 25*(3), 799–805. http://doi.org/10.1177/0956797613508790.

Tangney, J. P., Stuewig, J., & Mashek, D. J. (2007). Moral emotions and moral behavior. *Annual Review of Psychology, 58*, 345–372. http://doi.org/10.1146/annurev.psych.56.091103.070145.

Thornton, D., Mann, R., Webster, S., Bkud, L., Travers, R., Frienship, C., & Erikson, M. (2006). Distinguishing and combining risks for sexual and violent recidivism. *Annals of the New York Academy of Sciences, 989*(1), 225–235. http://doi.org/10.1111/j.1749-6632.2003.tb07308.x.

Tracy, J. L., & Robins, R. W. (2004). Putting the self into self-conscious emotions: A theoretical model. *Psychological Inquiry, 15*(2), 103–125. http://doi.org/10.1207/s15327965pli1502_01.

Van Vugt, E., Gibbs, J., Stams, G. J., Bijleveld, C., Hendriks, J., & van der Laan, P. (2011). Moral development and recidivism: A meta-analysis. *International Journal of Offender Therapy and Comparative Criminology, 55*(8), 1234–1250. http://doi.org/10.1177/0306624X10396441.

Volbert, R., & Dahle, K.-P. (2010). *Forensisch-psychologische Diagnostik im Strafverfahren.* Göttingen: Hogrefe.

Wakeling, H. C., Howard, P., & Barnett, G. (2011). Comparing the validity of the RM2000 scales and OGRS3 for predicting recidivism by internet sexual offenders. *Sexual Abuse: A Journal of Research and Treatment, 23*(1), 146–168. http://doi.org/10.1177/1079063210375974.

Wakeling, H. C., Mann, R. E., & Milner, R. J. (2011). Interrater reliability of Risk Matrix 2000/s. *International Journal of Offender Therapy and Comparative Criminology, 55*(8), 1324–1337. http://doi.org/10.1177/0306624X11386933.

Ward, T., & Brown, M. (2004). The good lives model and conceptual issues in offender rehabilitation. *Psychology, Crime & Law, 10*(3), 243–257. http://doi.org/10.1080/10683160410001662744.

Ward, T., Mann, R. E., & Gannon, T. A. (2007). The good lives model of offender rehabilitation: Clinical implications. *Aggression and Violent Behavior, 12*(1), 87–107. http://doi.org/10.1016/j.avb.2006.03.004.

Weiner, B. (2006). *Social motivation, justice, and the moral emotions: An attributional approach*. Mahwah, NJ: Lawrence Erlbaum.

Weiner, B. (2014). The attribution approach to emotion and motivation: History, hypotheses, home runs, headaches/heartaches. *Emotion Review, 6*(4), 353–361. http://doi.org/10.1177/1754073914534502.

Wischka, B., Foppe, E., Griepenburg, P., Nuhn-Naber, C., & Rehder, U. (2004). *Das Behandlungsprogramm für Sexualstraftäter (BPS)*. Lingen: Kriminalpädagogischer Verlag.

Personality Traits of Juveniles Convicted of Sexual Assault

11

GAYANE A. VARTANYAN
SERGEY V. GORBATOV

Contents

Contemporary Russian society is characterised by fundamental transformations in socio-economic, political and other spheres. However, certain social groups experience a decrease in living standards and deterioration of moral ideals. This has a strong negative effect on the younger generation. Juveniles' consciousness and stereotypes of sexual behaviour are altered, and their sexual ethics suffer deformation, which is a matter of particular concern (Azletskiy, 1999). Juveniles increasingly often satisfy their sexual desires through illegal means, which requires comprehensive psychological research into the underlying factors.

In fact, Russian psychologists are only starting comprehensive research into the psychology of sexual crimes. Both lawyers and psychologists are interested in studying aggressive behaviour in general and criminal aggression in particular, and their studies are described in a number of works (A.M. Antonyan, V.V. Guldan, M.I. Enikeev, S.N. Enikolopov, L.P. Kolchina, M.M. Kochenov,

I.A. Kudryavtsev, A.R. Ratinov, N.A. Ratinova, A.A. Rean, E.V. Romanin, S.E. Roschin, T.G. Rumyantseva, F.S. Safuanov and others). Meanwhilst, the number of research works on sexual aggression is insufficient (G.E. Vvedenskiy, P.N. Ermakov, I.S. Kon, O. Yu. Mikhaylova, Z. Starovich and B.V. Shostakovich).

When analysing research works dedicated to juvenile delinquency, we came across the same problem. There are numerous papers on the peculiarities of juvenile delinquent behaviour (M.A. Alemaskin, S.A. Belicheva, A.I. Dolgova, P.N. Ermakov, G.I. Zabryanskiy, A.A. Kokuev, V.V. Korolev, I.A. Kudryavtsev, A.E. Lichko, G.M. Minkovskiy, O.A. Potapenko, A.A. Rean, D.I. Feldshteyn, A.M. Yakovlev and others). However, the studies on sexual crimes committed by juveniles are scarce (Yu. M. Antonyan, L.M. Balabanova, O. Yu. Mikhaylova and A.A. Tkachenko). There are hardly any studies on (a) psychological mechanisms of juvenile group sexual crimes and (b) the personality of such criminals, with a few exceptions (L.P. Konysheva, V.F. Pirozhkov and Ch. Chapuv).

The number of juvenile sexual crimes is on the rise. This fact has aroused a research interest in the issues of juvenile criminal sexual conduct. According to the data of criminological statistics, in January–February 2014, more than 340,000 crimes were registered in Russia, and 1 out of 23 (4.4%) was committed by juveniles or with their participation. Meanwhilst, the rate of juvenile crimes remains practically at the same level of the last years; there is only a slight decrease – in the first quarter of 2013 juveniles committed or took part in 1 of 21 crimes.

The academic community is particularly concerned that at present juvenile sexual crimes are most often perpetrated against male children. The experts of the Karolinska Institute have analysed the research works on juveniles committing sexual crimes. They found that the considerable part of all sexual crimes is carried out by juveniles assaulting younger children of the immediate family. Also, the majority of these criminal acts remain latent for both surrounding people and the police. This trend is also observed in Russia, especially in recent years (Vartanyan & Gorbatov, 2013). The given facts prompt the following question: If juveniles commit sexual assaults on children of the same gender, can we classify them as paedophiles or homosexuals?

11.1 Analysis of Theories Describing the Reasons for and Factors of Homosexuality and Paedophilia

Contemporary science offers a number of theories describing the reasons for and factors of homosexuality. We shall briefly analyse some of them. The Austrian psychiatrist Sigmund Freud supposed that homosexuality results from the inborn predisposition to bisexuality, which is typical of all people. Under normal conditions, children's psychosexual development occurs in a heterosexual direction; however, in some cases normal development may stop at an 'immature' stage which will eventually lead to homosexuality. Freud's idea – that incorrect parent–child relations may result in homosexuality – was tested by Bieber et al. (1962). They examined the family life of their patients amongst which 106 were homosexuals and 100 were heterosexuals. As a result, they revealed that many homosexuals had a too authoritative mother and a weak-willed, passive father; meanwhilst, heterosexuals rarely had a similar correlation between their parents. In light of the data received, Bieber declined Freud's concept about psychological (inborn predisposition to) bisexuality and voiced an opinion that homosexuality stems from the fear of relations with persons of the opposite sex.

Later studies on the causes of male homosexuality yielded controversial results. According to Nicolosi, Byrd and Potts (2002), fathers of homosexuals seem emotionally removed, avoiding communications and incapable of changing the relationship with their sons (Ross, 1983). According to Greenblatt (1966), however, the fathers of homosexual men are kind and caring people, whilst their mothers are distinguished neither by excessive care, nor by authoritativeness (Masters et al., 1998). Siegelman (1974) notes the absence of any significant differences in parent–child relations between groups of psychologically well-adapted heterosexuals and homosexuals (Ross, 1983; Master et al., 1998). The research performed by Bell, Weinberg and Hammersmith (1981) did not support Bieber's conclusions either.

Marmor (1980), who studies the phenomenon of homosexuality, writes that homosexuals can occur in families where mothers are unfriendly and untender, with fathers having close relations with children; they may occur in families where relations with elder brothers are 'ambiguous'; they may come from families where a mother or a father is constantly absent and they may as well be encountered in families where fathers are idealised, whilst mothers play the role of a servant (Masters et al., 1998). There is a high probability that male children from problem families can become homosexuals, but many of them actually do not.

In their two-volume work *Sexual Preference: Its Development in Men and Women*, Bell, Weinberg, and Hammersmith (1981) tried to examine various theories related to the origin of homosexuality. Using a complicated statistical method, they sought to identify the correspondence between the results obtained and one of the theoretical models. The studies performed led to the following conclusions:

1. There is a very low possibility that homosexuality amongst men can arise from abnormal family relations such as an authoritative mother or a weak-willed father.

2. The stereotype that homosexuality often stems from perversion on the part of adults of the same sex is wrong.
3. Sexual preference is firmly established in adolescence; amongst grown-ups there rarely occurs significant changes in sexual orientation.
4. In childhood and adolescence, homosexuals take part in heterosexual intercourse as often as their heterosexual peers do; however, it gives them less or no satisfaction at all.
5. The lack of correspondence between the play behaviour of children and their gender – for example, the love of playing with dolls amongst male children – is an important but not an absolute sign that they will further become homosexuals.

Thus, theories about development of homosexuality remain purely academic and can fit one specific case but fail to explain the general origin of the issue. The most widespread theories include: behaviourist theories (Gagnon & Simon, 1973; Grandlach, 1977; Masters & Johnson, 1979; McGuire, Carlisle, & Young, 1965); and biological theories which focused on the influence of genetic factors on development of homosexuality (Heston & Shields, 1968; Kallman, 1952; Zuger, 1976) and on the influence of hormonal factors (Dorner, 1968/1976; Hutchison, 1978; Masters & Johnson, 1979; Meyer-Bahlburg, 1977/1979; Money & Ehrhardt, 1972; Money & Schwartz, 1977; Tourney, 1980) (Masters et al., 1998).

There is a similar situation regarding the views on paedophilia in contemporary society. Researchers offer theoretical and empirical information on the issue. We shall try to sum this up. In accordance with the *Diagnostic and Statistical Manual of Mental Disorders*, 5th edition (*DSM-5*), a paedophile sexual interest is not a mental disorder. This sexual interest can be ascribed to persons above 16 years old, based on the fact of at least 6-months-long intensive sexual motives and dreams related to involvement in sexual activity of children under puberty age. However, if a person suffers because of his peculiarities or inflicts harm on other people, he can be diagnosed with 'peadophilia disorder'. In this case, for this diagnosis it does not matter whether a subject's sexual interest is aimed at his own or other children (American Psychiatric Association, 2013).

In compliance with the 10th revision of the International Classification of Diseases (ICD-10) maintained by the World Health Organization (WHO) and used in its member countries (including Russia), the following general criteria must be satisfied for giving a diagnosis of paedophilia:

1. A person has unusual sexual motives and dreams (G1) which cause him distress.
2. A person acts in accordance with these motives and dreams (G2).

3. The sexual motives continue for at least six months (G3).
4. A person gives sexual preference to children of pre-puberty age and early puberty age; and this person is above 16 years old, according to special criteria F65.4 (WHO, 1993).

Thus, following the classifications offered both by the American Psychiatric Association and by the World Health Organization, a person with sexual attraction to children may be acknowledged as mentally ill if he implements his sexual motives through actions or suffers because of these actions.

However, when a subject has no possibility of or is not capable of entering relations with an adult sexual partner due to constant frustrations and he turns to children as sexual objects, such paedophile behaviour may have a substitutive nature (Tkachenko, 1997).

There is no general agreement amongst scientists concerning the definition of paedophilia as a mental disorder. In the article 'Is Pedophilia a Mental Disorder?', American psychiatrist Richard Green (2002) questions the definition of paedophilia as a mental disorder. He notes that such behaviour was considered normal in many ancient cultures. Sexologist Charles Allen Moser has summed up the information on the issue raised by Green and now requests that the American Psychiatric Association should fully exclude the category of 'paraphilia' from *DSM-5*. According to him, exclusion of the paedophilia diagnosis does not mean that a sexual intercourse between an adult and a child is not a crime. Moser emphasises that after this elimination, the judicial system will focus on the criminal aspect of an action, and criminals will not be able to justify themselves saying they suffer a mental disorder.

Nevertheless, the problem related to classification of paedophilia types still remains debatable. Depending on whether sexual preference is given to male or female children, *DSM-5* differentiates between heterosexual, homosexual and bisexual paedophilia; it also singles out exclusive paedophilia when sexual attraction is shown only to children of pre-puberty age, and non-exclusive paedophilia when sexual attraction is shown both to children and to adults. ICD-10 does not include the category of paedophilia diagnosis (WHO, 1993).

We shall try to find out the aetiology of this phenomenon and shall examine a few points of view.

To describe sexual preference, American sexologist John Money introduced the concept of a lovemap. It denotes the image of an ideal sexual partner and optimal sexual activity with this partner. The image is unique to every person and firmly imprinted on his brain. The disturbance of psychosexual development leading to a paraphilia was termed a vandalised lovemap. According to Money, a vandalised lovemap includes unusual components existing in the society outside the sexual context, such as the worship of talismans, atonement for sin and others.

Ray Blanchard and his colleagues (2002) performed research indicating paedophiles were exposed to craniocerebral injuries before the age of 13. As is well known, such injuries can be linked with both hyposexuality and hypersexuality and sometimes with paraphilias. Following the research conclusions, early craniocerebral injuries increase the possibility of paedophilia development, whilst a prenatal disturbance of the nervous system development equally raises the probability of paedophilia and of early craniocerebral injuries.

The studies performed by a Canadian group of researchers showed that paedophiles are of lower height and have a lower IQ. There are also a heightened percentage of left-handers and ambidexters amongst them (Cantor et al., 2007). The low height and the lower IQ may testify to the impact of various harmful factors during the period of prenatal and postnatal ontogenesis. Meanwhilst, the high percentage of left-handers and ambidexters indicates that a paedophile's brain may have suffered various detrimental conditions in the mother's womb. At a lecture of the Association for the Treatment of Sexual Abusers devoted to the study of paedophilia, James M. Cantor noted that paedophilia could result from brain pathology; however, researchers have not yet identified what brain mechanisms are traumatised and how. At the same time, the established correlations – including neuroanatomical ones such as a shortage of white matter – are not a necessary condition for development of paedophilia (Cantor, 2012).

Russian researchers also suggest that the primary source of paedophilia, as well as of all other paraphilias, is an organic lesion of the brain, most often a prenatal one. However, Andrey Tkachenko, who carried out research with his colleagues, believes that, in the event of paraphilias, traumas are caused to the brain systems responsible for developing a basic identity. As a result, the subsequent psychosexual ontogenesis is disturbed; this ontogenesis comprises development of gender identity, sex-role behaviour and psychosexual orientation. Tkachenko's research group revealed that disturbance of gender identity was observed amongst all paraphiliacs. Kurt Freund and his co-authors did not identify this disturbance in the childhood of paedophiles; it was detected only amongst homosexuals (Freund & Blanchard, 1987).

In 2012, Cantor reviewed the current state of research on paraphilias and homosexuality. His study delivered data indicating that homosexuality is caused by a disturbance of defeminisation and masculinisation of the brain. In childhood, this disturbance can be manifested as disruption of gender identity. At the same time, there is no proof that any paraphilia stems from the aforementioned process (Cantor, 2012).

Blanchard discovered that birth order can influence on the development of homosexual paedophilia. He thinks that the more older biological brothers a man has, the higher the possibility of him becoming a homosexual (Blanchard, 1997). The birth-order effect was confirmed in the research of Canadian sexologist Antoni Bogaert. He emphasised that the effect comes into force only on condition that there are biological brothers (Bogaert, 2006). Researchers suppose that the birth-order effect occurs due to an increase in the sensitisation of a mother's immune system to the proteins of the Y chromosome which are important for defeminisation and masculinisation of the brain. The increase takes place because the proteins get into the circulatory system of the mother whose immune system generates antibodies to them. After the antibodies break through the placental barrier, they can influence the sex differentiation of the brain. The more sons a mother has, the more sensitised her immune system to the proteins of the Y chromosome becomes; hence there is a higher risk of disrupting defeminisation and masculinisation in the foetus's brain and therefore of giving birth to a homosexual child. Cantor's research group hypothesises that paedophilia is the disturbance of basic instincts which trigger the sex instinct amongst paedophiles when they see children. Meanwhilst, non-paedophiles have an instinct for 'protection and upbringing' in this case.

According to Vernon Quinsey and Hubert Van Gijseghem, who reported at the parliament session in Canada in February 2011, paedophilia should be regarded as a sexual orientation due to its stable and incurable nature. The psychologists asserted that people who committed sexual crimes against children and were released from prison were inclined to a high percentage of repeated crimes; for this reason, the task of psychiatry consists in the effort to teach paedophiles how to control their desires but not to cure them (Millette, 2011).

Boris Schiffer studied paedophiles using neuroanatomical magnetic resonance tomography in 2007. Schiffer and colleagues detected a decreased quantity of grey matter in the orbitofrontal cortex, ventral striatum and cerebellum. Relying on this fact, Schiffer classified paedophilia as an obsessive-compulsive disorder, because the identified neuroanatomical peculiarities are typical of the spectrum of obsessive-compulsive disorders. Later, Schiffer came to the conclusion that, due to the malfunction of the orbitofrontal cortex and of the neural networks connected with it, the paedophile's cognitive stage of sexual excitement – at which sexual partners are recognised – is disturbed (Schiffer et al., 2008).

In the same year, Kolja Schiltz published his research data; he revealed that paedophiles had a decreased quantity of grey matter in the right amygdala, septal area, hypothalamus, the substantia innominata and the nucleus of the terminal strip bed. Schiltz thinks that the brain structures where the shortage of grey matter was identified perform an important role in sexual behaviour and its development (Schiltz, 2007).

The research based on functional magnetic resonance imaging indicated that sexual excitement activates the same brain structures in paedophiles' brains as in the brains of healthy people. The difference is that the activation is stimulated by images of children, not the images of adults.

Pierre Flor-Henry and his colleagues (Perehov & Buhanovskaya, 1998) revealed that paedophiles have electroencephalography changes associated with sinistrocerebral dysfunction, an activation decrease in frontotemporal lobes. They supposed that, due to the sinistrocerebral dysfunction, paedophiles have the disrupted formation of 'normal' verbal and ideational patterns of sexual activity. Tkachenko with co-authors received similar results in their research employing electroencephalography (Eliseev, Tkachenko, Petina, & Kunikovskiy, 1997).

Tkachenko and his co-authors detected unconscious disorders of gender identity and disturbances of sex-role behaviour amongst paraphiliacs most of which are paedophiles. Studying the compulsive forms of paraphilias, the researchers discovered a heightened content of free and conjugated forms of noradrenaline, adrenalin, dopamine and dioxyphenylacetic acid (dopamine metabolites) in blood plasma and daily urine; as well as a heightened rate of serotonin capture by platelets (Kogan et al., 1997).

Dutch researchers identified a lowered level of cortisol and prolactin in paedophiles' blood plasma and, upon injecting meta-chlorophenylpiperazine, registered a more significant increase in the cortisol level exceeding that of the control group. This fact made them suppose that paedophiles have disorders in the serotoninergic system. In another study, the same authors detected a higher increase of the adrenalin concentration in paedophiles' blood plasma upon injecting meta-chlorophenylpiperazine as compared to the control group.

Fred Berlin and his colleagues assumed that paedophiles have a dysfunction in the hypothalamic–pituitary–gonadal axis (Gaffney, 1984).

Canadian scientists have recently performed a study that reveals an interesting fact: the possibility of recidivism amongst paedophiles positively correlates with the level of luteinising hormones and follicle-stimulating hormones (Kingston et al., 2012).

Apart from the studies described, scientists also performed genetic research for studying the personal peculiarities of paedophiles and the factors stimulating paedophile behaviour. The first study of this kind was carried out by Fred Berlin in 1984. It confirmed the possibility of genetic investigation into paedophilia, because paedophilia occurred much more often amongst the relatives of paedophiles, rather than in the families of people who do not suffer from this disease. The results of the second genetic research were published by Finnish scientists in 2013. According to this study, the concordance of paedophilia amongst identical twins is higher than that amongst fraternal ones.

According to Abel and Harlow, paedophilia is a disorder that develops at an early age (Kershner, 2015). A person affected by this type of disorder starts offending against younger children. Sixty-eight per cent of the children who fell victim to paedophiles say that they are exposed to sexual abuse in their own families. Approximately 40% of child molesters assault children from the families of their acquaintances.

Contemporary experts think that therapy should be aimed at increasing the self-control of paedophiles and reducing their distress, rather than at changing their sexual preference (Seto, 2009).

11.2 Organisation of Research

11.2.1 Methods

In our research we employed the following group of mutually complementary techniques which we divided into three units:

1. Techniques designed to study the personal peculiarities of adolescents
   a. Raymond Cattell's 16 Personality Factors Questionnaire (Form C), aimed at exploring the individual psychological peculiarities of a person
   b. The Pathocharacterological Diagnostic Questionnaire by Lichko and Ivanov, designed to study the accentuations of adolescents' character and their disposition to psychopathy
   c. Timothy Leary's Interpersonal Diagnosis of Personality, for studying the preferred style of interpersonal relations
2. Techniques designed to research parent–child relations
   a. The Social Well-Being of Children, an author questionnaire consisting of 29 questions
   b. The Analysis of Family Relationships by Eidemiller and Yustitskis, aimed at studying various disturbances of an upbringing process, types of incorrect pathological upbringing and some of the psychological causes of these disturbances
   c. Sex Education in Family, an author questionnaire consisting of two forms: the one for parents (19 questions) and the other for children (16 questions)
3. Techniques for mathematical data analysis
   a. Basic descriptive statistics
   b. The Kolmogorov–Smirnov test (Z value)
   c. Student's t-test for two independent variables
   d. The Mann-Whitney U-test for two independent variables
   e. Pearson's correlation analysis

11.2.2 Participants

In the first research stage, 120 adolescents took part. They were divided into 6 groups, each comprising 20 participants:

1. Juveniles convicted of violent sexual crimes
2. Juveniles convicted of violent crimes
3. Juveniles convicted of acquisitive crimes
4. Juveniles under a suspended sentence, that is, the ones who are not put in penal colonies

5. Juveniles brought up in boarding schools, that is, social and biological orphans (control group 1)
6. Juveniles growing in a socially favourable environment (control group 2)

In the second research stage, 200 participants were involved:

1. Juveniles convicted of violent sexual crimes and their parents (84 people)
2. Juveniles growing in a socially favourable environment (a control group) and their parents (116 participants)

The general sample of participants comprised 320 people.

11.2.3 Procedure

The research consisted of three stages. At the first stage, we performed the comparative analysis of results obtained from studying the six groups of male adolescents. At the second stage, we examined the parent–child relations in the families of the aforementioned adolescent groups, supposing that there would be a significant difference between them. At the final third stage, we tried to investigate the interconnection between the peculiarities identified and the parenting style of the adolescent groups. It should be noted that, when making a correlation analysis, the data related to the analysis of family relationships were collected only from the mothers of the adolescent groups. The reason is that, as the author questionnaire showed, only 35% of the convicts were brought up in two-parent families. We find it insufficient for a joint correlation analysis of parenting styles adopted by the fathers and mothers of the adolescents. Participants were recruited from prisons for juveniles and boarding schools. An agreement was signed with the institutions. All adolescents and their parents voluntarily agreed to participate in the research. The data collected in the study consists of confidential information which is not disclosed. However, at the request of institutions, we have provided common facts without any personal data of participants.

11.3 Results

11.3.1 First Research Stage

As Table 11.1 demonstrates, practically all the data obtained using Cattell's 16 Personality Factors Questionnaire (Form C) are within normal limits. Meanwhile, the values at the reasoning (B) scale proved to be below the standard for all groups of convicts and for the group of boarding school children. This testifies to the prevalence of concrete thinking, difficulties in solving

Table 11.1 Results of Comparison between the Groups' Values Obtained Using Cattell's 16 Personality Factors Questionnaire (Form C)

Group	MD	A	B	C	E	F	G	H	I	L	M	N	O	Q1	Q2	Q3	Q4
Juveniles convicted of violent sexual crimes	6,5	6	3	7	5	5	6	6	5	6	6	6	6	6	6	5	5
Juveniles convicted of violent crimes	7,5	7,7	3,5	7,5	5,3	4,9	7,5	5,9	6,2	6,1	5,6	6,5	5,3	6,8	5,6	7,6	5,3
Juveniles convicted of acquisitive crimes	8,8	7,2	3	7,4	6,9	6,2	6,8	7,7	5,3	6,2	4,8	6,7	6,6	6,6	6,2	6,9	4,7
Juveniles under a suspended sentence	8,3	6,5	2,6	7,4	4,7	5,6	5,2	5,9	5,6	5,6	5,6	6,2	6,6	6,2	6,9	6	4,6
Juveniles brought up in boarding schools	8	5	1	7,5	8	5	5	5	4	8	6	9	5	4	8	8	7
Juvenile schoolchildren growing in a socially favourable environment	7	8	5	8	6	5	7	7	5	6	6	5	6	7	5	5	5

Note: MD, self-esteem; A, warmth; B, reasoning; C, emotional stability; E, dominance; F, liveliness; G, rule-consciousness; H, social boldness; I, sensitivity; L, vigilance; M, abstractedness; N, privateness; O, apprehension; Q1, openness to change; Q2, self-reliance; Q3, perfectionism; Q4, tension.

abstract tasks and low intelligence in the groups of convicts and boarding school children in general. As Table 11.1 shows, we did not identify any significant differences in psychological peculiarities of six adolescent groups. Nevertheless, we can single out some characteristics typical of each group. For example, juvenile convicts and boarding school children are characterised by prevalence of concrete thinking, a poor ability in solving abstract tasks and low intelligence in general.

Studying the accentuation of personality traits and disposition to psychopathy, we revealed that adolescents convicted of violent sexual crimes and those convicted of acquisitive crimes are characterised by the epileptoid psychological type (Table 11.2). The data obtained signify that such adolescents are distinguished by emotional tension, instability, affective explosiveness and impulsiveness. Lichko and Ivanov (1995, p. 7–8) provide the following description of these adolescents in their book:

> Their major peculiarity is manifested in the inclination to angry and melancholy states of mind and search for an object to vent their anger on. Regarding

Table 11.2 Results of Comparison between the Groups' Values Obtained Using the Pathocharacterological Diagnostic Questionnaire (A. Lichko and M. Y. Ivanov)

Group	H	C	L	A	S	P	Sch	E	Hys	U	Con
Juveniles convicted of violent sexual crimes	7	4.7	5.8	3.2	4.1	5	4.6	8.5	3	5.3	3.5
Juveniles convicted of violent crimes	7.2	4.3	4.7	2.5	3.4	4.1	5.1	7.4	5.8	4.7	2.5
Juveniles convicted of acquisitive crimes	7	5.2	5.9	3.8	3.9	4.3	5.4	8.6	5.2	5.5	2.6
Juveniles under a suspended sentence	7.3	4.6	5	3.6	5.1	4.5	6	9.2	9.2	5.1	2.6
Juveniles brought up in boarding schools	8.2	4.2	3.1	2.4	3.4	4.5	4.6	6.7	4	3.1	1.5
Juvenile schoolchildren growing in a socially favourable environment	1.8	6.6	6.7	3	5.2	8.7	5.3	6.6	6.2	4.8	3.2

Note: H, hyperthymic type; C, cycloid type; L, labile type; A, asthenoneurotic type; S, sensitive type; P, psychasthenic type; Sch, schizoid type; E, epileptoid type; Hys, hysteroid type; U, unstable type; Con, conformal type.

interpersonal relations, they show great jealousy towards their partner. Leadership shows in the striving for ruling over others. Such people adapt well under strict disciplinary regimes, where they seek to fawn on authorities by giving an appearance of industrious workers and to acquire a status that enables controlling other adolescents. The processes in their nervous system are characterised by inertness, stiffness, and 'viscosity', which in turn leaves an imprint on the entire psyche – from movements and emotions to thinking and personal values. They like developing their physical strength and give preference to strength sports. They make decisions without haste and in rather a prudent manner. This is why they sometimes miss an opportunity requiring quick action. However, their sluggishness disappears in an affective state. For this reason, they easily lose control of themselves, act on impulse, and may burst into swearing and beat someone in an unsuitable situation. Adolescents are very vindictive and inventive in methods of their revenge. Carefulness in details, scrupulousness, meticulous abidance by any rules, even to the detriment of business, and annoying pedantry are considered a compensation for one's own inertness. They usually have one-sided self-esteem. As far as the rest is concerned, they present themselves as being more conformist than they actually are.

The adolescents convicted of violent crimes are characterised by the mixed hyperthymic and epileptoid type. However, Lichko and Ivanov (1995) remark that such accentuations of character are extremely rare, whilst the data obtained may testify to the discordance of character, which may, in turn, point to mental problems.

The adolescents under a suspended sentence usually belong to the mixed epileptoid and hysteriod type. Such a combination is determined by endogenous and primarily genetic factors. At the same time, they do not deny the impact of development peculiarities in early childhood. The adolescents of the mixed epileptoid and hysteroid type are self-centred; thirst for attention and are emotionally strained, unstable, vindictive and unforgiving. They can fall in an affective state which can be strong and long at the same time. The juveniles under a suspended sentence are inert and stiff; they speak slowly, with authority and never make fuss. They are also slow in decision-making, which is why they sometimes miss an opportunity requiring quick action. The leadership of such adolescents is manifested in an effort to control others and combines with the striving for imposition of one's own rules and with intolerance to opposite points of view. They demand constant attention to and admiration for themselves. They are distinguished by deceitfulness and daydreaming. They are scrupulous and committed to order and neatness which is obvious in their clothes, haircut and preference for order in everything. The self-esteem is usually one-sided and far from being objective. Normally they present themselves in a way so as to most easily produce the required impression at the moment (Lichko & Ivanov, 1995).

Hyperthymic accentuation of character is peculiar to juveniles at boarding schools. The authors of that research write the following about such juveniles:

These juveniles are distinguished always by a good, even slightly heightened mood, increased vigour, excessive energy, unstoppable activity, and constant aspiration to informal leadership. A good sense of the new combines with unstable interests; while high sociability, with lack of selectiveness in choosing friends. As a result, they can imperceptibly find themselves in a bad company, tasting alcohol, drugs, and other intoxicants. Typically, they do not violate the law alone – they do it in a group. They easily adapt to unfamiliar and fast-changing conditions, but overestimate their possibilities and make too optimistic plans for the future. They are unselective in choosing their friends and partners, which is why they are often faced with betrayals. These adolescents can hardly bear solitude, a strictly regulated discipline. Other people's effort to suppress their activeness and leader's qualities often result in their heated, but short fits of irritation. They are forgiving and easily reconcile with the people they have a quarrel with. When socialising with others, they are talkative, have a quick speech, lively facial expressions and gestures. A high biological tone is always manifested in a good appetite and sound sleep – they get up in a cheerful mood and full of energy. Quite early they start feeling sexual attraction which is rather strong. They often have good self-esteem, but usually seek to give an appearance of being more conformist than they really are. The first signs of hyperthymic type are often shown in childhood: tirelessness, noisiness, an aspiration to command peers, and excessive independence. (Lichko & Ivanov, 1995, p. 4–5)

The control group of juvenile schoolchildren, who are in a socially favourable environment, typically belong to the psychasthenic type.

They are indecisive, mistrustful, inclined to self-analysis, and subject to fixed ideas. They often find it the most difficult task to be responsible for themselves and particularly for others. Imaginary objects and invented rituals help alleviate their constant anxiety about chimerical troubles and misfortunes. They become more indecisive when it comes to making an independent decision on insignificant everyday problems. Serious issues having a marked effect on the future are, on the contrary, often tackled with surprising hastiness. As regards their self-esteem, they tend to ascribe the characteristics of different psychological types to themselves, including the ones that are absolutely alien to them. They are excessively pedantic and committed to principles even in terms of minor issues, sometimes becoming despotic. As a result, they are rarely compatible with representatives of almost all other accentuations of character. Psychasthenics' pedantry is also considered to calm their fears for the future. (Lichko & Ivanov, 1995, p. 6–7)

In addition, the researchers identified that all the groups of juvenile convicts have a pure or mixed epileptoid accentuation of character, that is, they are characterised by emotional tension, instability, affective explosiveness and impulsiveness.

Studying adolescent interpersonal relations, we found that juveniles convicted of violent sexual crimes and violent crimes, and juveniles under a suspended sentence prefer a friendly style of interpersonal relations. Meanwhilst, juveniles convicted of acquisitive crimes, boarding-school children and schoolchildren growing in a socially favourable environment usually seek to dominate in interpersonal relations (Table 11.3).

The obtained data indicate that juveniles convicted of sexual crimes and violent crimes, and juveniles under a suspended sentence are shy, timid and yielding towards other people. They are disposed towards cooperation and compromise, and seek to agree with others when resolving problems and conflict situations.

Such adolescents are usually polite, follow the rules of etiquette and can be cordial. They take initiative in achieving group objectives and seek to help others and to be in the limelight, thus trying to win acknowledgement and love. They always sacrifice their interests and aspire to help and feel compassion for everybody. This is why they may impose their assistance and be too active in relation to others. They also tend to take on responsibility for other people. In return, they expect help and advice. However, their behaviour can be a mask hiding the personality of an opposite nature.

Conversely, juveniles convicted of acquisitive crimes, boarding-school pupils and schoolchildren growing in a socially favourable environment are confident and persistent. Their egoistic traits of character prevail; they are self-centred and inclined to competition. They are often stubborn and critical with regard to all social events and to surrounding people. Also, they aspire to leadership and dominance.

11.3.2 Second Research Stage

Nevertheless, the data received in our second research stage did not reveal any significant differences between the adolescent groups; we identified only some typical characteristics of each group. For this reason, at the following research stage we focused on parent–child relations in the adolescents' families. First, we studied their social well-being.

In our view, three peculiarities are of special importance. To begin, it is the family membership of the adolescent groups. Juveniles convicted of sexual crimes are brought up mainly in single-parent families (35% of juvenile convicts versus 75% of the control group of schoolchildren). The second peculiarity is the previous convictions amongst close relatives. Amongst juvenile convicts, 35% of parents and 15% of siblings have or had a criminal record. The third peculiarity consists in escapes from home, which are more typical of convicts rather than of law-abiding adolescents (25% of juvenile convicts versus 5% of the control group of schoolchildren).

Table 11.3   Comparison of Values Obtained Using Leary's Interpersonal Diagnosis of Personality

Group	Autocratic	Narcissistic	Sadistic	Rebellious	Masochistic	Dependent	Cooperative	Hypernormal
Juveniles convicted of violent sexual crimes	7.7	6.2	7.1	5.3	6.2	6.5	7.4	9
Juveniles convicted of violent crimes	6.7	6.4	6.5	5.9	4.8	5.6	6.8	7.7
Juveniles convicted of acquisitive crimes	7.6	5.8	6.5	5.6	4.6	5.3	6.9	7
Juveniles under a suspended sentence	7.3	5.8	5.8	4.4	5	5.2	6.5	7.6
Juveniles brought up in boarding schools	6	4.8	3	3.5	2	3.8	5	4
Juvenile schoolchildren growing in a socially favourable environment	7.9	7	7.1	5.4	4.4	5.5	6.6	7.1

Table 11.4   Results of Comparison between the Groups' Values Obtained Using the Analysis of Family Relationships Technique (E. G. Eidemiller and V. V. Yustitskis)

Scales	M_{score} Sex Offenders	M_{score} Control Group	t	$p \leq 0.01$; $p \leq 0.05$
	Groups			
Minimum of restricting requirements to a child	3	47	−1.638	0.002
Minimum of sanctions	3	82.3	−2.813	0.001
Parents' lack of confidence in upbringing	2	47	0.737	*
Preference for male qualities	3	23.5	4.147	0.046
Preference for female qualities	1	11.7	5.721	0.036

* $p < .001$.

Further we analysed family relationship and established that the families of juvenile convicts are distinguished by insufficient requirements to or restrictions on children, as shown in Table 11.4. In this case a child offender is allowed to do everything. Even if parents impose some restrictions, an adolescent feels free to break them. Parents either do not want to or cannot establish any conduct rules for their child. The given upbringing style fosters the development of the hyperthymic and unstable accentuations of character in an adolescent. As Eidemiller and Yustitskis (authors of the Analysis of Family Relationships technique) point out, an inharmonious parenting style always stems from a parent's personal problem which he or she seeks to dissolve on account of a child. The cause of this was not identified amongst the parents of juvenile convicts.

In the families of schoolchildren, the prevalent parenting style implies the minimum of sanctions (punishments). Parents prefer either to go without punishments at all or impose them extremely rarely, thinking it useless. The given parenting type arises from the parents' lack of confidence concerning upbringing matters (the corresponding scale is provided in Table 11.4). As a consequence, children stop obeying their parents. Apart from that, studying the parents of schoolchildren, researchers identified a shift in their attitude to a child, depending on the gender (Eidemiller & Yustitskis, 2007).

The final point in studying family relationship was sex education in the adolescent's family and in the family of his parents. We also examined the attitude of juveniles and their parents to sex education. The general conclusion is that the sex education of juvenile convicts significantly differs from that of the adolescents brought up in a socially favourable environment. Particularly, convicted adolescents do not have a conception of sexual education and its role in life because their parents did not pay attention to it during child-rearing.

11.3.3 Third Research Stage

These data enabled us to detect more significant differences between the groups by comparison with the first research stage focused on adolescents' psychological characteristics. For this reason, at the final research stage we examined the interconnection between the identified psychological characteristics of adolescents and the parenting style in their families. The following results were obtained.

First, as Figure 11.1 shows, the mothers of juvenile convicts often seek to ignore the growing-up of their children and to stimulate preservation of their infantile qualities such as spontaneity, naivety and playfulness.

The mothers of juvenile convicts are inclined to subconsciously reject their male children. In this case we encounter the general stereotypes about men. As Eidemiller and Yustitskis note, under these conditions parents may assume a parenting model based on either emotional rejection or hyper-patronage and pandering. This can in turn cause damage to children's accentuation of character. The mothers of juvenile convicts can also project their own undesirable qualities onto their sons. The problem is rather often parents see in their children the qualities they have themselves, but fail to admit it. This may lead to such deviations as emotional rejection and abusive treatment. In this case, convicts' mothers may also employ the opposite parenting style without imposing any restrictions on children's behaviour. Such

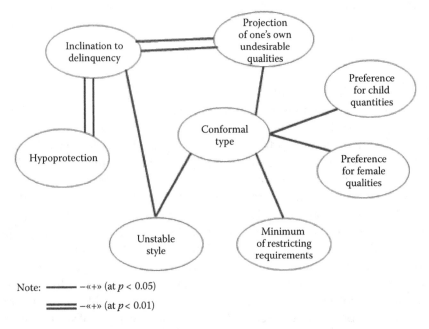

Figure 11.1 Interconnection between family upbringing styles and psychological peculiarities of convicts.

replacement of one parenting style with another, that is, emotional rejection on the one hand and permissiveness on the other, is the sign of an unstable pattern of parenting. According to Karl Leonhard, an unstable parenting style contributes to development of such personality traits as stubbornness and inclination to resist any authority, and often occurs in the families of children with deviations of character.

The aforementioned parenting styles are positively interconnected with the conformal accentuation of convicts' character. It signifies that such adolescents follow the rules: 'Think as others do', 'Act as others do' and 'Be similar to others in everything'.

Apart from that, making the correlation analysis, we revealed a positive correlation of psychological inclination to delinquency with hyper-patronage and an unstable parenting style.

Second, we identified a negative correlation between such parenting styles (the minimum of sanctions/punishments, an excessive number of restricting requirements) and personal problems of parents (a fear of losing a child) with the friendly style of interpersonal relations (Figure 11.2).

Third, as is shown in Figure 11.3, there is a positive correlation between family upbringing styles and the psychological peculiarities of law-abiding adolescents.

Accentuation of juvenile qualities – such as indecisiveness, anxiety about the future and inclination to self-analysis – positively correlates with a mother's effort to maximally and uncritically satisfy a child's needs. In addition, the given parenting style is positively interconnected with high susceptibility to

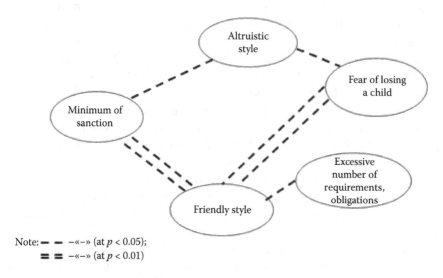

Note: ▬ ▬ –«–» (at $p < 0.05$);
　　 ▬ ▬ –«–» (at $p < 0.01$)

Figure 11.2 Interconnection between parenting styles and psychological peculiarities of convicts.

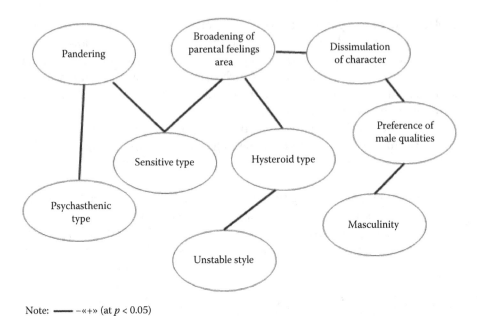

Note: ▬ – «+» (at $p < 0.05$)

Figure 11.3 Interconnection between family upbringing styles and psychological peculiarities of schoolchildren.

impressions and an inferiority complex amongst adolescents. Accentuation of the given type is positively correlated with personal problems of mothers such as broadening the area of parental feelings. It means that a mother subconsciously wants her child to satisfy at least part of the needs which, in a normal family, belong to the psychological relations between spouses. Amongst juvenile convicts, such an attitude to male children positively correlates with egocentrism, a thirst for attention to oneself and daydreaming. We also identified a positive interconnection between the given peculiarities of a person and the aforementioned unstable parenting style. The latter is, in turn, interconnected with the asthenoneurotic accentuation of character. In other words, a frequent change of parenting styles leads to increased fatigability, irritability and inclination to hypochondria and, to a lesser degree, to timidity and compliance in interpersonal relations.

We also revealed a positive correlation between a juvenile's refusal to disclose his personality traits and a mother's preference for male qualities in her son. The given preference is positively correlated with male qualities amongst adolescents.

Fourth, there is a positive correlation between (a) egoistic and leadership qualities of schoolchildren and (b) a parent's lack of confidence with regard to upbringing (Figure 11.4). As a result, children stop obeying their parents.

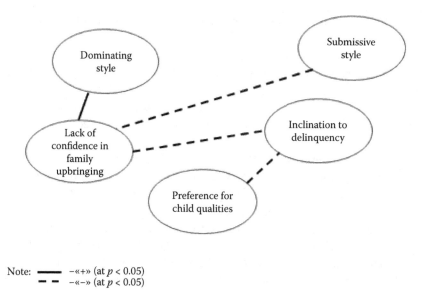

Note: ——— –«+» (at $p < 0.05$)
       – –   –«–» (at $p < 0.05$)

Figure 11.4 Interconnection between parenting styles and psychological features of schoolchildren.

There is a negative correlation between a mother's personal problems and a schoolchild's psychological disposition to delinquency and domination in interpersonal relations.

Thus, the research carried out enables us to suppose that the development of personality traits peculiar to juveniles convicted of violent sexual crimes is affected by their mothers' parenting style. This style is, in many respects, determined by a mother's personal problems which she seeks to resolve on account of children. In our view, these problems are strongly connected with family relations between spouses.

11.4 Discussion

The research has confirmed a considerable increase in juvenile crimes against children of the same gender, which gave rise to a number of issues to be studied. The issues are

1. Is it correct to classify juveniles committing sexual crimes against children of the same gender as paedophiles and to attribute paedophile characteristics to them, if these adolescents themselves are underage?
2. Is it correct to regard such juveniles as homosexuals if they commit sexual crimes against people of the same gender?

3. What are the causes of or the factors in development of such criminal behaviour?
4. Is the given group of criminals similar to any other category of
   offenders in their psychological type? Or does it essentially differ
   from other criminal groups?

We suppose that juvenile delinquency of this type is a predictor of paedophilia in adulthood.

Apart from these issues, there are a number of others to be resolved by
contemporary researchers in the struggle against sexual and repeated sexual
crimes and for the sake of ensuring the sexual safety and integrity of children. The problems described are not restricted by a specific region or country. Regrettably, they extend to the whole international community. This is
why we deem it necessary to join the efforts of doctors, psychologists, lawyers
and other specialists in the sphere of human behaviour to ensure sexual and
psychological safety of children. Moreover, we should more actively foster
international cooperation in the sphere.

11.5 Conclusions

The development of personality traits peculiar to juveniles convicted of sexual violence depends on the parenting style adopted by the mother. This style
is, in many respects, determined by her personal problems which she seeks to
resolve on account of her children. In our view, these problems are strongly
connected with family relations between spouses.

References

American Psychiatric Association (APA). (2013). *Diagnostic and statistical manual
of mental disorders* (5th ed., text rev.). Washington, DC: American Psychiatric
Publishing.

Azletskiy, O. O. (1999). Criminal psychology [Abstract]. *Criminal Psychology, 27.*

Bell, A. P., Weinberg, M. S., & Hammersmith, S. K. (1981). *Sexual preference: Its development in men and women.* Bloomington: Indiana University Press.

Bieber, I., Dain, H. J., Dince, P. R., Drellich, M. G., Granel, H. G., & Gundlach, R. R.
(1962). *Homosexuality: A psychoanalytic study of male homosexuals.* New York:
Basic Books.

Blanchard, R. (1997). Birth order and sibling sex ratio in homosexual versus heterosexual males and females. *Annual Review of Sex Research, 8*(1), 27–67.

Blanchard, R., Christensen, B. K., Strong, S. M., Cantor, J. M., Kuban, M. E., Klassen, P.,
Dickey, R., & Blak, T. (2002). Retrospective self-reports of childhood accidents
causing unconsciousness in phallometrically diagnosed pedophiles. *Archives of
Sexual Behavior, 31*(6), 511–526.

Bogaert, A. F. (2006). Biological versus nonbiological older brothers and men's sexual orientation. *Proceedings of the National Academy of Science of the United States of America, 103*(28), 10771–10774.

Cantor, J. M. (2012). Homosexuality a paraphilia? The evidence for and against. *Archives of Sexual Behavior, 41*(1), 237–247.

Cantor, J. M., Kuban, M. E., Blak, T., Klassen, P., Dickey, R., & Blanchard, R. (2007). Physical height in pedophilic and hebephilic sexual offenders. *Sexual Abuse: A Journal of Research and Treatment, 19*(4), 39–5407.

Eidemiller, E. G., & Yustitskis, V. V. (2007). *Family psychology and psychotherapy* (4th ed.). Saint Petersburg, Russia: Piter.

Eliseev, A. V., Tkachenko, A. A., Petina, T. V., & Kunikovskiy, Yu. E. (1997). *Neurophysiological mechanisms of abnormal sexual behaviour* (Chap. 6). Moscow: Serbsky State Scientific Center for Social and Forensic Psychiatry.

Freund, K., & Blanchard, R. (1987). Feminine gender identity and physical aggressiveness in heterosexual and homosexual pedophiles. *Journal of Sex & Marital Therapy, 13*(1), 25–34.

Gaffney, G. R., & Berlin, F. S. (1984). Is there hypothalamic-pituitary-gonadal dysfunction in paedophilia? A pilot study. *British Journal of Psychiatry.* Dec; 145.

Green, R. (2002). Is pedophilia a mental disorder? *Archives of Sexual Behavior, 31*(6), 467–471.

Kershner, S. (2015). *Pedophilia and adult-children sex: A philosophical analysis.* Lanham, MD: Lexington Books.

Kingston, D. A., Seto, M. C., Ahmed, A. G., Fedoroff, P., Firestone, P., & Bradford, J. M. (2012). The role of central and peripheral hormones in sexual and violent recidivism in sex offenders. *Journal of the American Academy of Psychiatry and Law, 40*(4), 476–485.

Kogan, B. M., Drozdov, A. Z., Tkachenko, A. A., Talitskiy, A. V., Kovaleva, I. A., Philatova, T. S., Mankovskaya, I. V., Perezhogin, L. O., & Kunikovskiy, Yu. E. (1997). *The state of monoaminergic systems in paraphilia cases* (Chap. 7). Moscow: Serbsky State Scientific Center for Social and Forensic Psychiatry.

Lichko, A., & Ivanov, M. Y. (1995). *The Pathocharacterological Diagnostic Questionnaire for Adolescents* (10th ed.). Moscow: Folium.

Masters, W., Johnson, V., & Kolodny, R. (1998). *Fundamentals of sexology.* Moscow, Russia: Mir.

Millette, R. (2011). *Pedophilia a 'sexual orientation' experts tell Parliament.* Ottawa, Ontario: LifeSiteNews.com (Mon Feb 28, 2011 – 3:13 pm EST). Date accessed: 06.28.2014.

Nicolosi, J., Byrd, D., & Potts, R. W. (2002). A meta-analytic review of treatment of homosexuality. *Psychological Reports, 90*, 1139–1152.

Perehov, A. Ya., & Boukhanovskaya, O. A. (1998). Clinical and pathophysiological correlation at autoerotic paraphilia leading to serial sexual offenses [Abstracts]. *Abstracts of the 2nd International Conference 'Serial murders and social aggression',* 200.

Ross, M. W. (1983). Homosexuality and social sex roles. *Journal of Homosexuality, 9*(1), 1–6.

Schiffer, B., Paul, T., Gizewski, E., Forsting, M., Leygraf, N., Schedlowski, M., & Kruger, T. H. (2008). Functional brain correlates of heterosexual pedophilia. *Neuroimage, 41*, 80–91.

Schiltz, K., Witzel, J., Northoff, G., Zierhut, K., Gubka, U. et al. (2007). Brain pathol-
    ogy in pedophilic offenders: Evidence of volume reduction in the right amyg-
    dala and related diencephalic structures. *Archives of General Psychiatry, 64*(6).
Seto, M. (2009). Pedophilia. *Annual Review of Clinical Psychology, 5*(1), 391–407.
Tkachenko, A. A. (1997). *The boundaries of the sexual norm and contemporary classi-
    fications of psychosexual orientation disorders* (Chap. 1). Moscow: Serbsky State
    Scientific Center for Social and Forensic Psychiatry.
Vartanyan, G. A., & Gorbatov, S. V. (2013). Personal features of teenagers convicted
    of sexual offenses [Abstract]. *Abstracts of the 17th International Conference of
    Young Scientists 'Phycology of XXI century: The path of integration into the inter-
    national scientific and educational space'.*
World Health Organization (WHO). (1993). *The ICD-10 classification of mental and
    behavioural disorders: Diagnostic criteria for research.* Geneva: World Health
    Organization.

Risk-Taking Behaviour Values and Attitudes towards Traffic Safety amongst Street Racers in St. Petersburg

12

J. V. GRANSKAYA
V. A. ZAICEV

Contents

Traffic safety is an issue of paramount importance. In Russia, the number of serious traffic accidents and the risk related thereto are alarmingly high. There are a few ways to lower the rate of traffic accidents. One of them is to toughen traffic regulations. Another is to make driver training better. The third is to improve the quality of roads. Bad roads, however, do not entail risky driving behaviour directly. On the contrary, foreign research shows that high-quality road surface and new cars are connected with increased speed and lack of safety (Lund & Rundmo, 2009).

The human factor (e.g. alcohol intake, speeding and other violations of traffic rules) remains the primary cause of traffic accidents. For this reason, various experts are deeply interested in analysing the psychological aspect of the problem. It is extremely important to study the psychological mechanisms of risky driving behaviour, because it will help, inter alia, create effective preventive programmes.

According to the research presentations at the Fifth International Congress 'Road Safety for the Safety of Life',* young drivers aged 22 to 32 made up more than one third (35.8%) of the total number of deaths on the roads in Russia. Therefore, the road safety of the younger generation and the decrease of road traffic injuries amongst them are of vital importance.

Modern society is increasingly advanced in the technical sense. Automobiles are no more associated with a luxury, having turned into an ordinary means of transportation. Moreover, cars are regarded as a hobby: some people collect exquisite models, whilst others enjoy street racing. The latter has recently increased the rate of traffic accidents. Street racing is gaining popularity, and therefore poses an increasing threat. Obviously, there is a pressing need to research this issue. It is necessary to reveal the causes of risky driving, learn the characteristics of people inclined to such behaviour and design appropriate preventive measures.

Street racing is becoming a popular hobby amongst young drivers in Russia. During the night, they organise dangerous competitions on the streets of big cities without taking into consideration the presence of other cars. Statistics show the increase of accidents due to the risky behaviour of such drivers (Fifth International Congress, 2014; GIBDD, n.d.). Moreover, street racing involves more participants every year.

Street racing was brought to Russia approximately in the mid-1990s, and it shortly spread throughout the country, involving thousands of fans. Today the Internet offers a few hundred websites devoted to various teams or 'gangs' of street racers. The websites display all sorts of information about auto races, racers, their cars and so on. As it has been noted, street racing came from abroad, and therefore it is not a new movement. For example, in the United States, street races were immensely popular in the 1950s–1960s, when the car industry started to produce high-performance automobiles – the so-called muscle cars (Senko, 2014). Initially, the movement was considered rebellious: it often consisted of real hooligans who not only violated traffic rules but also committed robberies and riots. Due to a great number of law violations, street racing was classified as asocial behaviour in the United States. Later, however, the social attitude to street racing changed. An increasing number of people were inspired with ideology of the movement and participated in it without infringing law. For this reason, street racers were no more associated with crimes.

---

* The Congress took place in St. Petersburg on September 25–26, 2014.

There are various types of street racing competitions, including, speeding away from traffic lights or sharp overtaking manoeuvres performed at high speed. These two types take place within a city's daily road traffic. Another type of competition is drag racing. Normally, drag races are organised in unpopulated, industrial districts of a city with few inhabitants and low traffic.

12.1 Street Racers and the Law

In Russia, street racing is prohibited, because, apart from violation of traffic rules, it poses a danger to traffic participants (including pedestrians) and racers themselves. Other countries, for example, the United States, implement tough measures against racers: participants are arrested, whilst their cars are destroyed under a hydraulic press. These steps decreased not only the number of street races but also the amount of car thefts, because racers often stole automobiles for their competitions. The aforementioned measures also reduced the number of deaths.

The Russian government is designing measures to bring the organisers and participants of illegal street racing to justice. Also, amendments are being drafted to the section of traffic rules related to dangerous and extreme driving. The amendments will allow law enforcement to penalise drivers who race within the city traffic. Street racers protested against such measures and demanded that authorities respect their hobby. Specifically, they requested special tracks for legal auto races. There are such tracks in St. Petersburg and Moscow. However, racing still takes place in prohibited areas.

One of the findings from the study conducted by Granskaya and Polkovnikova (2007) showed some psychological characteristics of persons inclined to risky driving behaviour. It is aggressiveness that most significantly contributes to high-risk driving, whilst aggressive driving presents the most serious threat to other motorists. This study also confirmed gender differences in risk behaviour, namely, compared to women, many more men are involved in traffic accidents. In addition, the study established that the attitude to road safety, not a subjective assessment of one's own risk behaviour, determines driving behaviour.

A cross-cultural study has shown Russian car drivers to be more willing to take risks in traffic and to have less safe attitude compared to Norwegians. At the same time, it was found that attitudes towards traffic safety predicted risk-taking behaviour in both countries (Rundmo, Granskaya, & Klempe, 2012).

Although drivers evaluate the possibility of a road accident and its consequences, they are not considerably affected by this evaluation (though there are slight differences between the countries studied). The research showed that, for Russian and Norwegian drivers, the perception of risk in evaluating the gravity of accidents is mainly determined by the general sensitivity to other risks. It was established that, both in Russia and in Norway, all traffic participants regard transport means as a serious source of danger similar to most considerable threats of contemporary life. For this reason, the researchers did not find any cultural differences between the studied countries in assessing the possibility of road accidents.

Drivers in Russia have not confirmed the connection between awareness of the consequences and actual driving behaviour. Mass media actively informs people on grave consequences of traffic accidents. Unfortunately, the influence is not strong enough to markedly change the actual behaviour of Russian drivers and pedestrians (Rundmo, Granskaya, & Klempe, 2012).

Contemporary international studies prove that perception of risk and the attitude to road safety are closely connected with risky driving behaviour (Rundmo & Iversen, 2004), preference for safe driving and the need for lowering risk (Oltedal et al., 2004; Oltedal & Rundmo, 2007).

Research confirms that, both in Russia and in Norway, risky driving behaviour depends mostly on the attitude to safety, although there are some cross-cultural differences (Granskaya, Klempe, & Rundmo, 2012). Consequently, behaviour modification programmes are the most effective solution, because they change the attitude to road safety. Judging from experience, such programmes indeed reduce risky behaviour amongst adolescent drivers who undergo psychological intervention (Iversen, Rundmo, & Klempe, 2005).

The value system performs one of the most important roles in regulation of human behaviour, including risk behaviour. Also the value system is one of the most significant characteristics of a person and his self-awareness.

Values mean ideals a person strives for. They impact greatly on his views, goals and actions, that is, they determine the focus of his attention, the way he evaluates events and what guides his behaviour. Thus, on the one hand, the value system determines the cognitive process of a person and, on the other, regulates his social behaviour.

By analysing the value system – identifying which values it includes, which are prioritised and how they are interconnected – we can make predictions about the primary goals of a person's life and his behaviour in specific situations. When examining values, psychologists normally assess personal significance, because it basically motivates and regulates human behaviour.

There are a great number of approaches to classifying personal values. The classification made by Schwartz and Bilsky (1990) is the most widespread. To understand the nature of individual values, the authors suggest regarding them as (often unconscious) criteria for choosing and assessing one's actions as well as for assessing other people and events. They single out 10 basic values typical of every person and these values determine one's entire life as well as concrete actions.

Aim. The main aim of our study was to examine differences in attitudes towards traffic safety, values and risk-taking behaviour between street racers and ordinary drivers. Another goal of this study was to explore whether values and attitudes to safety are related to risk-taking behaviour amongst these groups.

12.2 Method

12.2.1 Participants

- 60 male car drivers, 20–29 years old, from St. Petersburg, with car-driving experience not less than 2 years
- 30 were members of a street racing club with the average driving experience of 4.2 years (average age 24.8)
- 30 males with the average driving experience of 3.9 (average age 23.7)

12.2.2 Instruments

12.2.2.1 *Attitudes towards Traffic Safety and Risk-Taking Behaviour*

Attitudes towards traffic safety and risk-taking behaviour on the roads were examined by a self-completion questionnaire. A previously validated measurement instrument was used to measure attitudes towards road traffic safety (Rundmo & Iversen, 2004). Responses were scored on a 5-point Likert scale ranging from *strongly disagree* to *strongly agree*. Factor analysis carried out by Rundmo and Iversen (2004) found that the attitude indicators fell into the six following dimensions: (1) attitudes towards unsafe driver, (2) drinking and driving, (3) speeding, (4) rule violations and related sanctions, (5) knowledge of traffic rules and (6) attitudes towards pedestrians. The first dimension consisted of two indicators: 'If my friends were passengers of an unsafe driver, I would join them' and 'In the absence of other good alternatives, I would let an unsafe driver drive me home'. The second factor concerned the respondents' attitudes to driving whilst intoxicated by alcohol or to being passengers of a driver who they knew had consumed alcohol. The third factor included these indicators: 'If you are a decent driver it is acceptable to drive a bit faster' and 'It makes sense to increase speed to overtake cars which are driving too slowly'. The two test indicators of factor number four were related to the respondents' willingness to violate traffic regulations, such as speed limits. The fifth attitude factor related to the respondents' general awareness and knowledge of traffic regulations. The final factor contained indicators such as 'If a pedestrian is run down by a car, the pedestrian is to blame'. Summary scores for each scale were calculated using direct or back order where a higher score always indicates less risky attitudes to traffic safety. Thus, the scales attitudes towards unsafe driver, drinking and driving, rule violations and related sanctions, knowledge of traffic rules and attitudes towards pedestrians have two items each, meaning summary scores could vary from 2 to 10, and the scale speeding has three items, so the summary score was calculated from 3 to 15.

Driver behaviour was also measured by a questionnaire previously validated by Rundmo and Iversen (2004). This instrument asked about the driver's judgements of how often they carried out certain actions in traffic. The responses were scored on a 5-point Likert-type scale ranging from *never* to *very often*. Factor analysis identified six dimension of self-reported risk behaviour. These were the following: self-reported behaviour related to drinking and driving, rule violations, precautionary behaviour, speeding, seat-belt use and driver behaviour near children playgrounds. The first factor included four indicators related to how often the respondents used their car when intoxicated by alcohol or how often they travelled as passengers with a driver who they knew had consumed alcohol. The second factor included six indicators related to how often they carried out acts such as driving above the speed limit in order to reach important appointments and how often they kept on driving when they felt tired. The third factor consisted of four indicators. These items related to how often the respondents slowed down due to cues that communicated caution (e.g. traffic signs). Speeding constituted the fourth factor. The three indicators making up this factor related to how often the respondents slowed down in densely populated areas or when pedestrians approached them. The fifth factor included two indicators concerning how often the drivers used seat belts on longer and shorter trips, respectively. The final factor only contained one indicator related to how often the drivers reduced their speed when a road sign stated that children were playing in the designated area. Summary scores for each scale were calculated using direct or back order where a higher score always indicates less risky behaviour. Thus, the scale rule violations has six items, which means summary scores could vary from 6 to 30; the scales drinking and driving and precautionary behaviour have four items each, which means summary scores could vary from 4 to 20; speeding has three items with summary scores from 3 to 15; seat-belt use has two items with summary scores from 2 to 10 and behaviour near children playgrounds has only 1 item so the summary score was calculated from 1 to 5.

The reliability and internal consistency of the indices of road safety attitudes and self-reported risk behaviour have been tested in previous studies (Nordfjaern, Jørgensen, & Rundmo, 2009; Nordfjaern & Rundmo, 2009; Rundmo & Iversen, 2004). In Russia, the method was used for the first time in cross-cultural research involving 299 Russian drivers (Rundmo, Granskaya, & Klempe, 2012).

12.2.2.2 *Values*

To measure value orientations, Schwartz's Value Inventory (Schwartz, 1994) was used. The method consists of two parts. Part 1, the value survey, aims to identify the values at the level of views and ideals, and determine the ones that most significantly influence a person's personality but are not always manifested in his actual behaviour. The survey consists of two lists of words related to 57 values that have clear motives and are significant for various cultures. The first list contains terminal values expressed by nouns, for example, Social Power (control over others, dominance), Freedom (freedom of thoughts and actions) and Wealth (property, money). The second list contains instrumental values expressed by adjectives, for example, Brave (adventure seeking, risky), Healthy (not physically or mentally ill) and Successful (achieving goals). A respondent is asked to rate the importance of each value as a guiding principle of his life. The rating is performed on a scale between 1 and 7. The more points a value receives, the more important it is for the respondent. These basic values are categorised into 10 value types (see Table 12.3).

Part 2, the personal profile, is designed to identify values at the level of human behaviour, that is, individual priorities that are most often manifested in the actual behaviour of a person. The profile offers a list of 40 personal descriptions related to 1 of 10 types of values (see Table 12.4). Respondents are asked to rate how much the given descriptions fit their own personality. The rating scale is based on five positions: from *very similar* to *absolutely dissimilar* (Schwartz & Bilsky, 1990). For example, the universalism value is identified by expressions such as 'He/she believes everyone should be treated equally' and 'He/she wants justice for everyone even for the people that he/she doesn't know personally'. The Russian version of this method is widely used by Russian researchers (Karandashev, 2004; Lebedeva, 2001).

A Russian version of Kuhn and McPartland's test 'Who am I?' was used to study the characteristics of personal identity (Rumyanceva, 2006). The question 'Who am I?' is directly connected with personal self-awareness, that is, one's self-concept. Respondents are asked to give 20 answers to the question 'Who am I?' These answers give an idea of person's self-identification. For example, answers can be man, husband, father, brother, Russian, young, brave, easy going and so on.

12.3 Results and Discussion

12.3.1 Attitudes towards Traffic Safety

The results given by the comparative analysis of the attitude to traffic safety are presented in Table 12.1. The research showed statistically significant differences

Table 12.1 Differences in Attitudes towards Traffic Safety between Street Racers and Ordinary Drivers

	Street Racers		Ordinary Drivers		Student's	
	M	σ	M	σ	t-Test	p
Attitudes towards unsafe driver	5.27	2.840	6.67	3.032	1.846	0.070
Drinking and driving	7.43	2.944	9.30	1.685	3.014	0.004
Speeding	5.77	1.695	9.97	2.157	8.384	0.000
Rule violations and related sanctions	4.67	1.918	8.50	1.383	8.879	0.000
Attitudes towards pedestrians	5.03	1.790	6.63	2.042	3.227	0.002
Knowledge of traffic rules	6.27	1.741	9.27	0.868	8.447	0.000

Note: Higher score indicates less risky attitudes.

between the studied groups in six indicators of attitude to traffic safety. The differences in speeding confirmed our expectations. Street racers are more inclined to violate speed limits and drive at an extremely high speed. The second indicator – rule violations and sanctions – demonstrates that, by comparison with street racers, ordinary drivers have a considerably more serious attitude to traffic regulations, seek to observe them and more often realise the responsibility imposed in case of a violation. The third indicator of the most significant differences – knowledge of traffic rules – also testifies to greater respect for traffic regulations amongst ordinary drivers as compared to street racers. Besides, there are significant differences in the attitude to pedestrians. Street racers have a worse attitude to pedestrians and tend to shift responsibility to them for a road accident. The study also identified differences, although less considerable, in the attitude to drinking and driving. Again, street racers hold more risky views compared to ordinary drivers. This may, in turn, greatly influence their risky driving behaviour. The results of the comparative analysis of the self-reported risky driving behaviour indicators are presented in Table 12.2.

Table 12.2 Differences in Self-Reported Risk Behaviour

	Street Racers		Ordinary Drivers		Student's	
	M	σ	M	σ	t-Test	p
Drinking and driving	15.59	3.855	18.80	1.690	4.175	0.000
Rule violations	15.37	3.643	22.27	2.840	8.181	0.000
Precautionary behaviour	7.23	3.066	13.93	2.828	8.807	0.000
Speeding	7.50	3.008	13.57	1.501	9.877	0.000
Seat-belt use	5.42	2.924	8.83	2.069	5.220	0.000
Behaviour near children playgrounds	2.66	1.285	4.40	0.724	6.478	0.000

Note: Higher score indicates less risky behaviour.

All the indicators show statistically significant differences between the studied groups. Street racers more often violate traffic regulations. Also street racers more frequently exceed the speed limit and drink alcohol whilst driving. Moreover, they are distinguished by a general neglect for laws and inclination to their infringement. They demonstrate the same level of risk behaviour even near children's playgrounds. Street racers more rarely use car safety features, such as a seat belt. Thus, street racers tend to take various actions posing a threat to themselves and other people.

12.3.2 Value System of Street Racers

Table 12.3 provides the results from the comparative analysis of values rated depending on their preference. These values take a dominant position in drivers' personality, that is, street racers are striving for them.

Hedonism received the most points with a considerable advantage, and thus occupies the key role in street racers' value system. In other words, street racers prioritise entertainment. Stimulation takes the second place in the list of preferred values, that is, street racers seek novelty and like to experience new feelings. Further, there follows self-direction. Street racers seek independence and are ready to assume responsibility for their actions and choose their own way of living.

Benevolence ranks fourth in the list. It is manifested in an effort to be open and friendly to other people. Achievement takes the fifth place. It reflects the need for being successful in a personal activity or hobby. Power is the sixth preferred value. It shows how important it is for a person to influence others, realise his own weight and feel respect from others.

Security occupies the seventh position in the rating. Thus, street racers attach minor importance to this value. Conformity, tradition and universalism are not important, either; they rank eighth, ninth and tenth, respectively.

Table 12.3 The Value System: Part 1

Values – Part 1	Street Racers		Ordinary Drivers		Student's t-Test	p
	M	σ	M	σ		
Conformity	4.500	0.746	4.983	0.973	2.159	0.035
Tradition	4.353	0.737	4.553	0.811	1.000	0.322
Benevolence	5.007	0.586	5.060	0.776	0.300	0.765
Universalism	4.242	0.862	4.388	1.016	0.600	0.551
Self-direction	5.107	0.930	5.020	0.707	0.406	0.686
Stimulation	5.400	0.458	3.900	1.122	6.781	0.000
Hedonism	7.022	7.376	4.367	0.984	1.954	0.055
Achievement	4.933	0.709	4.758	1.043	0.760	0.451
Power	4.875	0.512	4.267	1.349	2.310	0.024
Security	4.840	0.745	4.847	0.984	0.030	0.976

In general, the research shows that street racers prioritise entertainment, seek absolute independence and like to realise their importance and uniqueness.

An absolutely different hierarchy of values was demonstrated by the control group of ordinary drivers in the same age category: benevolence ranks first; self-direction, second; conformity, third; security, fourth; achievement, fifth; tradition, sixth; universalism, seventh; hedonism, eighth; power, ninth and stimulation, tenth.

Hedonism – valued by street racers most of all – was rated eighth by ordinary drivers. Meanwhilst, security went up to the fourth position. Another important street racers' value, stimulation, was, on the contrary, put at the very end of the list. Thus, the data presented clearly show the differences in prioritised values between the two studied groups.

There are statistically significant differences between the groups concerning stimulation, conformity and power. The primary difference lies in the following: street racers constantly seek new sensations, want self-assertion and do not restrict their actions and motives causing harm to other people. To a large degree, these peculiarities account for street racers' attitude to road safety and risky driving behaviour.

Table 12.4 presents the values characterising drivers' actions (not expectations), that is, the values manifested in their everyday behaviour. We rated street racers' values in descending order of importance: stimulation ranks first; hedonism, second; achievement, third; self-direction, fourth; power, fifth; benevolence, sixth; security, seventh; universalism, eighth; conformity, ninth and tradition, tenth. The comparison between the lists of desired values and the values manifested in real behaviour shows insignificant difference. In real behaviour, stimulation overshadows hedonism. However, in both cases street racers prioritise the same values (stimulation, hedonism, achievement and self-direction) and attach the least importance to universalism,

Table 12.4   The Value System: Part 2

Values – Part 2	Street Racers		Ordinary Drivers		Student's t-Test	p
	M	σ	M	σ		
Conformity	1.683	0.557	2.558	0.753	5.116	0.000
Tradition	1.342	0.709	1.750	0.851	2.020	0.048
Benevolence	2.242	0.547	2.558	0.697	1.957	0.055
Universalism	1.750	0.532	2.057	0.597	2.092	0.041
Self-direction	2.392	0.611	2.417	0.638	0.155	0.877
Stimulation	2.844	0.399	1.722	0.918	6.139	0.000
Hedonism	2.600	0.702	1.878	0.735	3.891	0.000
Achievement	2.483	0.533	2.142	0.882	1.815	0.075
Power	2.322	0.681	1.922	1.019	1.787	0.079
Security	1.980	0.569	2.387	0.703	2.464	0.017

conformity and tradition. Street racers value independence, new experience (feelings) and strong emotions, and like to stand out from the crowd. For this purpose, they are ready to neglect rules and traditions.

The control group of ordinary drivers also has the same priorities in the list of values manifested in real behaviour: benevolence and conformism rank first and second; self-direction, third; security, fourth; achievement, fifth; universalism, sixth; power, seventh; hedonism, eighth; tradition, ninth and stimulation, tenth.

Ordinary drivers value independence, but at the same time assign great importance to social regulations. Security is not prioritised, but it still ranks high (fourth place). This group of drivers is not really inclined to risk behaviour and does not constantly seek novelty and extreme feelings.

There are even more statistically significant differences between the groups in the values manifested in real behaviour, namely, stimulation, hedonism, conformity, tradition, universalism and security. In reality, ordinary drivers more often respect and observe established rules, cultural norms and traditions, as well as road safety requirements.

12.3.3 Personal Identity

Manifestation of values was qualitatively analysed using the test 'Who am I?'. The structure of self-identity is similar in both groups. However, the qualitative self-evaluations of street racers testify to their high self-esteem and positive self-attitude. Here are some examples of their self-descriptions: a genius, a perfect guy, a leader, successful, correct, the best, the most handsome (beautiful), strong, brave, a good boy, clever, independent, a fine fellow, talented.

12.3.4 Correlation Analysis

The results from the correlation analysis with the use of the Pearson product–moment correlation coefficient of street racers' attitude to safety and values at the level of ideal expectations (Part 1) are presented in Table 12.5.

The general attitude to safety is linked with values such as self-direction, hedonism and security. In other words, there is an interconnection between the positive emotions experienced in driving, the feeling of independence and drivers' attitude to their own safety. Risk behaviour is connected with hedonism and achievement. The table demonstrates that hedonism is most often associated with the attitude to safety and risky driving behaviour. According to the present research, street racers' driving behaviour and attitude to safety is determined mainly by hedonism.

The results from the correlation analysis with the use of the Pearson product–moment correlation coefficient of street racers' attitude to safety, risky driving behaviour and values (Part 2) are presented in Table 12.6.

Table 12.5 Correlation Analysis: Attitude to Road Safety, Risky Driving Behaviour and Values (Part 1) amongst Street Racers

	Benevolence 1	Self-Direction 1	Stimulation 1	Hedonism 1	Achievement 1	Power 1	Security 1
Attitudes towards unsafe driver	0.185	0.289	0.383*	0.515**	0.060	0.125	0.350
Drinking and driving	0.198	0.330	0.123	0.490**	0.039	0.060	0.410*
Speeding	0.009	0.108	-0.024	0.246	-0.085	-0.154	0.073
Rule violation and sanctions	-0.115	0.318	0.222	0.522**	-0.232	-0.149	0.270
Attitudes towards pedestrians	0.407*	0.474**	0.193	0.093	0.422*	0.409*	0.397*
Knowledge of traffic rules	-0.178	-0.137	0.092	-0.354	0.168	-0.126	-0.067
Drinking and driving	0.160	-0.329	-0.274	-0.573**	0.103	-0.040	-0.070
Rule violations	-0.021	-0.543**	-0.414*	-0.643**	0.060	-0.317	-0.173
Precautionary behaviour	0.256	0.330	0.125	-0.203	0.501**	0.162	0.348
Speeding	0.256	0.162	-0.132	-0.287	0.398*	0.115	0.107
Seat-belt use	0.369*	0.021	0.186	-0.037	0.112	-0.194	-0.044
Behaviour near children's playgrounds	0.095	0.182	0.223	0.160	0.213	0.050	0.360

$*p < .05$, $**p < .01$.

Table 12.6 Correlation Analysis: Attitude to Road Safety (AS), Risky Driving Behaviour (RB) and Values (Part 2) amongst Street Racers

	Conformity 2	Tradition 2	Self-Direction 2	Stimulation 2	Hedonism 2	Achievement 2	Power 2	Security 2
AS1	-0.234	-0.244	-0.082	0.190	0.205	-0.168	0.002	-0.095
AS2	-0.418*	-0.379*	-0.074	0.108	0.276	-0.144	-0.175	-0.283
AS3	0.357	-0.068	0.158	0.098	0.334	0.310	0.267	0.217
AS4	0.027	-0.027	0.034	0.035	0.154	0.062	0.006	0.013
AS5	-0.119	0.011	0.279	0.056	-0.126	0.326	0.095	0.014
AS6	0.241	0.021	-0.085	0.178	0.241	-0.079	0.090	-0.008
RB1	-0.101	-0.049	-0.159	0.266	0.201	0.022	0.061	0.281
RB2	0.361	0.481**	-0.187	0.120	-0.287	-0.046	0.118	0.306
RB3	0.155	0.085	0.385*	0.791**	0.705**	0.756**	0.657**	0.790**
RB4	0.270	0.060	0.308	0.766**	0.664**	0.771**	0.680**	0.760**
RB5	0.402*	0.012	0.304	0.715**	0.696**	0.682**	0.595**	0.628**
RB6	-0.089	0.020	0.211	0.723**	0.659**	0.639**	0.643**	0.688**

$*p < .05$, $**p < .01$.

In most cases, the risky driving behaviour demonstrated by street racers stems from such values as stimulation, hedonism, achievement, power and security. Street racers associate risk with pleasure, new experience and self-assertion. Stimulation – the striving for new experience and intense emotions – is the determining factor in real driving behaviour. Thus, the correlation analysis confirms the results of comparative analysis: hedonism or striving for constant entertainment, stimulation, self-direction and achievement underlie street racers' attitude to road safety and risky driving behaviour.

The results from the correlation analysis of ordinary drivers' attitude to safety, risky driving behaviour and values shows that the behaviour of ordinary drivers (of the given age group) is primarily determined by such values as tradition, respect for the existing standards of conduct and benevolence or support for the well-being of the surrounding people. Their attitude to safety negatively correlates with hedonism, stimulation and power.

12.4 Summary and Conclusion

The research indicates that hedonism and the desire of new, extreme emotions (or stimulation) are determining values amongst street racers, both at the level of their ideals and at the level of their real behaviour. Street racers do not seek approval by their actions, and they are less motivated to follow social standards. Meanwhilst, the behaviour of ordinary drivers is determined exactly by social approval. Neither street racers nor ordinary drivers rank security amongst their top-priority values. We should note, however, that street racers rate security lower than ordinary drivers do. This fact undoubtedly causes high-risk driving behaviour in the given age group. Street racers more often violate traffic rules, have a negative attitude to compliance with laws and are inclined to infringe them. They neglect safety measures and less often use various car safety features, such as a seat belt. They associate drunk driving with the pleasure from driving. They violate traffic rules under the influence of such values as independence, uniqueness, entertainment and sensation-seeking stimulations.

It was established that the difference between street racers and ordinary drivers consists in their value system. Also, street racers are inclined to risky driving behaviour and tend to neglect safety measures. They connect risky driving with pleasure, and this is one of the most important motives for risk behaviour.

For street racers, an automobile signifies much more than an ordinary means of transport. They may invest half of their monthly pay in their car improvement, which testifies to its high significance. Street racers exhibit an aggressive manner of driving and prefer high speed. They are distinguished by high self-esteem and increased confidence in driving. They display a high level of inclination to and readiness for risk behaviour. Besides, such people constantly seek new, intense emotions.

They prefer movement and action. They find life interesting and emotionally charged. Street racers are characterised by a high level of independence manifested in self-assertion and immense courage indicated by their readiness for risk. The data obtained suggest that street racers' inclination to risk behaviour is affected by their desire of new emotions; they satisfy this desire, indulging themselves in speeding.

As a result, street racers more often have traffic accidents and they regularly break traffic rules. They are characterised by aggressive driving, an indifferent attitude to safety and inclination to unreasonable risk. The comparative research on the attitude to safety and street racers' level of risk behaviour indicate an acute need for serious correctional work in this risk group and for active incorporation of psychological programs designed to increase road safety amongst young drivers.

References

Fifth International Congress. (2014). Road safety for the safety of life. St. Petersburg, Russia, September 25–26. www.road-safety.ru.

GIBDD (Russian State Road Traffic Inspection). (n.d.). www.gibdd.ru.

Granskaya, J., & Polkovnikova, I. V. (2007). Lichnostnie osobennosti sklonnix k risku v situacii dorozhnogo dvizheniya [Personality characteristics of drivers who demonstrate risky behavior on the roads]. *Materiali nauchno-prakticheskoi konferencii 'Ananevskie chteniya'*. St. Petersburg: St. Petersburg University Press.

Granskaya, J., Klempe, H., & Rundmo, T. (2012). Cross-cultural comparative study of attitudes towards traffic safety, risk assessment and risk-taking behavior among Russian and Norwegian car drivers. *Vestnik St. Petersburg University*, *12*(3), 121–127.

Iversen, H. H., Rundmo, T., & Klempe, H. (2005). A comparison of the effects of a behaviour modification program and a traffic safety campaign on risk attitudes and behaviour amongst Norwegian adolescents. *European Psychologist*, *10*(1), 25–38.

Karandashev, V. N. (2004). *Metodika Schwartza dlya izucheniya cennostei lichnosti* [Schwartz's method for measuring value orientations]. St. Petersburg: Rech.

Lebedeva, N. M. (2001). Cennostno-motivacionnaya struktura lichnosti v russkoi culture [Value-motivational structure of personality in the Russian culture]. *Psychological Journal*, *22*(3), 26–36.

Lund, I. O., & Rundmo, T. (2009). Cross-cultural comparison of traffic safety, risk perception, attitudes and behaviour. *Safety Science*, *47*, 547–553.

Nordfjærn, T., & Rundmo, T. (2009). Risk perception, worry and demand for risk mitigation in transport in the Norwegian public – Years 2004 and 2008 compared. In T. Rundmo & S. H. Jørgensen (Eds.), *Studies of risk perception and transport safety* (pp. 365–379). Trondheim, Norway: Rotunde Publ. no. 90.

Nordfjærn, T., Jørgensen, S. H., & Rundmo, T. (2009). Driver attitudes and behaviour in rural, peri-urban and urban areas in Norway. In T. Rundmo & S. H. Jørgensen (Eds.), *Studies of risk perception and transport safety* (pp. 347–361). Trondheim, Norway: Rotunde Publ. no. 90.

Oltedal, S., Moen, B. E., Klempe, H., & Rundmo, T. (2004). *Explaining risk perception: An evaluation of cultural theory.* Trondheim, Norway: Rotunde Publikasjoner no. 85.

Oltedal, S., & Rundmo, T. (2007). Using cluster analysis to test the cultural theory of risk perception. *Transportation Research Part F: Traffic Psychology and Behaviour, 10*(3), 254–262.

Rumyanceva, T. V. (2006). *Psyhologicheskoe konsultirovanie: Diagnostika otnoshenii v pare* [Psychological consulting: Diagnostic of couple relationships]. St. Petersburg: Rech.

Rundmo, T., & Iversen, H. H. (2004). Risk perception and driving behaviour among adolescents in two Norwegian counties before and after a traffic safety campaign. *Safety Science, 42*(1), 1–21.

Rundmo, T., Granskaya, J., & Klempe, H. (2012). Traffic culture as symbol exchange – A cross-country comparison of Russia and Norway. *Safety Science, 50*(5), 1261–1267.

Schwartz, S. H. (1994). Are there universal aspects in the structure and content of human values? *Journal of Social Issues, 50*(4), 19–45.

Schwartz, S. H., & Bilsky, W. (1990). Toward a theory of the universal structure and content of values: Extensions and cross-cultural replications. *Journal of Personality and Social Psychology, 58*, 878–891.

Senko, E. V. (2014). Diggerstvo, streetracing I prochie uvlecheniya [Diggers, street racing and other 'hobbies']. *Russkaya Rech, 4*, 73–75.

Interviewing, Memory and Deception IV

The Eye-Closure Interview
The Practical Utility of Instructing Eyewitnesses to Close Their Eyes

13

ANNELIES VREDEVELDT
COLIN G. TREDOUX

Contents

13.1 Introduction

It is an unfortunate fact that most crimes are never solved, regardless of where in the world they occur (e.g. the Netherlands: Centraal Bureau voor de Statistiek, 2014; the United Kingdom: Home Office Statistical Bulletin, 2014; South Africa: Leggett, 2003). Whether a crime is solved will often depend on the quality and quantity of information obtained from eyewitnesses (Fisher, 1995; Kebbell & Milne, 1998). Over the past three decades, psychologists have helped to improve the collection and use of evidence from eyewitnesses during multiple stages of the process from statement taking to conviction or acquittal (e.g. Wells et al., 2000). An important set of interventions has been the design and testing of various interviewing methods to help witnesses remember more and better. Two well-known examples are the Cognitive Interview (Fisher & Geiselman, 1992; Geiselman et al., 1984) and the National Institute of Child Health and Human Development (NICHD) interview protocol (Lamb, Orbach, Hershkowitz, Esplin, & Horowitz, 2007;

Orbach et al., 2000). These interviewing procedures have proven to be highly effective at improving memory for events, yielding up to 35% more information in field settings (Fisher, Geiselman, & Amador, 1989).

Unfortunately, these complex interviewing procedures have also proven difficult to implement in practice. For example, Clarke and Milne (2001) found that the Cognitive Interview had not been used in 83% of investigative interviews in the United Kingdom (see also Dando, Wilcock, & Milne, 2008; Kebbell, Milne, & Wagstaff, 1999). Along with some colleagues, we have recently explored a very simple alternative to the Cognitive Interview, which we call the *Eye-Closure Interview* (ECI; Vredeveldt, Tredoux, Nortje et al., 2015). The crux of this procedure is getting eyewitnesses to attempt memory retrieval with their eyes closed – one of the optional components of the Cognitive Interview and one shown in a number of laboratory investigations to be an effective aid in memory retrieval. The present chapter will briefly review evidence from laboratory studies showing that eye-closure improves memory for events, but our main focus will be on the applied value of the Eye-Closure Interview in improving evidence obtained from eyewitnesses. Specifically, we will review empirical evidence addressing (a) whether Eye-Closure Interviews can be effective in naturalistic settings, (b) whether Eye-Closure Interviews are feasible and effective when interviewing eyewitnesses in field settings and (c) whether Eye-Closure Interviews can improve facial identification performance.

13.2 Laboratory Studies of Eye-Closure Effectiveness

Readers of this chapter will likely share the common experience of closing one's eyes when performing difficult cognitive tasks. Does this everyday habit make our mental work any more accurate, though? Glenberg, Schroeder, and Robertson (1998) empirically tested whether such eye-closure is functional. In a series of experiments, they corroborated the everyday observation that people spontaneously close their eyes for more difficult tasks. They also found evidence that participants instructed to close their eyes recalled more words correctly in a memory task. Replications and extensions of this work were reported by Wagstaff and colleagues (2004), who found that eye-closure improved memory for a public event that was televised 5 years earlier, and by Doherty-Sneddon and colleagues (Doherty-Sneddon, Bonner, & Bruce, 2001; Phelps, Doherty-Sneddon, & Warnock, 2006), who found that children perform better on a range of cognitive tasks when they are instructed to close their eyes or to avert their gaze from the interviewer's face. These studies do appear to show that the commonplace tendency to close one's eyes whilst thinking is functional: It improves our performance on cognitive tasks.

Notwithstanding the cognitive effectiveness of closing one's eyes, it is clearly not always easy or appropriate to do so. One important context of particular concern to us is that of the eyewitness interview. Eyewitnesses may well feel uncomfortable closing their eyes during a police interview (cf. Nash, Nash, Morris, & Smith, 2015), for many reasons.* Indeed, witnesses are unlikely to spontaneously close their eyes during police interviews (Vredeveldt, Tredoux, Nortje et al., 2015), but it could nevertheless be beneficial to encourage them to close their eyes in order to help them better remember the events they witnessed. Perfect and colleagues (2008) tested the effectiveness of the eye-closure instruction for memory of recently witnessed events. In five laboratory studies, interviewees who closed their eyes under instruction remembered significantly more about events that they had just witnessed than interviewees in a control condition who were not instructed to close their eyes. Moreover, information retrieved by participants who closed their eyes was significantly more accurate. In a subsequent study, Vredeveldt, Baddeley and Hitch (2014) found that eye-closure was still effective when witnesses were interviewed after a one-week delay and repeated recall attempts. The finding that eye-closure improves the quantity and quality of event memory has now been replicated in many laboratory studies and is thus robust to variations in materials and procedure (e.g. Mastroberardino, Natali, & Candel, 2012; Nash et al., 2015; Vredeveldt, Baddeley, & Hitch, 2012; Wagstaff, Wheatcroft, Burt et al., 2011).

Why does memory improve when witnesses close their eyes? There is evidence for several possible mechanisms, and these might operate independently or in concert. On the one hand, eye-closure reduces cognitive load, thereby freeing up resources for the task at hand (Glenberg, 1997; Glenberg et al., 1998; Perfect et al., 2008). Support for this conjecture comes from studies showing that eye-closure can improve recall of both visual and auditory stimuli (e.g. Nash et al., 2015; Perfect et al., 2008), and can even reduce the cross-modal impairment caused by auditory distractions (Perfect, Andrade, & Eagan, 2011), suggesting that eye-closure results in general cognitive benefits. On the other hand, eye-closure reduces modality-specific interference from visual stimuli in the environment, thus facilitating visualisation of witnessed events (Baddeley & Andrade, 2000; Baddeley & Hitch, 1974; Vredeveldt, Hitch, & Baddeley, 2011). Support for this conjecture comes from studies that show that eye-closure may selectively enhance recall of visual (but not auditory) information (Mastroberardino & Vredeveldt, 2014; Vredeveldt et al.,

---

* A recent national probability survey of South Africans, for instance, found that 35% of South Africans fear the police (FutureFact, 2012). They may presumably carry this fear into an interview situation, and thus be reluctant to close their eyes during the interview.

2012, 2014). Taken together, this suggests that the eye-closure effect involves both general and modality-specific processes (Vredeveldt et al., 2011).

An additional potential mechanism through which eye-closure may improve memory is that of 'mental context reinstatement'. Context reinstatement can be a powerful memory aide: Witnesses asked to mentally place themselves back into the context surrounding the event, and to re-experience the sights, sounds, smells, feelings and emotions that they experienced at the time of the event, remember more about the witnessed events (Clifford & George, 1996; Hammond, Wagstaff, & Cole, 2006; Wagstaff, Wheatcroft, Caddick, Kirby, & Lamont, 2011). When witnesses close their eyes, this seems to shift the focus to internal mental processes (cf. Vredeveldt & Sauer, 2015), which may facilitate mental reinstatement of context. Indirect support for this idea comes from studies showing that eye-closure leads to enhanced mental simulation of hypothetical events (Caruso & Gino, 2011) and an enhanced rating of emotionality for negative music (Lerner, Papo, Zhdanov, Belozersky, & Hendler, 2009). Importantly, Caruso and Gino found that eye-closure encouraged mental simulation of events in the absence of mental-simulation instructions. Thus, it is possible that eye-closure improves eyewitness memory through spontaneous mental reinstatement of context. We will return to this issue in the next section.

In sum, the finding that eye-closure improves memory for events has proven to be robust, replicating across laboratory studies that use different materials and methods. This is promising from the perspective of investigative interviewing: Because information from eyewitnesses plays a crucial role in police investigations, we must develop optimal procedures for interviewing witnesses. Although several more complex interview protocols were effective in the laboratory, they have proven difficult to implement in practice. The Eye-Closure Interview could serve as a simple alternative, with the significant added attraction that it does not require much extra training or time in addition to that presently spent by police officers on witness interviews. In the remainder of the chapter we explore the practical utility of the Eye-Closure Interview in police interviews. We discuss three studies that involved realistic settings when implementing the Eye-Closure Interview and addressed some important applied questions in the area of psychology and law that emerged during the course of the studies.

13.3 Naturalistic Experiment

Nearly all studies showing that eye-closure improves event memory have used videotaped or televised events as stimulus material. An exception is the research reported by Perfect and colleagues (2008; Experiments 4 and 5), who examined memory for live events. It is fair to say, however, that they used a somewhat mundane live event as stimulus material: A confederate in an adjacent waiting room received a phone call, and then left the room. People who witness crimes are likely to be exposed to events that are considerably more arousing, and it is important to show that eye-closure can be effective with such witnesses. To simulate more closely the type of event witnessed by real eyewitnesses (but simultaneously observing ethical standards of research), Vredeveldt and Penrod (2013) staged a live altercation on a street in New York City. They invited students from a local university to participate in a study on 'social interactions'. One to four participants per session arrived in the laboratory, and an experimenter told them that they needed to walk, with the experimenter, to a different building in order to commence the experiment. The experimenter then guided the participants along several streets in an area of New York City, where they met up with two research assistants on a street corner, whose ostensible role was to guide participants to the actual building where the experiment was to take place. The research assistants started addressing the participants but almost immediately started arguing. The argument was at first about the assignment of locations, and then escalated into an argument about something that 'happened this morning at Starbucks'. After a heated exchange, one of the research assistants threw her clipboard onto the ground in a fit of apparent displeasure, then walked off.

This closely scripted event was staged 38 times, for 96 witnesses in total. To obtain an independent record of what happened on each occasion (e.g. who walked by during the event and whether the participants interfered in the argument), each incident was unobtrusively videotaped from a nearby phone booth. Immediately after they had witnessed the event, the participants were separated. Each participant was taken to a different interview location by one of the researchers, where they were interviewed about the event, either with their eyes open or with their eyes closed. The interview consisted of a free-recall phase, in which participants were asked to report everything they could remember about the event, and a cued-recall phase, in which participants were asked 16 predetermined questions about the event (8 questions about visual aspects and 8 about auditory aspects).

The primary finding in Vredeveldt and Penrod's (2013) study was that the eye-closure effect replicated in a naturalistic setting (see Table 13.1). In the free-recall phase, participants who closed their eyes remembered 38% more correct visual information and 19% more correct auditory information than the control group. In the cued-recall phase, eye-closure significantly increased the number of precise correct responses about visual details, by 24% ($d = 0.43$), but had no significant effect on auditory details ($d = -0.25$). Thus, closing the eyes helped participants to remember an altercation witnessed on a busy street in New York.

Although police officers typically interview witnesses at the police station or in the witness's home, it is sometimes necessary to conduct interviews

Table 13.1 Effectiveness of the Eye-Closure Interview

Study	Dependent Variable	Effect Size	
	Event Recall	*d*	95% CI
Naturalistic experiment[a]	Number correct (free recall)	0.51	0.10–0.92
	Number correct (cued recall)	0.05	−0.35–0.45
Book-theft experiment[b]	Number correct (free recall)	0.55	0.14–0.96
	Number correct (cued recall)	0.76	0.35–1.18
Field study[c]	Number of details	−0.01	−0.42–0.40
	Forensic relevance	0.48	0.07–0.90
	Person identification	OR	95% CI
Book-theft experiment[b]	Lineup accuracy	1.31	0.73–2.35
Face-recognition experiment[b]	Recognition accuracy	0.98	0.78–1.21

Note: Cohen's *d* greater than 0 and odds ratio (OR) greater than 1 reflect higher scores in the eyes-closed condition than in the eyes-open condition.

[a] Vredeveldt and Penrod (2013).
[b] Vredeveldt, Tredoux, Kempen et al. (2015).
[c] Vredeveldt, Tredoux, Nortje et al. (2015).

at the scene of the crime or in a public place (Gabbert, Hope, & Fisher, 2009; Vredeveldt, Tredoux, Nortje et al., 2015). To simulate that type of situation, half of the witnesses in Vredeveldt and Penrod's (2013) study were interviewed outside on the street, a 5 minute walk from the 'scene of the crime' (i.e. where the altercation had taken place). The other half were interviewed indoors, on a quiet corridor inside a university building. Thus, participants were assigned to one of four conditions: They were interviewed (1) indoors with their eyes open, (2) indoors with their eyes closed, (3) outdoors with their eyes open or (4) outdoors with their eyes closed. The authors outlined two competing hypotheses regarding the potential role of interview location in the eye-closure effect. On the one hand, if reduction of distraction is what predominantly drives the eye-closure effect, one would expect eye-closure to be most effective in an environment with many distractions – in this case, outside on a busy street. On the other hand, if spontaneous mental context reinstatement is the primary mechanism behind the effect, one would expect eye-closure to be most effective in an environment that is very different from the context in which the event took place – in this case, indoors, on a quiet corridor. The findings provided more support for the latter hypothesis than for the former. There was a marginally significant interaction between eye-closure and interview location for free-recall performance, suggesting that eye-closure was more effective for participants interviewed indoors ($d = 0.88$) than for participants interviewed outdoors ($d = 0.16$). Thus, the eye-closure instruction was most effective when the retrieval context was highly different from the encoding context, which provides indirect support for the idea that closing one's eyes facilitates mental context reinstatement.

In sum, Vredeveldt and Penrod (2013) extended the eye-closure effect to a more realistic eyewitness setting. Their setup provided nearly the same level of experimental control as in laboratory settings (e.g. they obtained an independent record of what happened during each staged event), yet simulated conditions experienced by real eyewitnesses more closely than previous research. Nevertheless, it will always be difficult to ethically simulate the arousal component of real-world crimes, which frequently involve a high degree of violence. It is thus not clear whether Vredeveldt and Penrod's findings would extend to real-life situations. To examine the applied value of the Eye-Closure Interview further, specifically for crime events that contain high degrees of violence and arousal, Vredeveldt, Tredoux, Nortje et al. (2015) followed up Vredeveldt and Penrod's naturalistic experiment with a field study.

13.4 Field Study

To evaluate the effectiveness of the Eye-Closure Interview with real eyewitnesses, Vredeveldt, Tredoux, Nortje et al. (2015) conducted a large-scale field study in collaboration with the South African Police Service (SAPS). We chose to work with the Facial Identification Unit (FIU) of the SAPS, since this unit routinely interviews eyewitnesses and is considered by the Investigative Psychology Unit of the SAPS to be a well-run and well-trained team. All 12 of the police officers who work in the FIU in the Western Cape region of South Africa were trained in a one-day workshop to implement the study procedure and video- and audio-record their interviews (conditional on witnesses' consent to participate in the project). Interviewers were informed that the project concerned an evaluation of a new interview procedure, and that half of them would be trained to use the procedure immediately, whereas the other half would be trained at the end of the project. Participating interviewers were assigned to six pairs matched on gender, age and years of experience, and each pair member was randomly assigned to the Eye-Closure Interview condition or the control condition (which involved no eye-closure instruction). After data collection had been completed, all police interviewers again attended a workshop, during which those in the control condition were trained in the use of the Eye-Closure interview, and the researchers presented some preliminary findings and a set of general interviewing guidelines.

Over a period of seven months, we collected 95 video- and audio-recorded witness interviews, conducted by police interviewers at five police stations in the Western Cape region. Witnesses who were interviewed had been exposed to crimes ranging in seriousness: 20% of the crimes involved rape or murder, 49% armed or violent robberies, 28% unarmed or non-violent robberies and 3% other crimes. Forty interviews were collected in the Eye-Closure Interview condition and 55 in the control condition. Analysis of video-recordings of the interviews showed that witnesses in the Eye-Closure Interview condition kept their eyes closed during 97% of the relevant portions of the interview. This finding should assuage potential worries that witnesses in real life might have difficulty or be unwilling to close their eyes during a police interview. At least in this sample, witnesses adhered to the eye-closure instruction extremely well. Additionally, the analysis showed that witnesses in the control condition closed their eyes during only 0.2% of their descriptions. This suggests that witnesses rarely close their eyes spontaneously, and that the introduction of the Eye-Closure Interview, if found to be effective, could thus make a real difference.

To evaluate the amount of information reported by witnesses, all interviews were transcribed verbatim and coded by two independent coders. On average, witnesses reported 33 details about the perpetrator, 24 details about the modus operandi, 4 details about other witnesses present during the crime and 23 details about other aspects of the crime. Contrary to expectation, the Eye-Closure Interview did not significantly affect the overall amount of information reported (see Table 13.1). However, there was a significant interaction between interview condition and type of detail: Witnesses in the Eye-Closure Interview condition tended to report more details about the perpetrator and fewer other details than witnesses in the control condition (see Figure 13.1).

Because there was no independent record of what had happened during the crime, it was impossible to assess the accuracy of the information reported by witnesses in the field study. We did however assess the extent to which the interviews yielded quality information, namely, the *forensic relevance* of reported information in terms of its value to the police investigation or in court (cf. Roberts & Higham, 2002). Two independent coders – a senior

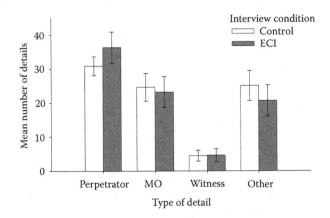

Figure 13.1 Field study with South African Police Services. Mean number of details reported about the perpetrator, modus operandi (MO), other witnesses and other aspects of the crime, in the control and Eye-Closure Interview (ECI) conditions. Error bars reflect 95% confidence intervals.

police officer and the lead researcher – rated the forensic relevance of each interview transcript on a 7-point Likert scale, blind to experimental condition. Interestingly, transcripts in the Eye-Closure Interview were rated as significantly more forensically relevant than transcripts in the control condition (see Table 13.1). Thus, introduction of the Eye-Closure Interview appeared to elicit more valuable information from witnesses.

Of course, the field study had some limitations. Unlike in laboratory research, there was little control over the behaviour of the interviewers (e.g. the types of questions asked), and the accuracy of witness reports could not be verified. However, unlike laboratory studies, the field study involved real eyewitnesses reporting about highly arousing, objectively dangerous events. To establish whether a new interview protocol is effective at helping witnesses remember more, we should rely on a combination of laboratory research findings, which involve high levels of experimental control, and field research findings, which involve high levels of realism. In the case of the Eye-Closure Interview, converging evidence suggests that eye-closure increases the amount and accuracy of event memories in the laboratory and enhances the forensic value of reported information in the field. Based on these findings, we would recommend that witnesses are instructed to close their eyes whilst they are trying to remember a witnessed event.

Extant evidence on the effectiveness of eye-closure as a memory aide appears solely relevant to recall memory. It is important to improve the ability of witnesses to recall details of an event, but it is also important to find ways of improving recognition memory. In the next section, we examine whether the Eye-Closure Interview can also help witnesses to recognise a perpetrator in identification procedures typically used by law enforcement agencies.

13.5 Eyewitness Identifications

In addition to reporting what happened during a crime, eyewitnesses are often faced with an additional task, namely, identifying the perpetrator from a line-up. Analyses of the many cases in which falsely convicted perpetrators were later exonerated reveal that the majority of wrongful convictions involved mistaken identifications made by eyewitnesses (e.g. Connors, Lundregan, Miller, & McEwen, 1996; Gross & Shaffer, 2012). In light of the influential role, both positive and negative, of eyewitness identifications in legal systems, Vredeveldt, Tredoux, Kempen, and Nortje (2015) investigated whether the Eye-Closure Interview could assist witnesses to recognise perpetrators of crime.

We recruited 192 participants for a study ostensibly about 'ethical dilemmas'. Participants watched a video in which a student steals a book from a shop after haggling about its price. After watching the video, participants completed a filler task and were interviewed about what happened during the videotaped event. At the end of the interview, they were asked to 'think about the face of the book thief' for 30 seconds. Half of the participants were instructed to keep their eyes closed during the interview and the subsequent mental rehearsal of the perpetrator's face, whereas the other half received no eye-closure instruction. Once the rehearsal period had passed, participants viewed a nine-person line-up that either contained the perpetrator (target-present) or not (target-absent). They were asked to indicate which member of the line-up (if any) was the book thief. We hypothesised that eye-closure during mental rehearsal of a face would improve subsequent line-up identification performance, either by helping participants conjure a more vivid mental image of the face or by helping them assign more helpful verbal labels to the face.

Replicating previous findings, participants who closed their eyes during the interview remembered significantly more correct information about the witnessed event than participants who kept their eyes open (see Table 13.1). The main variable of interest, however, was performance on the line-up task. Eye-closure during the interview and during mental rehearsal of the face had no significant effect on participants' accuracy on the subsequent line-up task. A more targeted analysis of correct identifications in target-present line-ups revealed that 54% of the participants who closed their eyes made a correct identification, compared to 42% in the control condition. This difference was not statistically significant. Thus, these data provided no evidence for the idea that the Eye-Closure Interview might improve subsequent line-up performance.

Because absence of evidence is not the same as evidence of absence, Vredeveldt, Tredoux, Kempen et al. (2015) did a follow-up experiment in which they increased statistical power. Although the line-up study had sufficient power to detect a medium-sized effect ($d = 0.40$), the population effect of the Eye-Closure Interview on recognition accuracy may be small, partly due to the dichotomous scale used to assess performance. Therefore, Vredeveldt and colleagues conducted a simple face recognition experiment with a sample size that allowed them to detect even a small effect ($d = 0.13$), if it existed. One-hundred-and-forty-four participants took part in 20 trials in which they viewed a photo of a face, completed a filler task, mentally rehearsed the face with eyes open or closed, were presented with another photo of a face and were asked to indicate whether this was the same person as the one they had seen 2 minutes earlier. Despite the high power of the study, the authors again found no significant effects of eye-closure during mental rehearsal of the face on subsequent accuracy rate, discrimination accuracy (d') or response criterion (c).

When considered alongside the other studies we have discussed in this chapter, the Vredeveldt, Tredoux, Kempen et al. (2015) findings suggest that the Eye-Closure Interview improves recall of events but does not improve performance on line-up identification tasks. From a practical perspective, these findings are disappointing: one would have hoped that the Eye-Closure Interview improves both recall and recognition memory. Nevertheless, if there are limits to the effectiveness of the technique, it is equally important that these be made clear. Recently, a legal practitioner asked the first author whether eye-closure improves face recognition. An attorney in a legal case had argued that the police had followed the correct procedures in administering a line-up, since the detective had asked the witness to close her eyes before attempting to make an identification. Presumably, the attorney in question had read about the effectiveness of eye-closure for recall memory (it has been covered to some extent in the popular press in various countries), and had made the understandable but mistaken inference that eye-closure is also effective for facial identification. This question illustrates the importance of investigating the boundary conditions of investigative techniques such as eye-closure. Although the Eye-Closure Interview can be used to help witnesses remember more about events, it does not seem to help them identify a perpetrator from a line-up with greater accuracy.

13.6 Conclusions and Future Directions

Since Glenberg and colleagues' (1998) pioneering research, various studies have documented the benefits of eye-closure for memory performance (e.g. Doherty-Sneddon et al., 2001; Perfect et al., 2008; Wagstaff et al., 2004). The series of studies discussed in this chapter enhanced the ecological validity of this research by examining the Eye-Closure Interview in eyewitness contexts. Vredeveldt and Penrod (2013) examined memory for a staged altercation witnessed on the street and found that the benefits of eye-closure extended to this naturalistic setting. Vredeveldt, Tredoux, Nortje et al. (2015) conducted a field evaluation of the Eye-Closure Interview and found that eye-closure enhanced the forensic relevance of information reported by witnesses. Vredeveldt, Tredoux, Kempen et al. (2015) examined the Eye-Closure Interview for a different type of memory task faced by eyewitnesses, namely, line-up identification and face recognition, and found benefits of eye-closure for event recall but not for facial identification. Taken together, these findings provide robust support for the effectiveness of the Eye-Closure Interview in helping witnesses remember events.

We propose at least two directions that future research on the Eye-Closure Interview could take. First, eyewitnesses are often exposed to misleading information – for example, from the news, from other witnesses or from police investigators (e.g. Loftus, 2005; Paterson & Kemp, 2006). Therefore, it is important to investigate whether the Eye-Closure Interview can mitigate the impact of such misleading information on memory. Previous research shows that witnesses who close their eyes typically report fewer errors than witnesses who keep their eyes open, but it is not clear whether this would also apply to erroneous information adopted from other sources encountered after the event. Second, future research could investigate the applied value of the Eye-Closure Interview in other settings. For example, in medical settings, patients often need to provide an accurate and complete medical history. Similarly, in educational settings, students need to remember a large amount of information. Other interview protocols originally developed for eyewitness settings, such as the Cognitive Interview, have been found to benefit recall performance in alternative settings as well, including recall of daily physical activities (Fisher, McCauley, Falkner, & Trevisan, 2000) and recall of foods eaten, which could be relevant for medical diagnoses of food poisoning or allergies (Fisher & Quigley, 1992). Given that the Eye-Closure Interview is such a simple and cost-effective procedure, it could easily be applied in medical and educational settings, but its effectiveness in these settings would first need to be investigated.

In conclusion, we believe it is important that psychologists working in the applied area of psychology and law, particularly on the specific topic of eyewitness memory, use their knowledge and research to aid in both the conviction of the guilty and the acquittal of the innocent. Some critics have pointed to a strong tendency for psychologists to appear as expert witnesses for the defence and have questioned whether this reveals a bias on the part of the discipline (e.g. McCloskey & Egeth, 1983). One way in which our research on eyewitnesses can make a contribution to both the prosecution and the defence is to improve the quantity and quality of evidence obtained from eyewitnesses. Pioneers of this approach have developed sophisticated interview protocols that adduce information from eyewitnesses that is demonstrably better than regular police interviews (cf. Fisher, Milne, & Bull, 2011). These protocols are rigorous and well-tested, but research in situ has shown a low uptake in some police forces, due to their complexity and length. In this chapter we have reported on the first decade of research on a simple alternative, the Eye-Closure Interview. This disarmingly simple interview technique requires witnesses to close their eyes when attempting to recall information about an event, and we have reviewed evidence here from laboratory and field studies that shows its effectiveness across a range of materials and methods. We believe that there is enough evidence for it to be used in practice by police officers, but simultaneously concede that a 'study space analysis' of the kind outlined by Malpass and colleagues (2008) would undoubtedly show that research on eye-closure is still at an early stage of elaboration. We see continued work on the Eye-Closure Interview as an important line of applied psychology and law research for the next decade.

References

Baddeley, A. D., & Andrade, J. (2000). Working memory and the vividness of imagery. *Journal of Experimental Psychology: General, 129*, 126–145. doi:10.1037/0096-3445.129.1.126.

Baddeley, A. D., & Hitch, G. J. (1974). Working memory. In G. A. Bower (Ed.), *Recent advances in learning and motivation* (Vol. 8, pp. 47–89). New York: Academic Press.

Caruso, E. M., & Gino, F. (2011). Blind ethics: Closing one's eyes polarizes moral judgments and discourages dishonest behavior. *Cognition 118*, 280–285. doi:10.1016/j.cognition.2010.11.008.

Centraal Bureau voor de Statistiek. (2014). *Criminaliteit en rechtshandhaving 2013: Ontwikkelingen en samenhangen*: Boom Lemma.

Clarke, C., & Milne, R. (2001). *National evaluation of the PEACE investigative interviewing course*. Police Research Award Scheme. London: Home Office.

Clifford, B. R., & George, R. C. (1996). A field evaluation of training in three methods of witness/victim investigative interviewing. *Psychology, Crime & Law, 2*, 231–248. doi:10.1080/10683169608409780.

Connors, E., Lundregan, T., Miller, N., & McEwen, T. (1996). *Convicted by juries, exonerated by science: Case studies in the use of DNA evidence to establish innocence after trial*. NIJ Research Report NCJ 161258. Washington, DC: National Institute of Justice.

Dando, C. J., Wilcock, R., & Milne, R. (2008). The cognitive interview: Inexperienced police officers' perceptions of their witness/victim interviewing practices. *Legal and Criminological Psychology, 13*, 59–70. doi:10.1348/135532506x162498.

Doherty-Sneddon, G., Bonner, L., & Bruce, V. (2001). Cognitive demands of face monitoring: Evidence for visuospatial overload. *Memory & Cognition, 29*, 909–919. doi:10.3758/BF03195753.

Fisher, R. P. (1995). Interviewing victims and witnesses of crime. *Psychology, Public Policy, & Law, 1*, 732–764. doi:10.1037/1076-8971.1.4.732.

Fisher, R. P., & Geiselman, R. E. (1992). *Memory-enhancing techniques for investigative interviewing: The cognitive interview*. Springfield: Charles Thomas.

Fisher, R. P., & Quigley, K. L. (1992). Applying cognitive theory in public health investigations: Enhancing food recall with the cognitive interview. In J. M. Tanur (Ed.), *Questions about questions: Inquiries into the cognitive bases of surveys*. New York: Sage.

Fisher, R. P., Geiselman, R. E., & Amador, M. (1989). Field test of the cognitive interview: Enhancing the recollection of actual victims and interviewees of crime. *Journal of Applied Psychology, 74*, 722–727. doi:10.1037/0021-9010.74.5.722.

Fisher, R. P., Milne, R., & Bull, R. (2011). Interviewing cooperative witnesses. *Current Directions in Psychological Science, 20*, 16–19. doi:10.1177/0963721410396826.

Fisher, R. P., McCauley, M. R., Falkner, K. L., & Trevisan, M. (2000). Adapting the cognitive interview to enhance long-term (35 years) recall of physical activities. *Journal of Applied Psychology, 85*, 180–189. doi:10.1037/0021-9010.85.2.180.

FutureFact. (2012). South Africa's big 5 social forces. Retrieved February 5, 2015, from http://www.futurefact.co.za/system/files/filedepot/4/FF%20SA%27s%20 Big%205%20Forces%202012%20HIGHLIGHTS.ppsx.

Gabbert, F., Hope, L., & Fisher, R. (2009). Protecting eyewitness evidence: Examining the efficacy of a self-administered interview tool. *Law and Human Behavior, 33*, 298–307. doi:10.1007/s10979-008-9146-8.

Geiselman, R. E., Fisher, R. P., Firstenberg, I., Hutton, L. A., Sullivan, S., Avetissian, I., & Prosk, A. (1984). Enhancement of eyewitness memory: An empirical evaluation of the cognitive interview. *Journal of Police Science and Administration, 12*, 74–80.

Glenberg, A. M. (1997). What memory is for: Creating meaning in the service of action. *Behavioral and Brain Sciences, 20*, 1–55. doi:10.1017/S0140525X97470012.

Glenberg, A. M., Schroeder, J. L., & Robertson, D. A. (1998). Averting the gaze disengages the environment and facilitates remembering. *Memory & Cognition, 26*, 651–658. doi:10.3758/BF03211385.

Gross, S. R., & Shaffer, M. (2012). *Exonerations in the United States, 1989 through 2012: Report by the National Registry of Exonerations*. University of Michigan Law School.

Hammond, L., Wagstaff, G. F., & Cole, J. (2006). Facilitating eyewitness memory in adults and children with context reinstatement and focused meditation. *Journal of Investigative Psychology and Offender Profiling, 3*, 117–130. doi:10.1002/jip.47.

Home Office Statistical Bulletin. (2014). *Crime outcomes in England and Wales 2013/14*. London: Home Office.

Kebbell, M. R., & Milne, R. (1998). Police officers' perceptions of eyewitness performance in forensic investigations. *Journal of Social Psychology, 138*, 323–330. doi:10.1080/00224549809600384.

Kebbell, M. R., Milne, R., & Wagstaff, G. F. (1999). The cognitive interview: A survey of its forensic effectiveness. *Psychology, Crime & Law, 5*, 101–115. doi:10.1080/10683169908414996.

Lamb, M. E., Orbach, Y., Hershkowitz, I., Esplin, P. W., & Horowitz, D. (2007). A structured forensic interview protocol improves the quality and informativeness of investigative interviews with children: A review of research using the NICHD Investigative Interview Protocol. *Child Abuse & Neglect, 31*, 1201–1231. doi:10.1016/j.chiabu.2007.03.021.

Leggett, T. (2003). The sieve effect: South Africa's conviction rates in perspective. *SA Crime Quarterly, 5*, 11–14.

Lerner, Y., Papo, D., Zhdanov, A., Belozersky, L., & Hendler, T. (2009). Eyes wide shut: Amygdala mediates eyes-closed effect on emotional experience with music. *PLoS ONE, 4*, e6230. doi:10.1371/journal.pone.0006230.

Loftus, E. F. (2005). Planting misinformation in the human mind: A 30-year investigation of the malleability of memory. *Learning & Memory, 12*, 361–366. doi:10.1101/lm.94705.

Malpass, R. S., Tredoux, C. G., Compo, N. S., McQuiston-Surrett, D., MacLin, O. H., Zimmerman, L. A., & Topp, L. D. (2008). Study space analysis for policy development. *Applied Cognitive Psychology, 22*, 789–801. doi:10.1002/acp.1483.

Mastroberardino, S., Natali, V., & Candel, I. (2012). The effect of eye closure on children's eyewitness testimonies. *Psychology, Crime & Law, 18*, 245–257. doi: 10.1080/10683161003801100.

Mastroberardino, S., & Vredeveldt, A. (2014). Eye-closure increases children's memory accuracy for visual material. *Frontiers in Psychology, 5.* doi:10.3389/fpsyg .2014.00241.

McCloskey, M., & Egeth, H. E. (1983). Eyewitness identification: What can a psychologist tell a jury? *American Psychologist, 38,* 550–563. doi:10.1037/0003-066X .38.5.550.

Nash, R. A., Nash, A., Morris, A., & Smith, S. L. (2015). Does rapport-building boost the eyewitness eyeclosure effect in closed questioning? *Legal and Criminological Psychology,* Advance online publication. doi:10.1111/lcrp.12073.

Orbach, Y., Hershkowitz, I., Lamb, M. E., Sternberg, K. J., Esplin, P. W., & Horowitz, D. (2000). Assessing the value of structured protocols for forensic interviews of alleged child abuse victims. *Child Abuse & Neglect, 24,* 733–752. doi:10.1016 /S0145-2134(00)00137-X.

Paterson, H. M., & Kemp, R. I. (2006). Comparing methods of encountering post-event information: The power of co-witness suggestion. *Applied Cognitive Psychology, 20,* 1083–1099. doi:10.1002/acp.1261.

Perfect, T. J., Andrade, J., & Eagan, I. (2011). Eye-closure reduces the cross-modal memory impairment caused by auditory distraction. *Journal of Experimental Psychology: Learning, Memory and Cognition, 37,* 1008–1013. doi:10.1037/a0022930.

Perfect, T. J., Wagstaff, G. F., Moore, D., Andrews, B., Cleveland, V., Newcombe, S., Brisbane, K. A., & Brown, L. (2008). How can we help witnesses to remember more? It's an (eyes) open and shut case. *Law and Human Behavior, 32,* 314–324. doi:10.1007/s10979-007-9109-5.

Phelps, F. G., Doherty-Sneddon, G., & Warnock, H. (2006). Helping children think: Gaze aversion and teaching. *British Journal of Developmental Psychology, 24,* 577–588. doi:10.1348/026151005X49872.

Roberts, W. T., & Higham, P. A. (2002). Selecting accurate statements from the cognitive interview using confidence ratings. *Journal of Experimental Psychology: Applied, 8,* 33–43. doi:10.1037/1076-898X.8.1.33.

Vredeveldt, A., & Penrod, S. D. (2013). Eye-closure improves memory for a witnessed event under naturalistic conditions. *Psychology, Crime & Law, 19,* 893–905. doi: 10.1080/1068316x.2012.700313.

Vredeveldt, A., & Sauer, J. D. (2015). Effects of eye-closure on confidence-accuracy relations in eyewitness testimony. *Journal of Applied Research in Memory and Cognition, 4,* 51–58. doi:10.1016/j.jarmac.2014.12.006.

Vredeveldt, A., Baddeley, A. D., & Hitch, G. J. (2012). The effects of eye-closure and 'ear-closure' on recall of visual and auditory aspects of a criminal event. *Europe's Journal of Psychology, 8,* 284–299. doi:10.5964/ejop.v8i2.472.

Vredeveldt, A., Baddeley, A. D., & Hitch, G. J. (2014). The effectiveness of eye-closure in repeated interviews. *Legal and Criminological Psychology, 19,* 282–295. doi:10.1111/lcrp.12013.

Vredeveldt, A., Hitch, G. J., & Baddeley, A. D. (2011). Eyeclosure helps memory by reducing cognitive load and enhancing visualisation. *Memory & Cognition, 39,* 1253–1263. doi:10.3758/s13421-011-0098-8.

Vredeveldt, A., Tredoux, C. G., Kempen, K., & Nortje, A. (2015). Eye remember what happened: Eye-closure improves recall of events but not face recognition. *Applied Cognitive Psychology, 29,* 169–180. doi:10.1002/acp.3092.

Vredeveldt, A., Tredoux, C. G., Nortje, A., Kempen, K., Puljević, C., & Labuschagne, G. N. (2015). A field evaluation of the Eye-Closure Interview with witnesses of serious crimes. *Law and Human Behavior, 39*, 189–197. doi:10.1037/lhb0000113.

Wagstaff, G. F., Wheatcroft, J. M., Caddick, A. M., Kirby, L. J., & Lamont, E. (2011). Enhancing witness memory with techniques derived from hypnotic investigative interviewing: Focused meditation, eye-closure, and context reinstatement. *International Journal of Clinical and Experimental Hypnosis, 59*, 146–164. doi: 10.1080/00207144.2011.546180.

Wagstaff, G. F., Brunas-Wagstaff, J., Cole, J., Knapton, L., Winterbottom, J., Crean, V., & Wheatcroft, J. (2004). Facilitating memory with hypnosis, focused meditation, and eye closure. *International Journal of Clinical & Experimental Hypnosis, 52*, 434–455. doi:10.1080/00207140490889062.

Wagstaff, G. F., Wheatcroft, J. M., Burt, C. L., Pilkington, H. J., Wilkinson, K., & Hoyle, J. D. (2011). Enhancing witness memory with focused meditation and eye-closure: Assessing the effects of misinformation. *Journal of Police and Criminal Psychology, 26*, 152–161. doi:10.1007/s11896-010-9082-7.

Wells, G. L., Malpass, R. S., Lindsay, R. C. L., Fisher, R. P., Turtle, J. W., & Fulero, S. M. (2000). From the lab to the police station: A successful application of eyewitness research. *American Psychologist, 55*, 581–598. doi:10.1037/0003-066X.55.6.581.

Understanding False Memories

14

Dominant Scientific Theories and Explanatory Mechanisms

JULIA SHAW

Contents

14.1 Introduction

False memories are a form of illusory recollection where an individual believes they have a memory of something that never actually occurred. Their recollection does not fit with reality. Individuals can have false memories of small details, such as whether a word was mentioned as part of a list (Roediger & McDermott, 1995), but they also have the potential to develop richly detailed false memories of entire autobiographical events. These can include relatively benign events such as getting lost in a shopping mall as a child (Loftus, 1997). They can also include highly emotional events such as being attacked by an animal (Porter, Yuille, & Lehman, 1999) or nearly drowning (Hyman, Husband, & Billings, 1995). They can even include false memories of committing aggressive acts in adolescence (Laney & Takarangi, 2013) or of committing crimes that never actually occurred (Shaw & Porter, 2015).

What makes these false memories ever more fascinating from a research perspective is the realism often associated with these accounts. Rememberers do not realise they are generating false memories, and it seems that the memories can be experienced in the same manner as real memories. This realism has been demonstrated in a number of ways. Individuals have been known to report high confidence in their memory illusions, insisting that their faulty recollection is correct (Laney, Fowler, Nelson, Bernstein, & Loftus, 2008; Laney & Loftus, 2008). They have also been shown to report the same kinds of multi-sensory components observed in real memories (e.g. Laney & Takarangi, 2013; Shaw & Porter, 2015). These reported rich memory experiences can include seeing, hearing, feeling, tasting and smelling components of autobiographical memories. And, independent observers of these recollections seem to have difficulty differentiating between true accounts and false memory accounts (Shaw, 2014). But what can explain this realism?

Whilst it can be difficult to fathom how exactly one would come to generate such false accounts, researchers in this area have worked hard to try to understand the mechanisms and explanatory frameworks that can lead to these memory illusions. In an ever-persistent empirical examination of these theories, researchers have developed a number of creative methods to replicate and examine the phenomenon of false memory in the lab. These researchers have also been able to then take the knowledge gained from the lab and to successfully apply it to the real worlds of psychotherapy, policing, law and medicine.

This chapter will provide an overview of the current theories of false memory. This is a chapter that will help the reader understand why false memories should look and feel like real memories and how the research has gone about demonstrating this.

14.2 Theories

A number of theories have been proposed in order to help us understand the nature of false memories – the mechanisms that allow their existence, their prevalence and their possible prevention. Whilst at times these theories are complementary, they can also be contradictory. So contradictory, in fact, that incompatible theories and beliefs have led to what is sometimes referred to as the *memory wars* (e.g. Loftus & Brewin, 1997). This term captures the heated debate and the animosity that has been generated by experts in various fields who have fundamentally disagreed about issues related to false memories. Some have argued that false memories, particularly of entire auto-biographical events, may merely be a misinterpretation of other phenomena by eager researchers. Others have claimed that the interview methods used in research settings have little to do with the memory retrieval techniques used by practitioners in psychotherapy and policing. However, whilst there are (and always will be) dissenters, the research literature overwhelmingly indicates that false memories exist, can be studied and that this research has extremely important implications.

14.2.1 A Fundamental False Memory Framework

Memory researchers have long called into question a common lay conceptu-alisation of memory as reliable and accurate. A great quote about this comes from Elizabeth Loftus, who is often considered one of the founders of false memory research. In a talk she gave at a large annual TED (Technology, Engineering and Design) conference, she proclaimed the following:

> Many people believe that memory works like recording device. But decades of research has shown that's not the case. Memory is constructed and recon-structed. It's more like a Wikipedia page – you can go change it, but so can other people. (Loftus, 2013)

A similar sentiment seems to be echoed throughout memory research more generally. In many ways, it could even be argued that *all memory is essentially false*. It can be false because of basic perceptual biases and abilities that we bring into situations. It can be false because of what we do, and do not, pay attention to. It can be false because of the accounts of others melding with our own. It can be false because of problems in the way memory is stored physiologically in the brain. It can be false because suggestive retrieval tech-niques, or poor interviewing, can cause us to construct or distort events. There are simply so many parts of the remembering process that can be fraught with error that it seems almost naïve to assume that our memory is ever perfect. Instead, it seems in many ways that we are consistently and repeatedly the post-hoc creators of our perceived personal past. Theories that help us understand this are biological theories, associative activation and fuzzy-trace theory.

14.2.1.1 Biological Theories
Utilising technological advances that allow researchers to study the bio-logical and chemical mechanisms underlying memory processes, research-ers have been able to examine purely physiological theories to explain false memory formation. One such theory of false memory suggests that

declarative memory in humans can be selectively rewritten during reconsolidation (Chan & LaPaglia, 2013). This 'retrieval induced forgetting' has to do with the manner in which these experiences are consolidated into long-term memories in the brain.

According to Chan and LaPaglia (2013), in order to stamp new experiences into long-term memory, a synthesis of new proteins is required to make connections between neurons – connections that have the potential to be long lasting. If the synthesis of these proteins is blocked, for example by introducing a drug, it is not possible to consolidate the memory. This block has to be introduced quickly, however, as the biochemical process of biological stamping begins to happen almost immediately during a learning exercise or personal experience. What makes this process important for understanding false memories is that every time an experience stored in long-term memory is recalled, this cycle of encoding and storage repeats. This makes the recalled event vulnerable to corruption and forgetting. By introducing a protein synthesis inhibitor immediately after recalling a long-term memory, the reconsolidation of the memory is stopped, and the memory is no longer stored in the brain. Similarly, if misinformation or suggestive interviewing occurs, it can actually lead to a restructuring of the biological stamps of declarative memories in the brain with non-medical procedures (LaPaglia, Wilford, Rivard, Chan, & Fisher, 2014; Wang, Paterson, & Kemp, 2014). This is how retrieval, if interrupted, can actually induce forgetting in a number of ways. It also means that at this point, when our brains are vulnerable to corruption, we are also potentially more vulnerable to generating false memories that help compensate for these missing memories.

Further in search of biological processes that can explain false memories, researchers have generated false memories by directly altering neuronal connections. Because a specific memory is thought to be stored by a small selection of neurons in the brain, remembering for a single event can be directly changed if those particular neurons are altered. Researchers have examined this in mice (Liu et al., 2012; Ramirez et al., 2013) and have found that activating a small but precise ensemble of neurons can lead to reactivation of a memory. The researchers were able to erroneously pair old memories with new situations, therein generating false memories. Mice who had previously learned to associate fear of pain with one environment, after having this memory activated in another environment, now associated it erroneously with an otherwise non-threatening environment. This meant that the mice essentially had a false memory of experiencing pain, in an environment where they had never actually been in pain.

These examples show that the manner in which memories are stored in the brain can be directly altered, and false memories can be facilitated or created directly by tampering with physiological processes in the brain.

14.2.1.2 Associative Activation Theory

Also highlighting the importance of physiological processes, but examining them without intrusive brain procedures, we are led to associative activation theory. The notion that memory is associative in nature has been part of our understanding of fundamental memory processes since the early 1900s (e.g. Ebbinghaus, 1913). The term *associative activation* was an elaboration on this original proposition, and it refers to an increase in activity for concepts stored in memory when other, similar concepts are processed (Anderson, 1983). For example, if you think about swimming, you will almost certainly automatically activate the associated concepts of water, pool and bathing suit. This notion assumes that individuals develop a set of frequently used words and concepts called 'nodes' (Anderson & Pirolli, 1984). Nodes that have similar meanings are thought to have stronger bonds than nodes that are not as strongly associated. So, the concept *police officer* is likely to be very strongly associated with the concept *law* and very weakly with the concept *table*. This kind of activation is thought to be quick and automatic, and dissipates quickly (Gallo, 2013).

In terms of false memory formation, this associative activation can contribute to false memory formation at two points in time – encoding and recall (Roediger, Balota, & Watson, 2001). During encoding, it is possible to present a number of concepts to an individual, without ever mentioning the target concept. So, a researcher could mention the concepts law, man and uniform, without ever mentioning the concept police officer. However, because this concept was activated automatically, it may be subsequently recalled by the participant as an event that actually happened – that the concept was directly mentioned or experienced. This is because the node police officer was activated during encoding due to its association with the other discussed concepts. Alternatively, when trying to remember which concepts were engaged with earlier, an individual may remember that the concepts law and uniform were mentioned, and the sense of familiarity with the concept police officer (because it is automatically activated) may encourage the individual to incorporate this into their recall.

Associative activation thus implies that false memories are the downside of powerful associations (Roediger, McDermott, & Robinson, 1998). This also means that if associations between memories or concepts can be strengthened or weakened, this can affect the likelihood of false memories being generated. Tying it in with fuzzy-trace theory (see next section), it would suggest that the strength of associations between gist and verbatim memories is important for understanding the generation of false memories. For a more in-depth exploration of the role of associative activation in false memory formation, refer to Roediger, Balota, and Watson (2001) and Gallo (2013).

14.2.1.3 Fuzzy-Trace Theory

One theory that attempts to more precisely explain why false memories exist, and builds on the theory of associative activation, is called fuzzy-trace theory. This elegant dual-processing theory can be used to explain a lot of memory phenomena and posits that remembering involves two primary processes: gist and verbatim memory traces (Brainerd & Reyna, 2002a). Put simply, this theory suggests that a gist trace is the 'meaning content' of a memory, and a verbatim trace is the 'surface form' of a memory. Most memories contain both gist and verbatim components.

One example that can help illustrate these concepts is to think about conversations. Individuals are likely to remember both what a conversation was generally about (the gist) and exact words or sentences that were said (verbatim). In another example, one could ask individuals to describe their best friend. In their description they will likely give verbatim descriptors such as what the friend *looks* like, details such as the friend's hair colour, facial features and body type. They will likely also provide gist descriptors regarding what the friend *is* like, such as the friend being kind and funny.

According to Brainerd and Reyna (2002b), this theory can explain a diverse set of false memory phenomena. As also described in Shaw (2016), the primary explanatory principles are as follows:

Principle 1: Parallel processing and storage. The first principle is that there is a parallel processing of stimuli – individuals encode both the verbatim and gist memory traces simultaneously and store them as dissociated representations. For example, looking at a scene, one simultaneously processes what the scene looks like (verbatim) and what meaning or interpretation is assigned to it (gist), and these two sets of information are stored separately.

Principle 2: Separate recall. The second principle is that these gist and verbatim traces are also recalled separately. This also means that one type of these two memory traces can be stronger than another. It also means that one, both or neither types of memory traces can be accessible. This helps explain why sometimes we may remember someone's name (verbatim trace) but cannot remember what the person was like (gist trace), and other times we may remember what the person was like but cannot remember their name. Worst-case scenario we remember neither the person's name nor what they were like. Best case scenario we remember both. Similarly, the recall of verbatim and gist memory can be independent of one another, with gist memory being generally more stable over the passing of time than verbatim memory.

Principle 3: Error-proneness. The independent recall of the two types of memory traces opens individuals to a host of potential memory illusions. The inherently imprecise nature of gist memory fragments allows feelings of familiarity to cause the fabrication of verbatim details. For example, an individual may recollect a gist trace that they had a conversation with their friend about coffee (gist), and this could lead to an attempt to make sense of the gist recollection by erroneously placing the conversation at a specific local coffee shop (verbatim). This is a normal process in which an individual tries to make sense of their gist memories in a manner that fits with their personal narrative. Alternatively, an individual may have a strong verbatim memory of talking to their friend in a specific coffee shop – remembering the exact seats they took and what they were wearing – but forgetting the gist of why they were there. Building on the strong verbatim trace, the individual may extrapolate and generate a false memory about why they were there.

Whilst these illusions can happen spontaneously, researchers are also able to generate them by intentionally misleading an individual's connections between gist and verbatim memory fragments. For example, a researcher may make up a story wherein the participant committed a crime in their hometown with their best friend (as in Shaw & Porter, 2015). If the participant believes this story about a crime event, he or she may begin to try to make sense of this misinformation. One way this could be done is by accessing real gist and verbatim fragments, but linking them in inaccurate ways.

For example, the participant may access a true verbatim memory of a specific park, verbatim memory of what their best friend looked like, verbatim memory of someone they disliked, gist memory of what their hometown is like and gist memory of the kinds of things that would have done with their best friend. Together, all of these true memories could quite easily be used to create a plausible memory for the participant of an event that never actually occurred. Whilst this example helps illustrate the fundamental memory error-proneness that fuzzy-trace theory proposes, it is also an oversimplification; there are a number of other mechanisms through which an individual in this situation may generate such a false memory of an event (which will be explained later in this chapter).

Principle 4: Vividness. The fourth principle is that both verbatim and gist processing cause vivid remembering. When verbatim traces are recalled, individuals often seem to re-experience the items and specific contexts. Gist trace retrieval is sometimes considered more generic remembering, and is associated with experienced familiarity and the perception that something occurred but cannot be explicitly recalled. When gist traces are particularly strong, they can encourage what are referred to as phantom recollective experiences and take this familiarity as an indicator that the gist is a good cue for verbatim interpretations. For example, an individual could feel a sense of familiarity when asked whether a friend partook in an event ('I feel like he was there') and could then use this to generate an erroneous verbatim memory of actually seeing the friend at the event ('He was there'). In other words, the realism of gist and verbatim memory traces can be sustained when these traces are separated from each other and recombined in a way that generates a false combination – a false memory.

These four principles give fuzzy-trace theory a broad explanatory framework that can encompass many of the mechanisms proposed by researchers that help explain when, how and why false memories are generated. For research and further discussion on the theoretical foundations of and evidence for fuzzy-trace theory, refer to Brainerd and Reyna (2002), Reyna (2013) and Flegal and Reuter-Lorenz (2014).

14.3 Mechanisms

Biological theories, associative activation and fuzzy-trace theory all help us understand the underlying processes that contribute to the generation of false memories. They provide a foundation for understanding the kinds of mechanisms that can cause false memories. These mechanisms include plausibility, fluency and familiarity, thematic consistency, explanatory coherence, imagination inflation and source monitoring. These mechanisms are all interlinked, and it appears there are cumulative effects when more than one mechanisms is activated at once. The more mechanisms are activated in an interpersonal or experimental setting, the more likely an individual is to generate a false memory and the more richly detailed the memory is likely to become. Expanding on each in turn should help explain how each mechanism can contribute to false memory generation.

14.3.1 Plausibility

It has been argued that the plausibility of a false memory will determine the success that this memory can be implanted into a participant. This suggests that if an individual believes that the event makes sense for their personal narrative – fits within the kinds of things they would expect themselves to experience – they should be more likely to accept it and develop a false memory (Pezdek, Blandon-Gitlin, & Gabbay, 2006). For example, an individual who is a zookeeper should be more likely to internalise a false narrative involving an elephant than the average person, because this is the kind of event they are already likely to experience. Alternatively, one would expect that it should be difficult to convince an individual who has never been in contact with law enforcement that they committed a crime. It seems, however, that the role of plausibility is not quite this simple.

Mazzoni, Loftus, and Kirsch (2001) have found some support for the notion of plausibility but have suggested that perceived plausibility needs to pass only a relatively low threshold in order for a personalised manipulation to produce changes in belief that may then be incorporated into memory. In other words, if the elephant story or crime accusation incorporates personalised details, such as the participant's best friend, and is said to take place in their hometown, this may be enough to make the event plausible to that particular individual. Once an individual believes the event is possible, they may begin to make sense of the event by searching for memory representations that feel familiar and make associations with those memory components. This may then encourage the formation of new associations between previously unrelated gist and verbatim memory fragments.

Further empirical support. For a general overview of the role of event plausibility for false memories, see Mazzoni (2013). For research demonstrating that individuals have less scepticism and more acceptance of plausible than of implausible false details see Hinze, Slaten, Horton, Jenkins, and Rapp (2014). For research demonstrating that false autobiographical beliefs can be generated in both forensic and clinical contexts, even for initially implausible events, see Mazzoni, Loftus, and Kirsch (2001). For research demonstrating that even in situations with low plausibility false memories and false confessions can be generated, see Horselenberg and colleagues (2006).

14.3.2 Fluency and Familiarity

One way in which personalised false memory manipulations, which include real details mixed with false information, may increase the formation of false memories is through fluency and familiarity. Fluency is the ease with which information about a target can be processed (Kelley & Jacoby, 1998), because associations between related nodes are strong. For example, it is generally very easy for individuals to generate details about their best friend – what he or she looks like, how they behave and what they do. This would be indicative of high fluency for both gist and verbatim memory fragments. A related concept, familiarity, has to do with the perception that a stimulus was previously encountered, but the feeling is accompanied by a sense of ambiguity and lack of clarity (e.g. Koriat & Levy-Sadot, 2001). Familiarity is often considered a type of gist memory. By incorporating real details that an individual has encountered, a sense of familiarity is bestowed upon an otherwise inaccurate account, lending the event plausibility and increasing false-memory rates.

Further empirical support. For a summary of how we can create false memories using bits of reality, see Loftus, Coan, and Pickrell (1996). For a review of 30 years of research on the role of familiarity for memory, see Yonelinas (2002). For research on the importance of familiarity for gap-filling memory errors and age-related changes, see Lyons, Ghetti, and Cornoldi (2010). For research on the importance of prototype familiarity for false memory, see Whittlesea (2002).

14.3.3 Thematic Consistency

Individuals are more likely to form false memory details that fit with the theme of the event or stimuli they are trying to remember. For example, individuals are more likely to confabulate that they remember encountering the word *sleep* if they hear words that are all sleep related such as rest, bed and night. In line with associative activation, this may be due to the strength of the connections between memory nodes. In line with fuzzy-trace theory, this may particularly help explain why a sense of familiarity (this feels familiar) can facilitate the retrieval of a verbatim trace (this happened). This also fits with research that indicates participants are likely to generate false memory details that fit with their personal schemas, prototypes and expectations.

Further empirical support. For research showing that gist consistency affects suggestibility and false memory formation, see Roberts and Powell (2006). For research demonstrating that expectations affect the likelihood of accepting fabricated political events, see Frenda, Knowles, Saletan, and Loftus (2013). For research demonstrating that thematic consistency influences false memory generation, particularly for children, see Otgaar, Howe, Peters, Smeets, and Moritz (2014).

14.3.4 Explanatory Coherence

When reading stories, individuals often try to identify the causal forces that drive interactions and link events. This is referred to as explanatory coherence, and it has been demonstrated to play a role in the memory errors that result from suggestive interviews. In particular, it has been shown that forced-fabrication paradigms can lead participants to incorporate causally relevant misinformation into memory over time to help make sense of events that participants believe happened but cannot remember (e.g. Chrobak & Zaragoza, 2008). In other words, imagined memory elements regarding what something *could* have been like can turn into elements of what it *would* have been like, which can become elements of what it *was* like. Although the interviewer may provide only a small, predetermined set of misinformation, it is possible that participants increasingly try to make sense of the introduced false events by spinning explanatory frameworks around what they think could have happened.

Further empirical support. For research on how causal explanations can facilitate false memory development, see Chrobak and Zaragoza (2013). For research showing that conceptual elaboration can result in high confidence false memories and a strong experience of remembering, see Zaragoza, Mitchell, Payment, and Drivdahl (2011).

14.3.5 Imagination Inflation

Imagination has been linked to the generation of false memories. In particular, in some versions of context-reinstatement exercises and false narrative paradigms (in which participants picture what it would have been like to engage in events that never actually occurred) imagination inflation may help explain how false memories are generated (Pezdek, Blandon-Gitlin, & Gabbay, 2006). Imagining an event taking place activates related nodes in the brain and can lead to new connections between concepts that were previously not associated. This may help explain why repeatedly imagining an event has been shown to increase ratings of the probability that the event was actually experienced. It also demonstrates the potential for the separate encoding of a verbatim fragment regarding how a thought was encountered (imagination) and the gist fragment regarding what the thought was (visualising the experience). Imagination seems to be able to generate new memory fragments that can later become mixed with real fragments to cause memory illusions.

Further empirical support. For the original imagination inflation research, showing that imaging events increases the confidence that they actually occurred, see Garry, Manning, Loftus, and Sherman (1996). For research demonstrating that imagination can cause false memories of autobiographical accounts, see Mazzoni and Memon (2003). For evidence that imagination can even create bizarre false memories, see Thomas and Loftus (2002). For research demonstrating that even individuals with superior autobiographical memory are prone to imagination inflation effects, see Patihis and colleagues (2013).

14.3.6 Source Confusion

Source confusion, mistaking the source of information stored in memory, has been proposed as a reason why false memories may develop. Individuals may mistake where they experienced or learned something and then proceed to erroneously combine it with another memory. For example, individuals who are recalling details from visualisation exercises or experimenter misinformation can forget the source of their ideas and may think they are recalling details from a genuine experience (e.g. Johnson, Hashtroudi, & Lindsay,

1993). This can also be explained by the separate encoding of gist and verbatim memory fragments, as an individual can encode the gist of a memory without encoding the specifics of where the memory was acquired. Subsequently, this means that during recall there may only be a very weak memory fragment (or none) regarding the source of the memory, or a fragment that is only very weakly associated with the gist memory. By not remembering the source of a memory, it is possible for a new or erroneous source to be attributed to the memory. For example, an individual may believe they remember seeing a blue car, forgetting that in reality another witness or interviewer had provided this detail on a previous occasion.

Further empirical support. For an exploration of how source confusion fits with fuzzy-trace theory and false memories, see Lindsay and Johnson (2000). For research demonstrating that source monitoring errors allow for the production of false memories, see Hekkanen and McEvoy (2002). For research showing that individuals both young and old generate false memories, but have different associated source-monitoring abilities, see Dehon and Brédart (2004).

Together, these mechanisms can help explain how false memories can form and the different kinds of situations that can facilitate their development. Whilst there are many different types of false memories – from rich autobiographical memory details, to false recognition of faces in line-ups, to misreporting words never mentioned in lists – it appears that the current theoretical foundations and explanatory mechanisms can capture this seemingly diverse set of experiences. There appear to be aspects fundamental to memory processes that open them up to errors, and this makes all memories potentially prone to corruption or fabrication. Because of the fundamental and possibly universal nature of memory errors, these conceptualisations of false memory formation point to the overriding importance of conducting more research on the manifestation and prevention of these universal memory errors, and a lesser focus on individual differences in false memory susceptibility.

References

Anderson, J. R. (1983). A spreading activation theory of memory. *Journal of Verbal Learning and Verbal Behavior, 22*(3), 261–295.

Anderson, J. R., & Pirolli, P. L. (1984). Spread of activation. *Journal of Experimental Psychology: Learning, Memory, and Cognition, 10*(4), 791.

Brainerd, C. J., & Reyna, V. F. (2002a). Fuzzy-trace theory: Dual processes in memory, reasoning, and cognitive neuroscience. *Advances in Child Development and Behavior, 28*, 41–100.

Brainerd, C. J., & Reyna, V. F. (2002b). Fuzzy-trace theory and false memory. *Current Directions in Psychological Science, 11*(5), 164–169.

Chan, J. C., & LaPaglia, J. A. (2013). Impairing existing declarative memory in humans by disrupting reconsolidation. *Proceedings of the National Academy of Sciences, 110*(23), 9309–9313.

Chrobak, Q. M., & Zaragoza, M. S. (2008). Inventing stories: Forcing witnesses to fabricate entire fictitious events leads to freely reported false memories. *Psychonomic Bulletin & Review, 15*(6), 1190–1195.

Chrobak, Q. M., & Zaragoza, M. S. (2013). When forced fabrications become truth: Causal explanations and false memory development. *Journal of Experimental Psychology: General, 142*(3), 827.

Dehon, H., & Brédart, S. (2004). False memories: Young and older adults think of semantic associates at the same rate, but young adults are more successful at source monitoring. *Psychology and Aging, 19*(1), 191.

Ebbinghaus, H. (1913). *Memory: A contribution to experimental psychology* (No. 3). Teachers College, Columbia University.

Flegal, K. E., & Reuter-Lorenz, P. A. (2014). Get the gist? The effects of processing depth on false recognition in short-term and long-term memory. *Memory & Cognition, 42*(5), 701–711.

Frenda, S. J., Knowles, E. D., Saletan, W., & Loftus, E. F. (2013). False memories of fabricated political events. *Journal of Experimental Social Psychology, 49*(2), 280–286.

Gallo, D. (2013). *Associative illusions of memory: False memory research in DRM and related tasks.* New York: Psychology Press.

Garry, M., Manning, C. G., Loftus, E. F., & Sherman, S. J. (1996). Imagination inflation: Imagining a childhood event inflates confidence that it occurred. *Psychonomic Bulletin & Review, 3*(2), 208–214.

Hekkanen, S. T., & McEvoy, C. (2002). False memories and source monitoring problems: Criterion differences. *Applied Cognitive Psychology, 16*(1), 73–85.

Hinze, S. R., Slaten, D. G., Horton, W. S., Jenkins, R., & Rapp, D. N. (2014). Pilgrims sailing the Titanic: Plausibility effects on memory for misinformation. *Memory & Cognition, 42*(2), 305–324.

Horselenberg, R., Merckelbach, H., Smeets, T., Franssens, D., Ygram Peters, G. J., & Zeles, G. (2006). False confessions in the lab: Do plausibility and consequences matter? *Psychology, Crime & Law, 12*(1), 61–75.

Hyman, I. E., Husband, T. H., & Billings, F. J. (1995). False memories of childhood experiences. *Applied Cognitive Psychology, 9*(3), 181–197.

Johnson, M. K., Hashtroudi, S., & Lindsay, D. S. (1993). Source monitoring. *Psychological Bulletin, 114*(1), 3.

Kelley, C. M., & Jacoby, L. L. (1998). Subjective reports and process dissociation: Fluency, knowing, and feeling. *Acta Psychologica, 98*(2), 127–140.

Koriat, A., & Levy-Sadot, R. (2001). The combined contributions of the cue-familiarity and accessibility heuristics to feelings of knowing. *Journal of Experimental Psychology: Learning, Memory, and Cognition, 27*(1), 34.

Laney, C., Fowler, N. B., Nelson, K. J., Bernstein, D. M., & Loftus, E. F. (2008). The persistence of false beliefs. *Acta Psychologica, 129*(1), 190–197.

Laney, C., & Loftus, E. F. (2008). Emotional content of true and false memories. *Memory, 16*(5), 500–516.

Laney, C., & Takarangi, M. K. (2013). False memories for aggressive acts. *Acta Psychologica, 143*(2), 227–234.

LaPaglia, J. A., Wilford, M. M., Rivard, J. R., Chan, J. C., & Fisher, R. P. (2014). Misleading suggestions can alter later memory reports even following a cognitive interview. *Applied Cognitive Psychology, 28*(1), 1–9.

Lindsay, D. S., & Johnson, M. K. (2000). False memories and the source monitoring framework: Reply to Reyna and Lloyd (1997). *Learning and Individual Differences, 12*(2), 145–161.

Liu, J., Dietz, K., DeLoyht, J. M., Pedre, X., Kelkar, D., Kaur, J., Vialou, V., Lobo, M. K., Dietz, D. M., Nestler, E. J., Dupree, J., & Casaccia, P. (2012). Impaired adult myelination in the prefrontal cortex of socially isolated mice. *Nature Neuroscience, 15*(12), 1621–1623.

Loftus, E. (2013). *The fiction of memory*. TED talk.

Loftus, E. F. (1997). Creating false memories. *Scientific American, 277*(3), 70–75.

Loftus, E. F., & Brewin, C. R. (1997). Dispatch from the (un)civil memory wars. In J. D. Read & D. S. Lindsay (Eds.), *Recollections of trauma* (pp. 171–198). New York: Springer.

Loftus, E. F., Coan, J. A., & Pickrell, J. E. (1996). Manufacturing false memories using bits of reality. In L. M. Reder (Ed.), *Implicit memory and metacognition* (pp. 195–220). Mahwah, NJ: Lawrence Erlbaum Associates.

Lyons, K. E., Ghetti, S., & Cornoldi, C. (2010). Age differences in the contribution of recollection and familiarity to false memory formation: A new paradigm to examine developmental reversals. *Developmental Science, 13*(2), 355–362.

Mazzoni, G. (2013). Metacognitive processes in creating false beliefs and false memories: The role of event plausibility. In J. Dunlosky & R. A. Bjork (Eds.), *Handbook of Metamemory and Memory* (pp. 315–332). New York: Taylor & Francis.

Mazzoni, G. A., Loftus, E. F., & Kirsch, I. (2001). Changing beliefs about implausible autobiographical events: A little plausibility goes a long way. *Journal of Experimental Psychology: Applied, 7*(1), 51.

Mazzoni, G., & Memon, A. (2003). Imagination can create false autobiographical memories. *Psychological Science, 14*(2), 186–188.

Otgaar, H., Howe, M. L., Peters, M., Smeets, T., & Moritz, S. (2014). The production of spontaneous false memories across childhood. *Journal of experimental child psychology, 121*, 28–41.

Patihis, L., Frenda, S. J., LePort, A. K., Petersen, N., Nichols, R. M., Stark, C. E., McGaugh, J. L., & Loftus, E. F. (2013). False memories in highly superior autobiographical memory individuals. *Proceedings of the National Academy of Sciences, 110*(52), 20947–20952.

Pezdek, K., Blandon-Gitlin, I., & Gabbay, P. (2006). Imagination and memory: Does imagining implausible events lead to false autobiographical memories? *Psychonomic Bulletin & Review, 13*(5), 764–769.

Porter, S., Yuille, J. C., & Lehman, D. R. (1999). The nature of real, implanted, and fabricated memories for emotional childhood events: Implications for the recovered memory debate. *Law and Human Behavior, 23*(5), 517.

Ramirez, S., Liu, X., Lin, P. A., Suh, J., Pignatelli, M., Redondo, R. L., Ryan, T. J., & Tonegawa, S. (2013). Creating a false memory in the hippocampus. *Science, 341*(6144), 387–391.

Reyna, V. F. (2013). Fuzzy-trace theory and false memory. In D. L. Best & M. J. Intons-Peterson (Eds.), *Memory distortions and their prevention*. New York: Psychology Press.

Roberts, K. P., & Powell, M. B. (2006). The consistency of false suggestions moderates children's reports of a single instance of a repeated event: Predicting increases and decreases in suggestibility. *Journal of Experimental Child Psychology*, 94(1), 68–89.

Roediger III, H. L., Balota, D. A., & Watson, J. M. (2001). Spreading activation and arousal of false memories. In H. L. Roediger, J. S. Nairne, & I. Neath (Eds.), *The nature of remembering: Essays in honor of Robert G. Crowder* (pp. 95–115). Washington, DC: American Psychological Association.

Roediger III, H. L., & McDermott, K. B. (1995). Creating false memories: Remembering words not presented in lists. *Journal of Experimental Psychology: Learning, Memory, and Cognition*, 21(4), 803.

Roediger III, H. L., McDermott, K. B., & Robinson, K. J. (1998). The role of associative processes in creating false memories. In M. A. Conway, S. E. Gathercole, & C. Cornoldi (Eds.), *Theories of memory II* (pp. 187–245). East Sussex, UK: Psychology Press.

Shaw, J. (2014). *False memories look real: Generating and evaluating rich false memories of committing crime.* Paper presentation at the annual International Conference of Investigative Psychology, London.

Shaw, J. (2016). *The memory illusion: Remembering, forgetting, and the science of false memory.* London: Random House.

Shaw, J., & Porter, S. (2015). Constructing rich false memories of committing crime. *Psychological Science.* doi:10.117/0956797614562862.

Thomas, A. K., & Loftus, E. F. (2002). Creating bizarre false memories through imagination. *Memory & Cognition*, 30(3), 423–431.

Wang, E., Paterson, H., & Kemp, R. (2014). The effects of immediate recall on eyewitness accuracy and susceptibility to misinformation. *Psychology, Crime & Law*, 20(7), 619–634.

Whittlesea, B. W. (2002). False memory and the discrepancy-attribution hypothesis: The prototype-familiarity illusion. *Journal of Experimental Psychology: General*, 131(1), 96–115.

Yonelinas, A. P. (2002). The nature of recollection and familiarity: A review of 30 years of research. *Journal of Memory and Language*, 46(3), 441–517.

Zaragoza, M. S., Mitchell, K. J., Payment, K., & Drivdahl, S. (2011). False memories for suggestions: The impact of conceptual elaboration. *Journal of Memory and Language*, 64(1), 18–31.

Verbal Lie Detection 15

ALDERT VRIJ
GALIT NAHARI

Contents

15.1 Verbal Lie Detection

Verbal lie detection has a long history. Around 900 B.C. a papyrus of the Vedas mentioned that a poisoner 'does not answer questions, or gives evasive answers; he speaks nonsense' (Trovillo, 1939, p. 849). In the 1850s the French forensic expert Tardieu reported that 'quantity of detail' needs to be considered in children's alleged sexual abuse cases (Lamers-Winkelman, 1999), and in 1886 the American forensic medical doctor Walker noted that in alleged child sexual abuse cases, in contrast to physical examinations, the way in which children tell their stories in their own words and the expressions they use are amongst the best cues to distinguish truth from deception (see Lamers-Winkelman, 1999).

The systematic search for verbal cues to deceit has accelerated since the 1950s (DePaulo et al., 2003; Hauch, Blandón-Gitlin, Masip, & Sporer, 2015; Masip, Sporer, Garrido, & Herrero, 2005; Vrij, 2008a). Sometimes verbal cues are measured in isolation (Hauch et al., 2015), but they are often examined as part of a verbal veracity assessment tool. The three tools most frequently used by scholars or practitioners are Criteria-Based Content Analysis (CBCA), Reality Monitoring (RM) and Scientific Content Analysis (SCAN).

CBCA, the core part of Statement Validity Analysis (SVA), is the most frequently researched verbal veracity tool to date and more than 50 studies have been published examining the working of this tool. The CBCA is used as evidence in criminal courts in several European countries. RM is to our knowledge is never used in real life, but it is popular amongst scholars because it has a solid theoretical background. More than 30 RM deception studies have been published to date. SCAN is popular in the field and probably frequently used. However, it has hardly been researched. The current chapter only provides brief outlines of these three tools. For more detailed information about SVA, see Gumpert and Lindblad's (1999), Köhnken (2004), Raskin and Esplin (1991), Steller and Boychuk (1992) and Vrij (2005, 2008a, 2015b). For more detailed information about RM, see Masip, Sporer, Garrido, and Herrero (2005), Sporer (2004) and Vrij (2008a, 2015b). For more detailed information about SCAN, see Armistead (2011), Driscoll (1994), Nahari, Vrij, and Fisher (2012), Smith (2001) and Vrij (2008a, 2015b).

A fourth verbal veracity assessment tool is the Verifiability Approach. This is a new approach and thus it has not yet been considerably examined. We believe that the findings are promising and that the tool has potential. We will discuss the Verifiability Approach in the last part of this chapter.

Police manuals generally ignore all these developments in verbal veracity assessments and continue to pay attention mainly to non-verbal cues to deception. We will start this chapter arguing that the notion that non-verbal behaviour tells us more about deception than speech content is a misconception, and that paying attention to non-verbal behaviour results in less accuracy and in a lie bias.

15.2 Non-Verbal Lie Detection: Misconception and Disadvantages

Many books convey the idea that non-verbal behaviour is revealing about deception, including *Lie Spotting* (Meyer, 2010) and *Spy the Lie* (Houston, Floyd, & Carnicero, 2012). Also police manuals typically pay considerably more attention to non-verbal cues than to verbal cues to deceit (see Vrij & Granhag, 2007, for an overview of such manuals).

Research findings shed a pessimistic light on the relationship between non-verbal behaviour and deception. Meta-analyses have concluded that non-verbal cues to deceit are faint and unreliable (DePaulo et al., 2003) and that people's ability to distinguish truth tellers from liars is poor by observing people's behaviour (Bond & DePaulo, 2006).

DePaulo et al.'s (2003) meta-analysis included 116 deception studies in which different non-verbal cues were examined. Focusing on 32 non-verbal cues that were examined in five or more deception studies, DePaulo et al.

found that six cues (19%) showed a significant relationship with deception. The average effect size of these six significant cues was $d = .19$. Effect sizes around .20 represent an effect that is a barely perceptible but real difference, the equivalent of the difference in height between 15- and 16-year-old girls (Cohen, 1988; Rice & Harris, 2005). Bond and DePaulo's (2006) meta-analysis included studies that examined the veracity judgements made by observers who paid attention to non-verbal behaviour. They obtained an average accuracy rate of 52%, whereas 50% would be obtained just by tossing a coin. In their meta-analysis, Hartwig and Bond (2011) concluded that people perform poorly in lie detection tasks because the differences in nonverbal behaviour between truth tellers and liars are too small to make the task achievable. This lack of diagnostic cues to deceit also explains why training people to detect lies, by informing them about 'diagnostic non-verbal cues to deceit', has hardly any effect (Frank & Feeley, 2003; Vrij, 2008a).

There is evidence that examining non-verbal behaviour (a) impairs accuracy in discriminating between truth tellers and liars and (b) results in a lie bias. In a meta-analysis the ability of (typically) laypersons to detect truths and lies of people they do not know were examined under three conditions: when they (1) watched videotapes without sound, (2) watched videotapes with sound and (3) listened to audiotapes (Bond & DePaulo, 2006). The accuracy levels were 52%, 56% and 63%, respectively. In other words, these findings revealed that having access to visual cues only impairs lie detection. This was replicated in a study in which police officers watched real-life videotaped police–suspect interviews or listened to audiotapes of these interviews (Mann, Vrij, Fisher, & Robinson, 2008). The officers who listened to the audiotapes were more accurate than those who watched the videotapes.

Apart from lower accuracy, Bond and DePaulo's (2006) meta-analysis showed that messages judged from visual cues only were perceived as less truthful than messages judged from audiovisual or audio presentation. In other words, paying attention to visual cues only results in a lie bias (the tendency to judge someone a liar). This is perhaps due to people having stereotypical beliefs about the behaviour of liars rather than of truth tellers (e.g. liars lack eye contact and fidget; Global Deception Team, 2006; Mann, Vrij, & Bull, 2004; Strömwall, Granhag, & Hartwig, 2004; Taylor & Hick, 2007; Vrij, Akehurst, & Knight, 2006). Being exposed to visual cues only encourages the use of these stereotypes, because, when speech and vocal cues are unavailable and only visual cues can be taken into account, observers have little other than their stereotypical beliefs to rely on (Bond & DePaulo, 2006).

Sometimes high accuracy rates of classifying truth tellers and liars based on analyses of non-verbal behaviour are reported. In one study an analysis of televised footage of 78 individuals who made an emotional plea for the return of their missing relative (35 turned out to be liars and had murdered their relative) obtained an accuracy rate of 90.4% (Ten Brinke & Porter, 2012).

Importantly, this accuracy rate was not obtained by observers who watched the televised footage. Instead, they were based on meticulous coding of the footage, which resulted in a few diagnostic cues. A statistical procedure (discriminant analysis) then obtained a 90.4% accuracy rate based on four of these cues. However, the statistical model underlying this 90% accuracy rate was specifically designed for this particular data set. It is far from certain that the same four cues will emerge as diagnostic cues to deceit with a different sample of individuals who plea for the return of their missing relatives, and the chance is very small that the same statistical model will again achieve a 90% accuracy rate with that different data set. And given the meticulous coding scheme that was required to obtain these four diagnostic cues, the chance is equally small that observers who would be informed about these four diagnostic cues would achieve such high accuracy rate if they would watch the televised footage bearing those four cues in mind.

Given this, why do people overemphasise the relevancy of non-verbal cues to deception? We believe that four factors contribute to this misconception. First, people often overestimate the importance of non-verbal behaviour in the exchange of information. Those who argue in favour of examining non-verbal cues to detect deceit often use quotes such as 'according to various social studies as much as 70% of a message communicated between persons occurs at a nonverbal level' (Inbau, Reid, Buckley, & Jayne, 2013, p. 122). The social studies referred to are from the psychologist Albert Mehrabian, who published in his book *Silent Messages* in 1971. Mehrabian's research dealt with the communication of positive or negative emotions *via single spoken words*. Obviously, if someone says little, speech content cannot have much influence on the impression information. This does not mean that Mehrabian's findings can be generalised to police interviews, or any other interview setting, where interviewees say considerably more than a single word.

Second, expectancies about the truthfulness of a person may influence what people pay attention to. Police officers readily assume that a suspect is guilty (Kassin, 2005; Moston, Stephenson, & Williamson, 1992; Stephenson & Moston, 1994). When lying is expected, police officers may have little interest in listening to a suspect's flat denials and prefer to look at bodily signs to detect deceit (Millar & Millar, 1998).

Third, conducting interviews in criminal investigations may be a mentally taxing task. It may be difficult to listen and interpret the incoming substantive information whilst simultaneously processing the same verbal channel for cues to deceit. To use a different channel to determine deceit, the non-verbal channel, would be the result (Patterson, 2006).

The fourth factor that may contribute to the misconception about the importance of non-verbal behaviour in lie detection is the notion that it is more difficult to control behaviour than speech (DePaulo & Kirkendol, 1989; Vrij, 2000, 2008b). First, automatic links exist between emotions and non-verbal behaviour (e.g. the moment people become afraid, their bodies jerk backwards), whereas automatic links between emotions and speech content do not exist. Second, people are more practiced in using words than in using behaviour, and this practice makes perfect. Third, people are more aware of what they are saying than of how they are behaving, and this awareness makes people better at controlling their speech. Fourth, verbally people can pause and think what to say, whereas non-verbally people cannot be silent. Yet, one should not underestimate the difficulty of telling a lie that sounds convincing and plausible, particularly when interviewees are invited to provide elaborative statements (i.e. 'Could you please describe, in as much detail as possible, what you did yesterday between 2 and 5 P.M.?'). Research has revealed that in those lengthy responses verbal differences occur between truth tellers and liars, particularly in the number and type of details they provide, as we will discuss later. Research has also shown that telling a convincing and plausible lie can be made even more difficult by using specific interview techniques. The Verifiability Approach, described later, is an example of such a technique, so are the Strategic Use of Evidence (Granhag & Hartwig, 2015; Hartwig, Granhag, & Luke, 2014) and the Cognitive Lie Detection technique (Vrij, 2015a).

15.3 Verbal Veracity Assessment Tools: Criteria-Based Content Analysis (CBCA) and Reality Monitoring (RM)

Statement Validity Analysis (SVA) is a tool designed to determine the credibility of *child* witnesses' testimonies in trials for *sexual offences*. It is not surprising that a veracity assessment technique has been developed to verify whether a child has been sexually abused. It is often difficult to determine the facts in an allegation of sexual abuse, since often there is no medical or physical evidence. Frequently the alleged victim and the defendant give contradictory testimony and often there are no independent witnesses to give an objective version of events. This makes the ability to accurately assess the credibility of the defendant and alleged victim important. The alleged victim is in a disadvantageous position if he or she is a child, as adults have a tendency to mistrust statements made by children.

SVA assessments are accepted as evidence in some North American courts and in criminal courts in several West European countries, including Germany, the Netherlands, Spain and Sweden (Vrij, 2008a). The tool originates from Sweden (Trankell, 1972) and Germany (Undeutsch, 1982) and consists of four stages (Vrij, 2008a): (1) a case-file analysis, (2) a semi-structured interview, (3) a Criteria-Based Content Analysis (CBCA) that systematically assesses the quality of the transcribed interviews and (4) an evaluation of the CBCA outcome via a set of questions (Validity Checklist). For this chapter about verbal cues to deceit, the CBCA component is particularly important. It is also the component that has attracted most research to date. We limit ourselves here to presenting an outline of CBCA.

CBCA comprises 19 different criteria and CBCA-trained evaluators judge the strength of presence of each of these criteria in an interview transcript. The presence of each criterion strengthens the hypothesis that the account is based on genuine personal experience. In other words, truthful statements will have more of the elements measured by CBCA than false statements.

According to Köhnken (1996), both cognitive and motivational factors explain why truth tellers will have higher CBCA scores than liars. With regard to cognitive factors, it is assumed that the presence of several criteria (Criteria 1 to 13) are likely to indicate genuine experiences as they are typically too difficult to fabricate. Therefore, statements which are coherent and consistent (*logical structure*), whereby the information is not provided in a chronological time sequence (*unstructured production*) and which contain a significant amount of detail (*quantity of detail*), are more likely to be true. Regarding details, accounts are more likely to be truthful if they include *contextual embeddings* (references to time and space: 'He approached me for the first time in the garden during the summer holidays'), *descriptions of interactions* ('The moment my mother came into the room, he stopped smiling'), *reproduction of conversation* (speech in its original form: 'And then he asked: Is that your coat?'), *unexpected complications* (elements incorporated in the statement which are somewhat unexpected, e.g. a witness mentions that the perpetrator had difficulty with starting the engine of his car), *unusual details* (details which are uncommon but meaningful, e.g. a witness who describes that the man she met had a stutter) and *superfluous details* (descriptions which are not essential to the allegation, e.g. a witness who describes that the perpetrator was allergic to cats). Another criterion that might indicate truthfulness is when a witness speaks of details that are beyond the horizon of his or her comprehension, for example, when he or she describes the adult's sexual behaviour but attributes it to a sneeze or to pain (*accurately reported details misunderstood*). Finally, possible indicators of truthfulness are if the witness reports details which are not part of the allegation but are related to it (*related external associations*, e.g. a witness who describes that the perpetrator talked about various women he had slept with and the differences between them); when the witness describes his or her feelings or thoughts experienced at the time of the incident (*accounts of subjective mental state*) or describes their interpretation of the perpetrator's feelings, thoughts or motives during the incident (*attribution of perpetrator's mental state*: 'He was nervous, his hands were shaking').

Other criteria (Criteria 14 to 18) are more likely to occur in truthful statements for motivational reasons. Truthful persons will not be as concerned with impression management as deceivers. Compared to truth tellers, deceivers will be more keen to try to construct a report which they believe will make a credible impression on others and will leave out information which, in their view, will damage their image of being a sincere person (Köhnken, 1996). As a result, a truthful statement is more likely to contain information that is inconsistent with the stereotypes of truthfulness. The CBCA list includes five such criteria: *spontaneous corrections* (corrections made without prompting from the interviewer: 'He wore black trousers, no sorry, they were blue'), *admitting lack of memory* (expressing concern that some parts of the statement might be incorrect: 'I think', 'Maybe', 'I am not sure', etc.), *raising doubts about one's own testimony* (anticipated objections against the veracity of one's own testimony: 'I know this all sounds really odd'), *self-deprecation* (mentioning personally unfavourable, self-incriminating details: 'Obviously it was stupid of me to leave my door wide open because my wallet was clearly visible on my desk') and *pardoning the perpetrator* (making excuses for the perpetrator or failing to blame him or her, such as a girl who says she now feels sympathy for the defendant who possibly faces imprisonment).*

Reality Monitoring (RM) is a second verbal veracity assessment tool we discuss and is to our knowledge only used in scientific research. The core of RM is that memories of experienced events differ in quality from memories of imagined events (Johnson & Raye, 1981). Memories of real experiences are obtained through perceptual processes and amongst other things are therefore likely to contain *perceptual information* (details of sound, smell, taste, touch or visual details) and *contextual information* (spatial details about where the event took place and details about how objects and people were situated in relation to each other, e.g. 'Fred stood behind me' and temporal details about time order of the events, e.g. 'First he switched on the video-recorder and then the TV' and details about duration of events). These memories are usually clear, sharp and vivid. Accounts of imagined events are derived from an internal source and are therefore likely to contain *cognitive operations*, such as thoughts and reasoning ('I must have had my coat on, as it was very cold that night'). They are usually vague and less concrete. RM may be relevant for detecting deception as it could be argued that truth telling often involves describing 'experienced events', whereas lying can involve describing 'imagined events'. Similar to the CBCA coding protocol,

---

* A final, 19th, criterion relates to *details characteristic of the offense*. This criterion is present if a description of events is typical for the type of crime under investigation (for example, a witness describing feelings that professionals know are typical for victims of, say, incestuous relationships). It is difficult to see how this criterion fits into the cognitive and motivational theoretical framework. Raskin and Esplin (1991) pointed out that this criterion is not related to the statement itself but to the particular crime to which the statement refers to. They argue that this criterion should not be included in the CBCA criteria list.

oral statements are transcribed, and trained RM coders judge the strength of presence of the RM criteria in the transcripts.

Several reviews of CBCA (Vrij, 2005) and RM (Masip et al., 2005; Sporer, 2004) research have been recently published, but Vrij's (2008a) review is the most comprehensive to date. It contains 38 samples in which the relationship between CBCA criteria and deception were examined and 29 samples concerning the relationship between RM and deception. The results regarding the individual CBCA criteria revealed a consistent pattern. Sometimes a CBCA criterion was not related to deception but when it was related nearly always the association predicted in the CBCA hypothesis emerged: Truthful statements are more likely to contain CBCA criteria than deceptive statements. The support for *quantity of details, contextual embeddings* and *reproduction of conversation* were the most impressive. For example, in 22 out of 29 samples where quantity of details was examined, truthful statements included significantly more details than deceptive statements, whereas in the remaining 7 studies no difference in quantity of details was found between truthful and deceptive statements. (Thus, in not one single study was it found that truthful statements included fewer details than deceptive statements.) Criteria with the least diagnostic value included *raising doubts about one's own memory, self-deprecation* and *pardoning the perpetrator*. For example, in none of the ten studies where it was examined, did a difference in self-deprecation emerge between truth tellers and liars.

CBCA experts are taught to take multiple criteria rather than the individual criteria into account. In 20 samples a total CBCA score was calculated (combining the results for the individual criteria). In 16 out of these 20 samples the CBCA score was significantly higher in truthful statements than in deceptive statements, whereas in 3 samples no difference was found. Only in one sample (Ruby & Brigham, 1998) did truthful statements receive a lower CBCA score than deceptive statements, but the procedure used in that study deviated in several important aspects from the procedure promoted by CBCA users, and the study is therefore not a fair test of the CBCA procedure (see Vrij, 2008, for details). Finally, the extent to which CBCA analyses can discriminate liars from truth tellers was examined in 25 samples. The average accuracy rate in these studies was 71%.

Several individual RM criteria also received consistent support, particularly *spatial details* and *temporal details*. For example, in 10 out of 11 samples where temporal details were examined, truthful statements did contain more temporal details than deceptive statements, whereas in the remaining sample no difference was found. In 8 samples a total RM score was calculated. In 7 of those samples the RM score was higher for truth tellers than for liars, whereas in the eighth sample no difference between truth tellers and liars was found (Vrij, 2008a). In the 10 samples in which RM was used to discriminate liars from truth tellers, the average accuracy rate was 69%, very similar to the 71% obtained in CBCA research. In fact, in 8 out of those 10 samples accuracy rates based on CVCA scores were also calculated. RM obtained the highest accuracy rates in five samples and CBCA in three samples. The fact that CBCA and RM yield similar results is not surprising given that the three criteria that received the strongest support in CBCA research – *quantity of details*, *contextual embeddings* and *reproduction of conversation* – are also RM criteria.

In sum, research findings suggest that the accuracy rates obtained with CBCA and RM assessments are similar and that both methods are effective in discriminating between truth tellers and liars.

15.4 Verbal Veracity Assessment Tools: Scientific Content Analysis (SCAN)

A third verbal lie detection tool we discuss is Scientific Content Analysis (SCAN), developed by Avinoam Sapir, a former Israeli police lieutenant and polygraph examiner. SCAN is popular amongst practitioners but there is not much research into this tool (Nahari, Vrij, & Fisher, 2012). In the SCAN procedure, the examinee is asked to write in detail all his/her activities during a critical period of time in such a way that a reader without background information can determine what actually happened. The handwritten statement is then analysed by a SCAN expert on the basis of a list of criteria. It is thought that some SCAN criteria are more likely to occur in truthful statements than in deceptive statements, whereas other criteria are more likely to occur in deceptive statements than in truthful statements (Sapir, 1987/2000). However, no theoretical justification is given as to why truth tellers and liars would differ from each other in the stated ways.

There is not a fixed list of SCAN criteria and different experts seem to use different sets of criteria. A list of 12 criteria is mostly used in workshops on the technique (Driscoll, 1994), in research (Smith, 2001) or by SCAN users in a field observation (Bogaard, Meijer, & Vrij, 2014). *Denial of allegations* refers to whether the interviewee directly denies the allegation in the statement. Denials are perceived as truthful. *Social introduction* refers to how the persons described in the statement are introduced. Honest social introductions are thought to be unambiguous (e.g. 'My wife Lisa …'), whereas a failure to introduce someone (e.g. 'We went outside' without mentioning who 'we' are) is interpreted as the writer trying to hide something. *Spontaneous corrections* refers to the presence of corrections in the statement, such as crossing out what was written. Although explanations and additions are allowed, interviewees are explicitly instructed not to cross anything out. A failure to follow this instruction is believed to indicate deceit. *Lack of conviction or memory* is the interviewee being vague about certain elements in the statement

('I believe ...', 'I think ...', 'kind of ...') or when the interviewee writes that he or she cannot remember something. SCAN users interpret these phrases as suspicious. *Structure of the statement* refers to the balance of the statement. It is thought that in a truthful statement the first 20% is used to describe activities leading up to the event, the next 50% to describe the actual event and the final 30% to discuss what happened after the event.

Emotions refers to whether there are emotions described in the statement. This criterion also refers to where the emotions are mentioned in the statement. It is thought that deceivers will mention emotions just *before* the climax of the story, whereas truth tellers are more likely to mention emotions *throughout* the story but particularly *after* the climax of the story. *Objective and subjective time* refers to how different time periods are covered in a statement. Objective time is the actual duration of events described in the statement, whereas subjective time is the amount of words spent describing these events. It is thought that in a truthful, but not in a deceptive statement, the objective and subjective time will correspond with each other. *Out of sequence and extraneous information* refers to whether the statement recounts the events in chronological order. A deviation of the chronological order may be deceptive. It also refers to extraneous information that does not seem relevant. It is thought that examinees could include extraneous information to hide more important information.

Missing information refers to phrases in the statement that indicate that some information has been left out. Examples are the use of words such as 'sometime after', 'finally', 'later on' and 'shortly thereafter'. Missing information is seen as a sign of deceit. *First person, singular tense* refers to the format in which a statement is written. It is thought that truthful statements are written in the first-person singular, past tense because the writer describes an event that has taken place ('I saw the smoke coming out of the window'). Deviations from this norm are viewed with suspicion. *Pronouns* include words such as 'I', 'my', 'he', 'his', 'they' and 'their'. Pronouns signal commitment, responsibility and possession. Omitting pronouns ('Left the house' rather than 'I left the house') suggests reluctance on the writer's part to commit him-/herself to the described action. The use of 'we' instead of 'I' is believed to suggest that the writer is trying to absolve him/herself of personal responsibility. Leaving out pronouns that indicate possession ('my' etc.) suggests that the writer denies ownership. *Change of language* refers to the change of terminology or vocabulary in the statement. A change in language indicates that something has altered in the mind of the writer. For example, if a suspect describes in his statement all verbal interactions he had as 'conversations' but one verbal interaction as a 'discussion', it is considered likely that he perceived this conversation differently from the other conversations.

There is overlap between some SCAN criteria and some CBCA criteria although, intriguingly, SCAN and CBCA users draw different conclusions about the veracity of a statement from the presence of the very same criterion. *Spontaneous corrections* is similar to CBCA Criterion 14 *spontaneous corrections* but CBCA experts believe that spontaneous corrections indicate truthfulness whereas SCAN experts interpret it a sign to deceit. *Lack of conviction or memory* is similar to CBCA Criterion 15 *lack of memory*. Again, CBCA experts interpret lack of memory as a sign of truthfulness and SCAN experts as a sign of deceit. *Emotions* is similar to CBCA Criterion 12 *accounts of subjective mental state*. However, unlike CBCA, in SCAN this criterion also refers to when the emotions are mentioned in the statement. *Out of sequence and extraneous information* is a combination of two CBCA criteria: *unstructured production* (Criterion 2) and *superfluous details* (Criterion 9). CBCA experts rate these criteria as signs of truthfulness and SCAN experts rate them as signs of deceit.

SCAN users refer to Driscoll's (1994) field study as evidence that SCAN works. However, a serious limitation of the study was that the ground truth could not be established. That is, it was unknown who of the examinees were actually truth tellers and who were actually liars. The Driscoll study can therefore not be used to assess the accuracy of SCAN. Nahari et al. (2012) tested the efficiency of SCAN in a laboratory experiment. Truth tellers truthfully wrote down their activities during the last half hour, whereas liars were asked to fabricate an account. The statements were analysed with SCAN and, by way of comparison, also with RM. SCAN did not distinguish truth tellers from liars above the level of chance but RM did. With RM analyses 71% of truth tellers and liars were correctly classified, a typical result for RM research (see earlier). Moreover, regarding the criteria for which SCAN and CBCA come to different predictions (see earlier), research supports the CBCA predictions in all cases (these criteria indicate truthfulness rather than deceit as CBCA suggests). In sum, there is no evidence to date to suggest that SCAN actually works.

15.5 Verbal Veracity Assessment Tools: The Verifiability Approach

A fourth approach we discuss here is a new approach called the Verifiability Approach. Central to the Verifiability Approach are two assumptions. First, truth tellers typically include more detail into their accounts than liars (Vrij, 2008a). Observers seem to be aware of this, as the richer an account is perceived to be in detail, the more likely it is to be believed (Bell & Loftus, 1989). As a result, liars will be inclined to provide many details in order to make an honest impression on observers, and they reported such a strategy in Nahari et al. (2012). Second, liars prefer to avoid mentioning too many details out of fear that investigators can check such details and will discover that they are lying (Nahari et al., 2012). Those two assumptions put liars in a dilemma. On the one hand, they are motivated to include many details so that they make an honest impression, and, on the other hand, they are motivated to avoid providing details to minimise the chances of being caught. A strategy that compromises between these two conflicting motivations is to provide details that cannot be verified. When attempting to make an honest impression, liars may choose to provide details that are difficult to verify (e.g. 'Several people walked by when I sat there') and may avoid providing details that are easy to verify (e.g. 'I phoned my friend Zvi at 10:30 this morning'). If so, liars may report fewer details that can be checked than truth tellers. This was indeed found in all five Verifiability Approach studies published to date (Harvey, Vrij, Nahari, & Ludwig, 2016; Nahari, Leal, Vrij, Warmelink, & Vernham, 2014; Nahari & Vrij, 2014; Nahari, Vrij, & Fisher, 2014a,b). The accuracy rates in these studies ranged from 61% to 88% and are, on average, not different from accuracy rates obtained with CBCA and RM (around 70% accuracy).

Verifiable detail include (a) activities with identifiable or named persons who the interviewer can consult; (b) activities that have been witnessed by identifiable or named persons who the interviewer can consult; (c) activities that the interviewee believes may have been captured on CCTV and (d) activities that may have been recorded through technology, such as using debit cards, mobile phones or computers.

In the study that obtained 88% (Nahari & Vrij, 2014), the Verifiability Approach was used to verify a suspect's claim that s/he was together with someone else (an innocent person) at the time of the crime. In such a case the innocent person is an alibi for the suspect and demonstrates the suspect's innocence. So-called alibi witnesses are frequently used by defendants in court. Burke and Turtle (2003) reviewed 175 Canadian and American criminal court cases in which an alibi was presented at the trial, and found that in 86% of the Canadian cases and 68% of the American cases a witness corroborated the alibi provided by the defendant.

Sometimes a guilty suspect asks an acquaintance to cover up for him/her and to falsely claim that they were together at the time the crime took place. A well-known case in the United Kingdom in which this happened was the Ian Huntley–Maxime Carr case. Ian Huntley was a caretaker in a school in southern England and was suspected of having murdered two young children. Huntley denied it and said that he was together with his then-girlfriend Maxime Carr on that particular day. Carr confirmed that they were together. At a later stage of the investigation, conclusive evidence linked Huntley with the crime and that made clear that Huntley and Carr had lied about being together on that particular day. Huntley and Carr's strategy – introducing a false alibi witness – is likely to be common. In a survey study, it was found that 61% of the participants thought they could find a witness to corroborate a false alibi (Culhane, Hosch, & Kehn, 2008). Another study showed that people are willing to lie for others, especially for those with whom they have a close relationship (Hosch, Culhane, Jolly, Chavez, & Shaw, 2011). In the study 82% of the participants said they would lie for their romantic partner and 68% would lie for their oldest/best friend. These studies showed that 61% of the 'Ian Huntleys' thought they would find a 'Maxime Carr' and that 82% of the 'Maxime Carrs' would be willing to lie for their romantic partner.

In the experiment we focussed on this 'witness alibi' tactic (Nahari & Vrij, 2014). We sent pairs of liars to conduct activities outside the laboratory. Member 1 of the pairs of liars carried out non-criminal activities, whereas Member 2 carried out criminal activities. When they returned to the laboratory, the pairs were told that they were suspected of conducting criminal activities in the last hour, and that they needed to provide a written statement about their activities during the last hour. We instructed them to use Member 1's activities as an alibi and to pretend that Member 2 was with Member 1 during the last hour (Member 1 would thus serve as a witness alibi). In comparison, pairs of truth tellers carried out together the same non-criminal activities as Member 1 of the pairs of liars, and thus had a true alibi to provide when they came back to the laboratory.

Importantly, all pairs also received the following information: 'To convince the interviewer that neither of you committed the crime, you should try to convince him that you were together at all times during the mission and describe in as much detail as possible all activities conducted by you as a pair'. The results indicated that truth tellers gave more details to verify that they carried out the activities as a pair than liars, and based on this difference 88% of the truth telling and lying pairs were classified correctly.

Intriguingly, research has shown that the verifiability effect became stronger when interviewees were informed about the lie detection method (Harvey et al., 2016; Nahari et al., 2014b). In Nahari et al. (2014b) truth tellers truthfully wrote down their activities during the last half hour, whereas liars were asked to fabricate an account. Half of the examinees were informed that the investigator would read their statement carefully and check whether the details they provided could be verified. To avoid confusion they were also told what checkable details are (e.g. phone calls, presence at places with closed-circuit television, activities that were carried out together with another identified person [such as a friend, librarian, lecturer] or that were witnessed by another person who can be identified and consulted). Truth tellers who received this instruction included more verifiable details into their account than truth tellers who did not receive this instruction, whereas this instruction had no effect on liars. As a result the difference between truth tellers and liars in providing checkable details was the largest in the condition where the participants were told that the investigator would look for verifiable detail, and the accuracy rates went up from 61% to 67%.

This experiment thus showed that informing examinees about the working of the lie detection technique improved the ability to discriminate amongst truth tellers and liars (hence, the reason for including such an instruction in the witness alibi study, discussed earlier). Typically, in lie detection research it is assumed that informing examinees about the lie detection method impairs the efficacy of that method, because examinees will then be able to fool the examiner by employing effective countermeasures (responding in such a way that makes them appear convincing). Indeed, studies have shown that participants can fool CBCA and RM coders (give stories that are rich in CBCA and RM criteria) if they are informed about the tool (Caso, Vrij, Mann, & DeLeo, 2006; Vrij, Akehurst, Soukara, & Bull, 2002, 2004). There is no reason to believe why people would not be able to fool SCAN coders.

Note that the Verifiability Approach differs in some important aspects from what investigators currently do. Indeed, investigators examine checkable details in statements, but they typically do not ask interviewees at the beginning of their free recall to include as many checkable details in their account as they possibly can. In addition, the Verifiability Approach works from the perspective of the interviewee rather than investigator. An interviewee can report that he spent an hour in the library on a specific afternoon. For the investigator this is a checkable detail if the investigator is aware that the library has a CCTV camera at the entrance. However, for the Verifiability Approach this only counts as a verifiable detail if the interviewee refers to the CCTV camera in his/her statement ('And you can check the CCTV camera at the entrance'), because the interviewee may not be aware of this.

The Verifiability Approach is still in its early development but has shown promising results. We believe it has several strong features, and we will report eight of them. First, as we just explained, the Verifiability Approach may be less sensitive to countermeasures. Second, it attempts to exploit differences in truth tellers' and liars' strategies (truth tellers are more willing and able to provide checkable details than liars), and interview protocols based on exploiting different strategies used by truth tellers and liars have shown good results in recent years. Prime examples are the Strategic Use of Evidence (SUE) (Granhag & Hartwig, 2015; Hartwig, Granhag, & Luke, 2014) and cognitive lie detection research (Vrij, 2015a). Third, since truth tellers provide more checkable detail after been instructed to do so, the tool helps to make truth tellers sound more convincing, which may reduce the risk of a false accusation of lying. Fourth, investigators do not have to check the truthfulness of the evidence mentioned by the interviewee to form a credibility assessment but only to count the number of checkable details reported, and in that respect it is a time-efficient tool.

Fifth, the tool focuses on obtaining evidence, which is the key part of any investigation. Thus, by using the Verifiability Approach, investigators are involved in credibility assessment and gathering evidence at the same time. Sixth, a definite answer about whether someone has been lying can often be found in the evidence available 'on the street' and not in the interview room. The verifiability approach focuses on this 'on the street' evidence. Seventh, with the exception of CBCA, credibility assessments are never used as evidence in court. In that respect, credibility assessments per se do not make the case for the prosecution any stronger, and efforts solely focused on credibility assessments are thus limited. The verifiable detail provided by interviewees in the Verifiability Approach may help the prosecution case. Eighth, technology is on the side of the Verifiability Approach. In the past it would have been difficult to use the Verifiability Approach when someone uses an alibi such as 'I stayed at home all night on my own and went to bed early' because liars as well as truth tellers would have found it difficult to provide verifiable detail to back up this claim. Nowadays, virtually everyone has modern technology (mobile phone, tablet, computer) and uses it frequently. Activities on this technology can be traced and it can be determined where this equipment is used.

15.6 Conclusion

In this chapter we briefly outlined four verbal veracity assessment tools. We discussed the empirical research related to these four tools and found that three of them – Criteria-Based Content Analysis (CBCA), Reality Monitoring (RM) and the Verifiability Approach – can be used to distinguish truth tellers and liars at a level above chance (around 70% accuracy), whereas no such evidence could be has been found yet for the fourth tool, Scientific Content Analysis (SCAN). We recommend practitioners to consider using CBCA, RM and the Verifiability Approach in their investigations to make credibility assessments and to use them as alternatives for the popular, but inefficient SCAN, and analyses of non-verbal behaviour.

References

Armistead, T. W. (2011). Detecting deception in written statements: The British Home Office study of scientific content analysis (SCAN). *Policing: An International Journal of Police Strategies & Management, 34*, 588–605.

Bell, B. E., & Loftus, E. F. (1989). Trivial persuasion in the courtroom: The power of (a few) minor details. *Journal of Personality and Social Psychology, 56*, 669–679. doi:10.1037//0022-3514.56.5.669.

Bogaard, G., Meijer, E. H., & Vrij, A. (2014). Using an example statement increases information but does not increase accuracy of CBCA, RM, and SCAN. *Journal of Investigative Psychology and Offender Profiling, 11*, 151–163. doi:10.1002/jip.1409.

Bond, C. F., & DePaulo, B. M. (2006). Accuracy of deception judgements. *Personality and Social Psychology Review, 10*, 214–234. doi:10.1207/s15327957pspr1003_2.

Burke, T. M., & Turtle, J. W. (2003). Alibi evidence in criminal investigations and trials: Psychological and legal factors. *Canadian Journal of Police and Security Services, 3*, 286–294.

Caso, L., Vrij, A., Mann, S., & DeLeo, G. (2006). Deceptive responses: The impact of verbal and nonverbal countermeasures. *Legal and Criminological Psychology, 11*, 99–111. doi:10.1348/135532505X49936.

Cohen, J. (1988). *Statistical power analysis for the behavioral sciences* (2nd ed.). Hillsdale, NJ: Erlbaum.

Culhane, S. E., Hosch, H. M., & Kehn, A. (2008). Alibi generation: Data from US Hispanics and US non-Hispanic Whites. *Journal of Ethnicity in Criminal Justice, 6*, 177–199. doi:10.1080/15377930802243395.

DePaulo, B. M., & Kirkendol, S. E. (1989). The motivational impairment effect in the communication of deception. In J. C. Yuille (Ed.), *Credibility assessment* (pp. 51–70). Dordrecht, the Netherlands: Kluwer.

DePaulo, B. M., Lindsay, J. L., Malone, B. E., Muhlenbruck, L., Charlton, K., & Cooper, H. (2003). Cues to deception. *Psychological Bulletin, 129*, 74–118. doi:10.1037/0033-2909.129.1.74.

Driscoll, L. N. (1994). A validity assessment of written statements from suspects in criminal investigations using the SCAN technique. *Police Studies, 17*, 77–88.

Frank, M. G., & Feeley, T. H. (2003). To catch a liar: Challenges for research in lie detection training. *Journal of Applied Communication Research, 31*, 58–75. doi.org/10.1080/00909880305377.

Global Deception Team. (2006). A world of lies. *Journal of Cross-Cultural Psychology, 37*, 60–74.

Granhag, P. A., & Hartwig, M. (2015). The Strategic Use of Evidence (SUE) technique: A conceptual overview. In P. A. Granhag, A. Vrij, & B. Verschuere (Eds.), *Deception detection: Current challenges and new approaches* (pp. 231–251). Chichester, UK: Wiley.

Gumpert, C. H., & Lindblad, F. (1999). Expert testimony on child sexual abuse: A qualitative study of the Swedish approach to statement analysis. *Expert Evidence, 7*, 279–314.

Hartwig, M., & Bond, C. F. (2011). Why do lie-catchers fail? A lens model meta-analysis of human lie judgments. *Psychological Bulletin, 137*, 643–659. doi:10.1037/a0023589.

Hartwig, M., Granhag, P. A., & Luke, T. (2014). Strategic use of evidence during investigative interviews: The state of the science. In D. C. Raskin, C. R. Honts, & J. C. Kircher (Eds.), *Credibility assessment: Scientific research and applications* (pp. 1–36). Oxford: Academic Press.

Harvey, A., Vrij, A., Nahari, G., & Ludwig, K. (2016). Applying the verifiability approach to insurance claims settings: Exploring the effect of the information protocol. *Legal and Criminological Psychology*.

Hauch, V., Blandón-Gitlin, I., Masip, J., & Sporer, S. L. (2015). Are computers effective lie detectors? A meta-analysis of linguistic cues to deception. *Personality and Social Psychology Review, 19*, 307–342. doi:10.1177/1088868314556539.

Hosch, H. M., Culhane, S. E., Jolly, K. W., Chavez, R. M., & Shaw, L. H. (2011). Effects of an alibi witness's relationship to the defendant on mock jurors' judgments. *Law and Human Behaviour, 35*, 127–142. doi:10.1007/s10979-010-9225-5.

Houston, P., Floyd, M., & Carnicero, S. (2012). *Spy the lie*. New York: St. Martin's Press.

Inbau, F. E., Reid, J. E., Buckley, J. P., & Jayne, B. C. (2013). *Criminal interrogation and confessions* (5th ed.). Burlington, MA: Jones & Bartlett Learning.

Johnson, M. K., & Raye, C. L. (1981). Reality Monitoring. *Psychological Review, 88*, 67–85. doi:10.1037/0033–295X.88.1.67.

Kassin, S. M. (2005). On the psychology of confessions: Does innocence put innocents at risk? *American Psychologist, 60*, 215–228. doi:10.1037/0003-066X.60.3.215.

Köhnken, G. (1996). Social psychology and the law. In G. R. Semin & K. Fiedler (Eds.), *Applied social psychology* (pp. 257–282). London: Sage Publications.

Köhnken, G. (2004). Statement validity analysis and the 'detection of the truth'. In P. A. Granhag & L. A. Strömwall (Eds.), *Deception detection in forensic contexts* (pp. 41–63). Cambridge, UK: Cambridge University Press.

Lamers-Winkelman, F. (1999). Statement validity analysis: Its application to a sample of Dutch children who may have been sexually abused. *Journal of Aggression, Maltreatment & Trauma, 2*, 59–81.

Mann, S., Vrij, A., & Bull, R. (2004). Detecting true lies: Police officers' ability to detect deceit. *Journal of Applied Psychology, 89*, 137–149. doi:org/10.1037/0021 -9010.89.1.137.

Mann, S., Vrij, A., Fisher, R., & Robinson, M. (2008). See no lies, hear no lies: Differences in discrimination accuracy and response bias when watching or listening to police suspect interviews. *Applied Cognitive Psychology, 22*, 1062–1071. doi:10.1002/acp.1406.

Masip, J., Sporer, S., Garrido, E., & Herrero, C. (2005). The detection of deception with the reality monitoring approach: A review of the empirical evidence. *Psychology, Crime, & Law, 11*, 99–122. doi:10.1080/10683160410001726356.

Mehrabian, A. (1971). *Silent messages*. Belmont, CA: Wadsworth.

Meyer, P. (2010). *Lie spotting: Proven techniques to detect deception*. New York: St. Martin's Press.

Millar, M. G., & Millar, K. U. (1998). The effects of suspicion on the recall of cues used to make veracity judgments. *Communication Reports, 11*, 57–64.

Moston, S. J., Stephenson, G. M., & Williamson, T. M. (1992). The effects of case characteristics on suspect behaviour during police questioning. *British Journal of Criminology, 32*, 23–39.

Nahari, G., Leal, S., Vrij, A., Warmelink, L., & Vernham, Z. (2014). Did somebody see it? Applying the verifiability approach to insurance claims interviews. *Journal of Investigative Psychology and Offender Profiling, 11*, 237–243. doi:10.1002/jip.1417.

Nahari, G., & Vrij, A. (2014). Can I borrow your alibi? The applicability of the verifiability approach to the case of an alibi witness. *Journal of Applied Research in Memory and Cognition, 3*, 89–94. doi:10.1016/j.jarmac.2014.04.005.

Nahari, G., Vrij, A., & Fisher, R. P. (2012). Does the truth come out in the writing? SCAN as a lie detection tool. *Law & Human Behavior, 36*, 68–76. doi:10.1007 /s10979-011-9264-6.

Nahari, G., Vrij, A., & Fisher, R. P. (2014a). Exploiting liars' verbal strategies by examining unverifiable details. *Legal and Criminological Psychology, 19*, 227–239. doi:10.1111/j.2044-8333.2012.02069.x.

Nahari, G., Vrij, A., & Fisher, R. P. (2014b). The verifiability approach: Countermeasures facilitate its ability to discriminate between truths and lies. *Applied Cognitive Psychology, 28*, 122–128. doi:10.1002/acp.2974.

Patterson, M. L. (2006). The evolution of theories of interactive behavior. In V. Manusov & M. L. Patterson (Eds.), *The SAGE handbook of nonverbal communication* (pp. 21–39). Thousand Oaks, CA: Sage.

Raskin, D. C., & Esplin, P. W. (1991). Statement validity assessment: Interview procedures and content analysis of children's statements of sexual abuse. *Behavioral Assessment, 13*, 265–291.

Rice, M., & Harris, G. T. (2005). Comparing effect sizes in follow-up studies: ROC Area, Cohen's *d*, and *r*. *Law & Human Behavior, 29*, 615–620. doi:10.1007/s10979-005-6832-7.

Ruby, C. L., & Brigham, J. C. (1998). Can criteria-based content analysis distinguish between true and false statements of African-American speakers? *Law and Human Behavior, 22*, 369–388.

Sapir, A. (1987/2000). *The LSI course on scientific content analysis (SCAN)*. Phoenix, AZ: Laboratory for Scientific Interrogation.

Smith, N. (2001). *Reading between the lines: An evaluation of the scientific content analysis technique (SCAN)*. Police research series paper 135. London: UK Home Office, Research, Development and Statistics Directorate.

Sporer, S. L. (2004). Reality monitoring and detection of deception. In P. A. Granhag & L. A. Strömwall (Eds.), *Deception detection in forensic contexts* (pp. 64–102). Cambridge, UK: Cambridge University Press.

Steller, M., & Boychuk, T. (1992). Children as witnesses in sexual abuse cases: Investigative interview and assessment techniques. In H. Dent & R. Flin (Eds.), *Children as witnesses* (pp. 47–73). New York: John Wiley & Sons.

Stephenson, G. M., & Moston, S. J. (1994). Police interrogation. *Psychology, Crime, & Law, 1*, 151–157. doi.org/10.1080/10683169408411948.

Strömwall, L. A., Granhag, P. A., & Hartwig, M. (2004). Practitioners' beliefs about deception. In P. A. Granhag & L. A. Strömwall (Eds.), *Deception detection in forensic contexts* (pp. 229–250). Cambridge, UK: Cambridge University Press.

Taylor, R., & Hick, R. F. (2007). Believed cues to deception: Judgements in self-generated serious and trivial situations. *Legal and Criminological Psychology, 12*, 321–332.

Ten Brinke, L., & Porter, S. (2012). Cry me a river: Identifying the behavioural consequences of extremely high-stakes interpersonal deception. *Law and Human Behavior, 36*, 469–477. doi:10.1037/h0093929.

Trankell, A. (1972). *Reliability of evidence*. Stockholm, Sweden: Beckmans.

Trovillo, P. V. (1939). A history of lie detection, I. *Journal of Criminal Law and Criminology, 29*, 848–881.

Undeutsch, U. (1982). Statement reality analysis. In A. Trankell (Ed.), *Reconstructing the past: The role of psychologists in criminal trials* (pp. 27–56). Deventer, Netherlands: Kluwer.

Vrij, A. (2000). *Detecting lies and deceit: The psychology of lying and its implications for professional practice*. Chichester: John Wiley & Sons.

Vrij, A. (2005). Criteria-based content analysis: A qualitative review of the first 37 studies. *Psychology, Public Policy, and Law, 11*, 3–41. doi:10.1037/1076-8971.11.1.3.

Vrij, A. (2008a). *Detecting lies and deceit: Pitfalls and opportunities* (2nd ed.). Chichester, UK: John Wiley & Sons.

Vrij, A. (2008b). Nonverbal dominance versus verbal accuracy in lie detection: A plea to change police practice. *Criminal Justice and Behavior, 35*, 1323–1336.

Vrij, A. (2015a). A cognitive approach to lie detection. In P. A. Granhag, A. Vrij, & B. Verschuere (Eds.), *Deception detection: Current challenges and new approaches* (pp. 205–229). Chichester, UK: Wiley.

Vrij, A. (2015b). Verbal lie detection tools: Statement validity analysis, reality monitoring and scientific content analysis. In P. A. Granhag, A. Vrij, & B. Verschuere (Eds.), *Detection deception: Current challenges and cognitive approaches* (pp. 3–36). Chichester, UK: Wiley.

Vrij, A., Akehurst, L., & Knight, S. (2006). Police officers', social workers', teachers' and the general public's beliefs about deception in children, adolescents and adults. *Legal and Criminological Psychology, 11*, 297–312. doi:10.1348/135532505X60816.

Vrij, A., Akehurst, L., Soukara, S., & Bull, R. (2002). Will the truth come out? The effect of deception, age, status, coaching, and social skills on CBCA scores. *Law and Human Behaviour, 26*, 261–283. doi:10.1023/A:1015313120905.

Vrij, A., Akehurst, L., Soukara, S., & Bull, R. (2004). Let me inform you how to tell a convincing story: CBCA and Reality Monitoring scores as a function of age, coaching and deception. *Canadian Journal of Behavioural Science, 36*, 113–126.

Vrij, A., & Granhag, P. A. (2007). Interviewing to detect deception. In S. A. Christianson (Ed.), *Offenders' memories of violent crimes* (pp. 279–304). Chichester, UK: John Wiley & Sons.

Index

Printed in the United States
By Bookmasters